Readers' Guide to

The Mahatma Letters to A.P. Sinnett

Readers' Guide to The Mahatma Letters to A.P. Sinnett

Compiled and Edited by
GEORGE E. LINTON
and
VIRGINIA HANSON

THE THEOSOPHICAL PUBLISHING HOUSE
Adyar, Madras 600 020, India
Wheaton, Ill., USA • London, England

First Edition 1972
Second Edition 1988

ISBN 81-7059-113-9

Printed at the Vasanta Press
The Theosophical Society
Adyar, Madras 600 020, India

ACKNOWLEDGMENTS, FIRST EDITION

THE editors wish to express deep appreciation to the Trustees of the Mahatma Letters Trust, Mr Christmas Humphreys and Mrs Elsie Benjamin, for their kind consideration and approval of this project and for making available for comparison several chronologies of the *Letters* with which the editors were not familiar. Special appreciation is expressed also to Mr Boris de Zirkoff and Mr Geoffrey A. Barborka, both of whom reviewed the first draft of the book and made helpful suggestions. Mr Barborka generously supplied descriptions of some of the letters. Mrs Seetha Neelakantan's aid in proof-reading has been invaluable. To all who have helped with their encouragement and enthusiasm, the editors are sincerely grateful.

GEORGE E. LINTON
VIRGINIA HANSON

ACKNOWLEDGEMENTS, SECOND EDITION 1988

In connection with the preparation and issuance of the revised and enlarged 1988 edition of the *Readers' Guide,* the editors wish to add the following acknowledgments:

To the members and President of the Mahatma Letters Trust in London, they wish to express great appreciation for assistance in securing financial support for obtaining from the British Museum 35 MM colour slides of the original letters now filed in that institution; also to all others who contributed financial support for that project. To Daniel H. Caldwell, research student in Tucson, Arizona, sincere appreciation for supplying considerable valuable information on various aspects of the *Letters.*

INTRODUCTION TO SECOND EDITION

THIS work was originally the result of the efforts of several students of *The Mahatma Letters* who, through the experience of group and personal study of the book, realized the need for some kind of guide or manual to aid in understanding its varied contents. It became apparent that for a fuller appreciation of the background of the *Letters*, as well as of the *Letters* themselves, the serious student should have information concerning the persons, phenomena, events in the early history of the Theosophical Society, unfamiliar terms and names, and many other items referred to in the volume. This realization bore fruit, over a period of years, in the collection of the material which was presented in a form which, it was hoped, would be useful to other students.

It should be made clear at the beginning that this *Readers' Guide* is not intended as a commentary on the subject matter contained in the *Letters* but only as a basic guide to assist the student in understanding references which might otherwise prove confusing or distracting. Therefore, no attempt is made to discuss metaphysical, philosophical, or occult subjects; the material is limited primarily to a narrative of events, brief explanations of historical incidents, definitions, biographical information and descriptive material. Included also are a great many cross-references both within the book itself and to other books or published material directly related to the subject matter.

The *Guide* is arranged in four major categories: 1. CHRONOLOGY, 2. STUDY NOTES, 3. ALPHABETICAL NOTES, 4. APPENDICES. Following is a more specific description.

CHRONOLOGY. This section gives the sequence of events from the date on which the founders of the Theosophical Society, Madame H.P. Blavatsky and Colonel H.S. Olcott, arrived in Bombay from the United States, through the ensuing seven years, together with a listing of the letters received from the Adepts during that period. So far as has been possible, the letters have been arranged in their correct chronological order. Since the pagination of the third edition of the book differs from that of the two previous editions, both listings are given. The editors have consulted all the known chronologies for the *Mahatma Letters* and, although it is impossible in many instances to determine the exact order in which the letters should be placed, an attempt has been made to arrange them logically and, particularly, to reconcile the differences which exist between the two principal chronologies compiled by Mary K. Neff and Margaret Conger, as well as to correct a few seeming errors in both. Accurate dates cannot be determined for some of the letters, and for some others only approximate dates can be suggested. In the latter instances, estimated dates are given with the notation 'est.' to indicate this uncertainty.

STUDY NOTES. Identifying facts about each letter are shown in the heading. It has been suggested that the chronological order of the letters should be followed in the first study, as it helps the student to think of the letters sequentially, thus preserving the thread of events which have great bearing on the context. The chronological number is therefore shown first, followed in parenthesis by the number as shown in the book. Choosing a letter at random, this order would show as follows:

50 (ML-88)

This is followed by the page number. Since the pagination in the third edition differs considerably from that of the first and second editions (it begins to diverge at pages 69-70, and the gap continues to widen) both page numbers for the letter are shown: the number in the first and second editions followed by a diagonal line and the page number in the third edition, e.g. 410/404. Next is shown the folio number in the British

Museum in which the letter can be found. Last comes the date. In most instances the date of receipt is shown rather than the date on which the letter was written. Exceptions to this are noted. The letters are very seldom dated, but in most instances Mr Sinnett has shown the date of receipt. Quite obviously, however, he sometimes did not do this immediately and relied on his memory later, so that it is quite impossible to be absolutely certain in all instances. Sometimes the date is determined by the context of events. Using the letter we have selected for a sample, the heading would then be thus:

50 (ML-88) p. 410/404 Folio 3 Rec. 11 March 1882.

When a cross-reference to some other letter in the book is given, the chronological number is shown first, followed by the ML number, as shown above. Page numbers are also as shown in the heading. Throughout this section the same format is maintained and is largely self-explanatory.

Following the heading is a brief description of the physical appearance of the letter itself, as determined by inspection of the original in the folio in the British Museum. This is included partly because the letters themselves are fascinating documents, and partly because the description adds an element of personal interest to the study.

Next is given a statement of the circumstances existing at the time the letter was received by Mr Sinnett or, in a few instances, by some other person. This is believed desirable in order to give the reader a better understanding of the items mentioned in the text of the letter, since many references and statements are not readily grasped unless the situation existing at the time is understood.

The last portion is devoted to items appearing in the text of the letter itself. These pertain principally to names, events, obscure words, cross-references to other pages in the book, and references to other books. Cross-references are to page numbers unless specifically indicated otherwise.

ALPHABETICAL NOTES. This section is included for quick reference to names, words, phrases, events, etc., which appear in the letters. Page numbers of the text and cross-references between letters are listed. Additional references are given to other books containing pertinent material. While this section duplicates some of the information contained in the STUDY NOTES, it is included for the convenience of the student.

APPENDICES. This section contains a variety of items which have bearing on persons or events mentioned in the letters. These have been selected from a vast store of pertinent information and comment to be found in theosophical literature and represent only a small fraction of what may be discovered by the serious and determined student. The early issues of *The Theosophist*—particularly those published during the 1880's—are especially recommended.

SUMMARY CHRONOLOGY. As a last item in the book a 'Summary Chronology' is included. This is designed for easy identification of the page number in ML for any letter chronologically listed. It also contains a cross-reference for identifying the chronological number for any letter as shown in the ML itself.

* * *

For a full understanding of the events and circumstances of the period covered by the earlier letters, it is almost essential that the student have available copies of *The Occult World* and *Esoteric Buddhism* by A.P. Sinnett. Both of these books were out of print for a time but have been reprinted. The ninth edition of *The Occult World,* which is a reprint of the English second edition, appeared in 1969; it carries different pagination from the American (fifth) edition. All references in the *Readers' Guide* are to the ninth edition. *Esoteric Buddhism* was reprinted in 1972. Also of special value to the student is *Masters and Men* by Virginia Hanson, Theosophical Publishing House, Adyar and Wheaton, 1980.

SOME EXPLANATORY NOTES

THE book entitled *The Mahatma Letters to A.P. Sinnett,* first published in 1923, was compiled and edited by Mr A. Trevor Barker, an English Theosophist, from letters belonging to the estate of A.P. Sinnett, who died in 1921. The history of the publication is quite well covered in the preface to the third edition and need not be repeated here.

A short time after the publication of this volume, Mr Barker published a second volume, *The Letters of H. P. Blavatsky to A. P. Sinnett,* also from material left by Mr Sinnett. This book contains valuable information and many intriguing clues to the relationship between H.P. Blavatsky and her Teachers, and to the less obvious aspects of the events surrounding the early struggles of the Theosophical Society.

Mr Barker attempted to arrange *The Mahatma Letters* according to subject matter under several different headings, but because of the nature of the letters this was only partially successful. Most of the time sequence was lost, and this lack of continuity made less comprehensible many passages of personal value.

It is therefore strongly urged that, initially, the student read the letters in their chronological sequence. Once he has the narrative and history clearly in mind, he can better understand the text if he wishes to study a particular topic. In addition to the metaphysical and technical teachings, the book is a veritable gold-mine of information on such matters as the ways of the Adepts, the training of chelas for the probationary path, insights into character, and other profound subjects.

It is certainly a fortunate circumstance that the letters found their way into the British Museum, where they are carefully mounted in folios and cared for, and where they are accessible to those who wish to see them.

How the Correspondence Began

The story of how the correspondence between the Mahatmas and Messrs A.P. Sinnett and A.O. Hume began is covered quite well by Sinnett in his book, *The Occult World,* and the student is urged to read this account at the outset of his study. However, a few brief remarks at this point will not be out of order.

The story really begins with the arrival of Col. Olcott and Mme Blavatsky in Bombay in February of 1879, with few friends and perhaps a little uncertain what they were to do. Soon they received a letter from A.P. Sinnett, editor of the Allahabad *Pioneer,* a leading newspaper in India, in which he indicated interest in their ideas and stated that he would be pleased to have such information as might be used in his newspaper. Sinnett was a cultured and intellectual Englishman, perhaps best described as a 'true gentleman'. He was forty years of age at the time, married to a lady of equally fine endowments, named Patience, and they had a small son named Denny. As a result of Sinnett's letter, an acquaintanceship developed, and Mme Blavatsky and Col. Olcott were invited to visit the Sinnetts at Simla, the summer capital of India, during the fall of 1880.

During this visit with the Sinnetts, which lasted some six weeks, the Founders made the acquaintance of a number of prominent members of the British community, including a close personal friend of Sinnett's, Mr A.O. Hume, who had been for many years a high ranking member of the Government. Also during this time, H.P. Blavatsky produced a variety of psychic phenomena which she attributed mostly to the Mahatmas with whom she claimed to be in contact. Sinnett was much interested in these phenomena and realized their genuineness. Being of a practical and scientific turn of mind, he wished to know more about the laws which governed them and hoped to have some demonstrations that would silence the sceptics. He asked Mme Blavatsky whether it would be possible for him to get in contact with one of the Mahatmas and be instructed by him in such matters. She was doubtful but said that she would inquire. It is indicated that when she approached her own Master, Morya, on the question, he refused point-blank to have anything to do with such a correspondence. Apparently she tried others without success, but finally the Master Koot Hoomi agreed to undertake a limited correspondence with Sinnett. So Sinnett wrote a letter to the Mahatma and Mme Blavatsky transmitted it to him. In his letter, Sinnett suggested the production of a phenomenon which he considered to be so foolproof and irrefutable that it would compel the scientific world to admit the existence of powers in nature beyond their comprehension. This proposal was the production of *The Times* of London in Simla simultaneously with its production in London—Simla and London at that time being at least a month apart by all means of communication other than telegraph.

The reply which Sinnett received a few days later, marking the start of this unusual correspondence, began with this rather startling statement: 'Precisely because the test of the London newspaper would close the mouths of the sceptics, it is unthinkable.'

A few days later, A. O. Hume, who resided in Simla, wrote a long letter to this same Mahatma, in which he apparently proposed that if he were taught some of the hidden laws of nature and the secret wisdom of the Adepts, he would devote his efforts for the remainder of his life to spreading this wisdom in the Western world. The Mahatma Koot Hoomi stated in one of his later letters that he attached such great importance to this offer that he took the letter in person to his own superior for advice and counsel.

Methods of Correspondence

The question naturally arises as to just how the two Englishmen, Sinnett and Hume, carried on a correspondence over a period of years with persons whom they never saw and whose whereabouts were generally unknown to them. Apparently this involved a variety of methods. Much has been written on the subject, and some explanations are found in the letters themselves. Mme Blavatsky has given a number of hints and explanations in her various writings, but much is left to one's own comprehension and intuition. In general, the process appears to have been as follows: the two gentlemen would write their letters by hand, place them in envelopes, and either give or post them to Mme Blavatsky or some other designated agent of the Adepts. The letters would then be transmitted by the agent to the Adepts by occult methods. The replies followed much the same procedure, i.e., through an agent who precipitated the message onto paper or served as a psychic centre for the actual transmission of a letter through space. The message was then delivered, or posted, by the agent to the recipient. Apparently, in a few instances, the Adept himself wrote a letter and sent it through the regular post. Also it appears that there were occasional exceptions to all these methods. One point seems to be quite clear, and that is that it is very difficult for an Adept to produce such phenomena in connection with ordinary humans except through the agency of a chela, or someone who has the necessary psychic force. A useful reference in studying some of the occult laws involved in the production of the letters, including methods of precipitation, is the work of Geoffrey A. Barborka, *H.P. Blavatsky, Tibet and Tulku.*

Why the Letters Were Written

The question also naturally arises as to why the Adepts should take the time and make the effort to carry on a protracted correspondence with two such people. On this point we can only speculate. The letters give several hints which seem to indicate that the Adepts were seeking someone who could present the Eastern esoteric philosophy and metaphysics to the

Western scientific world in a logical and intelligent manner, so as to 'arrest the attention of the highest minds'. Apparently they wished to bring about acceptance of this philosophy by nineteenth century science and thus lead it away from strictly materialistic lines. They evidently foresaw the great revolutionary changes that were to take place in the near future and wished to channel them in more progressive directions and along more spiritual lines.

Perhaps these two Englishmen were likely prospects for initiating such a work, and they were situated so as to be reached without undue difficulty. Mme Blavatsky was not temperamentally suited for the presentation of such ideas in a form that would be acceptable to men of science, and Col. Olcott had not sufficient standing in the European scientific community for his ideas to carry much weight; besides, both had other important work to do. One should bear in mind that at the beginning of the correspondence the only available theosophical book of importance was *Isis Unveiled,* written by H.P. Blavatsky in New York in 1877—a book intended primarily as an 'opening wedge' for later and more detailed information on Theosophy.

There is much in the letters of a personal nature, some of which seems rather inconsequential. Nevertheless, these passages are of value and deserve careful reading by the student; they contain interesting character studies as well as many hints regarding the ways of the Adepts, the nature of their consciousness, their methods of training aspirants for the probationary path, and qualifications for discipleship.

The propriety of publishing the letters, especially the more personal parts, has been seriously questioned. Statements in the letters themselves indicate that they were written under very difficult circumstances and were never intended to be published verbatim. Rather, the teachings contained in them were to be worked over by Hume and Sinnett into a more suitable and coherent form for publication, and this was done by both of them. For example, Sinnett's work, *Esoteric Buddhism,* an early classic on the theosophical philosophy, was largely the result of the teachings conveyed to him through his correspondence with the Mahatmas. Hume contributed many articles to early issues of *The Theosophist.* But whatever the intentions of the Mahatmas concerning the ultimate disposal of their letters, these have been published, undoubtedly to the great benefit of the world and especially to students of Theosophy.

KEY TO ABBREVIATIONS

Books:

BTT	*H.P. Blavatsky, Tibet and Tulku,* Geoffrey A. Barborka
D	*Damodar and the Pioneers of the Theosophical Movement,* Sven Eek
Glossary	*Theosophical Glossary,* H.P. Blavatsky
HPB	H.P. Blavatsky, *Collected Writings,* vols. 1-10, ed. by Boris de Zirkoff
HPB Speaks	*H.P.B. Speaks,* vols. 1 & 2, C. Jinarājadāsa
Isis	*Isis Unveiled,* H.P. Blavatsky
Key	*The Key to Theosophy,* H.P. Blavatsky
LBS	*Letters of H.P. Blavatsky to A.P. Sinnett,* ed. by A.T. Barker
LMW	*Letters from the Masters of the Wisdom,* Ser. 1 & 2, ed. by C. Jinarājadāsa
MATL	*The Mahatmas and Their Letters,* Geoffrey A. Barborka
ML	*The Mahatma Letters to A.P. Sinnett,* ed. by A.T. Barker
ODL	*Old Diary Leaves,* Ser. 1-6, H.S. Olcott
OW	*The Occult World,* A.P. Sinnett, 9th ed., London, 1969
SD	*The Secret Doctrine,* H.P. Blavatsky, Adyar ed.
SH	*A Short History of the Theosophical Society,* Josephine Ransom

Persons:

AOH	A.O. Hume
APS	A.P. Sinnett
CWL	C.W. Leadbeater
DK	Djual Khul (various spellings)
DKM	Dāmodar K. Mavalankar

HPB	H.P. Blavatsky
HS	H.S. Olcott
KH	Mahatma Koot Hoomi
M	Mahatma Morya
MMC	Mohini M. Chatterjee
TSR	T. Subba Row

CONTENTS

CHRONOLOGY

Letter No.		Page No.		Date	Letters and Events
Chron.	*ML*	*1st & 2nd eds.*	*3rd ed.*		
				1879	
				Feb. 16	Founders arrive in Bombay on SS *Speke Hall,* accompanied by E. Wimbridge and Miss Rosa Bates. Also aboard was Ross Scott.
				Feb. (prob.25th)	A. P. Sinnett, Editor of *The Pioneer,* Allahabad, writes to HSO expressing interest in their work and asking for news.
				Summer	Temporary headquarters established in Malabar Hill district of Bombay.
				Aug. 3	Damodar K. Mavalankar joins TS.
				Oct. 1	First issue of *The Theosophist* published.
				Dec. 4	Founders arrive in Allahabad for their first visit to the Sinnetts. They meet AOH there. They remain about two weeks.
				Dec. 15-17	Founders make a short side trip to Benares and return to Allahabad. Mr and Mrs Sinnett join the TS.
				Dec. 30	Founders return to Bombay.

Letter No. Chron.	ML	Page No. 1st & 2nd eds.	3rd ed.	Date	Letters and Events
				1880	
				Mar. 18	Swami Dayanand of Arya Samaj breaks with TS (See Appendix C).
				Mar. 25	One of the Adepts passing through Bombay is visited by HPB, HSO & DKM.
				Mar. 28	Alexis & Emma Coulomb arrive in Bombay.
				May 7	Founders leave Bombay for a tour of Ceylon.
				July 14	Founders leave Ceylon for return to Bombay headquarters.
				Aug. 12	Rosa Bates and E. Wimbridge, who had accompanied the Founders to India, leave Bombay headquarters due to personal difficulties.
				Aug. 15	Henry Kiddle gives speech in US which is destined to be the cause of controversy later. ML-6, and ML-93.
				Aug. 27	Founders leave Bombay for first visit to Simla as guests of Sinnetts.
				Sept. 8	Founders arrive at Simla.
				Sept. 29	Pink Note phenomenon at picnic on Prospect Hill.
				Oct. 3	Cup and saucer phenomenon at picnic. Brooch No. 1 phenomenon at dinner at home of AOH.

Letter No. Chron.	Letter No. ML	Page No. 1st & 2nd eds.	Page No. 3rd ed.	Date	Letters and Events
				1880	
				Oct.13 (est.)	APS writes his first letter to an 'Unknown Brother'.
				Oct.15 (est.)	APS writes second letter to an 'Unknown Brother'.
1	1	1	1	Oct. 17	APS receives first letter from KH answering his two. AOH writes first letter to KH.
2	2	6	6	Oct. 19	APS receives second letter from KH.
3A	3A	10	10	Oct. 20	Phenomenon of Brooch No. 2 found inside pillow at picnic on Prospect Hill.
3B	3B	10	10	Oct. 20	
3C	3C	11	11	Oct. 20	
				Oct. 21	Founders leave Simla for Amritsar and tour of north-west India.
				Oct. 23	APS writes letter to KH and posts it to HPB in Amritsar for transmission.
				Oct. 24	Sinnetts leave Simla for home in Allahabad. Founders arrive at Amritsar.
				Oct. 27	HPB receives registered letter from APS and transmits it by occult means to KH, who is aboard train en route to Amritsar. He sends telegram to APS from Jhelum and instructs HPB to return the empty envelope to APS.

Letter No.		Page No.		Date	Letters and Events
		1st & 2nd	*3rd*		
Chron.	*ML*	*eds.*	*ed.*		
				1880	
4	143	488	481	Oct. 27	Sinnetts arrive home in Allahabad. APS receives note from KH (ML-143).
				Oct. 28-30	KH visits HPB in Amritsar; writes long letter to APS. Probably also his first long letter to AOH.
				Nov. 1	AOH receives first long letter from KH (See OW, p. 109). This was reprinted in *The Theosophist*, February 1959.
5	4	11	11	Nov.3 (est.)	APS in Allahabad receives KH's letter of Oct. 29. Founders leave Amritsar to continue tour of N.W. Provinces.
6	126	454	447	Nov. 3 (est.)	This is a postscript to ML-4.
7	106	443	436	Nov. (est.)	KH to APS.
				Nov. 17	Bombay headquarters moved to Breach Kandy (north-west suburb of Bombay) in absence of the Founders.
				Nov. 19	Letter written by APS to KH and mailed to HPB at Cawnpore for transmittal is abstracted from envelope en route by KH.
				Nov. 20	HPB ill with fever in Lahore—probably dengue. See ODL 2:266.

Letter No. Chron.	ML	Page No. 1st & 2nd eds.	3rd ed.	Date	Letters and Events
8	99	435	428	Nov. 20	AOH writes letter No. 99 to KH commenting on items in ML-4. He sends this to Sinnett in Allahabad to have him give it to HPB for forwarding to KH. Sinnett holds the letter until HPB's arrival on December 1st.
10	5	17	17	Nov.26 (est.)	KH to APS (in Allahabad) posted from Ambala where HPB was at the time. Probably not received by APS until about Dec. 1 or later.
9	98	434	427	Dec.1 (est.)	Sinnett gives HPB Hume's letter (No. 99) which she transmits to KH. Letter No. 98 is KH's quick response to Hume's comments.
11	28	207	205	Fall (est.)	KH to AOH in Simla.
				Dec. 1-11	Founders visit Sinnetts in Allahabad.
				Dec. 3	HSO goes to Benares for a short side trip to visit the Maharaja.
12	6	22	22	Dec. 10	KH to APS in Allahabad. Statements contained in this letter quoted by APS in OW, resulted in 'Kiddle Incident' (See Appendix E).

Letter No. Chron.	Letter No. ML	Page No. 1st & 2nd eds.	Page No. 3rd ed.	Date	Letters and Events
				1880	
				Dec. 11	HPB goes to Benares for a few days to join HSO. They visit the Maharaja. Motto of TS is adopted from the Maharaja's crest.
				Dec. 20	Founders return to Allahabad.
				Dec. 28	Founders leave Allahabad for return to Bombay.
				1881	
				Jan. 4	AOH starts writing continuing series of articles entitled 'Fragments of Occult Truth'.
				Jan. 20	Murad Ali Beg (Godolphin Mitford) comes to the Founders.
13	7	25	25	Jan. 20	KH to APS, received in Allahabad, enclosed with letter from HPB.
14	142A	486	479	Feb. (est.)	DKM to APS in Allahabad, with comments by KH.
14	142B	488	481	Feb. (est.)	Same.
				Feb. 19	One of the Adepts (probably the Master Hilarion) passes through Bombay on way from Cyprus to Tibet. ML, p. 36.
15	8	26	26	Feb. 20	KH to APS in Allahabad, through HPB in Bombay.
				Feb. (late) or early March	Sinnett family sails from Bombay for England, on vacation, via Ceylon. HSO receives note from KH enclosing ML-107 to be forwarded to APS.

Letter No.		Page No.		Date	Letters and Events
Chron.	*ML*	*1st & 2nd eds.*	*3rd ed.*		
				1881	
16	107	444	436	Mar. 1	KH to APS through HSO, received in Galle, Ceylon, *en route*. During the time APS was in England, he wrote and published his book, *The Occult World,* dealing with phenomena produced through HPB and his early correspondence with KH.
17	31	240	237	March 26	KH to APS, received in London.
				Apr. 23	HSO leaves Bombay for an extended tour of Ceylon.
				June	*Occult World* published.
				July 7	APS arrives in Bombay on his return trip from England. He remains a few days in Bombay, visiting HPB.
18	9	38	38	July 8	KH to APS. Received in Bombay
19	121	452	445	July 11 (est.)	KH to APS in Bombay.
				July 12	Probable date of return to Allahabad by APS. Patience and son Denny remain in England.
				July	HSO working with Buddhists in Ceylon; issues *Buddhist Catechism.*
				July 22	HPB leaves Bombay for Simla for visit to AOH family.
20	49	280	276	Aug. 5	KH to APS at Ambala. APS was *en route* to Simla at the time to join HPB at the Hume's home.

Letter No.		Page No.		Date	Letters and Events
Chron.	*ML*	*1st & 2nd eds.*	*3rd ed.*		
				1881	
				Aug. 21	Simla Anglo-Indian Branch formed (later Simla Eclectic).
21	27	204	202	Sept. (est.)	KH to APS, Simla. APS was staying with the Humes.
22	26	203	201	Sept. (est.)	KH to APS in Simla.
23	104	440	433	Sept. (late)	KH to APS in Simla. Informs APS of his proposed retreat for several months.
24	71	374	367	Sept. (late est.)	M to APS in Simla. This is M's first letter, thanking APS for the pipe which apparently APS had sent to him. (Method of transmission not indicated.)
				Oct. (early)	KH begins his retreat, presumably in order to prepare for and take his next initiation. M takes over the correspondence in his absence.
25	73	375	368	Oct. (early)	M to APS in Simla.
26	102	439	432	Oct. (est.)	M to APS in Simla.
27	101	439	431	Oct. (est.)	M to APS in Simla.
				Oct. 23	HSO crosses from Ceylon to tip of India to spend several days and then returns to Ceylon.
28	74	375	369	Oct. (est.)	M to APS in Simla
29	29	217	215	Oct. (est.)	M to APS in Simla (M's longest letter).

Letter No.		Page No.		Date	Letters and Events
Chron.	*ML*	*1st & 2nd eds.*	*3rd ed.*		
				1881	
				Oct. (late)	HPB leaves Simla for extended tour of N W India. She writes several letters to APS while on this tour.
				Nov.1 (est.)	APS returns to Allahabad from Simla.
30	134	461	454	Nov. 4	HPB writes to APS from Dehra Dun upon arriving there.
				Nov. (mid)	HPB visits Sinnetts in Allahabad, returns to Bombay towards end of month.
31	40	254	251	Nov.	M to APS in Allahabad.
32	114	449	442	Nov.13 (est.)	M to APS in Allahabad.
33	38	250	247	Dec. 19	M to APS in Allahabad.
				Dec. 13	HSO sails from Ceylon; arrives in Bombay on Dec. 19.
34	39	253	249	Dec. (est.)	M to APS in Allahabad.
35	41	256	252	Dec. (est.)	M to APS in Allahabad.
				Dec. 28	Ross Scott marries Minnie Hume, AOH's only daughter. Marriage was arranged by HPB on Master's instructions.
				1882	
				Jan.1	At the beginning of 1882, the Founders were in Bombay. APS was in Allahabad; his family was aboard ship *en route* to Bombay from England. AOH presumably was in Simla,

Letter No. Chron.	Letter No. ML	Page No. 1st & 2nd eds.	Page No. 3rd ed.	Date	Letters and Events
				1882	
					and KH had emerged from his retreat but had not yet put himself in contact with his correspondents.
36	36	248	244	Jan. (early)	M to APS in Allahabad.
37	37	248	245	Jan. (early)	DK to APS in Allahabad, telling of KH's return from his retreat.
				Jan.	APS goes to Bombay to meet his family who arrive on Jan. 6. They stay with Founders for a few days.
38	90	412	406	Jan. 6	Stainton Moses to APS, dated London Nov. 26. (This letter apparently came on the same ship with Mrs Sinnett.)
Note appended to ML-90					
		415	409		KH to APS, a note regarding the letter from MS which APS was waiting to show to HPB; this note was formed on blank paper in front of both of them.
				Jan. 10	D. M. Bennett arrives in Bombay on world tour. Sinnetts leave for home in Allahabad.
39	115	449	442	Jan. (before 12th)	M to APS in Bombay.

Letter No. Chron.	Letter No. ML	Page No. 1st & 2nd eds.	Page No. 3rd ed.	Date	Letters and Events
				1882	
				Jan. 12	Sixth Annual Convention of TS held in Bombay. APS did not stay for this, as suggested by the Mahatmas. The annual convention was held a month late this year due to Olcott's late return from Ceylon.
40	108	444	437	After	M to APS in Allahabad (both letters on a single sheet).
41	109	444	437	Jan. 12	
				Jan. (late)	Rev. Joseph Cook arrives in Bombay and denounces Theosophy and the Founders.
				Jan. (est.)	Cosmological Notes, M to AOH (See Appendix).
42	43	258	255	Jan. 28	M to APS in Allahabad.
43	42	257	253	Feb. (est.)	M to APS in Allahabad.
44	13	70	70	Jan. 28	M to APS in Allahabad (Cosmological Notes).
45	44	263	259	Feb. (est.)	M to APS in Allahabad.
46	12	66	66	Feb. (est.)	M to APS in Allahabad.
47	45	264	260	Feb. (est.)	KH to APS. First regular letter after his retreat.
				Feb. 17	HSO leaves Bombay on North Indian tour, is accompanied by Bhavani Shankar.

Letter No.		Page No.		Date	Letters and Events
Chron.	*ML*	*1st & 2nd eds.*	*3rd ed.*		
				1882	
48	47	271	267	Mar. 3	M to APS in Allahabad, through Damodar.
49	48	273	269	Mar. 3	KH to APS in Allahabad.
				Mar. 10	HSO and Bhavani Shankar Rao arrive in Allahabad, *en route* to Calcutta. Stop with Sinnetts for a few days.
50	88	410	404	Mar. 11	KH to APS in Allahabad, through HSO or Bhavani Shankar Rao, both of whom were at home of APS.
				Mar. 11	Plaster cast phenomenon by M. (Broken fragments transported occultly from Bombay to Allahabad.) One of the very few demonstrations of phenomenon made by M.
51	120	452	444	Mar. 12 (est.)	KH to Mrs Sinnett in Allahabad, enclosing lock of hair.
				Mar. 13	HSO and Bhavani Shankar Rao at APS home in Allahabad; leave to continue on their journey.
52	144	488	481	Mar. 14	KH to APS in Allahabad ('no power'). Seven words.
				Mar. 15	Wm. Eglinton, English medium, sails from Calcutta for England on s.s. *Vega*.
53	136	464	457	Mar. 17	HPB in Bombay to APS in Allahabad.
54	35	246	242	Mar. 18	KH to APS in Allahabad.

	Letter No. Chron.	Letter No. ML	Page No. 1st & 2nd eds.	Page No. 3rd ed.	Date	Letters and Events
					1882	
3					Mar. 22	'*Vega* phenomenon'. KH appears to Eglinton aboard ship at sea.
					Mar. 24	HPB in Bombay and HSO and Gordons in Calcutta receive instantaneous confirmation from Eglinton of visit by KH aboard ship at sea.
	55	89	410	404	Mar. 24	KH to APS in Allahabad *re: Vega* incident.
	56	100	438	431	Mar. 25	HPB to APS in Allahabad *re: Vega* incident with comment by KH (See LBS, p. 8).
					Apr. 1	HPB leaves Bombay for Calcutta, via Allahabad; joins HSO there on April 6. Bengal TS Branch formed.
					Apr. 19	Founders sail from Calcutta for Madras.
	57	122	452	445	Apr. 27	KH to APS in Allahabad; letter appears to have been transmitted through agent in London.
					May 3	Founders in Madras, start extended houseboat trip on Buckingham Canal.
	58	130	457	450	May 7	TSR to APS in Allahabad, offering to give him occult instructions as per request of M.
					May 31	Founders inspect Huddleston Gardens in Adyar and decide to purchase for headquarters. They then return to Bombay.

Letter No. Chron.	Letter No. ML	Page No. 1st & 2nd eds.	Page No. 3rd ed.	Date	Letters and Events
				1882	
59	132	459	452	June 3	TSR to HPB, with comments by KH to APS. Parts of the
60	76	376	369		same letter, accidentally separated in publishing the book.
61	17	117	113	June	KH to APS (Question and Answer series).
				June	Sinnetts go to Simla for the hot season.
62	18	119	115	June	KH to APS (Question and Answer series).
63	95	429	423	June	KH to APS (continuation of ML-18).
64	131	458	451	June 26	TSR to APS in Simla.
65	11	59	59	June 30	KH to AOH in Simla.
66	14	78	77	July 9	KH to AOH in Simla.
67	15	88	87	July 10	KH to AOH in Simla.
				July 15	HSO leaves Bombay for extended tour of Ceylon. ODL 2: 368.
68	16	99	97	July (after 5th)	KH to APS (Devachan letter).
69	69	373	366	July	KH to APS in Simla.
70A	20A	123	120	Aug. (early)	AOH to KH (with marginal notes by KH).
70B	20B	125	121	Aug. (early)	APS to HPB (with marginal notes by KH).

Letter No.		Page No.		Date	Letters and Events
Chron.	*ML*	*1st & 2nd eds.*	*3rd ed.*		
				1882	
70C	20C	127	123	Aug. (early)	KH to APS in Simla.
71	19	122	119	Aug. 12	KH to APS in Simla.
72	127	455	447	Aug. 13	KH to APS and AOH in Simla.
73	113	448	441	Aug.	KH to APS in Simla.
74	30	228	225	Aug. (est.)	KH to AOH (probably never delivered).
75	53	294	290	Aug. (after 23rd)	KH to APS in Simla.
76	21	134	131	Aug. 22	KH to APS in Simla (written Aug. 12).
77	50	286	282	Aug.	KH to APS in Simla.
78	51	287	283	Aug.22	KH to APS *re* Col. Chesney.
79	116	450	443	Aug.	KH to APS in Simla.
80	118	450	443	Aug. (est.)	KH to APS, sends lock of hair for Denny's health.
81	52	288	284	Aug. (est.)	KH to APS in Simla.
82	32	242	239	Aug.26 (est.)	KH to APS in Simla, *re* AOH
83	125	453	446	Aug. (end)	DK to APS, *re* Oxley.
84	111	446	439	Sept. (est.)	KH to APS in Simla.
85A	24A	178	175	Sept. (mid)	KH to APS in Simla (famous contradictions).

Letter No.		Page No.		Date	Letters and Events
Chron.	*ML*	*1st & 2nd eds.*	*3rd ed.*		
				1882	
85B	24B	180	177	Sept. (mid)	Same.
				Sept. (late)	HPB goes to Sikkim to visit M and KH for a few days, is rejuvenated and returns to Darjeeling for a period of rest.
86	112	447	440	Fall (est.)	KH to APS in Simla, *re* Col. Chesney and Oxley.
87	34	245	242	Fall (est.)	KH to APS in Simla.
88	10	52	52	Sept. 28	KH to AOH, *re* 'God'.
89	46	268	264	Fall (est.)	M to APS, *re* AOH and HPB's visit to Sikkim.
90	22	137	133	Fall (est.)	KH to AOH.
91	110	445	437	Oct. (early)	KH to APS from Sikkim.
				Oct. 7	APS elected President of Simla Eclectic TS.
92	54	302	298	Oct. (after 7th)	KH to APS in Simla. Written from Phari Dzong Monastery in Tibet, near the Sikkim border. Tells story of the goat eating his letters.
93A	23A	144	141	Oct. (est.)	KH to APS in Simla.
93B	23B	149	145	Oct. (est.)	KH to APS in Simla.
94	117	450	443	Oct. (est.)	KH to APS in Simla, introducing Mohini.
				Nov. 3	HSO arrives in Bombay from Ceylon tour.

Letter No.		Page No.		Date	Letters and Events
Chron.	*ML*	*1st & 2nd eds.*	*3rd ed.*		
				1882	
				Nov. (early)	Sinnetts return from Simla to Allahabad. HPB stops with them on her return trip from Darjeeling, where she had been resting, to Bombay.
95	72	374	368	Nov. (early)	KH to APS in Allahabad, *re* Mohini.
96	92	419	413	Nov. 23	KH to APS in Allahabad, giving him passwords which must appear on any genuine communication through a medium.
				Nov. 25	HPB arrives in Bombay from her Darjeeling trip, via Allahabad.
97	70	373	367	Dec. 7	KH to APS in Bombay. Seventh annual convention of TS held in Bombay. APS presided. Convention was held early due to pending move to Adyar.
98	105	441	434	Dec.	KH to APS, probably in Allahabad. APS had just received notice of his termination as editor of *The Pioneer*.
99	78	378	372	Dec.	KH to APS.
100	79	382	376	Dec.	KH to APS.
				Dec. 17	Bombay headquarters closed and Founders leave for Madras, arriving there on Dec. 19; they settle in the new quarters at Adyar, in Huddleston's Gardens.

Letter No. Chron.	ML	Page No. 1st & 2nd eds.	3rd ed.	Date	Letters and Events
				1883	
101	57	327	322	Jan. 6	KH to APS in Madras, where he apparently was on a business trip.
102	56	325	320	Jan. (est.)	KH to APS in Allahabad, *re* AOH.
103A	91A	415	409	Jan. 8 (est.)	KH to APS in Allahabad, *re* C.C. Massey.
103B	91B	416	409	Jan.8 (est.)	KH to APS in Allahabad *re* C.C. Massey.
104	25	191	188	Feb. 2	KH to APS in Allahabad (Devachan Notes).
105	80	383	377	Jan. (est.)	KH to APS in Allahabad, *re* proposed newspaper (*The Phoenix*).
106	103	440	432	Feb.	KH to APS in Allahabad.
				Feb. 20	HSO goes to Calcutta in effort to enlist support for proposed newspaper.
107	77	377	371	Mar. (late)	KH to APS in Madras. The Sinnetts had gone to Madras preparatory to returning to England, where they planned to stay until the 'Phoenix' affairs were settled.
108	58	336	331	Mar.	KH to APS in Madras.
109	119	451	444	Mar. (est.)	KH to unidentified person at Adyar.
				Mar. 30	Sinnett family sails for England. It was expected they would return in the autumn if *The Phoenix* venture proved successful. They arrived in England on April 26.

Letter No.		Page No.		Date	Letters and Events
Chron.	ML	1st & 2nd eds.	3rd ed.		
				1883	
				Apr. (est.)	APS begins another book on esoteric philosophy, based on the information received through the letters from the Mahatmas. This was published as *Esoteric Buddhism*.
110	67	371	364	May 27	KH to HSO (Forwarded to APS in London, re *Phoenix* business). Received June 16.
111	59	338	333	July	KH to APS in London. APS had published *Esoteric Buddhism* in June.
				July 7	HPB goes to Ootacamund to visit Gen. Morgan and family.
112	81	383	377	July	KH to APS in London, *re* spiritualistic phenomena.
113	82	387	381	Aug. (est.)	KH to APS in London. *Phoenix* business.
114	83	393	387	Sept. 16 (est.)	KH to APS in London. *Phoenix* business.
				Oct. & Nov.	HSO, DKM, and William T. Brown on an extended tour of North India. During this time, while the party is in Jammu, Kashmir, DKM disappears for a few days on visit to his Master.
115	128	456	449	Nov. 25	Two telegrams from HSO to HPB regarding DKM's dis-
116	129	456	449		appearance; note inserted by Mahatma KH in ML-129, probably in transit.

Letter No. Chron.	ML	Page No. 1st & 2nd eds.	3rd ed.	Date	Letters and Events
				1883	
117	93	420	413	Winter	KH to APS, explaining the 'Kiddle Incident'. See Appendix E.
118	96	431	424	Dec.	M to APS in London, advising him of fraud being perpetrated at spiritualistic seance.
				Winter	KH passes through Madras on his way to South East Asia. See ML, p. 421.
				Dec.	CWL and Sir William Crooks join TS. Subba Row medal established.
				1884	
119	86	403	396	Jan.	KH to APS in London, enclosing a letter to be read to the
120	85	398	392		London Lodge, dated 7 December 1883.
121	84	397	391	Jan.	KH to APS in London, *re* London Lodge affairs.
122	87	406	399	Feb. 7	KH to APS about London Lodge affairs, dated Jan. 17 from Adyar.
				Feb. 20	Founders, together with MMC, sail from Bombay for Europe. They arrive at Marseilles on Mar. 12. HPB stayed in Europe for three weeks and HSO went on to London.

Letter No.		Page No.		Date	Letters and Events
Chron.	*ML*	*1st & 2nd eds.*	*3rd ed.*		
				1884	
123	68	372	366	Apr. 7	KH to APS, giving him encouragement.
					HPB arrives unexpectedly at London Lodge election. She returns to Paris in about a week.
124	94	429	422	Apr. (est.)	KH to APS.
125	61	349	344	Apr. 15	M to APS, telling him of the poor treatment he has been giving MMC.
				May 14	Coulombs expelled from Adyar Headquarters.
				June 29	HPB goes to London, stays with Arundales until Aug. 15.
				May-June	Society for Psychical Research takes testimony from HSO, APS, & MMC.
				June	Laura C. Holloway, American psychic, comes to London to work with the Theosophists.
				June-July	H. Schmiechen, German portrait painter, paints portraits of the Mahatmas M and KH, under inspiration. (Originals now at TS Headquarters in Adyar.)
126	62	351	345	Jul. 18	KH to APS.
				Jul. 21	Farewell meeting in Princess Hall for Founders.
				Jul. 23	Founders go to Germany.

Letter No. Chron.	ML	Page No. 1st & 2nd eds.	3rd ed.	Date	Letters and Events
				1884	
127	133	460	453	Jul. (est.)	HPB to APS.
				Aug.	MMC and Holloway publish book, *Man, Fragments of Forgotten History*.
				Aug. 15	HPB at Elberfeld, Germany, is joined by MMC, Holloway, and others.
128	63	356	350	Summer (est.)	KH to APS in London, *re* publication of his letters.
				Sept. 15	H. Schmiechen paints portrait of HPB in Elberfeld. (Now in TS Headquarters in Varanasi.)
129	60	349	343	Sept.(end)	KH to APS in London, *re* portraits.
130	55	322	317	Oct.2 (est.)	KH to APS.
				Oct. 6	HPB returns to London.
131	66	366	360	Oct. 10	KH to APS, *re* Mrs Holloway.
132	135	464	457	Oct. (est.)	HPB to APS, both in London.
				Oct. 20	HSO sails from England for Madras, via Marseilles.
				Oct. (est.)	Mabel Collins publishes *Idyll of the White Lotus*.
				Nov. 1	HPB sails from England for Madras on s.s. *Clan Drummond*.

Letter No. Chron.	ML	Page No. 1st & 2nd eds.	3rd ed.	Date	Letters and Events
				1884	
133	137	467	459	Nov. 8	HPB to APS, written aboard ship and posted from Algiers.
134	64	358	352	Nov. 8	KH to APS in London.
				Nov. 10	HSO arrives in Bombay.
				Nov. 17	HPB, at Port Said, is joined by CWL.
				Dec. 18	R. Hodgson arrives in Madras to start investigations of TS for Society for Psychical Research.
				Dec. 21	HPB and party arrive at Adyar.
				Dec. 22	Hodgson visits Adyar.
				Dec. 24	Kingsford and Maitland resign from London Lodge.
				1885	
				Jan.	R. Hodgson from SPR conducts his inquiry into psychic phenomena and events at Adyar.
				Jan. 9	HPB gets plan for *The Secret Doctrine* from M.
				Jan. 14	HSO and CWL sail for tour of Burma.
				Feb. 23	DKM leaves Adyar on his trip to Tibet, never to return.
				Mar. 19	HSO returns to Adyar due to serious illness of HPB and other difficulties there.

Letter No. Chron.	Letter No. ML	Page No. 1st & 2nd eds.	Page No. 3rd ed.	Date	Letters and Events
				1885	
135	138	468	460	Mar. 17	HPB to APS in London, telling of troubles at Adyar.
				Mar. 25	R. Hodgson leaves Adyar.
136	65	362	356	Mar. 27	KH to APS in London (apparently enclosed in LBS-32).
				Mar. 31	HPB leaves Adyar for last time, accompanied by F. Hartmann, Mary Flynn, and Bawaji. Sails for Naples; starts getting material for *The Secret Doctrine*.
				Apr. 13	DKM leaves Darjeeling on final leg of his journey to Tibet.
				Apr. 29	HPB in Italy, spends spring and summer in Italy and Switzerland.
				Aug.	HPB moves to Germany.
137	97	433	426	Sept. or Oct.	M to APS in London, *re* his personal affairs.
138	145	488	481	Sept. or Oct.	KH to APS (six words of encouragement).
				Aug.	HPB settles in Germany to live. Works on *The Secret Doctrine*.
				Dec.	Countess C. Wachtmeister joins HPB at Würzburg. Official SPR report issued.

Letter No. Chron.	ML	Page No. 1st & 2nd eds.	3rd ed.	Date	Letters and Events
				1886	
				Jan. 1	HSO initiates construction of the Adyar Library.
139	140	478	470	Jan. 6	HPB in Würzburg to APS in London, *re* Hodgson report.
140	141	482	474	Mar. 17	HPB to APS.
141	139	475	468	Mar. 19	HPB to APS.
				July 8	HPB leaves Elberfeld, on her move to London.

LETTERS FOR WHICH NO DATES ARE ASSIGNED

Letter No. Chron.	ML	Page No. 1st & 2nd eds.	3rd ed.	Letters and Events
A	33	244	241	KH to APS
B	75	375	369	KH to unidentified person
C	123	453	446	KH to APS
D	124	453	446	KH to APS, *re* 'three pebbles'

STUDY NOTES

The chronological numbers of the Letters are shown first in each heading, immediately followed by the numbers as listed in ML, in parentheses. It is recommended that the Chronology be followed, along with the Study Notes, as pertinent events are listed therein.

1 (ML-1)   Page 1   Folio 1   Recd. Oct. 17, 1880 (est.)

DESCRIPTION

In dull black ink, on both sides of white paper. There are some smears and write-overs and, in a few instances, words have been crossed out. In the bottom right-hand corner of the first page are three rather large red dots in the form of a triangle with a small ink mark underneath which looks like an initial. The signature is in slightly blacker ink than the text, and the script is not quite the same. This characteristic is noticeable in several of the earlier letters. Note the formal type of address and the four-part signature. These change in a short while.

CIRCUMSTANCES

HPB and HSO were at Simla, the summer capital of India, as guests of the Sinnetts. Simla is located about 200 miles north-east of New Delhi and at an elevation of nearly 8000 feet in the foothills of the Himalayas. Many prominent Englishmen went there during the hot season and the Viceroy and his staff moved there for several months of the year. The capital of India at that time was in Calcutta. Earlier in the month a number of unusual phenomena had been produced there, through the agency of HPB, for the benefit of her hosts and other friends. APS desired to get in communication with some of the 'Mahatmas' to whom HPB gave most of the credit for the phenomena, and she had agreed to try to accomplish this.

In OW (pp. 81-83) Sinnett explains what he wrote in his first letter to the Mahatma and why he wrote it. In spite of his conviction of the genuineness of the phenomena performed by HPB during the summer of 1880 at Simla, he felt that they were not always surrounded by the necessary safeguards and that it would not be very difficult for any thoroughgoing sceptic to cast doubt on their validity. He was eager to have some phenomenon produced which would, as he expressed it, 'leave no opening for even the suggestion of imposture'. He wondered whether the 'Brothers' themselves might not always realize the necessity for rendering their test phenomena unassailable in every minor detail.

So Sinnett decided that, in his first letter to the Mahatma, he would suggest a test which he was sure would be absolutely foolproof and which could not fail to convince the most profound sceptic. This was the simultaneous production in Simla (in the presence of the group there) of one day's editions of the London *Times* and *The Pioneer*.

At that time, London and India were at least a month apart by all means of communication other than telegraph, and it would obviously have been impossible for the entire contents of *The Times* to have been telegraphed to India in advance of its publication in London, and to appear in print in India at the same time that it appeared in print in London. Further, such a project could not have been undertaken without the whole world knowing about it.

After he had written the letter and delivered it to HPB, a day or so passed before he heard anything about its fate. Finally, HPB told him he was to have an answer. This so encouraged him that he sat down and wrote a second letter, feeling that perhaps he had not made his first letter quite strong enough to convince his correspondent. After the lapse of another day or so, he found on his writing table, one evening, his first letter from the Mahatma KH. It answered both of his letters. By what means the letter reached his desk without any apparent intermediary, he does not attempt to say.

At the time of writing this letter, KH was at Toling Monastery in Tibet, apparently travelling from Shigatse to some point north-west of Kashmir. Toling is near the city of Gungotree (Gangotri) in Tibet, almost directly across the Himalayas from Simla.

REFERENCES

The letter opens abruptly with an explanation of why the phenomena suggested by APS are impracticable.

p. 2 (middle): '...does not quite date from 1662, when Bacon, Robert Boyle and the Bishop of Rochester transformed under the royal charter their "Invisible College"...' Sir Francis Bacon died in 1626. Charles Boyle was born in 1627. However, the *Encylopedia Britannica* says of Boyle: 'Boyle's great merit as a scientific investigator is that he carried out the principles which Bacon presented in Novum Organum.' According to the encyclopedia, the 'Invisible College' became the 'Royal Society of London for improving natural knowledge' in 1662. See also Alphabetical Notes on the Royal Society.

'Roma ante Romulum fuit': Rome was before Romulus.

'...the great Syracusan': Archimedes, one of the most celebrated of the ancient physicists and geometricians, '...the only one among the ancients who has left us anything satisfactory on the theory of mechanics and on hydrostatics' (*Encyclopedia Americana*).

'The *vril* of the "Coming Race".': A term used by Bulwer-Lytton in his novel, *The Coming Race*. It designated a mysterious form of energy. (See Alphabetical Notes.)

The *akas,* or *akasha,* to which the Mahatma refers is that first differentiation of the eternal primordial substance mentioned innumerable times in the SD and defined in Vol. 4

(4th Ed.), p. 81, as 'the Universal Soul, the Matrix of the Universe, the Mysterium Magnum from which all that exists is born by separation or differentiation. It is the cause of existence; it fills all the infinite Space, is Spapce itself in one sense. ...'

p. 3: '...Newton's fine discoveries ...' There are indications that Newton was much more conversant with occult science than he publicly dared to admit.

p. 4 (top to mid-page): Remarkable paragraph showing KH's wide range of knowledge. See Alphabetical Notes on individuals mentioned.

(bottom): '...the goddess Saraswati ...' Goddess of learning in the Hindu pantheon.

Just a brief mention of one sentence near the bottom of p. 4 which would be easy to miss: 'I listened attentively to the conversation which took place at Mr Hume's ...' Apparently this posed no problem for the Mahatma; it seems a rather casual comment involving so stupendous a power.

A bit later the Mahatma mentions three of the phenomena that had taken place at Simla and which had inspired Sinnett to learn more: the note, the cup, and the brooch. The description of these phenomena will be found in OW (9th ed.): Note, 54 *et seq;* cup, 58 *et seq;* and the brooch, 68 *et seq*.

p. 5: '...those who generally deal with the European mystics'. There are several references in the Letters to the existence of different sections of the Occult Brotherhood. The first contacts that Olcott had with the Adepts in New York came through the Egyptian Section.

'...the *Pioneer* ...': *The Pioneer,* Allahabad, of which APS was editor. This was the outstanding British newspaper in India at that time.

The letter closes with the admonition to 'TRY' and the Mahatma promises that if Sinnett will work on the material he already has, 'we will be the first to help you get further evidence'.

For a detailed commentary on the contents of this letter, see *The Mahatmas and Their Letters,* pp. 123-167 by Geoffrey A. Barborka.

It is believed that this first letter was dictated to and precipitated by the Master KH's disciple, Djual Khul (See Alphabetical Notes). The full signature, 'Koot Hoomi Lal Singh' was discontinued quite soon and the Master signed simply Koot Hoomi, or KH. To document the conclusion concerning Djual Khul: some time later, writing on other matters, the Mahatma comments on the 'Lal Singh' and says that it was probably 'invented as half a *nom de plume* by Djual Khul and carelessly allowed by me to take root without thinking of the consequences' (See ML p. 364/358).

2 (ML-2) Page 6 Folio 1 Recd. Oct. 19, 1880.

DESCRIPTION

Similar in appearance to ML-1 and in the same dull black ink. On 6 sheets of standard-size white paper, on both sides. Also, as in ML-1, the signature is in a somewhat different script from the text and in a slightly darker ink. It has a tinge of red in places. Also the signature varies a little from the previous one in that the last three parts are all joined together and the 'h' at the end is illegible or missing. There are three dots in the form of a triangle beneath the signature.

CIRCUMSTANCES

Similar to those of ML-1. The first letter received from the Mahatma KH was written from Toling Monastery, a relatively short distance over the border in Tibet. When the second was written (or precipitated), the Mahatma had left Toling Monastery and was somewhere in the Kashmir Valley on his way to consult with the Mahachohan about a letter he had received from A.O. Hume, and other matters.

As explained by Sinnett in OW (90-91), Hume had read the first letter from the Mahatma and, becoming enthused with the possibilities of such a correspondence, decided to write to KH himself. In that letter he offered to give up everything and go into seclusion if only he could be trained in occultism so that he could return to the world and demonstrate its realities.

REFERENCES

The opening sentences of letter 2 are only slightly less devastating than the first sentence of letter 1. 'We will be at cross-purposes in our correspondence until it has been made entirely plain that occult science has its own methods of research as fixed and arbitrary as the methods of its antithesis, physical science, are in their way. ...'

The Master cites Sinnett's suggestions about dealing directly with the Mahatmas. '...and yet,' he says, 'as you say yourself, hitherto you have not found "sufficient reasons" to even give up your "modes of life"—directly hostile to such modes of communications. This is hardly reasonable.' Sinnett's 'mode of life' was, of course, the popular one: alcohol, tobacco, meat-eating, etc. Several times in the letters, the Mahatma reminds him that they cannot have personal contact until or unless he is willing to give up these habits. 'He who would lift up high the banner of mysticism and proclaim its reign near at hand, must give the example to others. He must be the first to change *his* modes of life; and regarding the study of occult mysteries as the upper step in the ladder of Knowledge, must loudly proclaim it such despite exact science and the opposition of society.'

The Mahatma mentions that he has received a letter also from Mr Hume but says that since the 'motives and aspirations' of the two Englishmen are 'diametrically opposite in character' he must answer the two letters separately.

The Mahatma's reply to Hume's letter is not included

in ML but is found (with the exception of some personal references) in OW, p. 100 *et seq* (9th ed.) It is a most remarkable letter, containing many revealing and important statements concerning the philosophy and practices of the Adepts. Pertinent to these notes is the statement: '...we do not refuse to correspond with, and otherwise help, you in various ways. But what we do refuse is to take any responsibility upon ourselves than this periodical correspondence and assistance with our advice and, as occasion favours, such tangible, possibly visible proofs as would satisfy you of our presence and interest.' Mrs Sinnett made a copy of this letter and it is included with the letters to Sinnett in the British Museum.

The Master then outlines Sinnett's motives for seeking special conditions under which to continue the correspondence. The student should study this paragraph on p. 7. The Mahatma then continues: 'To our minds then, these motives, sincere and worthy of every serious consideration from the worldly standpoint, appear—*selfish*...because you must be aware that the chief object of the T.S. is not so much to gratify individual aspirations as to serve our fellow men. ... Perhaps you will better appreciate our meaning when told that in our view the highest aspirations for the welfare of humanity become tainted with selfishness if, in the mind of the philanthropist, there lurks the shadow of desire for self-benefit or a tendency to do injustice, even when these exist unconsciously to himself. ...'

The Mahatma's statements in this letter are unequivocal. The matter of establishing a separate branch, independently of HPB and Col. Olcott, is rejected. Sincere tribute is paid to these two who have ventured so much in the cause of Theosophy. '...would it not be a palpable injustice to ignore them as proposed in an important field of theosophical effort? Ingratitude is not one of our vices. ...'

The Adepts throughout the correspondence stressed the question of *motive*. KH takes Sinnett to task for wanting to receive occult instruction without subscribing to the basic concept of the parent Theosophical Society—that is to say, 'Universal Brotherhood'.

p. 9: '...Mad. B. ...' HPB. Some of the other names by which she is designated in the Letters are 'the Old Lady', 'the Old Woman', 'Upasika' (a female disciple).

'... the contemplated Anglo-Indian* Branch...': Reference to a branch of the TS proposed to be formed in Simla by APS and AOH for the study of occultism and phenomena. The Mahatma states that neither HPB nor Olcott has the 'least inclination' to interfere with the management of such a branch but that, if formed at all, it 'must' be a branch of the Parent Society 'and contribute to its vitality and usefulness by promoting its leading idea of a Universal Brotherhood and in other practicable ways'.

p. 10 (top): 'Our visible agent': HPB.

'...the "brooch" affair ...': This refers to the so-called No. 1 brooch phenomenon which occurred on October 3 at a dinner-party in the Hume house. This was a brooch belonging to Mrs Hume and not the one referred to in 3B(ML-3B). The occurrence is described in OW, pp. 68-75. The incident is referred to a number of times in ML.

This letter is signed 'Koot' Hoomi Lal Sing' (the name seems to be spelled both 'Singh' and 'Sing').

3A, B & C (ML-3A, B & C) Page 10 Folio 1
Recd. Oct. 20, 1880.

DESCRIPTION

The explanatory note by APS preceding the message from KH is on smooth white notepaper, written in black ink.

* Today, an Anglo-Indian is one with mixed European and Indian blood. Formerly the term applied to a person of British birth but living or having lived long in India.

ML-3A is on this same type of folded notepaper and in black ink. The script is finer than in the previous two letters. Again, the signature is in a darker ink and different script from the body of the letter. ML-3B is on a full-sized sheet of white paper. The writing is in the same ink and, as in ML-3A, the signature is in a different script and slightly darker ink. Part of it has a slight reddish tinge. The paper has been folded both ways so as to make a square and then folded twice diagonally. On one of the triangular folds is the following:

A.P. Sinnett, Esq.
c/o Mrs Sinnett

ML-3C is on a sheet of paper about 8″ x 7″, folded, in ink and script similar to parts of A & B. All three notes were received by APS on the same day. It is interesting that all the letters received while HPB was at Simla during that season are in this colour of ink.

CIRCUMSTANCES

The circumstances are partially explained in APS's note preceding 3A (ML-3A). The Founders were still in Simla as guests of the Sinnetts. The student should read OW, pp. 98-101 (9th ed.) for a description of events.

REFERENCES

The story of these three letters is usually called the 'pillow incident' although sometimes it is referred to as the 'brooch 2 incident'. It seems to show that the Mahatma was willing to go to considerable trouble (especially considering that he was physically miles away from Simla) to gratify to some extent the longings of his correspondent and to give him direct evidence of his existence.

'...pink paper...': This refers to an earlier phenomenon which occurred on September 20, when Mrs Sinnett received a note from KH written on a piece of HPB's pink paper. See OW, pp. 4-56 and ODL, 2:232. 3B, p. 10: 'This brooch,

No. 2...': Brooch No. 1 was involved in the phenomenon at the home of AOH at a dinner-party on October 3. See Study Notes on Letter 2 (ML-2). See OW, p. 70.

The second paragraph refers to the question of how correspondence with the Mahatma was to be carried on after HPB left Simla, which she expected to do soon. 'One of our pupils will shortly visit Lahore and N.W.P.' (North-West Province). [See Letter 5 (ML-4), pp. 15-16 for a description of some of the difficulties.]

KH informed APS on several occasions that the Adepts are not allowed to waste energy, and that in order to communicate with the public, they have to have certain conditions, which are usually accomplished through their chelas or special agencies.

p. 11 (top): '...through—pillows'. Refers to the phenomena then being performed. (See p. 34 near the end of the first full paragraph.)

'... a Kashmir Valley ...': KH was travelling through Kashmir to somewhere in the north-west. (For the story of KH's many travels see Appendix F.) 3C: This note was received by APS at dinner time. The reference to 'your last note' is to a note written by APS to KH just as the party was leaving for a picnic on Prospect Hill. See OW, pp. 100-1.

'...pillow-*dak* ...': Dak is an Indian term meaning, generally, postal service or post office, and is often used in combining form to indicate delivery of some sort. See Alphabetical Notes.

The 'amorous major' mentioned at the end of the note was Major Philip D. Henderson. He was present on the occasion of the cup and saucer phenomenon and helped dig them out of the ground. He joined the TS on that day, his membership certificate being produced phenomenally on the spot. However, the next day he became suspicious and resigned, thereafter joining HPB's critics.

See Sinnett's account of the cup and saucer phenomenon

in OW 58 et seq. See also Josephine Ransom's *Short History of the Theosophical Society,* Adyar, Theosophical Publishing House, 1938, pp. 146-148, for the story of Major Henderson's involvement with the Theosophical Society. Nowhere is there a hint of why the Mahatma described him as 'amorous'.

4 (ML-143) Page 488/481 Folio 3 Recd. Oct. 27, 1880

DESCRIPTION

APS's message is on one side of a card; the Mahatma's reply is on the other side. Dull black ink.

CIRCUMSTANCES

The Founders had left Simla on Oct. 21 for a tour of NW India. The Sinnetts had returned to Allahabad on Oct. 24. Just before leaving Simla, APS had written the short note to KH asking whether the latter wished him to include the story of the 'pillow phenomenon' of Oct. 20 in his newspaper, *The Pioneer*. He received the reply (appended to this note) after he had arrived at his house in Allahabad. He published the story in the paper on Nov. 7. See OW, pp. 96-101 for a description of the phenomenon.

REFERENCES

'Our much ill-used friend...': A reference to HPB.

Note also KH's remark about using his first name. He soon ceased to use the 'Lal Singh'.

5 (ML-4) Page 11 Folio 1 Recd. Nov. 3, 1880, Dated Oct. 29, 1880

DESCRIPTION

In dull black ink on both sides of 8 sheets of full-sized white paper. The script varies somewhat in weight and appearance. The signature is in four separate parts. The 'K' has a backward turned curl at the top of the upper arm. Beneath the signature in Devanagari characters, is a transliteration of 'Koot Hoomi Lal Singh'.

CIRCUMSTANCES

HPB and HSO left Simla on October 21 for Amritsar and a tour of the North-West Provinces. Before leaving Simla, HSO had written an account of some of the phenomena that had occurred there during the previous few weeks and had sent this to DKM in Bombay to be reproduced and circulated to the TS members. It was entitled 'A Day with Madame Blavatsky'. This was to have repercussions.

The Sinnett family left Simla on October 24 for their home in Allahabad. Just before leaving, APS wrote a letter to KH which he sent by registered mail to HPB at Amritsar for her to transmit to the Mahatma.

Shortly after the arrival of the Founders at Amritsar, HPB became aware of trouble caused by the story that HSO had sent to DKM. One of the newspapers had somehow procured a copy of it and had published it. Unfortunately, HSO, in his account, had mentioned the names of several prominent Englishmen as being involved in the phenomena, and some of these persons were very unhappy about this. HPB became frantic and called (occultly) upon KH to help her. He was at the time *en route* (in his physical body) through Ladakh, in the far north of India, on his return from a visit to the Mahachohan. After receiving her urgent message he decided to alter his route and come to Amritsar to see her. Meanwhile,

HPB, then at Amritsar, received APS's letter (Oct.24) and transmitted it occultly at once to KH who was at that moment aboard the train on his way to see her. He instructed her to return the empty envelope to APS and he himself got off the train at the next stop (Jhelum), and went into the station and sent a telegram to APS acknowledging receipt of the letter. He wrote out the text of the telegram by hand on the standard form, which of course was filed by the telegraph agent. At a later date APS obtained this telegram form, which is the one in the British Museum folio. After arrival in Amritsar, KH wrote a long letter [5 (ML-4)] to APS in Allahabad. APS did not receive the letter until about Nov. 3. Since HPB was available at this time for transmission of the letter and it is in dull black ink on her type of paper, it seems probable that the letter was precipitated by her. (See OW, pp. 103-7 and ML, p.19.) It is probable also that while at Amritsar, Mahatma KH wrote his long letter to Hume in reply to Hume's first letter to him. (See OW, p.110 et seq.)

REFERENCES

'Amrita Saras': Literally the 'Fount of Immortality', the name of the Golden Temple of the Sikhs in the lake in Amritsar. See ODL 2:251.

p.11 (bottom): Regarding references to the impending Russo-Chinese war, see 7 (ML-106), p. 443/436; also comments by AOH in 8 (ML-99), p. 209/207 and OW, p. 110.

' " Olcott has raised the very devil again!" ': Reference to the article sent by HSO to DKM, mentioned above under 'Circumstances'. See also explanation in the middle of p. 19.

p. 12: 'Saraswati': Goddess of speech and of sacred or esoteric knowledge and wisdom. (Glossary)

p. 12: 'Nagas'; Exoterically serpent gods or dragons; esoterically, wise men endowed with great knowledge and wisdom.

'... forgot that she was speaking English': A very interesting comment. Both KH and HPB were fluent in French and seemingly used that language in their verbal intercourse, as a general rule.

'Marcus Aurelius', Roman Emperor AD 161-80, author of *Meditations*. See Alphabetical Notes.

'...*Yog Vidya* ...': Occult Wisdom. See p. 436/428, last paragraph.

'Vakil': An Indian lawyer.

p. 13 (top): '... your letter of the 24th inst'. The letter which APS had written to KH just before leaving Simla. Apparently APS had written up some of the Simla happenings for his newspaper. KH then proceeds to explain the receipt of this letter as mentioned under 'Circumstances' above.

'Mr Hume's proposition...': As contained in his first letter to KH. The reply referred to is printed in part in OW, p. 110 et seq.

'Our Mahat...': The Mahachohan, KH's superior, whom he had just recently visited. See Alphabetical Notes.

'...an Anglo-Indian Branch...': The first reference to a branch of the TS which had apparently been suggested by APS and AOH, but which actually did not come into existence for a number of months.

'...our friends... Simla visit...': Reference to HPB and HSO and their recent visit to Simla. This was their first real contact with anyone in India but Indians.

'... Bombay publication ...': Again a reference to the newspapers publishing the article HSO had sent to DKM, intended only for members of the TS. ('A Day with Madame Blavatsky')

p. 14 (middle): '...A.I.B. ...': The Anglo-Indian Branch.

p. 15 (middle) '...our holy Shaberons ...'. Superior adepts.

'...designate an agent between yourself and us...': KH was seeking means for transmitting letters between himself and APS while HPB was away. See 3B (ML-3B), p. 10, and

6 (ML-126), p. 454/447. See ODL 2:252-3 for HSO's description of the incident involving 'the young gentleman' spoken of here and mentioned in 6 (ML-126) as being 'unfit for the useful office of intermediary' because of his 'sentimentalism'.

p. 16 (middle): '...A.I.T.S. ...': Anglo-Indian TS. See 11(ML-28), p. 209/207.

(bottom) '... a *Cis* and *Trans*-Himalayan "cave dweller"...': Reference by KH to himself.

p.17: ' "Many are the grains of incense ..." remarked a great man ...': Seemingly a reference to Marcus Aurelius, Roman emperor and philosopher, who is reputed to have made such a statement after having been refused admission into the Eastern Mysteries.

(middle): '...renewal of the vision ...': See 3A (ML-3A), p. 10.

'... Simla is 7,000 feet higher than Allahabad ...': An indication that geographical elevation has something to do with psychic atmosphere. There are other similar references in the letters.

(last par.): ' "Universal Brotherhood" ...': APS and AOH were not as yet interested in this aspect of Theosophy.

'...my letter to Hume...': This is the letter found in OW p. 110 et seq. It is a long and important letter and apparently the first one written to Hume.

6 (ML-126) Page 454/447 Folio 3 Recd. Nov. 3, 1880 (est.)

DESCRIPTION: KH to APS

On a sheet of heavy rough greyish paper, about 6″ x 8″, in black ink. It appears to be a postscript to 5 (ML-4).

CIRCUMSTANCES

Similar to those of the preceding letter. KH is trying to find suitable means of carrying on the correspondence after HPB returns to Bombay. See Study Notes on 5 (ML-4), ref. to p. 15.

REFERENCES

'Both B. and I had counted much upon ...': Presumably 'B' means HPB.

'N.W.P.' North-West Provinces, now part of Pakistan.

The Adepts explain in several instances that they are not permitted to waste energy, and that in order to transmit letters occultly with non-members of their fraternity, they must have suitable conditions. Normally, for this purpose, they make use of one of their chelas or disciples as an intermediary. Letter 52 (ML-144), consisting of seven words, which KH sent to Sinnett without use of an intermediary, illustrates the excessive amount of power involved. KH remarks in Letter 54 (ML-35) that this effort cost him several days of recuperation.

7 (ML-106) Page 443/436 Folio 3 Recd. Nov. 1880 (est.)

DESCRIPTION

On a single folded sheet of rippled white rice paper, in blue ink, large lettering, and fine lines. The envelope is attached, addressed: 'A.P. Sinnett, Es.' in large script different from that of the letter.

CIRCUMSTANCES

The Founders had been touring NW India and were returning to Bombay via Allahabad. The Sinnetts were at home in Allahabad.

REFERENCES

'...authority of our Priestly King'. Seemingly a reference to the Dalai Lama, then ruler of Tibet. See Alphabetical Notes. Refer to ML, pp. 11 and 435/428 regarding this threatened invasion of Tibet.

8 (ML-99) p. 435/429 Dated Nov. 20, 1880
9 (ML-98) p. 434/427 Dec. 1 or later

DESCRIPTION: AOH to KH

Letter 8 (ML-99) is a letter from AOH to KH, forwarded to APS by KH with his comments thereon [Letter 9 (ML-98)]. AOH's letter is in black ink on folded paper.

Letter 9 (ML-98) by KH is on both sides of two sheets of standard size white paper, unfolded, in blue ink, with well-formed fine lettering. The signature is in a script different from the text and similar to that in the first four letters. The signature has a line extending from the final 'h' clockwise entirely around the name. The envelope is attached with comment thereon in pale blue pencil in KH script: 'Read and returned with thanks and a few commentaries. K.H.'[1]

Letters 8 and 9 have to be considered together. Letter 8 is dated 20 November 1880, but it was not transmitted to the Mahatma until 1 December 1880 or later. Letter 9 was received on 1 December 1880 or shortly thereafter, on the same date that 8 was transmitted to KH. Letter 8 is a letter from Hume to the Mahatma; Letter 9 is a reply to that letter but is directed to Sinnett rather than to Hume.

This may seem confusing. In OW, p. 122, Sinnett mentions that Hume wrote a long reply to the Mahatma's *first* letter to him and, subsequently, an *additional* letter to KH which he forwarded to Sinnett, asking him to read it and then seal it up and send or give it to HPB for transmission, since she was expected soon at Allahabad. Letter 8 is this *additional* letter.

HPB arrived at Allahabad on Dec. 1, and undoubtedly Sinnett gave the letter to her on that date or shortly thereafter.

In Sinnett's account in OW, p. 122, he describes the care with which he had sealed Hume's letter, using a stout envelope and gumming and sealing it thoroughly. When it was returned, Sinnett examined it carefully and found that '...it was absolutely intact, its very complete fastenings having remained just as I arranged them'. Undoubtedly one reason why Mr Hume's letter was returned was because of the numbered paragraphs; KH numbers his own paragraphs to correspond.

Hume's letter (8) is almost wholly concerned with comments the Mahatma had made to Sinnett in Letter 5 (ML-4). Hume takes a rather superior attitude and obviously intends to give the Mahatma a 'set down'. Hume's pride —which he was never able to conquer and of which, unfortunately, he was unaware (it being so ingrained in his nature)—had been pricked by the Mahatma's letter to Sinnett, which the latter has shared with him. He feels that KH doesn't understand him and goes to some length to state some of his views and to 'set the Master straight' on a number of points.

In the first paragraph of Letter 8 (ML-99), the Mahatma has inserted an asterisk after the statement. 'And yet every letter I see of yours, shows me that you do not yet realize what I think and feel.' In letter 9 (ML-98) the Mahatma has begun by using a corresponding asterisk and saying, 'I realized it perfectly...'

The Mahatma's first numbered paragraph in 9 refers to Hume's implied criticism of the governments of Tibet and India, which does seem to carry a certain self-righteous tone. The 'English speaking vaquil' referred to by Hume refers to a comment made by the Mahatma in Letter 5 about the English speaking 'vakil' (different spelling of no consequence) who had spoken slightingly of Theosophy and yoga (see ML p. 12).[2] Hume takes occasion to voice his questions concerning the manner in which the Mahatmas guard their knowledge.

Obviously, in this paragraph, Hume sees himself as the man willing to come forward 'gratuitously, manifestly at the sacrifice of his own time, comfort and convenience', to teach 'what he believes to be for the good of mankind to know'. He never quite understood why his offer to become a chela of the Mahatmas was rejected.

At the end of Letter 9, the Mahatma tells Sinnett that he mailed a letter to him 'the other day from Umballa [usually spelled Ambala]; I see you did not receive it.' It is the next letter to be considered.

Footnotes to Letters 8 and 9

1. It is not clear why the two letters are reversed numerically in the book. Perhaps it was just a slip on the part of A.T. Barker.

2. A 'vaquil' is a native lawyer who speaks English; presumably a person of some education.

10 (ML-5) Page 17 Folio 1 Dated Nov. 26, 1880, Recd. after Dec. 1, 1880

DESCRIPTION

In dull black ink on both sides of five full-sized sheets of rippled white rice paper. The full signature appears at the end of the letter, but the 'Lal Singh' has been crossed out. The upper hook on the 'K' is looped to the right. The 'Lal Singh' was seldom used thereafter. See ML, p. 218.

CIRCUMSTANCES

HPB had recovered sufficiently from her attacks of fever while on tour in the NW Provinces to resume her travels, and the Founders were on their way south, planning to visit the Sinnetts in Allahabad on their way to Bombay. The letter was posted at Umballa (or Ambala).

REFERENCES

It is interesting to observe the change in salutation and complimentary closings which KH uses from this time on. The reason for this is explained by APS in OW, p.100.

p. 17 (first sentence): APS apparently had written a letter to KH and forwarded it, together with a note, to HPB at Cawnpore, asking her to transmit it to KH. Due to her weakened condition as a result of the fever from which she had just recovered, KH saved her energy by abstracting his part from the envelope *en route*.

p. 18 (top): See OW, p. 124, for explanation concerning the letter to AOH.

The warning that the proposed Anglo-Indian Branch could never be a success with Hume in it proved to be true.

(middle): '...consent to have "a nigger"...': The attitude of the British toward the Indians at that time was discriminatory.

'Desdemona...Othello': A reference to the Shakesperian play.

(bottom):'... an atmosphere of sandalwood and cashmere roses'. Several references in theosophical literature indicate that the Adepts often create an atmosphere of fragrant scent when they wish to make an appearance in surroundings not especially conducive to such a visit. It is also indicated that each Adept has his own distinctive fragrance.

p.19 (top): '...section of our fraternity...': Other references in the *Letters* indicate that there are several sections in the Adept Brotherhood which operate in various parts of the world and have different responsibilities.

'...across the threshold...': Perhaps this refers to Initiation.

p. 19 (top): '...section of our fraternity...': Other references in the *Letters* indicate that there are several sections in the acknowledgement of it from Jhelum [see Study Notes on 5 (ML-4)]. See p. 13 and OW, pp. 104-5. The telegram is in

Folio 6 in the British Museum, but not published by Barker. It is shown in facsimile on page 81 of HPB II, also on pp. 212-13 of Barborka's book, *The Mahatmas and Their Letters.*

'...multum in parvo...' Much in little.

p. 19 (middle) ' "A day with Madame B." ...': Reference to the article by HSO about the Simla phenomena, and which was intended for distribution to TS members only, but which unfortunately was published by some of the Indian papers.

p. 19 (bottom): The statement by KH that his letters are 'impressed' or precipitated was made at a time when this mode of transmission was being used. It is evident that this method was not used exclusively in later correspondence.

p. 19 (bottom): 'Et voici pourquoi nous n'irons plus au bois': 'And this is why we go no more to the woods.'

(bottom): 'Did you write "tune"?' See top of p. 14 ('out of time').

p.20 (near top): '...the Shaberon of Than-La'. The term 'Shaberon' is used to denote a superior adept. Presumably in this instance it is a reference to the Mahachohan.

p.20 (lower half): Sinnett was very much interested in psychic phenomena and retained this interest throughout his life. The Mahatma does not discourage him in this matter, but gives him some advice on how to proceed.

p. 21: 'Of course you ought to write your book.' This refers to APS's suggestion that he write up the phenomena which had taken place that summer at Simla and reveal some of the information received from KH. He did this later in *The Occult World.*

'...Dr Wyld...Mr Massey...Lord Lindsay...': See Alphabetical Notes.

'...on her way down home'. Reference to HPB's trip back to Bombay and her probable visit to the Sinnetts *en route.*

11 (ML-28) ***Page 207/205*** ***Folio 2*** ***Recd. Late autumn 1880 (est.)***

DESCRIPTION: KH to AOH

On both sides of eleven sheets of white paper, in black ink. The script is larger than usual and varies somewhat from the customary KH style. The complimentary closing is in the stilted formal style of that time and the signature is the full four-part name used in the early letters.

CIRCUMSTANCES

Since the exact date of this letter is not known, it is difficult to assign the circumstances. It is, however, probable that Hume was still at home in Simla, that the Sinnetts had just returned to their home in Allahabad, and that Olcott and HPB were on their tour of north-west India. Apparently the formation of the 'Anglo-Indian Branch' was under way. APS, in his notation on this letter, makes reference to a 'final break-off ' with AOH. This was obviously an earlier threatened break, as the Mahatmas corresponded with him for some time longer. See LBS-4, p. 5. In ML, p. 208/206, KH mentions that he must 'decline for the present any further correspondence'. It seems evident that this letter is in response to AOH's answer to KH's reply to Hume's original letter to KH.

REFERENCES

p.209/207: In connection with the comments on this page, the student might refer again to pp. 12 and 16; also to OW, p. 110 (KH's first letter to AOH).

The Master states unequivocally that the new Anglo-Indian Branch must be a branch of the parent T.S. and not an independent society.

p. 209/207: '...amidst the glaciers of the Himalayas': Again, a reference to a stratification of psychic atmosphere.

'...Lord Lytton's father ...': Bulwer Lytton. Lord Lytton was Viceroy of India at this time.

p. 210/208: '...our chiefs—they *hope*'. An indication that there exists in man a certain amount of free will. (See also p. 211/209 directly opposite.) The comment seems to indicate that even the Adepts are not always able to predict the direction of events.

p. 210/208 (middle): 'Then came yours—unexpectedly.' A reference to Hume's first letter in which he expressed his willingness to dedicate his life to the service of humanity or some such offer. Some students speculate that it was not the intent of the Master KH to have Hume as a correspondent.

p. 211/209 (top): This gives some of the reasons why the Adepts were willing to take part in the Simla phenomena.

(middle): '...brooch phenomenon...': A reference to Brooch No.1 phenomenon, which occurred in AOH's house at a dinner-party. See OW, p. 70 and ODL, 2:237.

p. 212/210 (bottom): '...*apres moi—le déluge*': After me, the deluge.

p. 213/211 (middle): '...*quid pro quo* ...' : Thing given as compensation.

p. 214/212 (near top): '...*entente cordiale* ...': A friendly understanding.

(middle): '..."Parthian arrow"...': Allusion to a trick used by the ancient Parthian horsemen who would pretend to flee and, when the pursuer was off guard, would shoot their arrows backward over their shoulders. Hence an expression denoting trickery by trying to lead the adversary into an unsuspected trap.

'...your "little birds"...': Reference to AOH's interest in ornithology. He maintained a large museum in his house. See Appendix B.

p. 216/214 (bottom): Some interesting comments on conscience and its limitations.

p. 217/215: A warning to AOH that the future held some dangerous situations in regard to his association with the T.S., which all too truly came about.

12 (ML-6) Page 22 Folio 1 Recd. Dec. 10, 1880

DESCRIPTION

In blue ink on both sides of four full-sized sheets of white paper. The signature has a circle drawn completely around it, similar to that of Letter 9 (ML-98), p. 427.

CIRCUMSTANCES

The Founders had been visiting the Sinnetts on their way back to Bombay. HSO had gone on a side trip to Benares, and HPB went over on the 11th to join him for a few days. KH (according to his statement; see last par., pp. 415-17) was on a long horseback trip and had been riding continuously for 48 hours during the time he was composing this letter, which was being precipitated by an inexperienced chela. This is the first of the 'blue ink' letters, the previous ones having all been in black ink on white letter paper and presumably precipitated.

REFERENCES

The first paragraph appears to be in reply to some question by APS concerning the method used by the Mahatma in preparing his letters.

p. 22: '...*lithophyl* (or lithobiblion) ...': Rock engravings, or the records of nature imprinted in rocks.

Paragraph 2 seems to answer an inquiry from APS as to whether he should write something in *The Pioneer* in refutation of the slanders being published as a result of the story sent by HSO to DKM. See pp. 12 and 19. This has reference to the account by HSO entitled 'A Day with Madame Blavatsky', in which he described some of the phenomena produced by HPB in Simla, and which account caused such a stir by the Englishmen whose names were given in the account.

Paragraph 3 also seems to be in reply to a question. The phrase 'I have my "proprietors" also' is an analogy to the management of a newspaper so familiar to APS: the Adepts have *their* superiors, to whose policies they must conform.

p. 23 (top): '... my *Essay* ...': See p. 20, about three-fourths down the page, where KH offers an essay.

'... do not fail to write to Lord Lindsay'. See Alphabetical Notes and p. 21, mid-page.

(near top) '... "Moggy" and Davison ...': 'Moggy' was Mrs Hume. Davison was a personal secretary to the Humes. See Alphabetical Notes.

p. 23 (middle): Here we have a succinct statement as to why the correspondence was permitted and undertaken.

p. 24: The passages here contain the alleged plagiarism of a speech by Henry Kiddle in Boston. For an explanation and a correct rendering of the text see Letter 117 (ML-93) beginning on. p. 420/413. See also Appendix E: 'The Kiddle Incident.' It is interesting that the Mahatma let Sinnett 'sweat it out' for two years before giving him an explanation of what happened in that letter.

p. 24: 'Planetary Spirits': The rulers or governors of the planets. In occultism the term is generally applied to the seven highest hierarchies pertaining to our earth globe.

13 (ML-7) Page 25 Folio 1 Recd. Jan. 30, 1881

DESCRIPTION

In blue ink on both sides of two sheets of regular-sized white paper, signed simply 'K.H.' Most of the letters after this date are signed in this fashion. The 'H' in this letter is, however, formed differently from later ones. It contains no date or salutation. The script is different from that of Letter 12 (ML-6).

CIRCUMSTANCES

The Founders had returned to Bombay after this stop in Allahabad on their way home from Northern India. APS was at home in Allahabad. This letter was enclosed with one from HPB mailed from Bombay on January 28.

REFERENCES

The first paragraph refers to the disappointment of APS that he had not been able to have personal contact with KH.

p. 25: '...found their *Ultima Thule* ...': The highest point of attainment. Another statement by the Mahatma that they avoid as much as possible living in the outside world. It also means somewhere 'at the end of the world'. In Letter 5 (ML-4) page 12 (bottom) KH remarks that he could not stand the atmosphere of Amritsar for more than a few days.

The second paragraph tells APS that he can expect little in the way of psychic development as long as he continues to live the life of an average Westerner.

'...our venerable Khobilgan ...': The Mahachohan.

'...the stone of Sisyphus ...': A metaphor for unceasing fruitless toil. It derives from the story of the avaricious king of Corinth who was doomed forever in Hades to roll a heavy stone to the top of a hill, only to have it roll back down again.

(bottom of page): KH makes some interesting comments on the subject of 'motive'.

p. 26: '...the "foreign Section"...': This is another reference to the fact that the Adept Brotherhood has sections in different parts of the world. See top of p. 19; also p. 5.

14 A & B (ML-142 A & B) Page 486/479 Folio 6
Recd. before Feb. 20, 1881 *(est.)*

DESCRIPTION: Damodar to APS

Not obtained.

CIRCUMSTANCES

Similar to those of Letter 13 (ML-7). DKM was at the Bombay headquarters. On p.26 (ML-8, Letter 15), KH explains the reason for this letter. ODL 2:291 *et seq* explains that DKM was living with the Founders and helping with the work.

REFERENCES

Sinnett, who was sincerely interested in the welfare of the TS, had asked for some suggestions. It does not seem to be specifically stated, but it seems reasonably safe to assume that the Mahatma instructed Damodar to write to Sinnett, giving the point of view of the Hindus. 14A (ML-142A) contains Damodar's suggestions.

p. 486/479: Devoted mostly to DKM's exposition of why the esoteric teachings should not be disseminated too freely to the public—an attitude common to many of the Indians.

p. 478/480 (middle): '...found inadvisable by our "Brothers" ...': The Adepts.

'...thought ... they could see phenomena...': Some people even today join the TS hoping to gain psychic powers or see phenomena. Frequently they become dissatisfied when this does not happen.

Letter 14B (ML-142B) would seem to be a note of transmittal that Damodar attached to his letter, which he evidently submitted through his superior, Mahatma KH, and to which KH added a few comments for Sinnett's benefit. Why Barker separated these into two letters is not clear.

15 (ML-8) Page 26 Folio 1 Recd. Feb. 20, 1881 (est.)

DESCRIPTION: KH to APS

In blue ink on both sides of 12 full-sized sheets of paper. Some words in the letter have been marked out. Just prior to the place where the note is inserted by DK (p. 34), the script becomes smaller and finer. A comment near the end of the letter would indicate that it was being written by KH himself somewhere in the high mountains. The salutation is on the same line as the opening of the text.

CIRCUMSTANCES

APS was in Allahabad. The Founders were in Bombay. KH and DK were apparently somewhere in a high altitude. APS indicates that he received the letter through HPB, presumably meaning through the post. The evidence would therefore seem to indicate that the letter was written down by KH or DK, transported occultly to HPB in Bombay, where it was rematerialized and then sent by regular post. This was the last letter received by APS before leaving for England on vacation, during which time he wrote and published *The Occult World*.

REFERENCES

p. 26: The opening paragraph apparently deals with some actions taken by APS with respect to modifying the 'Rules' of the TS, perhaps influenced by the comments in 14 (ML-142). It is a good example of KH's light way of expressing himself on occasion.

'...a kind of *Kalki Avatar* ...': One who appears at the end of the fourth and last Yuga of a Maha Yuga (Great Age), i.e. the Kali-Yuga, or dark age. See also Alphabetical Notes under Yuga.

'... the *fata morgana* ...': A mirage, from Morgan le Fay, the sorceress sister of King Arthur.

'... the word *fecit* ...': He did it, from the Latin verb *facio*, to do, or cause to be done.

'... the sternest of Khobilgans'. The Mahachohan.

'... somewhat lengthy farewell epistle ...': This was to be his last letter to APS before the Sinnetts left for England on holiday for three months.

p. 26 (near bottom): KH explains why he cannot appear in his physical body to Sinnett.

p. 26 (near bottom): 'When I am not permitted to do so for Olcott ...': It is worth while to comment on this statement. It seems to the careful student of the Mahatma Letters and from other available information that the Adepts do not visit very often in their natural physical bodies the world outside their retreats removed from the influences of the outside world. The number of these contacts in their natural bodies seems to be extremely few. Even HPB during her five years in India saw the two adepts in their physical forms only a very few times. From the Mahatma's statement here, it seems apparent that Olcott likewise had few such visits. The evidence seems to indicate that nearly all of the 'so-called' visits that were being had by various TS members in those early days of the Society by Adepts were in their Mayavi Rupas or 'illusory bodies' and not in their natural physical bodies. In the book of Mahatma Letters as edited by Barker, there are only two instances to be noted where HPB contacted KH in his natural body, once when he came to Amritsar to see her and once when she went to Sikkim to meet him and Master M. there.

pp. 26-27: '... Lord Crawford and Balcarres ...': See Alphabetical Notes. This is an interesting analysis and a long lament on what the Western social world and its obligations do to spiritual life. The rather lengthy comments about Lord Crawford would seem to be intended to serve the dual purpose of preparing Sinnett for his meeting with the Earl when he was in England on his vacation, and also perhaps as a help to Lord Crawford himself.

p. 27: '... become an English Dupotet ...': A reference to the French Dupotet who was one of the early investigators of mesmerism.

pp. 28-29: Here KH very patiently undertakes to explain how occult communication is carried on and the impediments to direct contact between them.

'... psycho-physiological *tamasha* ...': Playful mischief or fun.

p. 29 (top): KH suggests here that sound has also a higher medium of transmission than the air, a higher correspondence of some sort. Some scientists today favour a hypothesis similar to this.

On this page, KH tries to explain why it is so difficult for the Western mind to comprehend the things of the spirit.

p. 30 (bottom): '... semi-intelligent Forces ...': Probably referring to the grades of beings in the elemental kingdoms. The comments regarding their forms being composed of sound and colour are interesting in relation to clairvoyant sight.

p. 31: '... *vera pro gratis* ...': Unsolicited advice.

'... that *Missio in partibus infidelium* ...': Literally mission in the lands of the unbelievers.

p. 31 (bottom): This is in connection with APS's proposal to write a book about occultism and the Adepts. This appeared later as *The Occult World*.

p. 32: ' "Mejnour"... as an ideal character ...': The adept hero of Bulwer Lytton's occult novel, *Zanoni,* published in 1842. See Alphabetical Notes on author.

p. 22: 'Addison': English essayist, 1672-1719.

p. 32: 'Orphan Humanity': A phrase expressive of humanity's unique position in the scheme of things.

p. 33: '... inform Dr Wyld ...': President of the TS in England at the time; apparently a very orthodox man. See Alphabetical Notes.

p.33: 'Sannyasis': Ascetics who have renounced worldly things.

In the next paragraph we find the statement, 'Precipitation in your case having become unlawful...' There has been considerable speculation about the reason for the temporary prohibition against using precipitation in correspondence with the Englishman. We find the explanation rather buried in another letter and while not explicit as to details, it lays the responsibility squarely on the shoulders of

Hume, '... the unpleasant fact that we are forbidden to use one particle of our powers in connection with the *Eclectic* (for which you have to thank your President and *him alone*' (ML p. 181/178). This paragraph also underlines the supposition that KH may have been writing this personally. He is short of paper and apparently feels he would not be justified in using his occult powers to produce it—or ink, either. The phrase about being in a place where 'a stationer shop is less needed than breathing air' would imply that he is in some isolated spot in high mountains.

'A friend promises to supply me in case of great need with a few stray sheets, memento relics of his grandfather's will, by which he disinherited him and thus made his "fortune".' This friend is, of course, his chela, Djual Khul, who was accompanying him on this trip. He is frequently referred to in the letters as 'the Disinherited' a nickname given him because he was disinherited when he became a chela of the Mahatma KH. He is also sometimes called Benjamin, probably from the biblical story of Benjamin, the youngest son of Jacob, for whom his father showed a special affection.

p. 34: Obviously Sinnett had asked permission of KH to include in his proposed book certain of the letters (or extracts therefrom) which he had received from the Mahatma, and now, p. 34, the Mahatma tells him he places no restriction upon his letters *except* (and here is a strong hint that there is one letter from the Mahatma which was withheld from publication in the published letters, or it may not even now be in existence).

p. 34 (middle): KH's parenthetical statement requesting a recipe for making blue ink is very interesting since it indicates that he or DK actually wrote out some of the 'blue ink' letters. We have no indication whether or not APS ever complied with this request.

P. 34: '...my friend tells me...': Again, a reference to DK.

'... a *thirteenth* cup...': Reference to the phenomenal

production of the extra cup and saucer during the picnic at Simla on 3 October 1880. OW, p. 58 et seq.

'The pillow was chosen by yourself...': Reference to the Brooch No. 2 phenomenon at the picnic on Prospect Hill at Simla on 20 October 1880, when a brooch belonging to Mrs Sinnett was found inside a pillow (OW, p. 98 et seq). Several phenomena are described in OW and ODL.

'The "Disinherited" ': A nickname for DK.

p. 35 (near top): '... various thaumaturgists ...': From thaumaturgy. See Alphabetical Notes.

(near bottom): '... our two agents ...': HPB and HSO.

p. 36 (par. 2): '... the Maratha boy's letter ...': A reference to DKM and the letter he wrote to APS on KH's instructions about the rules of the Society [Letter 14 (ML-142)]

'Farewell until your return ...': Notifying APS that he would not be hearing from him during his vacation in England, but indicating that he might be able to impress ideas on his mind if circumstances were favourable.

There is a very interesting postscript to the letter. KH refers to the medium D. D. Home, a man of Scottish birth but brought up in the United States. He later went to England where he was active in spiritualist circles and became acquainted with Lord Lindsay and other interested persons. He even managed for a time to prejudice Lord Lindsay's mind. Apparently he was a rather unsavory character. Mephitis means an offensive smell, hence one concludes that the man was a 'stinker', or a 'real skunk'. (See Alphabetical Notes.)

16 (ML-107) Page 444/436 Folio 3 Recd. March 1, 1881 (est.)

DESCRIPTION: KH to APS

As in the case of several of the letters, it is written on a sheet of rippled white paper which has been folded. It is in dark blue ink, written with a sharp pen. The letter starts on the front in the normal manner, continues on right side of the inside of the fold, then crossways on the left side of the inside. The signature is unusual in that it is: 'KH and—'.

One further very short letter was received by Sinnett before he was well on his way to England. It came through Olcott. It had been sent to him from the Mahatma KH with instructions to deliver it to Sinnett without HPB's knowledge, for she was at that time very upset emotionally and in a critical state of health. Olcott received it after the Sinnetts had sailed but was able to forward it to him at Ceylon (now Sri Lanka), which was his first stop after leaving India.

The transmittal note with which this letter was sent is found in LBS, p. 363. Sinnett has noted that it was received at 8.30 p.m. on 1 March 1881, 'on journey to Europe'.

The note says: 'Dear O: Forward this immediately to A.P. Sinnett, and do not breathe a word of it to H.P.B. Let her alone, and do not go near her for a few days. The storm will subside.'

REFERENCES

p. 444/436: The letter to Sinnett begins with a rather light touch: 'My dear Ambassador—' The Mahatma had, in effect, given Sinnett some commissions to carry out during his visit to England. The first paragraph seems largely concerned with an attempt to reassure Sinnett concerning HPB. So, says the Mahatma, he is sending along this note to Olcott by a friend to have it forwarded without HPB's knowledge.

The letter contains a suggestion and a word of encouragement to Sinnett to 'consult freely with our friends in Europe and return with a good book in your hand and a good plan in your head'.

The 'good book' was, of course, *The Occult World.* Obviously, knowing that Sinnett was in—or was to be in—Ceylon, KH asks him to encourage the 'sincere brethren of

Galle' (Galle being at that time the principal seaport of Ceylon) thus showing that he was still in full accord with all the plans. It is not clear why he was to telegraph the Inspector of Police there: perhaps he was a member of the TS. Nor is it clear to whom he refers as 'another person' to whom HPB is to do the same. A still further mystery is the signature: 'K.H. and ...' Perhaps it is the 'friend' referred to above, in which case it was probably Djual Khul, since this chela was with him when he was writing his long farewell letter to Sinnett; he may have been the one who transmitted the letter to Olcott.

The friends in Europe with whom he was to 'consult freely' can be identified in previous letters—primarily, of course, Lord Lindsay, but also the members of the TS there, including Dr Wyld who had such 'original' ideas about the Brothers.

The Mahatma, all the way along, has been most encouraging to him about writing his book.

17 (ML-31) Page 240/237 Folio 2 Recd. March 26, 1881 (in London)

DESCRIPTION: KH to APS

In blue ink on two sheets of white paper, both sides in fine lettering. The transmittal envelope is in the British Museum Folio. It is addressed to 'A.P. Sinnett, Esq. F.T.S., c/o Herbert Stacks, Esq., 30 Kensington Park Gardens, London'. There is a 35¢ French postage stamp affixed to the lower right-hand corner of the envelope.

REFERENCES

This appears to be the only letter received by Sinnett from the Mahatma while he was in England. The envelope in which it was enclosed is with the original letter in the British Museum.

Two curious facts about the envelope are that it bears a French postage stamp, and that the writing of the address is quite different from KH's familiar script and also from that of the accompanying letter.

Geoffrey Barborka, in his book (MATL, p. 84) engages in some interesting speculation about these facts. He suggests that the Mahatma composed the letter and transmitted it from Terich-Mir, where he was at the time, to an adept member of the Fraternity somewhere in France. This adept then, Mr Barborka believes, put it in an envelope to which he affixed a French postage stamp and mailed it by regular post. The postage stamps bears the usual French cancellation mark. Sinnett received the letter in the regular post when it reached London.

p. 240/237: Terich-Mir is a mountain at the terminating point of the Hindu Kush Mountains, which lie mainly in Afghanistan; it has an elevation of 25,426 feet. It is 'from the depths of an unknown valley' that KH says he is sending the letter. It is here, he says, that he received Sinnett's 'affectionate homage' and it is where he expects to spend his 'summer vacation'—perhaps a light reference to the fact that Sinnett was on vacation or perhaps merely indicating that it was cool.

Obviously Sinnett has written him and he now is sending a letter 'from the abodes of eternal snow and purity' to 'the abodes of vice'—by which one infers he means the outer world, and specifically Europe.

Sinnett must have asked him whether he could visit astrally in London. The Mahatma says no—not in his astral or any other tangible form, but simply in thought.

'Your book is a little jewel': a very interesting statement, since KH had not seen the book physically. He knew generally what the book was about, of course, but he had no way other than by phenomenal means of knowing its actual contents. Apparently he had looked at it mentally.

In 'the wild jungle of Spiritualistic literature', says the Mahatma, it will undoubtedly prove a Redeemer. The Spiritualists will begin by rejecting and even vilifying it, but 'it will find its faithful twelve' and the seed sown 'will not grow up as a weed'.

p. 241/238: Nevertheless, it is 'a spirited and discriminative little memoir ... and far more useful than Mr Wallace's work'.

'It is at this sort of spring that Spiritualists ought to be compelled to slake their thirst for phenomena and mystic knowledge, instead of being left to swallow the idiotic gush they find in the *Banners of Light* and others.'

Special attention is called to the remainder of this paragraph—a piece of superb writing. Several items in this paragraph might be clarified:

Kailasa is the name of a mountain. In Hindu mythology, it is described as the residence of Kuvera—the deity of riches and treasures. It is also represented as the paradise of Siva—the third aspect of the Trimurti, or Hindu Trinity. Kailasa was fabled to be one of the loftiest peaks in the Himalayas, north of Lake Manasarooar. It is generally referred to as 'Mount Meru'. Lama Govinda describes his visit to it in his book, *The Way of the White Clouds.*

Yoga Shastras: Since the word 'sastra' means any sacred book of composition, or for that matter any treatise or book, this signifies the most important work on yoga, that which is ascribed to Patanjali. Known also as the Yoga Sūtras.

Max Müller: (1823-1900), a German-born and educated philologist and famous Sanskrit scholar. Translated many oriental works for European readers, his major works appearing in the series entitled *Sacred Books of the East.*

Monier-Williams, Sir Monier: (1819-99) Famous Sanskrit scholar. He became professor of Sanskrit at Oxford in 1860 and continued in that office until his death. He travelled extensively in India in connection with his translation of Indian writings.

We are indebted to Geoffrey Barborka for a succinct explanation of the philosophical groups mentioned in this paragraph (see fn. MATL, p. 9): 'The *Positivists* ... assert that man cannot have knowledge except that which is gained by means of facts and actual phenomena along with their interrelations. Further, that speculation concerning ultimate origins or causes is inadmissible. The *Sensationalists* are regarded as radical empiricists. They declare that all knowledge is derived from sensory experience. [The] *Intellectualists* hold that pure reason is wholly or largely the source of knowledge [and] affirm the doctrine that the ultimate principle of all reality is intellect or reason. [The *Sceptics*] assert that it is not possible to obtain absolute knowledge; therefore judgements must be questioned and doubts expressed, so that relative certainty may be obtained.'

According to the editors of the third edition of ML, the word *phanerosis* in the next paragraph means a making-visible. It derives from *phanero* a combining form meaning evident as opposed to cryptic.

p. 242/239: Becoming an adept and maintaining one's adeptship is, one can be sure, an extremely formidable task. The goal is not that of attaining personal power, but simply of aiding humanity. The Mahatma says that he has 'laboured for more than a quarter of a century night and day to keep my place within the ranks of that invisible but ever busy army which labours and prepares for a task which can bring no reward but the consciousness that we are doing our duty by humanity. ...'

The Mahatma then assures Sinnett that he has proved faithful and true and has done his best. 'If your efforts will teach the world but one single letter from the alphabet of *Truth*—your reward will not miss you.'

18 (ML-9) Page 38 Folio 1 Recd. July 5, 1881

DESCRIPTION: KH to APS

In blue ink on both sides of 13 full-sized sheets of white paper. There are some smears and write-overs. On the last sheet and the next to the last some of the text appears to have been erased. There is no date or salutation.

CIRCUMSTANCES

APS had just arrived in Bombay on his return trip from England, having left his family there for a while longer. He remained in Bombay for a few days visiting HPB. HSO was on an extended tour of Ceylon. Letter 17 (ML-9) was received on the day following APS's arrival while he was talking to HPB. See OW, p. 154 (an inclusion in a second edition of the book) for his account of its receipt. It was the first letter he received after his return and it marks the beginning of the real teachings he was to receive on metaphysics and occultism. It is a long and important letter.

REFERENCES

p. 38: '... brilliant author ...': *The Occult World* had just been published in England.

'...yards of drivel ...': This poses a problem for the student, since some of the later letters may contain passages of this type.

'...our "Rock of Ages", Cho-Khan'. The Mahachohan.

'*Le quart d'heure de Rabelais*': KH seems to suspect that publication of the OW is going to get him into trouble with the Mahachohan. The French phrase, about mid-page, means a time for settling accounts—'paying up time', hence a trying time. It will be remembered that the Mahatma has spoken of the Mahachohan as 'the sternest of Khobilgans'. We can see here, perhaps, some explanation for the 'sufferings' undergone by KH which HPB mentioned in the passage quoted in the notes on Letter 15. One may speculate that he must have gone through some very uncomfortable interviews with his Chief —perhaps the more severe in proportion to what he was trying to do, i.e., to bring some light into the materialistic western mind. It has been apparent also that while some of the results were excellent, some were not so good, and undoubtedly the Mahachohan was holding him responsible.

'...swamping me blue ink and all!' Why KH used blue ink or pencil generally and M used red ink is not explained. KH's reference is interesting, in as much as the first five letters are in black ink and some of the later letters are in blue pencil. Also a few letters are in green or red ink.

...'make me lose my situation': a light reference to the fact that Sinnett was in danger of losing his position as editor of *The Pioneer*.

There are several references in the letters to the effect that there are definite limits to the extent to which the occult wisdom can be given out to the unprepared public. This is quite clearly stated in letter No. 49 (pp. 282-83, 1st ed. and 278/79, 3rd ed.).

'... in company with S.M.': Stainton Moses. See Alphabetical Notes.

p. 39: Stainton Moses (1839-92) was a prominent member of the Spiritualist group in England. He had a guide called 'Imperator' (usually designated in ML as +). There is considerable speculation as to the identity of this control, and it is intimated that at one time it was one of the Brothers and at other times some other entity and, again, perhaps the Higher Self of Moses. Stainton Moses frequently used the pen-name of M.A. Oxon. (standing for Master of Arts, Oxford).

'... and Mrs K. ...' Mrs Anna B. Kingsford. See Alphabetical Notes.

p. 39: '...his Simla indiscretions ...' Reference to HSO's article, 'A Day with Madame Blavatsky'. See Study Notes on Letter No. 5 (ML-4).

'C.C. Massey?' An English Spiritualist and a charter

member of the TS in New York in 1875. See Alphabetical Notes.

'Dr Wyld?' First President of the London Lodge. See Alphabetical Notes.

'His is a weird, rare nature.' Meaning Stainton Moses.

p. 40 (top): '... Mount Athos...': In Greece, 40 miles east of Salonica. The Holy Mountain of Macedonia on which there are a number of monasteries of the Eastern Orthodox Church.

'... its presumable founder...': Reference to Jesus Christ. There are several comments throughout the *Letters* which seem to indicate that the Adepts did not consider Jesus Christ an historical figure.

p. 40 (towards bottom): '...he heard for the first time the voice of Imperator...': There are intimations that at this early stage of SM's mediumship, 'Imperator' was one of the adepts. In LBS, p. 22, HPB comments that 'the + of his early mediumship *is* a Brother, and I will assert it over and over again on my death bed'.

Moses, however, refused to believe that Imperator was an adept and continued to regard him as a 'spirit guide'. He was almost unbelievably stubborn about this, for he had a fixed idea that he was in communication with a disembodied spirit and nothing could change his view.

p. 40 (bottom): '... the *highest* Planetary Spirits ...' Members of the Occult Hierarchy who have passed through a stage of evolution corresponding to the humanity of earth, in long past cycles (*Glossary*).

p. 41 (lower middle): '... Elementals and Elementaries ...' Elementals: Spirits of the Elements; creatures evolved in the four elements of earth, air, fire and water. Elementaries: phantoms of disembodied persons, or the disembodied souls of the depraved (*Glossary*). See Alphabetical Notes.

p. 41 (bottom): 'Ever since 1876, acting under direct orders, she tried ...' It is interesting that even while still in New York, HPB was trying to get SM to understand better what was happening.

p. 42 (near bottom): 'Bulwer': A reference to Bulwer-Lytton, author of the occult novel, *Zanoni,* in which he uses the term 'Dwellers on the Threshold'. See Alphabetical Notes on author and on 'Dweller ...'

'... her Superior ...': HPB's Master, M.

p. 43 (top): The ' + ' sign is used most frequently in ML to designate 'Imperator'.

p. 44 (top): 'Tsong-ka-pa of Kokonor ...': Fourteenth century reformer of Buddhism in Tibet. See Alphabetical Notes.

(middle): '... Imperator & Co. ...': An intimation that the 'guide' of Stainton Moses was not always the same entity.

(bottom): '... what I said to G. Th. Fechner one day ...' Fechner was a professor at the University of Leipzig whom KH met when he was in Europe in the mid 1870's. See Alphabetical Notes. See also LBS, p. 105, about three-quarters of the way down the page, where HPB speaks of 'the centres one of the Masters lived in'.

p. 45 (top): '... assurance that spirits of the departed ...' In this discussion the reader should be aware that the Mahatma is using the word 'spirit' in a different connotation from that of the Spiritualists.

One wonders why the Mahatma spent so much time writing about Stainton Moses; one wonders even more why Sinnett took it upon himself to pass on all this to Moses himself. Perhaps he thought he would finally convince Moses that Imperator was not a disembodied spirit, but apparently he could not.

In a later letter [21, (ML-27), p. 204/202)] the Mahatma says, '... I advised you to be prudent as to what you allowed SM to learn of + and of his own mediumship, suggesting that he should be told merely the substance of what I said. When, watching you at Allahabad I saw you making instead copious extracts for him from my letter, I again saw the danger but did not interfere. ...' One rather wonders why the Mahatma did *not* interfere, but as mentioned a few paragraphs back, the

Adepts never subject the will of individuals to their own will; and elsewhere we are told they never interfere with karma. Besides, the Mahatma tells Sinnett, 'No powers whether human or superhuman can ever open the eyes of S.M.—it was useless to tear them open.'

Writing to Sinnett some time later (LBS, p. 23) HPB asked in some desperation: 'Oh why did you ever have the unfortunate idea of writing to him [Moses] what KH said! He was a· Theosophist, lukewarm, still open to conviction then, and now he is an *inveterate enemy* of K.H. ...'

p. 45 (bottom): 'Anima Mundi of the Greeks ...': The 'Soul of the World', the divine essence which permeates, animates, and informs all, from the smallest atom of matter to man and god (*Glossary*).

p. 46 (top): '... an epicycloid ...': The curve traced by a point on the circumference of a circle when this circle is rolled around the circumference of another larger circle.

p. 49 (top): 'Remembering thoughts are things ...': This is a very important paragraph.

p. 50 (near top): '...before my GUIDES ...': Presumably he means the other members of the Occult Hierarchy.

p. 50: 'The book is out ...': *The Occult World*

'Art Magic ...': A book by Emma H. Britten, American medium. See Alphabetical Notes.

(middle): 'The Thersites ...': In Greek legend, a loud abusive Greek soldier in the Trojan War, killed by Achilles.

'... literary Philistines ...': The enemy on the border who continually harasses and attacks. Biblical reference; used metaphorically, also smug and narrow.

'... the Organs of "Angels"...': A light reference to the publications of the Spiritualists.

' "So far beyond the science and philosophy of Europe"...' A quotation from the dedication in *The Occult World,* in which APS dedicated the book to KH in somewhat glowing terms.

(near bottom): '... Wallace and Crookes ...': Alfred Russel Wallace and Sir William Crookes. See Alphabetical Notes.

(bottom): '...as soon as installed in your sleeping chamber ...': See also p. 51 directly opposite. Apparently this refers to another attempt to be made by KH to impress APS during his sleep so that he will be able to bring the experience through into his waking consciousness. In both places portions of the letter have been erased, when and how is not certain. The trial did not seem to be a success.

p. 51: The poem 'Wakeful Dreamer' is not in Tennyson's familiar published works. This puzzled Sinnett for some time, for he was something of an expert on Tennyson. He finally located it in a collection of Tennyson's poems entitled 'Poems Chiefly Lyrical' in an 1830 edition. It does not appear in subsequent editions. The real title of the poem is 'The Mystics', written before Tennyson was twenty years old. During the time that Sinnett was searching for this poem, he must have asked KH about it, for the Mahatma says (p. 286/282) 'Quotation from Tennyson? Really cannot say. Some stray lines picked up in the astral light or in somebody's brain and remembered. I never forget what I once see or read.'

'... 17th of July and ...': A reference to the plan mentioned on p. 50 directly opposite. Here six lines have been erased. See p. 284/279.

19 (ML-121) Page 452/445 Folio 3 Recd. July 11, 1881 (est.)

DESCRIPTION: KH to APS

On a single sheet of rippled white paper, in blue ink. The sheet is about 4″ x 6″ in size, folded note style. The capital 'P' in 'Patience' near the end of the letter is heavy, and the ink has blotted near the top of the sheet where the paper was folded, indicating that the ink blot was still wet when the paper was folded.

CIRCUMSTANCES

APS had just returned from England and was staying for a few days at the TS headquarters in Bombay before returning home to Allahabad. *The Occult World* had been published in London just prior to his return.

REFERENCES

First sentence: The statement would indicate that APS had brought back with him some little presents for KH, presumably to be sent to him by occult means.

'You ought to go to Simla.' HPB was to go to Simla later in the month as a guest of AOH. Possibly KH considered that the three of them together could produce some worthwhile results.

'... *the* Book'. *The Occult World.*

'... by presenting *The Occult World* to the C—'s notice'. KH may have been to see the Mahachohan in person, as indicated in the last page of Letter 20 (ML-49) p. 286/282, or it may have been done occultly.

'The *blanks* are provoking and "tantalizing" but we cannot go against the inevitable.' Probably this refers to the erasures and deletions from the immediately preceding letter. This might suggest that these were not done by KH but perhaps by his 'superior'.

The closing of the letter with the word 'Patience' repeated a second time is a word that one finds reiterated a number of times in the correspondence.

In the British Museum there is a very interesting verse about patience in the KH script on a scrap of paper, unaddressed and undated. Apparently not knowing what to do with it, Barker (the compiler) used it as a frontispiece in the volume of Letters from HPB to APS. See LBS frontispiece which he published the following year.

20 (ML-49) Page 280/276 Folio 2 Recd. Aug. 5, 1881

DESCRIPTION: KH to APS

In blue ink, on both sides of six full-sized sheets of thin paper. The script is quite small. This is an interesting and very valuable letter for the aspirant.

CIRCUMSTANCES

HSO was in Ceylon. HPB had left Bombay on July 22 on her way to visit the Humes in Simla. APS had left Bombay about July 12 for his home in Allahabad. He was now on his way to Simla, also as a guest of the Humes. This letter was received by APS at Umballa (or Ambala) on his way to Simla. The Simla Eclectic TS was formed on August 21 with AOH as President, APS as Vice-President, and Ross Scott as Secretary. The first communication received from KH after APS's arrival in Simla was a short note found in LBS (No. 204), p. 365.

With the entrance of Ross Scott on the scene, we have one of those situations which help to make the story of the letters so interesting. He is not one of the major characters but is, one might say, a member of the supporting cast—always necessary to give depth and human interest to every drama.

Ross Scott was a young Irishman and British civil servant whom the Founders had met on shipboard when they were sailing from England to Bombay in 1879, and to whom both warmed at once. Col. Olcott called him 'a noble fellow and an Irishman of the better sort'. In a short postscript at the end of this letter (20) KH asks Sinnett to make friends with Scott and adds: 'I need him.'

REFERENCES

p. 280/276: 'Just home.' KH had apparently been on a long trip on horseback. See last paragraph of this letter.

'... your "future book" ...': The first indication that

APS was already considering writing another book. He later published *Esoteric Buddhism.*

'... those who *know best'.* The superior Adepts.

'... Art Magic ...': a light reference to Anna Kingsford's recently published book by that title.

'... Éliphas Levi ...': See Alphabetical Notes.

'Rosencreuz... Saint Germain...': Christian Rosenkreuz, who founded the original order of mystical students known as Rosicrucians. The Count de Saint-Germain, a mysterious personage, close friend of Frederic II, King of Prussia, and said to be 'the greatest Oriental Adept Europe has seen during the last centuries' (*Glossary*).

(near bottom): 'Isaac Newton understood them well...' Another reference to the fact that Newton was something of an occultist.

p.281/277 (middle): '...Bus ...' (or buss). An expression meaning 'That's all', or 'Enough for now'.

KH mentions Éliphas Lévi and his book, *Haute Magie (High Magic).* Éliphas Lévi was the pseudonym used by a French abbé, Alphonse Louis Constant, who was very much interested in occultism and the Cabbala and who wrote extensively on such subjects. He is referred to a number of times in the letters and the Mahatma seemed to think there was much of value in his writings if one had the right key. He was for a time a member of Bulwer-Lytton's club for practical magic.

The Saturday Review (not the current publication of that title) was one of the Spiritualist magazines in England. It carried a review of Sinnett's OW which, not unexpectedly perhaps, was not complimentary. Here the Mahatma quotes the reviewer as saying, in effect, that every scientist should begin with a negative assumption about everything he sees and then look for whatever will support that assumption. The magazine, *The Spiritualist,* also carried a review of the book. This magazine was habitually hostile to the Theosophists, and the Mahatma comments that *The Saturday Review* let Sinnett off easier than *The Spiritualist* did. 'Losing its footing on mediumistic ground, it fights its death struggle for supremacy of English adeptship over Eastern knowledge.' The author of the review was a rather pretentious intellectual named Julius Kohn, who signed merely his initials, also standing for 'Jewish Kabalist'.

The Mahatma comments that 'the formidable JK is certainly a dangerous enemy; and I am afraid our Bodhisatwas will have to confess some day their profound ignorance before his mighty learning'. KH confesses that he feels 'a little wrathful' at some of the utterances of JK but says that the Hobilghan to whom he showed the passage in *The Spiritualist* 'laughed till the tears streamed down his old cheeks'. He adds: 'I wish I could.' A rather wistful-seeming expression which again emphasizes his humanness. See CW III: 286-290 and 332-343, which together greatly clarify this situation.

p.282/278: Suddenly, almost parenthetically, the Mahatma reminds Sinnett that their correspondence may break off suddenly. This is not specifically explained, but it emphasizes the 'thus far and no further' condition in which the Mahatma worked. The inference is, of course, that his superiors may intervene.

(bottom and top) p. 282/279 and 283/279: This is a profound statement of the requirements for occultism. It should be studied carefully by all serious students.

p.283/279: '...Iamblichus...': Fourth century Syrian philosopher who greatly increased the mystical and magical beliefs of Neoplatonism.

p.284/279 (bottom): ' "Woke up sad on the morning of the 18th..." ' See pp. 50 and 51 and Study Notes on Letter 18 (ML-9). This refers to the experiment proposed by KH but to which APS had apparently not been able to respond.

p. 284/280: The Mahatma speaks of the Shammars and the Red Capped Brothers of the Shadow. These are terms given to those who follow the left-hand path—meaning the path of materialism. Their existence and aims are essentially selfish, opposed to evolution. They are sometimes called the 'Chohans of Darkness' (p.462/455) which implies that they are initiates and even adepts of the left-hand path, but necessary to some elements of involving life.

KH gives some information about where he is travelling at the moment. Sakya-Jong is probably a monastery about 60 miles south-west of Shigatse. 'To you the name will remain meaningless. Repeat it to the "Old Lady" and—observe the result.' Sakya Jong may have been one of the places in which HPB received her training in Tibet.

Some very pertinent comments are made before this very long paragraph ends: 'the misuse of knowledge by the pupil always reacts upon the initiator...'; 'in sharing his secrets with another, the Adept by an immutable Law, is delaying his own progress to the Eternal Rest ...'; 'a *Price* must be paid for everything and every truth by *somebody* and in this case WE pay it...' All this, he says, 'must remain between us two' and the letter is to be regarded as strictly confidential. However, the Mahatma suspects that if these facts were generally known to candidates for initiation 'I feel certain they would be both more thankful and more patient'.

p. 285/281: Then the Mahatma comes again to the fact that Sinnett has shared with Stainton Moses large extracts from KH's letter about him—in *two* letters as a matter of fact. But they will come to nothing; Moses will not be convinced, but the Mahatma predicts that Sinnett will receive a letter from Moses 'full of suspicion and with no few unkind remarks'. Sinnett did receive such a letter a few months later, dated 26 November 1881. It is included in ML and we come to it directly.

Another example of the Mahatma's fine sense of humour is shown as we near the end of the letter (p.285/281). Sinnett had asked the Mahatma for a portrait; KH tells him he never had but one taken in his whole life and that was a ferro type (essentially the same as a tintype—an early form of photography) 'produced in the days of the "Gaudeamus" '. This refers to merry-making of college students, a further reference to KH's days at a university in Germany—probably Heidelberg. The description of the picture is discouraging, but KH says he has no other to offer—but he 'may try—some day to get you one'. Notice how very guarded this half promise is. Elsewhere in the letters, KH says that he never promises what he is not sure he can fulfil. Apparently the Adepts do not care to have their pictures taken. The pictures available are all artists' paintings made under inspiration or direction, or by precipitation by one of the chelas. As far as is known by the writers, there are no authentic photographs of the two adepts available anywhere.

p. 286/281-82: The 'Quotation from Tennyson' was discussed in the notes on Letter 9. See the last paragraph preceding the footnotes in the notes on that letter.

p. 286/282(top): '...pilfered from Dr Wilder's brain...' Early Vice-President of the TS in New York. See Alphabetical Notes.

'From Gharlaring-Tcho Lamasery...': [See Letter19 (ML-121)], p. 452/445. Location is not determined, but it would seem to be in the vicinity of the Pamir Mountains north-west from Hunza Territory. Seemingly KH had been on another trip to see the Mahachohan in person.

PS: '...be in Bhutan'. The small Himalyan country just east of Sikkim and between Tibet and India.

'...make friends with Ross Scott'. See Alphabetical Notes.

21 (ML-27) Page 204/202 Folio 2 Recd. Sept. 1881 (est.)

DESCRIPTION: KH to APS

In dark blue ink on three large sheets of white paper

heavy lettering with blotched appearance towards the end. A strange feature of the script is that the dark blue frequently changes to light blue, suddenly, and for no apparent reason.

CIRCUMSTANCES

APS and HPB were in Simla as guests of AOH. HSO was in Ceylon. The Simla Eclectic TS had been formed on August 21.

REFERENCES

p.204/202 'In my Bombay letter ...': Reference to Letter No.12 (ML-9), which APS received in Bombay after his arrival there from England.

'...in *Light* ...': A Spiritualist publication in London (not to be confused with the *Banner of Light* published in U.S.A.

'..."shall lose S.M." ': Stainton Moses.

p.205/203 (top): 'S.E.T.S.'. Simla Eclectic TS.

p.205/203 (bottom): '... Angel's whispering...': A reference to the guides of the mediums.

p. 206/204: '...judge a man by his motives...': The Master lays great stress on *motive*. In another letter he states 'motive is everything'.

p.204 (bottom) '...leave you to yourselves for the period of three months'. The first intimation by KH that he was planning to go into retreat for an extended time.

p. 207/205: '...a poem written by Padshah ...': An early TS member. See Alphabetical Notes.

'...the *Grand Inquisitor* ...': A reference to a chapter in the book *The Brothers Karamazoff* by Dostoevski. See article, 'The Grand Inquisitor' in *The Theosophist,* November 1881, p. 38, and December 1881, p. 75.

'Society of Jesus.' The Jesuits.

P.S. The 'brandy atmosphere' referred to would have been in AOH's house, since that was where APS was staying at the time.

22 (ML-26) **Page 203/201** *Folio 2* ***Recd. Sept. 1881 (est.)***

DESCRIPTION: KH to APS

In bright blue ink on both sides of a full-sized sheet of white paper, with medium heavy, carefully formed script.

CIRCUMSTANCES

Similar to those of previous letter 21 (ML-27).

REFERENCES

This letter is a confidential memo to APS and AOH in which KH attempts to explain some of the seemingly strange characteristics of HPB's nature which are the principal cause of her oftimes trying behaviour. See LBS-156 (beginning on p. 305), a letter to HPB from AOH on which M has added marginal comments and underlined a number of passages. In that letter, on p. 307, AOH expresses scepticism about the explanation of HPB's 'missing principles' in the words: 'Now I know all about the Brothers' supposed explanation that you are a psychological cripple, one of your seven principles being in pawn in Tibet...' M has appended a comment: 'He is mistaken — *he does not*.' Further on in this letter, AOH speculates sarcastically on which of the seven principles it might have been, and M comments: 'Very clever — but suppose it is neither *one of the seven* particularly but all? Every one of them a "cripple" and forbidden the exercise of its full powers? And suppose such is the wise law of a far foreseeing power" ' (See also BTT, pp. 362-3). In letter 54, KH also explains in considerable detail some of HPB's idiosyncrasies.

p. 203/201: '...an Initiate of the "fifth circle"...': May refer to the fifth or 'Aseka' Initiation, i.e. an adept.

'...the *Bod-Lhas* ...': Divine rulers of Tibet. Probably refers here to the Adepts. See Alphabetical Notes — Bod.

'One of his seven principles has to remain behind.' This

statement has caused a lot of discussion. See comment in paragraph above as to M's comment.

p.204/202: 'the real baitchooly...': The meaning of this term is not determined, but it may be similar to the western slang expression, 'the real McCoy' (i.e. the real thing).

23 ML-104) Page 440/433 Folio 3 Recd. late Sept. 1881 (est.)

DESCRIPTION: KH to APS

In blue ink on both sides of a folded single sheet of rippled white paper. The envelope is in the folio. It is addressed to A.P. Sinnett, Esq., with 'P.p.c.' written in the lower right-hand corner. The script on the envelope is different from that of the letter. The writing is crossways on the folded sheet.

CIRCUMSTANCES

Similar to the several preceding letters. This is the last letter received by APS from KH prior to the latter's 'retreat' for a period of several months. In the interim, M took over the correspondence.

It will be remembered that, at the close of Letter 20 (ML-49) KH had said, 'I will be in Bhutan in October.' Here he gives the information that the Mahatma M will make that trip for him. The passage seems to underscore the likelihood that he left on his retreat in late September, for he comments that 'nothing whatever of the Society's original programme is yet settled upon...nor do I hope of seeing it settled for some time to come...' (He is, of course, referring to the Simla Eclectic Society and not to the parent organization.) Then he adds: 'We are at the end of September and nothing could be done by October 1st that might warrant upon my insisting to go thither...' The context of this statement hints that the journey may have had some connection with the Simla Society, but doesn't give any indication of what that connection might be.

The Mahatma KH's reason for choosing to go on his retreat at this time, he says, is that his Chiefs want him to be present at the New Year's festivities in February, and 'in order to be prepared for it I have to avail myself of the three intervening months'—i.e. October, November, and December—since he would certainly need some time for recuperation before participating in such observances. In fact, he intimates this later, but here he says, 'In January next I hope to be able to let you have news of me.' This, of course, means that his retreat would be ended.

REFERENCES

p. 440/433: '...*argumentum ad hominem* ...': An argument attacking one's opponent rather than dealing with the subject under discussion.

'..."catching up" any more of his letters ...': Indicating that for the duration of the retreat, KH will not be carrying on any correspondence with AOH, for which he is thankful.

'...give up my projected voyage to Bhootan ...': See P.S. on p.286/282. This part of the letter indicates a change of plans necessitating an earlier retreat than KH had anticipated.

'...obstinate Brother M ...': An affectionate reference to his Brother who had agreed to undertake to carry on the correspondence with APS.

'... Answer—through a third party—not HPB'. This was probably due to her state of health. Some of M's correspondence apparently was routed through Subba Row, who was one of his chelas. Normally, the adepts seemed to work through their own chelas.

p. 441/434: '...my Disinherited...': Djual Khul, a high chela and KH's principal assistant in the correspondence.

In Letter 23 (ML-104) the Mahatma KH expresses some doubt that he would be able to persuade the Mahatma M to take over the correspondence, for apparently he was reluctant to do so. He did, however, assume that task and some very remarkable letters resulted.

Towards the end of this letter: 'I leave orders with my "Disinherited" to watch over all as much as it lies in his weak powers.' This, of course, refers to Djual Khul who, as mentioned previously, was a first degree chela of the Mahatma KH and worked very closely with him. It is explained, that he was nicknamed 'the Disinherited' because his family disinherited him when he became interested in Theosophy and a chela of Mahatma KH.

The Mahatma closes, saying that he has but a few hours to prepare for his long, *very* long journey, meaning one would surmise, that the journey will be long in consciousness, not necessarily in distance.

24 (ML-71) Page 374/367 Folio 3 Recd. Sept. (near end) 1881 (est.)

DESCRIPTION: M to APS

In pale sepia ink on a single sheet of vellum notepaper. On the front of the sheet, the writing is diagonally on the page, and on the back, it is square with the paper. See OW, p. 158.

CIRCUMSTANCES

Similar to the preceding letters. KH was leaving for his long retreat, and M was taking over his correspondence. This is the first letter received by APS from M. See OW, p. 158. No indication as to how the letter was transmitted. APS was at home in Allahabad.

REFERENCES

'...thanks and salaams for the tobacco-machine'. Apparently APS on his return from England had sent M a present of a European-style pipe, since it was said by HPB that M habitually smoked a water-pipe (or hookah). There are several references in ML to M's smoking a pipe, but no indication as to what he smoked in it.

'Our frenchified and pelingized Pandit...' meaning KH. Peling was a common term among the Indians for any white Westerner. The 'frenchified' expression has reference to the fact that KH had studied in France when a young man and was fluent in the French language. Some of his correspondence with HPB seemingly was carried on in French.

'...has to be cooloted...': The meaning of this is not clear, but perhaps it has to do with the 'breaking-in' of the pipe.

p.374/368: '...go to Bombay to the Anniversary...': A suggestion that they would like APS to attend the Anniversary Celebration of the TS in Bombay, which was to be held on 12 January 1882. See ML, pp.260/256, 444/437, 449/442.

'...the Peling Sahib'. Western gentleman, meaning in this case APS. *Peling* is a Tibetan word meaning 'outsider' as contrasted with 'insider', i.e. one of their faith. In more or less common usage in Asiatic countries to designate Westerners, particularly Europeans and Americans. See ML index; BTT, p. 70.

25 (ML-73) Page 375/368 Folio 3 Recd: Oct. (early) 1881 (est.)

DESCRIPTION: M to APS

In bright red ink, in M script, on a single sheet of heavy rough vellum on one side only. Size about 5" x 7". The salutation looks a little like HPB's script. The writing is lengthwise on the paper.

CIRCUMSTANCES

APS and AOH were in Simla, as was also HPB. HSO was

still in Ceylon. KH was entering his retreat. DKM (Damodar K. Mavalankar) was at the Bombay headquarters. Master M. was now taking over the correspondence in KH's absence of about three months.

REFERENCES

'...the Brahmin Boy': DKM. Apparently the letter had been dictated earlier to DKM by KH. See Letter 27 (ML-101) p.439/431. Damodar was a member of a strict Brahmin family before joining the TS Headquarters in Bombay. M was concerned that Damodar had confused KH's message and that if AOH saw it, he would become angry.

'Tong-pa-ngi...': The Void, meaning the state or condition of KH during his retreat.

26 (ML-102) Page 439/432 Folio 3 Recd. Oct. 1881 (est.)

DESCRIPTION: M to APS

In red ink on one side only of a folded sheet of letter paper, with APS's name written on the reverse side. The writer ran short of space and crowded the writing close together near the bottom, with smaller letters, so that there was barely room in the corner for the initial 'M'.

CIRCUMSTANCES

APS was still in Simla with AOH. HPB had left Simla and was travelling about North India. KH was in his retreat. HSO was in Ceylon. M was now looking after the correspondence in KH's absence.

REFERENCES

'My dear young friend ...': APS was 41 years of age at the time!

'If he can stand ...': Meaning AOH.

The French expression, *ou tout ou rien,* means 'all or nothing'.

'... frenchified K.H. ...': A reference to KH's training in France as a young man and his fluency in the French language.

'...I had "Benjamin" stick a patch in the page...' Meaning Djual Khul. The letter referred to is the one mentioned in Letter 25 (ML-73), 28 (ML-74) and 27 (ML-101).

'Not having the right to *follow* K.H. ...' i.e. into his retreat.

M sometimes referred to KH as 'my boy', since the latter was somewhat his junior, both in age and status.

'... and refusal ...': Perhaps a reference to the first sentence of the letter.

'... the son of "a member of Parliament" '. AOH, whose father had served in that capacity, of which fact AOH was very proud.

It is characteristic of M's letters that he signed them with only the single initial.

27 (ML-101)　　Page 439/431　　Folio 3　　Recd. Oct. 1881 (est.)

DESCRIPTION: M to APS

In bright red ink, in a medium sized scrawl, on both sides of a single sheet of very heavy rough paper with uneven edges, about 4" x 6" in size. The initial 'M' at the end does not have the usual 'tail'. The letter is typical of M's brusque manner, having no salutation or complimentary closing.

CIRCUMSTANCES

Similar to those of Letter 26 (ML-102), p. 439/432.

REFERENCES

p. 439/431 (line 2): '...than his ...': AOH. This sentence has reference to material that Hume and Sinnett were writing for *The Theosophist* and other journals.

'...attended to the Brahmin boy's letter and erased the offensive sentence'. See Letter 25 (ML-73), 28 (ML-74) and 26 (ML-102).

p.439/432:'...Maha Sahib ...': AOH. Perhaps a bit of sarcasm by M.

'...written *through* Olcott'. HSO was in Ceylon at the time; HPB was away from Simla. What letter he is referring to is not indicated, but it is interesting that it was written 'through' Olcott.

'... Your AOH. *I know him better* ...': Probably APS sometimes thought the Mahatmas did not fully understand AOH. Hume was a very close friend of Sinnett's and the two shared much of the correspondence with the Adepts as well as correspondence with others on occult subjects.

28 (ML-74) Page 375/369 Folio 3 Recd. Oct. 1881 (est.)

DESCRIPTION: M to APS

In bright red ink lengthwise on a single sheet of bright blue paper, about 8"x12½", with a watermark of W & P. Some smearing and rubbing off of the ink is noticeable, and where the ink has run together in letters—as in the 'a'—a reddish black colour is produced. The sheet of paper is one that HPB had used to paste up a newspaper cutting from the *New York Sun,* but the cutting had been pulled off. The smearing of the ink and the noticeable rubbing off indicates that the writing is neither embedded nor waterproof.

CIRCUMSTANCES

Similar to previous letter, 27 (ML-101).

REFERENCES

This letter concerns DKM's letter, first mentioned in Letter 25 (ML-73). See also 27 (ML-101), and 26 (ML-102).

The next to last sentence shows the deep feeling which M had for his Brother KH, who had entered a retreat, probably to take his sixth or Chohan initiation, a very important stage in his evolution.

'...the tamasha produced...': A reference to the deletion and re-precipitation in the letter of KH's referred to.

29 (ML-29) Page 217/215 Folio 2 Recd. Oct. 1881 (est.)

DESCRIPTION: M to APS and AOH (jointly)

In red ink on 9 sheets of slick white paper, on both sides. Heavy lettering, blotched occasionally, with some evidence of corrections. This is M's longest letter.

CIRCUMSTANCES

Similar to previous letters, 28 (ML-74) and 27 (ML-101). Sinnett was still staying with Hume at his home (Rothney Castle) in Simla. HPB had left Simla and was travelling about North India. KH was in his 'retreat', and M was carrying on the correspondence in his absence.

REFERENCES

M says that he would not have troubled to write what promises to be a 'rather lengthy letter' but for 'a debt of profound gratitude for what he [Hume] is doing for my poor chela'.

In its issue of 3 September 1881, *The Saturday Review*, English Spiritualist publication, attacked HPB and Olcott as 'unscrupulous adventurers'. Hume wrote an article in their defence, apparently ignored by *The Saturday Review* but later published in the December 1881 and January 1882 issues of *The Theosophist*. In this article, Hume referred to letters of HPB from her uncle, Major-General H. Fadeev and from Prince Dondoukoff Korsakoff. We come a bit later to HPB's own mention of these letters which helped to establish her identity at a time when she was being accused of being a Russian spy, an adventuress, and so on. It may have been this article by Hume which partially occasioned the Mahatma's sense of obligation to him.

This statement is followed by some interesting and valuable comments on the ways of the Adepts. About one-third down page 218 of the 2nd ed., and near the top of page 216 of the 3rd ed., the word *dikshita* is used. This means an *initiate*.

It is interesting to compare these statements with those of KH in Letter 17 (ML-31) in which he states that 'the Adept is accorded an instantaneous, implicit insight into *every first truth*'.

p. 219/217: Here M describes the place of KH's 'retreat'. No hint is given as to the geographical location of this site, but it is evident from the description that it is located in mountainous country and quite isolated.

'...the new *Eclectic...*': The Simla Eclectic TS which had recently been organized in Simla. See ECLECTIC, Alphabetical Notes.

p. 222/220 (middle): '...like the Grecian *Saraswati* ...' Hindu goddess of esoteric knowledge and wisdom.

'...treating him *de haut en bas* ...': Literally, 'from top to bottom', or as an inferior.

p.223/221: '...be that person *Dev* or mortal ...' Reference to a Dev, or celestial being. (*Glossary*).

p.224/222: 'My Rajput blood ...': the Rajputs were a ruling class of northern India.

'*Cui bono* then?' What good then? or who gains by it?

'...his *fifth* principle...': Manas, or mind, according to the system they were using.

p.226/224: '...the meeting of 21st Aug....': The date of organization of the Simla Eclectic TS.

p.227/224: '...so long as men doubt...': A significant passage giving at least one reason why the occult knowledge has to be guarded.

'... set us up in the British Museum...': An interesting passage, considering that their *Letters* are now in that institution.

p. 227/224 (near bottom): '... trying to penetrate the things of the spirit...': A very pertinent expression and similar to some of HPB's graphic metaphors.

p. 227/225 (near top): '...asking me to go and tell O ...' HSO was in Ceylon at the time. It is intriguing that KH asked M to convey the message to HSO rather than doing it himself. It appears, from comments here and there, that the Adepts have rather strict rules regarding their contact with the chelas of other Adepts.

p. 228/225 (middle): '... I altered ... the memo ...': See p. 221/219, near top.

Closing paragraph: '... mark of the Adept is kept at — ...': This blank is in the original, and one can only speculate as to the location referred to. Some think that it refers to Shigatze.

At this point it might be well to consider a letter to Sinnett written early in November 1881—sometime before the 6th, probably—by HPB and listing seven items which she has been directed by the Mahatma M to pass on to Sinnett. This is Letter IV found in LBS, pp. 5-6:

Ordered by my Boss to tell Sinnett, Esq., the following:-
1. Not to lose the opportunity tonight of acquainting R[oss] S[cott] with every detail of the situation he can think of, whether relating to the Society or his projected matrimonial ideas.[1]
2. To insist upon having a true copy of the hitherto written sketches of Cosmogony with the Tibetan words, *M.*'s notes etc. HPB is also ordered to have one, as she has to know thoroughly

what Mr Hume has noted and how much he has elaborated of the explanations. Otherwise, when the reaction comes and Mr Hume begins studying once more—neither Mr Sinnett nor HPB will be *au courant*;[2] and he will begin once more abusing—like the quartette of musicians in Aesop's fable—the *instruments* on which he does not know how to play.[3]

3. Sinnett is advised, once he is in Allahabad, to announce the formation of the Allahabad Society, calling it 'The Anglo-Indian Investigation (Theosophical) Society' or some such name which would not jar upon the nerves of the unbelieving community. Let it be distinct from the other Branch in Allahabad called the 'Prayaga Theos. Society' though the Hindus in it might be very useful to Mr Sinnett and he will find wonderful *mesmeric* subjects in it if he but searches.[4]

4. Mr Sinnet is advised by M to make a special duty to prevent his little son being made to eat meat—not even fowls, and to write so to Mrs Sinnett. Once the Mother has placed the child under KH's protection, let her see nothing pollutes his nature. The child may become a powerful engine for good in a near future. Let him be trained as *his own nature* suggests it.

5. Mr S is reminded to telegraph O[lcott] not to answer one word to Mr Hume until he receives a letter from Mr Sinnett.[5]

6. Mr S is advised, now that he will be alone, to put himself in communication through [Prof.] Adytyarum B[hattachorus][6] with some Hindu mystics, not for the sake of philosophy but to find out what mental phenomena can be produced. At the *Mela*[7] there is a number of such visiting the town.

7. Whenever he feels like writing or needs M's advice, Mr Sinnett is invited to do so without hesitation. M will *always* answer him, not only for KH's sake but his own sake, as Mr S has proved that even an Anglo-Indian can have the true S—[8] SPARK in him, which no amount of brandy and soda and other stuff can extinguish and which will occasionally glitter out very brightly.

The above is followed by a note in the Mahatma M's handwriting in bold type in the book:

'It *was* my wish that she should read the letter to Fern last night. You can also show and read it to R[oss] S[cott] if you like. All of the above is correct.

Yours, M.'

Footnotes to LBS IV

1. Ross Scott and Minnie Hume were married on 28 December 1881.
2. *au courant:* fully informed.
3. This particular instruction relates to what amounted to a tabulation of such of the ultimate principles of the universe as the Mahatma M was prepared to set forth. Most of these statements were answers to questions asked by Hume, and the Master's replies were directed to getting them into his own notebook. Here he is instructed to make a 'true copy' and to see that HPB also has one. The Mahatma seems to feel that Hume might elaborate on these inaccurately. These 'Cosmological Notes' are found in full as Appendix 2, p. 376 of LBS. A little later in the ML we come to a letter which Sinnett has called 'Cosmological Notes' but these are mainly answers to his own questions and the text is not the same as that of the Appendix in LBS.
4. Opposite this item, Mary K. Neff has inserted a marginal note in her copy of LBS: 'The Prayag Psychic Theosophical Society was established Nov. 6, 81.'
5. A marginal note in Mary K. Neff's copy of LBS, opposite this item: 'Col. [Olcott] says in "Diary" Jan. 6, 82, worked on a long letter to Hume repelling his arguments against the Brothers.' This is followed by another item from Olcott's Diary: 'Jan. 27. Spent day in reading & preparing a reply to Hume's new pamphlet on Theos.'
6. An erudite Sanskritist.
7. *Mela* = a fair.
8. It is not known what word the Mahatma had in mind here, but it might possibly have been 'sannyasi' or holy man.

30 (ML-134) Page 461/454 Dated Nov. 4, 1881. Probably received about Nov. 4

DESCRIPTION: HPB to APS

On both sides of two folded sheets, in black ink, the major portion seemingly dictated by M.

CIRCUMSTANCES

This letter is from HPB (travelling about North India) to APS, who had left Simla for his home in Allahabad about Nov. 1. It incorporates, at M's dictation, his letter in reply to one from APS. Dehra Dun is a hill-station at the end of the railway, situated north-east of Delhi. See also LBS pp. 9, 10. She was starting on her way home in Bombay, expecting to go by a direct rail route which did not pass through Allahabad. However her Master M changed her plan and arranged for her to go by way of Allahabad and visit Sinnett there.

The bulk of the letter apparently is a direct dictation of M to HPB.

REFERENCES

The Mahatma mentions some 'foolish letters' from two Allahabad Theosophists. One of these was apparently the learned Sanskritist through whom M had advised Sinnett to get in touch with some Hindu mystics (see preceding letter copies from LBS). The other, Benemadhab, or Benee Madhab Battacharya, was the first President of the Prayag Theosophical Society in Allahabad. From the context of the Mahatma's letter, these two men had asked to be put in contact with the Mahatmas, which the Mahatma here refuses to consider. He mentions the only conditions on which they will agree to any kind of association with individuals other than the two Englishmen with whom they had been corresponding.

'...to become a theosophist of the II Section'. In those days the Society was divided into three sections: the first section consisted of the Mahatmas; the second of those who were in direct touch with the Mahatmas; and the third of ordinary members.

The following are definitions from various glossaries of terms used in the second page of the letter:

Arhats: those who have taken the fourth Initiation.

Sang-gyas: a Tibetan term meaning perfect, holy; used for Gautama, the Buddha.

Shastra: book of divine or accepted authority.

Fakir: a Moslem 'yogi'.

Sadhu: a Hindu ascetic.

Nastika: an atheist, or one who does not recognize gods and idols.

Fakirs, sannyasis and sadhus may lead lives of utmost purity, and yet be 'on the path of error' because they cling to many beliefs and superstitions. Sinnett and Hume have no *beliefs* and consequently are exceptions.

p. 463/456 (near bottom): '...the *C* and *M* ...': The *Civil and Military Gazette,* the semi-official organ of British officialdom. See LBS, p. 9, where HPB calls this publication 'the C. and M. Sewer'.

'... Prince Dondoukoff ...': See Alphabetical Notes.

'Mr Primrose': A newspaper publisher.

'Lord Ripon': Viceroy of India from 1880 to 1884.

'Gladstone': British Prime Minister

P. 464/457: 'Jeypur and Baroda'—cities on the western route from Delhi to Bombay, which HPB was planning to visit on her way home (See 'Circumstances' above).

At the end of this letter, HPB adds a short note complaining because her 'Boss' (M) wants her to go to Allahabad and she doesn't understand the purpose of such a journey or have the money to make it. No doubt this was in connection with receiving new members into the Society in Allahabad. She seemed to be admitting a considerable number of persons during her visits to various cities.

31 (ML-40) Page 254/251 Folio 2 Recd. Nov. 1881 (est.) APS's date of Feb. 1882 is obviously wrong.

DESCRIPTION: M to APS

On both sides of two sheets of standard size white paper, in dark red ink, except for four words in dark blue ink. The letter is very difficult to read.

CIRCUMSTANCES

APS was at home in Allahabad. HSO was still in Ceylon. AOH was in Simla. HPB's location not known precisely due to uncertain date of this letter. See ODL, 2:311. HSO had made a short trip from Ceylon to points on the tip of the Indian peninsula and then returned to Ceylon.

REFERENCES

p. 255/251: '...at Tinnevelly October 23rd ...': Tinnevelly is a city near the tip of the Indian peninsula.

Sinnett had asked the Master M whether he could do anything to help the Society, and the Master, with his usual blunt directness, answers: 'No: neither yourself nor the Lord Sang-yias Himself—so long as the equivocal position of the Founders is not perfectly and undeniably proved due to fiendish malice and a systematic intrigue—could help us on'. He mentions some of the measures against which the Founders had to work.

The Mahatma mentions the 'C. and M. of Lahore' as 'hardly missing a day' in attacking the Theosophists. This is the C & M *Gazette* mentioned in Letter 17 (ML-31) and which HPB had called 'the C & M Sewer'. This is a reference to the *Civil and Military Gazetteer* a newspaper which reflected the attitude of the British Government. See ML-134 (31) p. 463/456.

Olcott writes in his Diary: '...the Principal of the local Hindu College enclosed for my information a copy of a pamphlet which had been circulated through the town the day before, to prejudice the community against us; the copies being distributed by hand by the servants of the missionaries, with the verbal message that they were sent "with the compliments of the Secretary of the Tinnevelly Theosophical Society". In violation of the law which requires that the name of the printer and publisher shall appear on every printed work, this pamphlet revealed neither. Its contents were reprints of two meanly slanderous articles against us, from a London and a New York paper. This is the sort of warfare that we have had to encounter throughout the whole period of our Indian work; and almost invariably the offenders have been Protestant missionaries.'

'Rattigan': Newspaper publisher. See Alphabetical Notes. Owner of several papers, including *The Pioneer*. He had no sympathy with Sinnett's interest in Theosophy or in his defence of HPB and Col. Olcott, and he later (as will be seen) relieved Sinnett of his job as editor, giving him a year's salary in advance to get rid of him.

'... the Prince D...': Dondoukoff. He was to send an official document to prove HPB's identity. See p. 463/456, near bottom of page.

Suby Ram is mentioned next. This is the only time he is met in the Letters. He was a medium with a considerable following. The Mahatma speaks of him as 'a pure, unselfish, earnest soul, absorbed in misguided, misdirected mysticism'. He had a chronic disorder of that portion of the brain which responds to clear vision, which had been brought about by forced visions, hatha yoga, and prolonged asceticism — a clear warning against indulging in these practices without a bona fide teacher.

p. 255/252: This paragraph expresses, quite forcibly and plainly, M's opinion regarding mediumship. This paragraph should be carefully considered by those who are interested in mediumship and the results of mediums.

'...by joining his society'. Suby Ram's society.

'...Keshub Chunder Sen...': Leader of the 'New Dispensation' branch of the Brahmo-Samaj, a modern reform movement in Hinduism. See HPB, VI, pp. 12, 13 and 68.

'I think of sending her to you.' Intimation that M may ask APS to invite HPB to visit. This he does in the next letter, 32 (ML-114).

It seems clear that this letter to Sinnett was sent through someone other than HPB, and at that time she did not know about the plan to send her to Allahabad. She received a letter from Sinnett mentioning it, and, in a reply to him written from Dehra Dun sometime before Nov. 14, she says: 'What possessed you to write to me as if I was going decidedly to Allahabad?' (LBS 8, p. 10) She goes on in this letter to explain why she cannot do this; she has to go to several other places on Society business. So, at this point, she knows nothing of the plan.

The next letter in ML deals with this proposed meeting in Allahabad. It must have been written very shortly after this one, as the request to Sinnett to write to Bannerjee was what brought about the change in HPB's plans.

32 (ML-114) Page 449/442 Folio 3 Recd. Nov. 13, 1881 (est.)

DESCRIPTION: M to APS

In red ink on a single folded sheet of rippled paper, in medium sized script, more carefully done than some of the other letters. On the back, in different script, appears: 'A.P. Sinnett Sahib'.

CIRCUMSTANCES

APS was in Allahabad. HPB was en route from Dehra Dun to Meerut and Bareilly. She arrived in Meerut on the 13th or 14th of November, where she received the telegram from APS inviting her to come to Allahabad to visit. (The telegram was suggested by M in this letter.)

REFERENCES

Note: APS's date of February 1882 is obviously an error. See LBS, p. 12.

'...from a Baboo ...' (or babu): A person of status.

'... our friend of Simla...': A.O. Hume.

Bannerjee was a prominent Indian Theosophist in the early days of the Society. He was a magistrate and Deputy Collector at Barhampore, Bengal.

'Prayag': The ancient name for Allahabad. The Muslims changed the name to fit their religion.

'Then telegraph to her to Meerut ...': HPB acknowledged this telegram in a letter to APS dated Nov. 14, from Meerut. See LBS, p. 12.

The Mahatma encloses a letter from Bannerjee, whom, apparently, Sinnett does not like, since the Mahatma refers to him as 'your nausea-inspiring Bengalee'. The Mahatma asks Sinnett to try to overcome his queasiness at a possible meeting with Bannerjee and read the letter with attention. 'The lines underlined contain the germ in them of the greatest reform, the most beneficent results obtained by the Theosophical movement.'

He goes on to say, 'Were our friend of Simla [Hume] less cantankerous, I might have tried to influence him to draft out special rules and a distinct pledge with the applications and obligations for the Zenana women of India.'

It is this sentence which suggests that Bannerjee's letter may contain a suggestion for the formation of an organization for women in the Theosophical Society in Bengal. Obviously it meets with the approval of the Mahatma.

If one may be permitted a speculation about this, it may be that it was the reason why HPB was being sent to Allahabad without telling her all the circumstances surrounding such a visit. She seems not to have been altogether trustful of women generally and some doubt may have been felt about her sympathy with such a suggestion.

The last paragraph is a bit puzzling. Sinnett must have asked to see the Mahatma's letter to someone else, for the request obviously refers to some such circumstance; the response is negative.

33 (ML-38) Page 250/247 Folio 2 Recd. Dec. 10, 1881 (est.)

DESCRIPTION: M to APS

In purplish red ink on both sides of two sheets of letter-size white paper. This letter is difficult to read.

CIRCUMSTANCES

APS was in Allahabad. HPB had returned to Bombay from her trip in the north of India and had stayed with the Sinnetts on her way home. She arrived in Bombay during the latter part of November. HSO sailed from Ceylon on Dec. 13 and arrived in Bombay on Dec. 19.

REFERENCES

Note: APS's date of February 1881 appears to be incorrect.

p.250/247: 'Your "illustrious" friend...': A reference to himself, M, implying that APS may have addressed or referred to him in this fashion.

'...the two herein enclosed'. An exchange of letters between AOH and HPB which M apparently enclosed for HPB's perusal.

What was enclosed was an exchange of correspondence between Hume and HPB. In spite of the fact that Hume had gone to the trouble to defend HPB against some of the attacks in the newspapers, he frequently wrote her very sarcastic and even cruel letters; and she, with her fiery temperament, never failed to pick up the gauntlet.

How the Mahatma came to be in possession of these letters is not explained and perhaps does not need to be; he was aware—or could be aware—at any moment of what HPB was doing. Here he comments that 'The undignified, bitter, sarcastic tone of one [which probably refers to Hume's letter] will give him [KH] as little cause to rejoice as the undignified, foolish, and childish tone of the other' [obviously HPB's reply].

Hume, and sometimes even Sinnett, occasionally spoke of the Mahatmas as 'Their Highnesses' because they thought the Mahatmas deliberately made themselves unapproachable. One may perhaps assume that Hume had used this term in his letter to HPB. However, the Mahatma says that 'no epithet will hang to the shirt-collar of a Bod-pa'—meaning a man of Tibet. He proposes to pay no heed to it and advises Sinnett to adopt the same attitude.

The reference to something being 'libellous' is not explained but it is apparently dealt with in more detail in the next letter.

Now the Mahatma takes up the matter of a possible women's branch of the Theosophical Society and says there will certainly be trouble about it. He makes no bones about HPB's feeling for her own sex and says that 'she can hardly be persuaded that any good can ever come from that quarter'. Neither he nor KH could become involved with such an undertaking, but he believes that a great good might result from it, considering the influence which the women exert over their children and husbands. The Mahatma suggests that perhaps Sinnett ('with Mr Hume's help') might be of immense use to KH who knows nothing of women with the exception of his sister.

pp. 251-52/248: Some positive comments on brotherhood

and the role of the TS that are well worth the consideration of the student of occultism.

34 (ML-39) Page 253/249 Folio 2 Recd. Dec. (middle) 1881 (est.)

DESCRIPTION: M to APS

In bright red ink on both sides of two sheets of letter-size paper. Heavy M script, difficult to read.

CIRCUMSTANCES

Similar to those of previous letter, 33 (ML-38).

REFERENCES

The Mahatma begins this letter by saying that the 'real and true' situation has to be defined. Having pronounced his 'Arhat vows' (the vows pertaining to the initiatory status which he has achieved) he cannot seek revenge or help anyone else to do so. But he insists that HPB has every right to *defence*.

It seems that the information published in the *Statesman* was sent to that paper by someone named Macoliffe, whose handwriting was apparently illegible ('a calligrapher and scribe of my kind', the Mahatma calls him), and an error was made in deciphering it. The Mahatma believes this was a 'lucky mistake' and the vindication of HPB may be built upon it 'if you act wisely'. He must do this at once or he will lose the opportunity.

'I can help her with cash only...': Apparently a question concerning the costs in connection with a proposed libel suit by HPB against a slanderer. There are statements in a few of the *Letters* and other writings which indicate that the Adepts can, and do sometimes, supply funds to their chelas, but apparently only under certain circumstances.

'...I telegraphed to offer option...': Again about the libel situation. The telegram in question is dated 8 December 1881. It is not included in the published *Letters* but is found in Folio 6 in the British Museum.

Here the Mahatma abruptly drops this subject and tells Sinnett that HPB's aunt, 'the Odessa Old Lady' would like his (Sinnett's) autograph, since she considers him 'a great and celebrated writer'. He adds: 'She says she was very undisposed to part with your letter to the General but had to send you a proof of her own identity.' He refers to himself as the 'Khosayin' meeting manager or 'boss' and suggests that Sinnett tell HPB's aunt that he advised Sinnett to write to her and send her his autograph. Also Sinnett is to send back through HPB some portraits which apparently HPB's aunt had lent him, as she was very anxious to have them back.

p. 254/250: '..."the lovely maiden"...': An early photograph of HPB. It is shown opposite page 18 in *H.P. Blavatsky, Tibet and Tulku* by Geoffrey A. Barborka. It is, of course, found elsewhere also. It is perhaps the earliest good photograph that we have of HPB.

Then the Mahatma gives some suggestions for *The Theosophist*. He suggests publication of a 'superb address' by Hume, as well as an editorial by Sinnett in reply to material published in *The Spiritualist*.

'My object is twofold,' says the Mahatma, 'to develop your metaphysical intuitions and help the journal by infusing into it a few drops of real literary good blood.' An instance of the importance which the Adepts attached to *The Theosophist*.

'Meanwhile I have to create my dinner—you would scarcely like it—I'm afraid.' This suggests perhaps a type of oriental food not generally palatable to westerners. An intriguing statement. What does he mean by 'create'?

p.251: '...the Disinherited ...': Djual Khul.

'...Prayag and Shigatse...': Prayag was an old name for Allahabad, the 'Holy City'. Shigatse (many variations of spelling) is one of the larger cities in western Tibet and, before the

Chinese invasion, the home of the Panchen or Teshu Lama. It was also the site of the well-known Tashil-Humpo Monastery. The home of M and KH is believed to be near there.

35 (ML-41) Page 256/252 Folio 2 Recd. (late) Dec. 1881 (est.)

DESCRIPTION: M to APS

In bright red ink on both sides of a folded sheet of thin white paper; heavy lettering in M script.

CIRCUMSTANCES

Similar to previous letter 34 (ML-39).

REFERENCES

p. 256/252: '...issue it as a circular letter...': See page 253/250.

'Her letter B.G...': *Bombay Gazette.*

p. 256/253: 'If the laugh is not turned on the *Statesman*...': See first part of Letter 34 (ML-39).

p. 256/253 (second paragraph): This statement about HPB is very interesting. In effect, what M seems to be saying is that the crisis in HPB's life was brought on by her displays of phenomena, and that she is paying a heavy price for it.

(Third paragraph): Again M seems to be telling APS that by helping HPB in her crisis, he is working off some of his own karmic debts.

p. 257/253: 'I saw the lawyer's papers...': By occult means?

36 (ML-36) Page 248/244 Folio 2 Recd. early Jan. 1882 (est.)

DESCRIPTION: M to APS

On small sized sheet of heavy white paper in dark red ink, on both sides in M script.

CIRCUMSTANCES

APS was in Allahabad. HPB and HSO were in Bombay. Mrs Sinnett and son were *en route* from England to Bombay. The Simla Eclectic TS was apparently not progressing very fast. Hume was not doing much.

REFERENCES

p. 248/244: The opening statements are probably in regard to taking new members into the Simla Eclectic TS.

p. 248/245: '...his *index* ...': Probably a catalogue of birds. Hume was one of the leading ornithologists in India and was writing books on the subject.

(Last paragraph): '...those Prayag theosophists...': Prayag was the old Hindu name for the city of Allahabad, this latter name being the one given to it by the Mogul conquerors. Apparently the Simla Eclectic TS had recruited some members there or in Allahabad.

37 (ML-37) Page 248/245 Folio 2 Recd. (early) Jan. 1882 (est.)

DESCRIPTION: Djual Khul to APS

On thin creamy white paper, folded, in blue ink, in DK's script. size 6″ x 9″.

CIRCUMSTANCES

Similar to those of last letter 36 (ML-36)

REFERENCES

This letter is from DK. The first part informs APS that KH has completed his retreat but that, due to his sensitive condition, he will not be able to venture into the outside world for some time. DK then transmits a message from KH. One is impressed with KH's kindliness in sending word at once to his 'lay chela', as he considered Sinnett. A very real affection had developed between them.

The Mahatma KH did go to great lengths to help Sinnett, even to the extent of incurring occasional criticism from the Mahachohan, as has been mentioned in previous notes.

p. 249/246: 'Even Nirvana cannot obliterate GOOD'. A very intriguing statement, indicating that Mahatma KH during his retreat had been functioning at the Nirvanic level of consciousness.

DK takes occasion to thank Sinnett personally 'and very warmly for the genuine sympathy which you felt for me at the time when a slight accident...laid me on my bed of sickness'. It will be remembered that he was saved by a fellow chela from a possible fatal fall over a cliff. See ML, p. 254/251 and LBS-8, p. 12. Apparently it was not such a 'slight accident' for it laid him up for quite some time. The comment about APS's good wishes is intriguing.

DK then informs Sinnett that a man by the name of Bennett will soon be arriving from America. He seems to anticipate that Sinnett will not be favourably impressed by the American, which turns out later to be the case. Sinnett was repelled by Bennett because of his somewhat uncouth appearance (including dirty fingernails) and a certain coarseness which grated on the Englishman's fastidiousness. However, DK quotes the Mahatma: 'He is one of our agents (unknown to himself) to carry out the scheme for the enfranchisement of Western thought from superstitious creeds.' DK adds, 'If you can see your way toward giving him a correct idea of the actual present and potential future state of

Asiatic, but more particularly Indian, thought, it will be gratifying to my Master.'

D.M. Bennett was an American free-thinker and editor of *The Truth-seeker.* In ODL, 2:327-331, Col. Olcott gives considerable space to him, and the passage is worth reading. Olcott speaks of him 'as a very interesting and sincere person, a free-thinker who had suffered a year's imprisonment for his bitter—often coarse—attacks on Christian dogmatism'. A sham case was manufactured against him by an unscrupulous detective of a Christian Society in New York, and 'he was prosecuted and sent to prison. He was made to serve out his whole term of one year, despite the fact that a petition, signed by 100,000 persons, was sent to President Hayes on his behalf. When he was discharged, a monster audience welcomed him enthusiastically at the most fashionable public hall in New York, and a fund was subscribed to pay his expenses on a world-round tour of observation of the practical working of Christianity in all lands.' Interestingly enough, the Colonel learned, in conversation with Bennett, that he and his wife had been members of the Shaker Society for a number of years. 'His religious yet eclectic mind had revolted against the narrowness and intolerance of the Shakers and of Christian sectarians in general; he and the gentle Shakeress in question decided to marry and make a home of their own, and they left the Shaker community.' (See pages noted above in ODL for an interesting development which took place in India.) See also Letter 43 (ML-42) p.261/256 and Alphabetical Notes on Bennett.

p. 250/246: '...the work left undone from Mr Hume's hands'. This refers to the series of articles written by Hume and published in *The Theosophist* under the title 'Fragments of Occult Truth'. He was a brilliant writer, but soon grew tired of the undertaking and Sinnett took over. The teachings were later used in Sinnett's second book, *Esoteric Buddhism.*

The Mr Terry mentioned here was an Australian Theosophist, a Spiritualist and founder and editor of the magazine,

Harbinger of Light, published in Melbourne. It was in part some original questions of his which persuaded Sinnett and Hume to answer him at some length, and out of this grew the series of 'Fragments'. He seems otherwise not to have played a very great part in the letters.

p. 250/246: DK then mentions Hume and adds: 'As to our reverenced M: he desires me to assure you that the secret of Mr Hume's professed love for Humanity lies in, and is based upon, the chance presence in that word of the first syllable; as for "mankind"—he has no sympathy for it.' This is an excellent example of Master M's satirical humour.

The Mahatma KH will not be able to write to Sinnett for a month or two longer, says DK ...'He begs you to proceed for his sake with your metaphysical studies; and not to be giving up the task in despair whenever you meet with incomprehensible ideas in M. Sahib's notes...' During Master KH's absence, Master M had been giving Sinnett and Hume some very occult teachings, including the famous 'Cosmological Notes'.

P.S. This gives an indication that letters were transmitted sometimes by Damodar (DKM).

38 (ML-90) Page 412/406 Folio 3 Dated 'University College, London, W.C., November 26th, 81 ' Recd. Jan. 6, 1882.

DESCRIPTION

This is a letter from Stainton Moses to APS, with underlinings and comments by KH. It is written on both sides of two long narrow sheets, about 5″ x 16″ in size. The underlining and comments are in blue ink and the KH script. The comments are on the back side of sheet No.2.

CIRCUMSTANCES

HPB and HSO were in Bombay. APS had gone to Bombay in early January to meet his family arriving from

England. He received the letter after his arrival there, so presumably it came out on the same ship with his family.

It is frequently asked how the footnotes and underlining could have been done by KH, since he was in his retreat in November and December. However, he was out of it about the first of the year, as indicated by the letter from DK in 37 (ML-37), p. 248/245. It would seem likely that the notes were added to the letter in transit just before APS received it, probably through the agency of DK.

It will be recalled that Letter 18 (ML-9) p. 38, dealt at some length with Stainton Moses, pointing out some of his errors and mistaken ideas. It was mentioned in the notes on that letter that Sinnett copied long passages from it and later sent them to Stainton Moses.

This letter (38) is mainly concerned with Moses's response to those passages and with his insistence that Imperator (+) (whom he claimed was his spirit guide) was never one of the Brothers, as the Mahatma KH had said, and knew nothing whatever about them or their existence. Therefore Moses did not believe in them. It may be important to consider the Mahatma's inserted comments in this letter.

REFERENCES

p. 412/406 (first sentence): Mrs Sinnett was still in London when the letter was written.

On p. 413/407 the Mahatma has inserted: 'I will try one more honest medium—Eglinton, when he is gone; and see what comes of it. I will do so much for the Society.' The words 'when he is gone' must refer to the 'Magus' mentioned by Moses in a preceding sentence—someone apparently known to Imperator, since the mention is in a message from that 'guide'.

William Eglinton was a popular English medium who came to India early in 1882 and spent some time in Calcutta. Apparently he was an excellent medium but had a number of personal weaknesses.

p. 414/408: *'Mt Athos'* in Greece. Stainton Moses had spent some time there.

'There is no LACUNA.' A void or blank.

p. 414/408: 'Fragments of Occult Truth...': See Study Notes on Letter 37 (ML-37). The articles that AOH and APS wrote and which were published serially in *The Theosophist.*

p. 409: '...Edward Maitland...': An English Spiritualist (1824-97) and close friend and collaborator of Anna Kingsford. See ML index. For photograph see HPB, VI, 171.

39 (ML-115) Page 449/442 Folio 3 Recd. Jan. (before 12th) 1882 (est.)

DESCRIPTION: M to APS

In red ink on both sides of a single sheet of heavy smooth folded paper, about 9″ x 13″. The lettering is large and the script somewhat different from that of Letter 32 (ML-114).

CIRCUMSTANCES

This is a short letter from the Mahatma M received while Sinnett was in Bombay in January 1882. He had gone there to meet his wife and son Denny on the 6th. The Mahatma had not yet resumed correspondence.

However, both of the Mahatmas seem concerned that Sinnett should attend the anniversary celebration of the Theosophical Society. This was mentioned in an earlier letter [24 (ML-71), p. 374/367] when the Mahatma said: 'Could you but go to Bombay to the Anniversary you would confer upon K.H. and myself a great obligation and a lasting one—but that you know best.'

In a letter written by the Mahatma KH shortly before he left for his retreat (LBS 203, p. 365) he said: 'Your presence in Bombay would save *everything*, and yet seeing how reluctant you feel I will not insist.' In this letter (39) the Mahatma M says: 'But neither of us would force a course of action—against your wish—upon you.'

This meeting took place on 12 January 1882. It was a delayed celebration, as the anniversary of the founding of the Society was November 17. But in his Annual Report, the Colonel explained that while the meeting should have been held on November 17, that was impossible, as he was in Ceylon and did not return until 19 December 1881; it was being held at the first convenient date. However, APS decided against the stay, as he was apparently in a hurry to get home and was concerned about his job. In Letter 44 (ML-43), it is indicated that APS gave his 'wife and child's interests' as the excuse. See Letter 41 (ML-109), 42 (ML-43), and 24 (ML-71).

(Last part of letter): This would seem to indicate that Sinnett missed one more chance to have a contact of some sort with KH.

40 & 41 (ML 108-109) Page 444/437 Folio 3
Recd. Jan. (after 12th) 1881 (est.)

DESCRIPTION: M to APS

These two notes are in red ink on a single sheet of folded heavy white paper, about 6″ x 9″ in size. 40 (ML-108) is written diagonally acrosss the front side and 41 (ML-109) is written diagonally across the opened inside of the sheet. On 41 half of the first sentence is in black ink, and red and black are intermingled throughout the letter. The ending of the letter is in the lower right-hand corner where there is hardly room for M's initial.

CIRCUMSTANCES

The Sinnetts had returned to Allahabad from Bombay. The TS Anniversary had been observed in Bombay on January 12, without Sinnett in attendance as had been suggested by M and KH.

REFERENCES

40 probably pertains to membership in the Simla Eclectic TS. The last sentence indicates the ability of the Adepts to be constantly aware of the actions of those with whom they are concerned and especially their chelas.

41: '...the French woman...': Reference to Madame Coulomb, who was residing at the Bombay headquarters.

'Ramaswami(er) and Scott...': See Alphabetical Notes. Ramaswamier stated that on his trip to Sikkim, he had met M in person. Ross Scott was one of a group (which included Damodar) to whom the Mahatma M appeared at the Bombay headquarters of the TS early in 1882.

'...by attending the meeting..': Again a reference to the Anniversary celebration on January 12 which the Mahatmas had encouraged APS to attend, but which he did not choose to do.

42 (ML-43) Page 258/255 Folio 2 Recd. Jan. 1882 (est.)

DESCRIPTION: M to APS

In dark red ink on three full-sized sheets of white paper. The writing on two of the sheets is diagonally across. The signature is a bit different in that the initial has no 'tail' but has a line beneath it which is looped at both ends.

CIRCUMSTANCES

HPB and HSO were in Bombay. The Sinnett family had returned home to Allahabad from Bombay. KH had ended his 'retreat' but had not as yet put himself into communication with Sinnett and Hume.

REFERENCES

p. 259/255: '...my snake-like signature ...being pulled by the tail...': M's signature initial generally carried a looped tail with three dots in the form of a triangle.

'Why will you be so impatient?' Both Adepts were asking Sinnett to develop more patience.

'...the *Deva Lok* "Eclectic"...': The Simla Eclectic TS.

'...the "Parent"...': The Parent TS.

'...our too intellectual friend'. AOH.

'...call a Padri...': A light reference to the Christian missionaries.

'...our Ved-Vyasa...': Supposed compiler of early Vedas.

'...write as a *bhut* to you ...': Roughly translated, 'a has been'.

'...the best English I find lying idle in my friend's brain...': The brain of the Mahatma KH.

p.259/256: '...with the "visible" one...': The personality.

p. 260/256: '...the Bombay meeting'. Referring again to the January 12 anniversary meeting in Bombay, which the Mahatmas wanted APS to attend. See Letters 41 (ML-109), 39 (ML-115) and 24 (ML-71).

p.260/256: '...shine in a *Durbar* ...': See Alphabetical Notes.

(near bottom): 'His is a bird-killing and a faith-killing temperament...': Apparently the Mahatmas did not consider AOH to be a very compassionate person in some respects.

'...a singing bulbul...': A common bird in India.

'..."Stray Feathers"...': A quarterly bird journal published by AOH.

p. 260/257: '...Damodar thro' the D—': The Disinherited, DK.

'...Bennett had unwashed hands...': D.M. Bennett who arrived in Bombay on January 10 while APS was there. See Alphabetical Notes. See also Letter 37 (ML-37) and ODL, 2:327.

'...your bearer...': Personal servant.

'See how well KH read your character when he would not send the Lahore youth to talk with you without a change of dress.' This refers to the incident mentioned in the notes on Letter 5 (ML-4) concerning Rattan Chandra Bary.

p. 262/258: '...each man is personally responsible to the Law of Compensation for every word of his voluntary production'. This is a statement that all of us should remember and be aware of.

p.262/258: '...you (like your fabled Shloma) but choose...': Perhaps he means Solomon.

'Yes—your "cosmogony"!' It is not certain which Cosmological Notes are referred to here, but perhaps those which appear in the Appendix to LBS.

'...just now I am on duty'. There are several similar references throughout the *Letters* to being on duty, or being on watch. These expressions are not explained, so one can only speculate on what is implied.

The verse quoted at the bottom of p. 262/258 is from the poem 'Up-Hill' by Christina Rossetti.

'...our Simla Sage'. AOH.

'...the O.L. ...': HPB; the 'Old Lady'.

The closing word 'Namaskar' means 'homage' or 'I do homage.'

43 (ML-42) ***Page 257/253*** ***Folio 2*** ***Recd. Jan. 1882 (est.)***

DESCRIPTION: M to APS

In bright red ink on three small sized sheets of thin white paper, each of a different size. The letter is unsigned but is in the M script.

CIRCUMSTANCES

APS was in Allahabad. The Founders were in Bombay.

KH had returned from his retreat, but had not as yet resumed his correspondence with APS and AOH.

REFERENCES

p. 257/253: 'Whether the Chohan finds ... is another question.' Apparently it will be a decision of the Mahachohan as to how much of the technical occult teachings will be given to Sinnett and Hume.

p. 257/253: '...I will return to give room ...to him...' Reference to KH who will shortly resume the correspondence.

p. 257/254: 'Primrose and Rattigan...': Newspaper publishers.

p. 258/254: '...*Fragments* ...': The series of articles entitled 'Fragments of Occult Truth' being written by APS and AOH.

p. 258/254: 'Send both portraits...': These were to go back to HPB's aunt in Odessa, referred to as the 'Old Generaless'. See p. 254/250.

'...promise help for her niece'. HPB.

44 (ML-13) Page 70 Folio 1 Recd. Jan. 28, 1882

DESCRIPTION: M to APS

APS labels this document 'Cosmological Notes'. Another group of questions and answers generally referred to as 'The Cosmological Notes' is found in LBS, Appendix II, p, 376. The questions in this letter were written by APS on the left half of sheets of smooth white notepaper. The answers by M are mostly on the right-hand side of the sheets opposite the questions. Where space was insufficient, the answer was continued on the back of the sheet. But in some cases, even this was not enough space for the answer, and an additional sheet of a different type of paper was inserted. In the case of sheets 1 and 2, the right side has been cut off and a new right half pasted on. The replies are in M's script, but in *blue* ink, with a few exceptions. The third sheet (inserted) is in red ink and on both sides, diagonally in front, and square with the paper on the back. On the next sheet the writing is in red ink. This is followed by another inserted sheet, with writing in red ink.

The final word 'Prepare' is very interesting in that the first five letters are printed in upper and lower case letters mixed, and the last two letters are in M's script.

CIRCUMSTANCES

The Sinnett family had returned to Allahabad. The Founders were in Bombay. Sinnett was probably asking these metaphysical questions on his own and M was trying to give him basic information.

REFERENCES

No attempt is made to interpret the subject-matter of these Cosmological Notes, as that is beyond the scope of the *Guide.* The student is referred to various glossaries and to the Alphabetical Notes for definitions and names; also to *The Secret Doctrine* for technical items covered in the letter. The term 'Devachan' appears for the first time in this letter. See Alphabetical Notes.

One has to consider that the information given out here in these letters of M's and later by KH are the first basic metaphysical teachings that had been given to the western world. The only previous information along this line was in *Isis Unveiled,* and this was only an 'opening wedge' as KH expressed it.

This is a very long letter and it would be well to give it some study.

In the second edition of ML, some words and letters are missing from the answer to the first question. These have been supplied in the third edition. For the benefit of the student who is using the second edition, that portion of the completed passage is copied below, beginning with line 10 of the paragraph, the missing portions shown in italics.

> '...effect establishing *as you* go along, analogies between *the birth* of a man and that of a world. In our doctrine, *you* will find necessary the synthetic *method,* you will have to embrace the whole—that is to say to blend the macrocosm *and* microcosm together—before you are enabled...'

(The student may wish to write or print in the missing words and letters.)

45 (ML-44) Page 263/259 Folio 2 Recd. Feb. 1882 (est.)

DESCRIPTION: M to APS

In bright red ink, on two sheets of regular size white paper, on both sides, in medium weight M script.

CIRCUMSTANCES

After the closing of the last letter (44, ML-13) in which the Mahatma M told Sinnett he would not be hearing from him again for some time, it is somewhat surprising to come to another letter from him. There are yet more. However, it is seen from his first sentence that Sinnett, not being aware that the Mahatma KH had written to him, since he had not yet received the letter, had addressed another letter to M, who very kindly answered him.

REFERENCES

First paragraph: 'Do so by all means; go ahead.' This direction is not very intelligible since we don't know precisely what Sinnett had written to him. However, obviously it concerned the medium William Eglinton, whom the Mahatma here terms 'The poor sensitive lad'.

William Eglinton has been mentioned previously. He was a popular English medium who spent the spring of 1882 in Calcutta. His principal 'guide' was known as 'Ernest' and Eglinton had great faith in him.

Eglinton seems to have been a fine medium; it was said that he never resorted to trickery. He had, however, a number of personal weaknesses. It may be remembered that there was some indication that the Mahatma KH had considered bringing him to Simla for training so that he could be used in their work, but after Eglinton arrived in Calcutta, KH decided against this.

After a time, Eglinton became disappointed and returned to England in 1882. He had also some personal reasons for this. A very striking event took place during his voyage, which will be related in appropriate sequence.

Perhaps the comment in this first paragraph about allowing him to risk himself inside the lion's den had something to do with the earlier plan to bring him to Simla for special training.

p. 263/259: The Mahatma M next reminds Sinnett that on the 17th of the following November, the septenary term of trial given the Society at its foundation will expire. This was the real seventh anniversary of the founding of the Theosophical Society and was a serious testing time. In effect, the Mahatma says, 'Better get busy'.

An important passage follows; it has to do with the conditions under which the Theosophical Society was founded; how 'one or two of us' felt it was time to undertake such a venture; how consent was given for the trial; how HPB and Olcott were brought together and offered themselves for the undertaking, etc., and how they struggled against almost overwhelming odds, etc. 'In a few more months the term of probation will end', and if the question of the 'Brothers' is not settled by that time, they will 'subside out of public view... Only those who have proved faithful to themselves and to

Truth through everything, will be allowed further intercourse with us.' Even this possibility is qualified.

In the penultimate paragraph, the Mahatma mentions Hume's 'present pamphlet'. This is his small book entitled *Hints on Esoteric Theosophy,* which was published that year (1882).

The reference to 'cosmological questions' in the last paragraph probably refers to the next letter to be considered, —46 (ML-12)—in which the Mahatma answers questions.

46 (ML-12) Page 66 Folio 1 Recd. Feb. 1882 (est.)

DESCRIPTION: M to APS

The letter is without date or salutation. On both sides of four sheets of coarse rough paper, plus one sheet of thin white paper. The heavy sheets appear to be hand-cut out of larger sheets, being a bit uneven in size. The writing on the heavy sheets is in bright red ink, and this is somewhat blotted and has a few smears. One sheet has a spot which is evidently caused by wet ink from the next sheet. In the middle of sheet 4, the writer apparently changed to a reddish purple ink. Sheet 5 is written on one side only in purple ink, and the writing is from the middle outwards towards both ends. At the bottom of this sheet is the postscript in what looks like *red pencil* remarking about the penmanship, quality of paper, etc. This has been touched up a little in purple ink.

COMMENT

There are several places in the original letters where there appears to be blotting or smearing such as would occur in the use of ink for writing. W.Q. Judge also states that in a letter he received phenomenally from an Adept, he also noted a similar blotting effect. This is another of the mysteries surrounding the writing and transmission of letters by occult methods.

CIRCUMSTANCES

Similar to those of previous letter, 45 (ML-44).

REFERENCES

This letter deals principally with questions raised by APS about cosmology. The student is referred to the glossaries and *The Secret Doctrine* for information and definitions.

There was need at this time for a definite nomenclature, as there was considerable confusion in terms and no definite understanding concerning them had been reached. See the comments at the top of p.70. The student should keep in mind that the sevenfold constitution of man used here is that of the early period of the Theosophical Society and *The Secret Doctrine* and differs somewhat from that used by some later writers.

SPECIAL NOTE

The following comments on the text of the letter are included as an aid to students.

The 'hypothesis' to which the Mahatma seems to give some approval is not specifically given, but much can be inferred from the explanations given by the Mahatma. 'Almost unthinkably long as is a Mahayug...'[1] A Mahayuga is the same as the period more often called a 'Manvantara' or a period of manifestation, a 'life cycle' within which the whole descent and return of spirit must be accomplished.

The Mahatma then proceeds to discuss what later came to be called the doctrine of chains and rounds. It must be remembered that, at the time the Letters were written, the nomenclature which later came to be used was not in existence.

The Mahatma says: '...among the stellar galaxies, births and deaths of worlds ever follow each other in the orderly procession of natural law'. Planets die as the life wave leaves them, but they do not remain dead! They reincarnate. 'Motion is the eternal order of things and affinity or attraction its handmaid of all works.' So life swings around the chains, and each cycle 'gives birth to something still higher as moral and physical types than during the preceding manvantara'. It is a spiral process, never-ending, but not a continuous repetitive cycle.

One may wonder how this can be—but the end of evolution is inconceivable; new potentials are forever evolved out of past and present achievements.; 'Planetary development', says the Master, 'is as progressive as human or race evolution.'

'The hour of pralaya's coming catches the series of worlds at successive stages of evolution; each has attained to some one of the periods of evolutionary progress—each stops there until the outward impulse of the next manvantara sets it going from that very point, like a stopped timepiece rewound.'

At the coming of pralaya everything stops: no human, animal, or even vegetable is alive to see it, although the mineral kingdom does not disappear. Everything physically disintegrates yet is not destroyed, and everything will pick up again at the very point in the chain at which it stopped with the onset of pralaya. 'This, as we know, is repeated endlessly throughout ETERNITY. Each man of us has gone this ceaseless round, and will repeat it for ever and ever. The deviation of each one's course, and his rate of progress from Nirvana to Nirvana is governed by causes which he himself creates out of the exigencies in which he finds himself entangled.'

But, as already stated, this is a spiral: each Nirvana is higher than the one which preceded it, although there is probably a great deal of recapitulation each time—just as each of us has to recapitulate the periods of infancy, childhood, and adolescence before coming again to maturity. Each recapitulation, however, would be at a more advanced stage of evolution.

The Mahatma says that the picture of an eternity of action may appal the mind accustomed to look forward to a period of ceaseless repose. But this concept (ceaseless repose) is not supported by the analogies of nature. Periods of action and rest inevitably follow one another.

The Mahatma mentions the Monad and says that the periods that intervene between the manvantaras are proportionately long to reward for the thousands of existences passed on the various globes, and this same principle applies between births to compensate for any life of strife and misery.

'To conceive of an *eternity* of bliss or woe, and to offset it to any conceivable deeds of merit or demerit of a being who may have lived a century or even a millennium in the flesh, can only be proposed by one who has never yet grasped the awful reality of the word Eternity, nor pondered upon the law of perfect justice and equilibrium which pervades nature. Further instructions may be given you, which will show how nicely justice is done not to man only but also to his subordinates, and throw some light, I hope, upon the vexed question of good and evil.'

One may question what is meant by the term man's 'subordinates'. No doubt it refers to the so-called 'lower' kingdoms of nature which man has used or exploited; he must at some time 'pay' for this use. (This is not a dogmatic statement but a speculation of the compiler.)

'And now to crown this effort of mine [of writing],' says the Mahatma, 'I may as well pay an old debt and answer an old question of yours concerning earth incarnations. Koot'hoomi answers some of your queries—at least began writing yesterday but was called off by duty—but I may help him anyhow. I trust you will not find much difficulty—not as much as hitherto—in making out my letter. I have become a very plain writer since he reproached me with making you lose your valuable time over my scrawlings. His rebuke struck home, and as you see I have amended my evil ways.'

The Mahatma then discusses the scientific findings about the appearance of man on the planet, rather roughly correlated with the geological periods.[2]

The Mahatma speaks of the 'four races' of man then recognized by science and says that—like much else in the science of that day—this is wrong; there are five—'and we are that fifth with remnants of the fourth'.

The first race appeared on earth 'not half a million of years ago but several millions'.

'Nature shuts the door behind her as she advances.' A very pertinent comment and one which is verifiable by one's own studies.

In one of the Mahatma KH's earlier letters he commented on the need for a nomenclature for the expression of their idea, and here the Mahatma M says: '...you ought to come to some agreement as to the terms used when discussing upon cyclic evolutions. Our terms are untranslatable; and without a good knowledge of our complete system (which cannot be given but to regular initiates) would suggest nothing definite to your perceptions but only a source of confusion...'

At the end of the letter there is mention of Subba Row, a great occultist, who strenuously opposed revealing the knowledge to Westerners. Here the Mahatma says, '...he is very jealous and regards teaching an Englishman as a sacrilege'.[3]

Footnotes to Letter 46

1. *Mahayuga:* (Sk.) The aggregate of four *yugas* or ages, of 4,320,000 solar years; a 'Day of Brahma', in the Brahmanical system; lit., 'the great age'. *Theosophical Glossary,* H.P. Blavatsky, A photographic reproduction of the original edition, at first issued in London 1892. Los Angeles, California, The Theosophy Company, 1930. (See also *Yuga)*

2. The student will be aware of the vast changes that have taken place in scientific findings during the last century.

3. Subba Row is mentioned a number of times in the *Letters.* Later, he was 'ordered' (his term) by the Mahatma M to instruct the two Englishmen. [See Letter 58 (ML-130), p.457/450.]

47 (ML-45) Page 264/260 Folio 2 Recd. Feb. 1882 (est.)

DESCRIPTION: KH to APS

In medium blue ink, in a large clear script, on six sheets of white paper. The first four sheets are written on both sides, the fifth on one side, and the sixth on both sides.

CIRCUMSTANCES

APS was in Allahabad. The Founders were in Bombay. HSO left on February 17 for a tour of North India. This is the first letter received by APS from KH after the latter's return from his retreat. He had been out of correspondence for about three months, during which time Master M had been filling in for him with the correspondence.

REFERENCES

The careful student of the Mahatma Letters will note a decided change in KH's correspondence from this time on. He evidently had gone through a momentous time in his life, advancing a stage in his evolution and assuming the duties of a Chohan of his ray. We see a deeper aspect to his nature, a wider vista and added responsibility. As he says in his opening sentence, 'I have been on a long journey after supreme knowledge...' Meaning a journey in consciousness, not in distance.

p. 264/260: '...the New Year's festivities...' See Letter 23 (ML-104). No explanation is given of what festivities are meant, but it seems unlikely that it refers to the popular religious ones.

p. 264/261: '...exercises of patience'. Another comment to APS with regard to patience.

Par. 2: '...it is more difficult than before to exchange letters with you...' This may refer to an increase in the gulf between them as a result of the initiation KH had just undergone. We see in this paragraph and the next one the concerns of KH for the future of the TS, both in England and India.

p. 265/261: '...succeeded in bringing over to it Wyld...' Dr George Wyld. He was made chairman of the Committee on Mesmerism of the SPR. Dr Wyld was one of the charter members of a branch of the TS formed in London in 1878. Apparently he turned against the Society, as KH indicates in this letter.

p. 286/262: '...members with whom we can work *de facto* ...' The London Lodge did not accomplish much until the arrival of HPB and, after her, under Mrs Besant.

(middle): 'Like the needle the adept follows his attractions.' Meaning, of course, as the compass needle follows its attractions. There are a number of references in which the student is advised that he must draw the Master towards him by his own actions.

'In the imperishable RECORD of the Masters...' There are several references to these 'records' of the Adepts, although the meaning or method of operation of such records is not explained. Perhaps it is merely a reference to the Akashic Records.

p. 263: 'Tathagata.' In this context and on the next page, KH seems to be referring to the Buddhist teaching that everyone is potentially a Buddha and has the Buddha light or Buddha nature in his heart.

p. 268/264: '...the hill of Jakko'. The hill is in Simla where AOH's house was located. References in ML to 'Jakko' refer either to AOH or his home, Rothney Castle.

'...friends of S.B.L.' Probably the Simla Branch Lodge.

'...the Sisyphus' rock...' Reference to the Greek myth. See also Letter 12 (ML-7), p. 25.

p. 268/264 (last sentence): 'I am called to duty.' Another unexplained reference to the fact that the adepts are sometimes called to important 'duties'.

48 (ML-47) ***Page 271/267*** ***Folio 2*** ***Recd. Mar. 3, 1882***

DESCRIPTION: M to APS

In dark red ink, in rather fine M script, on three large-sized sheets of thin paper. The writing on the first page is diagonally across the sheet.

CIRCUMSTANCES

APS was in Allahabad. HPB and DKM were in Bombay. HSO was on his tour of North India, accompanied by an Indian chela named Bhavani Rao. They were planning to stop in Allahabad en route. APS notes that this letter was received 'Through Damodar'.

REFERENCES

'Cook is a *pump of filth*...' This refers to the Revd Joseph Cook, a Boston preacher who was visiting India at the time. He had at one time supported Spiritualism but in India he denounced both Spiritualism and Theosophy. Damodar took occasion to counter some of his accusations in the public press.[1]

'Your last letter to me was less a "petition" than a protest,' says the Mahatma. He comments favourably on it, however, because it was frank and outspoken. 'Europe is a large place but the world is bigger,' he says, and adds: 'The sun of Theosophy must shine for all, not for a part. There is more to this movement than you have yet had an inkling of, and the work of the T.S. is linked in with similar work that is secretly going on in all parts of the world...'

There is reference to a 'Greek Brother'—indicating that there are different sections within the Occult Brotherhood.

'You speak of Massey and Crookes...' and, later, 'Wild' (Wyld). Charles Massey, although primarily interested in Spiritualism, was one of the original seventeen persons present at the founding of the Theosophical Society, although he was not at the actual founding meeting: he had to leave on his return trip to England. Here the Mahatma comments on an opportunity which Massey declined.

Dr Wyld was President of the London Lodge—a man with strong orthodox leanings. HPB called him 'a bigoted ass' (LBS p. 22). He was later expelled from the London Lodge, and HPB says (LBS, p. 60) that if he hadn't been 'kicked out' (her term) there would have been a revolution against the lodge itself.

Dr William Crookes was an English physicist and scientist of note and a member of the Royal Society, the ultimate in prestige in scientific England. He achieved some remarkable results with experiments in what he called 'radiant matter'. He became a member of the Theosophical Society and was one of the five counsellors of the Society. HPB stated (LBS 224-225) that he was teaching a very occult doctrine and that the Mahatmas intended to help him. There are numerous references to him in both the Mahatma's Letters and in LBS.

'To say and point out to Edison[2] and Crookes and Massey—would sound much like boasting of that which can never be *proven.*' The Mahatma then points out how much greater is the whole Brotherhood than the two Mahatmas with whom Sinnett has had some experience.

There follows a defense of HPB and a rather surprising statement: '...she is ordered *in cases of need* to *mislead* people... She is *too truthful, too outspoken, too incapable of dissimulation,* and now she is being daily crucified for it.'

The Mahatma counsels patience. 'Let evolution take its course naturally...' Crookes and Edison and others may make other discoveries, 'So I say "WAIT".'

'Who knows what may be the situation in November?' This is a reference to the end of the seven-year probationary period of the Society—the seventh anniversary of the founding.

'Bide your time, the *record book is well kept*. Only look out sharp: the *Dugpas* and the *Gelukpas* are not fighting but in Tibet alone ...' The Dugpas were at that time largely regarded as sorcerers and adepts of black magic. The Gelukpas were 'the highest and most orthodox Buddhist sect in Tibet, the antithesis of Dugpa' *(Theosophical Glossary* by H.P. Blavatksy).

'...your acquaintance Wallace...' We have met him before. He was a prominent English naturalist, much interested in spiritualistic phenomena. He originated a theory of natural selection very similar to that of Darwin, although with some important differences. He was the author of a book entitled *Miracles and Modern Spiritualism*.

Shammars: the Tantric magicians of the Red Cap sect.

The Mahatma then comments that it is useless for Sinnett to say anything more about Olcott's eccentricities and the inferiority of America to England. The student will be aware that the two Englishmen rather looked down their noses at Olcott and, in general, had a rather superior attitude towards anything American. The Mahatma says that they are aware of whatever in this attitude has any basis, but that the rest of it is 'mere superficial prejudice'. He indicates that it might be a shock to Sinnett if he were sometime suddenly put in Olcott's place.

The Mahatma then says that he has written the 'Answers to Correspondents' in the Supplement to *The Theosophist*. This was the supplement to the March 1882 issue. It has already been noted that many contributions from the Mahatmas appeared in that magazine. In an article entitled 'Adepts and Adept Writings' appearing in *The Theosophical Forum* for August 1884, the author, John Rogers, lists 17 contributions which were unquestionably by the Mahatmas and he gives documentation in every instance.

(Much in this letter seems obscure because we do not have Sinnett's comments to which the letter is in reply.)

Footnotes to Letter 48

1. See *Damodar,* pp. 178-180. See also an interesting account of the Revd Mr Cook's activities in India, ODL 2: 329.

2. Thomas Edison was an early member of the Theosophical Society. His cheque in payment of his dues is preserved in the Archives at Adyar, the international headquarters of the Society.

49 (ML-48) Page 273/269 Folio 2 Recd. Mar. 3, 1882

DESCRIPTION: KH to APS

In medium blue ink on both sides of 7 sheets of thin paper. One sheet is missing for reasons unknown. The signature is in ink different from that of the body of the letter.

CIRCUMSTANCES

Similar to previous letter [48 (ML-47)], and received the same day. This was the second letter to be received by APS after KH's 'retreat'.

Refer to notes on Letter 38 (chronologically), a letter from Stainton Moses in which the Mahatma KH inserted some comments. In those comments, appended at the end of Moses's letter, the Mahatma said: 'My letter is private. You may use the arguments but not my authority or name.' In those notes it was mentioned that the Mahatma was referring to a letter which he was writing, or had written,but which Sinnett had not yet received. This is that letter. The fact that it is dated as received on March 3 strengthens the suggestion that the Mahatma's comments on Moses's letter were written late in February or very early in March. As a matter of fact, its length indicates that it may have taken several days to write. And at the end of this letter, he warns Sinnett: 'And now need I remind you that this letter is strictly *private*?'

REFERENCES

The first long paragraph is filled with metaphors, of which KH seems to be a master.

p. 273/269: The words 'however bitterly we may complain' are provocative. One cannot help but wonder whether there are times when personal longings assail the Mahatmas with terrific impact. Again and again, the Mahatma KH says, in effect, that if he had only his personal preferences to consider, he would do many things for Sinnett that he was not permitted by their rules to do.

The Mahatma goes on to say that they can never pursue the journey, even if hand in hand, along the crowded highway on which the many 'spiritualists and mystics, prophets and seers elbow each other now-a-day[s]'. All this 'motley crowd of candidates may shout for an eternity to come, for the *Sesame* to open. It never will, so long as they keep outside those rules'—the rules, or laws, by which the Adept must live.

The *Sesame* to open' is, of course, a reference to the 'Open Sesame' in the story of Ali Baba and the Forty Thieves in the *Arabian Nights*. We do not open the door to adeptship by saying a magic word, but only by the long, hard, and often bitter struggle through the jungle of the world, not allowing ourselves to be led astray by the glamour of awakened psychic faculties.

The Mahatma goes on to say that no one can ever violently break the rules 'without becoming the first victim to his guilt' even to the extent of losing his own immortality. '...too anxious expectation is not only tedious, but dangerous too'. Always, in studying occultism, one is warned against 'expectation'. To expect something is already to have formed in one's mind what the result is to be, and developments are almost always *un*expected. '...he who would gain his aim—*must be cold*'. This statement has caused difficulty, even consternation, with some readers. Perhaps it is used in the sense of impersonality or dispassion, not to be caught up in the emotions.

p. 274/270: the 'forthcoming number' of *The Theosophist*. These articles were 'The Elixir of Life' by Mirza Moorad Ali Beg (real name, Godolphin Mitford) and 'Philosophy of the Spirit' by William Oxley. The author of 'The Elixir of Life' was a member of a prominent English family which had produced several noted writers. He was, however, born in India. Olcott gives an extremely interesting, although tragic, commentary on him in ODL 2, beginning on page 289. The article by Oxley was actually a reply by him to a review of his book, *Philosophy of the Spirit*; the review was written by Djual Khul and was, in some respects, rather scathing. In his reply, Oxley took exception to it.

The quotations on this page and on p. 275/271 are from this article. See Alphabetical Notes.

As might be expected, HPB would not stand for Oxley's rather slighting reference to KH in his reply to the review: '...our blunderbuss Editor failed not to explode'. HPB might say all kinds of things about the Mahatmas when she was impatient and even angry with them, but she would never permit anyone else to criticize them and always rose to their defense. 'Nor would she be soothed', says the Mahatma here, 'until Djual Khul, with whom the famous review was concocted...was authorized to answer ... the Seer in a few innocent footnotes.' From the comments here, it seems he felt the review should never have been published in the first place, and he has some favourable things to say about Oxley and his book. Then after pointing out some of its inaccuracies (which, obviously, he knew all about) the Mahatma says: '...yet he is positively and absolutely the only one, whose general comprehension of *Spirit,* and its capabilities and functions after the first separation we call *death,* are on the whole if not quite correct, at least approximating very nearly Truth'.

'...Djual-Khul...' A first degree chela who later became an Adept. See Alphabetical Notes.

p. 275/271: 'Thus—S.M. is taught...' Stainton Moses.

'...and Mrs K ...' Mrs Anna B. Kingsford.

p. 275/272: '...the "Seeress"...' Mrs Kingsford.

p. 277/273: 'Mrs H. Billing...' Mrs Hollis Billing, an American medium. See Alphabetical Notes.

He mentions Stainton Moses and his Imperator and then Mrs Anna Kingsford (Mrs K.) and Edward Maitland. In spite of their haziness, 'those teachings are nearer to the mark than anything uttered so far by the mediums...When the "Seeress" is made to reveal that "immortality is by no means a matter of course for all" ...she is delivering herself of actual, incontrovertible facts.'

p. 277/273: 'Yes; I am indeed satisfied with your last article...' Probably a reference to an instalment of 'Fragments of Occult Truth', written by APS, who had taken over the writing of these articles after Hume had stopped writing them.

p. 278/274: '...the ways of the Siddhas...' Highly evolved sages.

p. 278/274: '...the humble, the derided journal of your Society'. A reference to *The Theosophist*. He then gives an interesting and somewhat amusing description of the cover on the magazine which carried the familiar picture of Lucifer descending from the sky.

p.279/274: 'Bhavani Shankar is with O...' The Indian chela who was accompanying HSO on his tour. Also spoken of as Bhavani Rao. See Alphabetical Notes. They were about to arrive in Allahabad.

p. 279/275:'...I am not a "Seraph" yet...' The Seraphim are considered next to the highest in the celestial hierarchy by the Christians.

p. 279/275: A little further on, we come to an interesting passage showing that the Mahatmas do not always agree on methods of teaching. KH says that 'Morya ... wanted me to acquaint you with the totality of the subtle bodies and their collective aggregate...' The Mahatma KH believed this was 'premature'. Obviously the two Mahatmas had different modes of teaching. Here the Mahatma KH says: 'What I blame him for is that he allows you to begin from the wrong end—the most difficult unless one has thoroughly mastered the preparatory ground...Indeed, when you complain of being unable to comprehend the meaning of Eliphas Lévi, it is only because you fail like so many other readers to find the key to their way of writing.'

An important statement follows: '...you will find that it was never the intention of the Occultists really to conceal what they have been writing from the earnest determined students, but rather to lock up their information for safety-sake, in a secure safe-box, the key to which is—intuition'.

The reference to the blue ink and the red ink relates to the fact that the Mahatma M habitually wrote in a heavy red ink, while the Mahatma KH generally used blue ink.

'O. [Olcott] will be with you shortly, and you ought to make the best of this opportunity...' Olcott was accompanied by Bhavani Rao, or Bhavani Shankar, a young man who was developing some ability in occult powers. As it turned out, he was able to perform a minor phenomenon, but less than Sinnett expected. (See *Masters and Men*, p. 136.)

50 (ML-88) Page 410/404 Folio 3 Recd. March 11, 1882

DESCRIPTION: KH to APS

In dark blue ink on a single folded sheet of white paper about 5″ x 8″. The signature is slightly smeared. This is one of the few instances where the Master has included the calendar date of his letter.

CIRCUMSTANCES

HSO, accompanied by the Indian chela, Bhavani Rao (or Shankar), was starting on a tour of North India. The two had stopped at the Sinnetts in Allahabad for a few days. HPB was in Bombay. The 'plaster cast' phenomenon described in OW, p. 163 et seq. also occurred on March 11. Perhaps this is the reason why the date of the letter is given.

REFERENCES

The short letter deals principally with reasons why phenomena cannot be produced except under suitable conditions.

Refer to Letter 54 (ML-35) p. 246/242; also OW, p. 168, where APS gives an account of the visit by HSO and mentions the brief note from KH [See Letter, 52 (ML-144) p. 488/481]

NOTE

For a narrative account of events that occurred during this visit, see notes on Letter 52 (ML-144) p. 488/481.

51 (ML-120) Page 452/444 Folio 3 Recd. Mar. (between 11 & 13), 1882

DESCRIPTION: KH to PATIENCE SINNETT

A note from KH to Patience Sinnett, written on a 3" x 4" sheet of folded paper in blue pencil. The envelope is attached—a small one, 2½" x 5" with a Chinese block print on one side, in rose pink.

CIRCUMSTANCES

HSO, accompanied by the chela Bhavani Rao, was visiting the Sinnetts on his tour to the north.

REFERENCES

The text of the letter indicates that KH enclosed a lock of

his hair for Mrs Sinnett to wear as an amulet. Her health was not robust and, for that reason, as indicated in Study Notes on earlier Letters, she had remained in England for some time after her husband returned to India. Later, KH sent a lock of hair to her son Denny to wear, Letter 80 (ML-118), p. 451/443. There is also an indication that APS himself had received a lock of KH's hair which he wore. Letter 111 (ML-59).

NOTE: For a narrative account of events that occurred during this visit of Olcott and Bhavani Rao to Allahabad, see notes included with Letter 52 (ML-144).

52 (ML-144) Page 488/481 Recd. March 14, 1882

DESCRIPTION: KH to APS

Seven words in KH script on one side of a sheet of paper. On back: 'A.P. Sinnett.'

CIRCUMSTANCES

HPB was in Bombay. APS was in Allahabad. HSO and Bhavani Rao had just left the Sinnetts' home for their tour in the north after their visit of a few days there.

REFERENCES

This was in response to a letter transmitted through Bhavani Rao just before he left Allahabad, in which APS had requested that certain phenomena be performed in the absence of HPB. Apparently APS was anxious to have this take place. APS describes the incident in OW p. 168. See also ML p. 246/242 and 410/404. On p. 246/243, KH adds the word 'here' after the word 'power' and mentions what the 'eight words' cost him in energy.

p. 246/243: '...in the state that I am in at present'. This is not explained but presumably it refers to the fact that his situation is changed since his return from his long retreat.

The following is a narrative account of the events that occurred during the visit of HSO and Bhavani Rao to the Sinnetts:

Letter 50 (ML-88),	p. 410/404	Dated by Mahatma KH 'March the 11th, 1882'.
Letter 51 (ML-121)	p. 452/444	Undated.
Letter 52 (ML-144)	p. 488/481	Undated.

In order to show how these three letters really constitute one event, they are considered together here. All were received at Allahabad during the visit of Col. Olcott and the chela Bhavani Rao (Shankar). The P.S. on Letter 50 states that it was written on 11 March 1882. It has to do with the conditions necessary for the performance of phenomena.

In OW, p. 168, Sinnett tells how, on the day before he received this letter he had written to KH and had given the letter to Bhavani Rao. The next morning Bhavani Rao found this note under his pillow. He explained that Sinnett's letter had been taken the evening before.

It happened that on the day this was written (March 11) Sinnett had returned home in the evening to find several telegrams awaiting him.[1] These, he said, were all enclosed in the usual way in envelopes securely fastened before being sent out from the telegraph office. The telegrams were all from ordinary people about business matters. However, inside one of the envelopes he found a little folded note from the Mahatma M. 'The mere fact that it had been thus transferred by occult methods inside the closed envelope was a phenomenon in itself,' he says, but the phenomenon about which the note gave him information was 'even more obviously wonderful'.

> The note made me search in my writing-room for a fragment of plaster bas-relief that M——had just transported

> instantaneously from Bombay. Instinct took me at once to the place where I felt that it was most likely I should find the thing which had been brought—the drawer of my writing-table exclusively devoted to occult correspondence; and there, accordingly, I found a broken corner from a plaster slab, with M——'s signature marked upon it. I telegraphed at once to Bombay to ask whether anything special had just happened and next day received back word that M——had smashed a certain plaster portrait and had carried off a piece. In due course of time I received a minute statement from Bombay, attested by the signatures of seven persons in all which was, as regards all essential points, as follows:[2]

Briefly, the statement was to the effect that several persons were seated at the dining-table at tea in HPB's verandah. They all heard a knock, as of something falling and breaking, behind the door of HPB's writing-room, which was unoccupied. This was followed by a still louder noise and all rushed into the writing-room. There, just behind the door, they found on the floor a plaster of Paris mould of a portrait broken into several pieces. The iron wire loop of the portrait was intact, and not even bent. The pieces of the plaster were spread on the table and it was found that one piece was missing. It was searched for but not found. Shortly afterwards, HPB went into the room and a minute or so later showed them a note in the handwriting of the Mahatma M, and with his signature, stating that the missing piece was taken by him to Allahabad and that she should collect and carefully preserve the remaining pieces.

Sinnett goes on to say that the fact that the piece received by him in Allahabad was 'veritably the actual piece missing from the cast broken at Bombay' was proved a few days later, 'for all the remaining pieces at Bombay were carefully packed up and sent to me, and the fractured edges of my fragment fitted exactly into those of the defective corner, so that I was enabled to arrange the pieces altogether again and complete the cast'.[3]

Sinnett adds that after he received this note (No. 50) through Bhavani Rao, he wrote again the next day to KH, thinking that he might take additional advantage of the conditions presented by the presence of Olcott and the young man. He gave this letter to Bhavani Rao on the evening of March 13. On the 14th he received a very short note from KH saying: 'Impossible: no power. Will write thro' Bombay.' In a still later letter, the Mahatma quotes this message and adds the word 'here' so that it reads: 'Impossible: no power here. Will write thro' Bombay.'

Sinnett comments that when, in due time, he received this letter written through Bombay,[4] he learned that the limited facilities of the moment had been exhausted and that his suggestions could not be complied with. But the importance of the whole thing, he said, was the fact that he did, after all, exchange letters with KH at an interval of a few hours at a time when HPB was at the other side of India.

In the meantime, between the 11th and the 13th of March, Letter 51 (ML-120) was received by Mrs Sinnett. The Mahatma gives a warning about not harbouring ill feelings. There is no indication of the identity of the 'enemy' mentioned in the note. Some time later, the Mahatma sent a lock of hair to the Sinnetts' son, Denny, to wear,[5] and there is also indication that Sinnett himself had a lock of KH's hair which he wore.[6]

The substance of Olcott's advice, which the Mahatma advised Mrs Sinnett to follow, is not given.

Footnotes to Letters 50, 51 and 52

1. OW, 9th ed., p.163 (all references here to 9th ed.).
2. OW, 164-166.
3. OW, 166.
4. See Letter 54 (ML-35), p. 246/242.
5. See Letter 80 (ML-118), p. 450/443.
6. See Letter 111 (ML-59), p. 338/333.

53 (ML-136) Page 464/457 Dated Bombay, 17 March 1882. Probably recd. about the 19th.

DESCRIPTION

HPB to APS on two folded sheets of letter paper in black ink.

CIRCUMSTANCES

HPB was in Bombay; APS was in Allahabad. HSO and Bhavani Rao had left Allahabad a few days previously.

REFERENCES

The first part of the letter indicates that the Sinnetts had invited HPB to visit them in Allahabad.

p. 465/457: '...you must not take these words *en mauvaise part'*. The French term means 'in bad part' or as meant to give offence.

p. 475/458: '...*pour mes beaux yeux* ...': 'for my beautiful eyes...'

'...become a C.S...' A rather caustic comment by HPB on the background of some of the British Civil Servants in India, who she felt were generally not of the best class of English citizenry.

'...Boss says...' Reference to M.

'...the Ripons and his Roman Catholics...' A suggestion that, in her opinion, Lord Ripon, Viceroy of India, had become a tool of the Roman Catholic Church. See ML, p. 392/386.

'....beneath the first cuticles of my *Real Self ?'* Another reference to the mystery that surrounded HPB's true nature.

p. 466/459 (near top): '...the day will come when you accuse K.H. ...' A rather significant prophecy, as in later years APS preferred to believe some of the statements of a medium rather than those of KH.

'I have now with me *Deb*; Deb "Shortridge" as we call

him...' Reference to a chela of KH. See Alphabetical Notes under Deb; also under Babaji and Dharbagiri Nath. There seemed to be a mystery regarding the real identity and relationship of these chelas.

'...dear little Dennie'. Only child of the Sinnetts, a young boy at this time.

54 (ML-35) Page 246/242 Folio 2 Recd. Mar. 18, 1882

DESCRIPTION: KH to APS

On three sheets of regular size white paper, on both sides, in KH script in dull blue ink.

CIRCUMSTANCES

HPB was in Bombay, APS in Allahabad, and HSO in Calcutta visiting the Gordons. William Eglinton, the English medium, who had been in Calcutta for some time and had been staying with the Gordons (See Alphabetical Notes), had sailed from Calcutta for England on March 15, aboard the ship *Vega*.

REFERENCES

p. 246/242: '...my note... of March 11th'. Reference to Letter 50 (ML-88), p. 410/404. It appears that APS was hopeful that while Olcott and the chela were at his house, he could have some phenomena independent of HPB.

'...Olcott and Mallapura...' HSO and the chela Bhavani Rao (Shankar), who had been visiting the Sinnetts. See OW, pp. 167-8.

'Mallapura': an example of the curious practice of the Adepts often referring to one of the chelas or a person by location or caste rather than by name. Bhavani Rao is the one referred to here.

p. 246/243: '...real dgiü...' True knowledge as distinct from knowledge of the ephemeral. M uses the word 'dgyu' in the Cosmological Notes in answer to Question 1. (See Appendix II, p.376 of LBS.)

'Oxon...' M.A. Oxon, a pen-name used by Stainton Moses, the British Spiritualist, who was a Master of Arts from Oxford.

(middle): 'Impossible; no power here...' Reference to Letter 52 (ML-144), p. 488/481. See also OW, p. 168. KH does not quote himself exactly in this matter. The word 'here' does not appear in Letter 52, there being only seven words instead of eight. Also, in Letter 52 the word 'through' is contracted to 'thro'.

'...your scheme of "Degrees" '. It appears that APS was endeavouring to work out some system of degrees within the Society (whether in the Simla Eclectic or in the Parent Society is not clear).

p. 247/244; '...and Carter Blake'. See Alphabetical Notes.

'...Moorad Ali Beg...' See Alphabetical Notes (Mitford).

'...your character—au fond': basically or essentially.

'Remember the proposed test of the *Times* ...' Reference to the test proposed by APS in his letter to KH in October 1880 for the appearance of *The Times* of London in Simla at the same time that it was published in England, etc.

'...phenomena ... shown by Eglinton...' William Eglinton, it seems, returned to England partly as the result of the unpleasant reception accorded him in Calcutta by those who disapproved of his spiritualistic phenomena. See Alphabetical Notes.

'... even to Mrs Gordon'. Mrs Alice Gordon, FTS, who, with her husband, Lt-Col. W. Gordon, was resident in Calcutta. See Alphabetical Notes.

The last paragraph deals with preparations being made to convince Eglinton of the reality of the Adepts, which his 'spirit' controls had been denying. Hence the appearance of M at one of his last seances in Calcutta, to set the stage perhaps for the planned appearance of KH to Eglinton at sea on the ss *Vega*. See ODL, 2:96 and D, p. 187; also OW, p. 169.

55 (ML-89) Page 410/404 Folio 3 Recd. Mar. 24, 1882.

DESCRIPTION: KH to APS

KH script in blue ink on two sheets of white paper, folded note fashion.

CIRCUMSTANCES

APS was in Allahabad, HPB in Bombay, HSO in Calcutta with the Gordons, and William Eglinton, the medium, was aboard ship somewhere in the Indian Ocean, en route home to England.

REFERENCES

p. 410/404: '...thro' a channel which few liked...': presumably meaning HPB.

p. 411/405: On this page, KH undertakes to advise APS in advance of the test to be made with Eglinton, how he will appear to Eglinton on board ship, and how Eglinton will be forced to recognize the existence of the Masters and their powers. KH of course would be appearing on board ship at sea in his illusory body. Why he chose to personate himself in another form is not explained. Eglinton, of course, did not know what KH looked like. There are several accounts of this phenomenon. See OW, 169, et. seq.; LBS-2, p. 3; D, p. 185 et seq. The incident is referred to several times in ML. See Letter 95 (p, 429/423).

(middle): 'before Fern...': a secretary to AOH. See Alphabetical Notes.

p. 412/406: 'Till the 25th of March ...' i.e. until after

Eglinton's letter from mid-ocean and was received in Bombay.

'...in death...three score and ten hence'. Perhaps a bit of KH's lightness as APS was past 40 at the time and could hardly be expected to live to the age of 110.

NOTE: The following is a narrative account of the 'Vega incident' and the transmission of messages from the ship to Bombay and Howrah:

On the 22nd of March, some hours after the *Vega* had left Ceylon (its first port of call out of India) KH visited Eglinton in his *mayavi rupa* (illusory body, which the Mahatmas were able to create) and they had a long conversation. Two days later, on the 24th, when the *Vega* was 500 miles out at sea, letters were transmitted instantaneously (or practically instantaneously) from the *Vega* to Bombay; and from there (along with some other items), again, almost instantaneously, to Howrah, to the home of Col. and Mrs Gordon.

Mrs Gordon describes the phenomenal delivery of Eglinton's letter. She stated that Col. Olcott had left Bombay on March 17 for another city and had gone from thence to Howrah, so that he was present when the letter was received from Eglinton. On the 22nd, HPB sent a telegram to Mrs Gordon, which arrived on the 23rd, saying that KH had seen Eglinton on the *Vega*. This wire corroborated a previous one sent by Olcott on the preceding evening. A still later telegram asked the Gordons and Olcott to fix a time when they could be together. They named 9 o'clock, Madras time, on the 24th. The three sat in a triangle with the apex to the north. In a few minutes, Olcott saw, outside the open window, the Mahatmas M and KH. One of them pointed into the room, over Mrs Gordon's head, and a letter dropped. The Mahatmas then vanished.

Mrs Gordon relates what happened next:

> I now turned and picked up what had fallen on me, and found a letter in Mr Eglinton's handwriting, dated on the *Vega* the

> 24th; a message from Madame Blavatsky, dated at Bombay on the 24th, written on the backs of three of her visiting cards; also a larger card, such as Mr Eglinton had a packet of and used at his seances. On this latter card was the, to us, well-known handwriting of K.H. and a few words in the handwriting of the other 'Brother' who was with him outside our window, and who is Colonel Olcott's chief. All these cards and the letter were threaded together with a piece of blue sewing silk.

The letter from Eglinton follows and affirms his now 'complete belief ' in the 'Brothers'.

As an additional interesting note, there was a postscript signed by six persons affirming that they had seen the arrival, in Bombay, of the letter from Eglinton.

56 (ML-100) Page 438/431 Folio 4 Recd. after Mar. 25, 1882 (est.)

DESCRIPTION: KH to APS

This letter is actually a postscript to LBS-2, p. 3, from HPB to APS, dated March 25. Hence the original is in *Folio 4* with her letters. Beginning at the end of HPB's letter, KH has added his 'few words' in blue ink, somewhat lighter in colour than that used by HPB. He continues on the back of the sheet and finishes by writing crosswise over her writing.

CIRCUMSTANCES

Similar to those of previous letter, 55 (ML-89).

REFERENCES

'The new "guide" has meanwhile a few words to say to you.' This refers to a comment made by HPB in her letter: 'Now it remains to be seen what kind of "guides" Eglinton will hook on KH.'

KH's letter is concerned with a proposal by Hume to go to Tibet and find the Adepts, an idea which KH considers 'insane' and wishes Sinnett to dissuade Hume from pursuing.

As a matter of fact, Hume did *not* make this attempt.

57 (ML-122) Page 452/445 Folio 3 Dated April 27, 1882, London.

DESCRIPTION: KH to APS

KH script in blue ink on both sides of a small heavy card, 3″ x 4½″ The lettering is small.

CIRCUMSTANCES

APS was in Allahabad. Eglinton was in London. HPB was in Bombay. HSO was on tour in India. There is no indication as to why the card is dated in London or of how it was delivered. One is perhaps entitled to speculate that it was transmitted through Eglinton as a trial of his abilities and the possibility of his use for this purpose if he returned to India. This is indicated in LBS-193 and 193A, p. 361. See also Letter 61 (ML-17), p. 118/115.

REFERENCES

'... now that Mr Davison is away'. (See Alphabetical Notes.) A suggestion that Eglinton be hired by AOH as a secretary so that he would be where he could be trained for use by the Adepts. This did not happen, and, instead, Fern was hired for the position, was tested by the Mahatmas, and failed.

'...there's a chance for you'. KH is suggesting that if Eglinton could be brought to Simla and trained by the Mahatmas, it might be possible for him (KH) to show himself to APS and AOH in his illusory body. This did not happen.

The comment concerning HPB's being 'too old' and having done too many services to 'be forced into it' implies that a considerable expenditure of psychic energy was involved in the transmission of letters.

'...after the danger that has threatened him at Calcutta on the very day of his departure'. Again, there is no explanation. It will be remembered that in Letter 54 (ML-35) the Mahatma mentioned the 'bitter hatred' that had been evoked by some of the phenomena produced by Eglinton. It is assumed that this was on the part of religious fundamentalists.

Hume seems to have been eager to have Eglinton return, and the Mahatma says here: 'If Mr Hume is anxious to have him, let him for want of something better—offer him the place of his private secretary for a year or so, now that Mr Davison is away.'

Davison (or Davidson, as it is spelled elsewhere in the Letters) was a scientific ornithologist who at one time worked for Hume in connection with the latter's bird hobby. He served in the capacity of a private secretary and was there at the time of the first visit of HPB and Olcott in 1880. Later, he became disgusted with Hume, left his employment and, after some little time, returned to England.

58 (ML-130) Page 457/450 Dated May 7, 1882

DESCRIPTION: TSR to APS

Letter to APS in the handwriting of TSR, on one folded sheet of paper.

CIRCUMSTANCES

APS was in Allahabad. TSR was in Madras. He was a young Advaiti Brahman of exceptional brilliance who was being urged by HPB and M to assist in instructing APS in his occult studies and training. See Alphabetical Notes.

As the letter to APS indicates, TSR laid down some very stringent rules and requirements for APS before he would agree to undertake the job of teaching him.

REFERENCES

p. 457/450: '...in the case of beginners like you...' Statements like this from a Hindu probably did not sit well with Sinnett. Of course APS did not accept Subba Row's conditions and nothing came of the Master M's request.

Later on, Subba Row again declined to assist HPB in the writing of *The Secret Doctrine*. These two refusals of his to comply with his Master's requests cause one to wonder if they had something to do with his early removal from the theosophical scene.

59 (ML-132) page 459/452
60 (ML-76) page 376/369 (no dates indicated)

DESCRIPTION

These two letters must be considered together, as they are actually not two letters, but one. Letter 59 consists of extracts from a letter from T. Subba Row to the Mahatma M concerning instructions to Sinnett (see notes on No. 58). Sinnett had written to Subba Row and the latter had forwarded the letter on to the Mahatma M with these comments. The Mahatma KH has extracted them from Subba Row's letter for Sinnett's benefit, since apparently he thinks the Mahatma M may not give the letter immediate attention. He has inserted his own comments on both sides of the sheet in blue pencil; these are printed in bold type. He indicates that he is not in accord with the Mahatma M's proposal to instruct Sinnett in true chela fashion so as to develop in him clairvoyant faculties and other Siddhis.

Letter 60 is then a continuation of the Mahatma KH's comments, which somehow got separated from the first part of the letter. The paper is different, which may explain why the two were not kept together.

CIRCUMSTANCES

The explanatory sentence preceding the beginning of Letter 59 indicates that Sinnett was curious enough to know what Subba Row had said about him to ask the Mahatma, and the latter obliged him by extracting some of Subba Row's remarks for his benefit. Part of this letter is missing, as indicated by the editor. It is tempting to speculate whether this was because the comments might have disturbed Sinnett or whether they contained information which KH felt Sinnett was not yet ready for. (The compiler leans toward the latter possibility.)

REFERENCES

The added paragraph in the Mahatma KH's writing is formidable. Further, it illustrates (as one or two other comments in the book do also) that the Mahatmas do not always agree concerning methods, although one in ultimate aims. Further, the Mahatma indicates that Sinnett does not understand the first principles of '*Chela* training'. (Here one must turn to Letter 60 for the last two words.)

The Mahatma then explains the dilemma in which Subba Row finds himself and advises Sinnett simply to learn what he can 'under the circumstances' although he will find Subba Row's terminology somewhat different from that of the Mahatmas. But since terminology doesn't change facts, the meaning is identical.

The rest of the letter mainly concerns Hume but there is a hint that, were he qualified to do so, he would change the way of things somewhat.

He closes with a short allegory and a provocative question.

61 (ML-17) Page 117/113 Folio 1 Recd. June 1882 (est.)

DESCRIPTION

A question and answer letter. Questions by APS are written on the left side of sheets of his notepaper. Answers by KH are on the right half of the sheets, or on the back, in dull red ink with heavy lettering. Reference numbers to APS's questions have been added in square brackets.

CIRCUMSTANCES

The Sinnett family had now gone to Simla for the summer. HPB was in Bombay or its vicinity.

Again several letters should be considered together. No. 61 is a Q & A letter; No. 62 is called 'Appendix' and contains comments referred to by the Mahatma in his answers in No. 62 as 'Appendix' No. I, II, and III. These are more or less elaborations on the answers he has given in No. 61. No. 63 is actually not a separate letter but a continuation of No. 62 which became separated and included in the volume as a separate letter.

Those two letters constitute a resumption of the technical teachings. It will be remembered that there was no clear definition of terms at this time, which may possibly lead to some confusion in trying to understand.

GENERAL COMMENTS

It is obvious to the present-day student that Sinnett was somewhat confused at that stage of the correspondence on the question of rounds and races. M told him that they needed to settle on the nomenclature of things before they could proceed properly with their correspondence.

REFERENCES

p. 117/114, Answer (2): The quotation from *Isis,* referred to in connection with the Buddha's 'overshadowing' a chosen individual who 'generally overturned the destinies of nations' is, in part, as follows:

> Thus, all those great characters who tower like giants in the history of mankind, like Buddha-Siddhartha, and Jesus, in the realm of spiritual, and Alexander the Macedonian and Napoleon the Great, in the realm of physical conquests, were but reflexed images of human types which had existed ten thousand years before, in the preceding decimillennium, reproduced by the mysterious powers controlling the destinies of our world. ...As the star, glimmering at an immeasurable distance above our heads, in the boundless immensity of the sky, reflects itself in the smooth waters of a lake, so does the imagery of men of the antediluvian ages reflect itself in the periods we can embrace in an historical retrospect.

Sinnett's third question concerns whether there is any essential spiritual difference between a man and a woman, or whether sex is a mere accident of birth, the ultimate future of the individual furnishing the same opportunities. The Mahatma answers: 'A mere accident—as you say...', and then he adds some qualifications which seem to take the matter out of the realm of accident: '...yet guided by individual karma—moral aptitudes, characteristics and deeds of a previous birth'.

p. 118/115: (Question 6, not numbered) '...sheet of "Pioneer" Notepaper...' This refers to LBS-193, p.361, from the medium Eglinton in London to APS in Allahabad. It was written on APS's office stationery, which had been obtained by Eglinton's control, 'Ernest'. APS was curious about how this was accomplished. See also Letter 62 (ML-18). See p. 122/119.

Last paragraph regarding Subbha Row: this relates to the unsuccessful attempt by M to get Subba Row to give Sinnett some instruction in metaphysics and occultism.

62 (ML-18)
63 (ML-95) Folios 1 & 3 Recd. June 1882

DESCRIPTION

Letter 62 (marked 'Appendix') is really an attachment to Letter 61 (ML-17). It is in dark blue ink on both sides of four sheets of heavy rough paper size 10″ x 11½″ very irregular in size, with the appearance of having been cut by hand. The script is heavy and somewhat different from the usual script.

Letter 63 is a continuation of Letter 62, which accidentally became detached. It is on two sheets of dissimilar paper, in dull blue ink. The first sheet is heavy folded notepaper bearing the letterhead of 'Government, N.W. Provinces and Oudh'. The second sheet is a thin one bearing the letterhead of 'The Pioneer, Allahabad'. Since the question of transporting writing-paper by occult means had been under discussion in the previous letter 61 (ML-17), p. 118/115, one is tempted to surmise that KH had abstracted a sheet of paper from both APS and AOH on which to write this portion of the 'Appendix', just by way of illustrating how easy it was to do. AOH had previously been District Officer of North-West Provinces and Oudh.

CIRCUMSTANCES

Similar to those of 61 (ML-17), p. 117/113.

REFERENCES

The Roman numerals refer to the similar numerals in Letter 61 (ML-17), i.e. 'I' refers to Q-1; 'II' refers to Q-4; 'III' refers to Q-5. The last paragraph refers to the last question in Letter 61.

p. 119 (top): '...during E's stay in Calcutta in Mrs G's atmosphere ...' This refers to Eglinton and Mrs Gordon; the latter was also somewhat psychic.

Turning now to the continuation of the letter which forms

Letter 63 (ML-95), p. 430/423: The first part of this page deals with the desirability of developing Eglinton as an intermediary and bringing him to India so as to relieve HPB of the work of transmitting letters, etc.

'M. had to prepare him for six weeks...' It is interesting to speculate how this was accomplished without Eglinton's knowledge.

'...what he saw was *not me*'. See p. 411/405. This has reference to KH's visit to Eglinton on board ship, known as the 'Vega incident' , on Eglinton's way back to England.

'I am not at all sure that E. will resist the tide ...' Subsequent events seem to have substantiated this doubt, as Eglinton never became of use to the Mahatmas.

p. 424: 'I will write to Mr Hume ...' This is Letter 65 (ML-11), p. 59.

'Your *Review* of the *Perfect Way* ...' Reference to APS's review of a book by Anna B. Kingsford, entitled *The Perfect Way* which she had just published in England. The review appeared in the May and June 1882 issues of *The Theosophist*.

64 (ML-131) Page 458/451 Folio 3 Dated June 26, 1882

DESCRIPTION: T. SUBBA ROW to APS

In the handwriting of TSR, both sides of white paper in sepia brown ink.

CIRCUMSTANCES

APS had gone to Simla for the summer. The contemplated plan for TSR to give APS instruction had not progressed very well. APS had demurred to the strict conditions outlined in the May 7th letter from TSR, Letter 58 (ML-130), p. 457/450. KH had recommended against his attempting anything so strenuous, Letter 59 (ML-132) p. 459/452.

REFERENCES

In this letter, TSR explains the situation and agrees that he will help both APS and AOH in their philosophical and theoretical studies in connection with occultism, but nothing further.

From the material available on the subject, it does not appear that he ever gave very much of such help.

65 (ML-11) Page 59 Folio 6A Recd. June 30, 1882.

DESCRIPTION

This letter from KH is to AOH in Simla. The copy available is one made by APS in his 'copy-book'. (Filed in British Museum as Folio 6A.)

CIRCUMSTANCES

APS and AOH were in Simla. HPB was in Bombay or its vicinity. This is the first of a series of three letters from the Mahatma KH directed to A.O. Hume. Apparently Hume had become dissatisfied with the responses of the Mahatma M to his inquiries and addressed some questions to the Mahatma KH. From the first sentence of the letter it is obvious that the Mahatma KH is well aware of the uncertain nature of the undertaking. The letter is in the folio in the British Museum in Sinnett's handwriting. It will be remembered that the Sinnetts had gone to Simla for the summer and Hume shared the letter with him. It is even probable that the two Englishmen compiled the questions together.

The Mahatma pays tribute to Hume's accomplishments and his desire to serve the Society. But, he says, before he can answer questions and give any further explanations of the doctrine, he has to preface his reply with 'a long introduction'.

It is not specifically so stated, but it would seem that Hume may have become a vegetarian, for the Mahatma says he has more chance than Sinnett who, even if he were to give up feeding on animals, would still crave such food, 'a craving over which he would have no control and the impediment would be the same in that case'.

REFERENCES

p. 59, first sentence: '...my new role ...' would seem to indicate that this is KH's first letter to AOH since returning from his 'retreat' in early January.

In this letter, some of KH's comments on scientific matters are difficult to understand from the ordinary Western point of view. No doubt he is viewing things from quite a different standpoint, hence the difficulty in presenting his ideas for the understanding of a Westerner.

Therefore, he prefaces his letter with a long introduction explaining some of the difficulties in the way of answering Hume's questions. He attempts to explain how their concepts of nature differ from those of science.

p. 64 (middle): '... our semi-European Greek Brother...' Probably the Mahatma Hilarion; possibly the Mahatma referred to in Letter 48 (ML-47), p. 271/267.

'Eclectic': the Simla Eclectic Theosophical Society.

p. 64: '...become a Zetetic': an inquirer after truth.

(near bottom): This paragraph explains the necessity for serenity and quiet for those who seek occult wisdom.

(bottom): 'Concerning Eglinton ...' This probably refers to the question of bringing Eglinton back to India and training him to serve as an intermediary between the Adepts and APS and AOH. See Letter 63 (ML-95), p. 430/423. Eglinton was still being tested, hence KH could not give Hume a definite answer.

p. 65 (top): There are indications that Mrs Hume may have been an alcoholic, and possibly was tuberculous. KH warns AOH against trying to make abrupt changes in her habits.

(last paragraph): 'Your suggestion as to the box ...' This would seem to indicate that AOH had some idea of making a psychically charged box which could be used for exchange of letters without the aid of HPB or others.

(near bottom): '...flower-shed ...' AOH's conservatory in Rothney Castle.

'...your museum ...' AOH's bird museum in Rothney Castle.

p. 66: 'Penang ...': a city on the Malay peninsula.

(last sentence): '...through little Deb or Damodar and Djual Kool will transmit them'. An interesting comment on one of their methods of transmitting letters. Deb and Damodar were at the Bombay Headquarters, Djual Kool was probably in Tibet with KH. Hume of course was up at Simla in northern India.

66 (ML-14) Page 78 Folio 6A Recd. July 9, 1882

DESCRIPTION

This letter consists of technical questions posed by AOH and answered by Master KH. The original is not available but was copied by APS in his 'copy-book' in which he preserved copies of a number of important letters. The copy-book is preserved in the British Museum. It seems reasonable that these are accurate copies of the original letters.

CIRCUMSTANCES

AOH and APS were both in Simla for the summer. The Founders were in Bombay. The method of transmision of these letters is not indicated, but it seems possible that DK was the intermediary, utilizing an agent at the Bombay Headquarters as stated in Letter 11, p. 66.

REFERENCES

No attempt is made in this Guide to provide a technical commentary on the subject matter of this and other letters of technical import.

The student is advised to refer to various glossaries and to such books as *The Secret Doctrine, The Divine Plan,* and other basic theosophical literature of a later date in which a more definite nomenclature had been agreed upon and more coherent explanations were made.

p. 84/83 (short note following the initials 'K.H.'): '... No.3 of Terry's letters ...' This refers to William H. Terry, a member in Australia. See SH, 163-4. See also Alphabetical Notes.

67 (ML-15) Page 88/87 Folio 6A Recd. July 10, 1882

DESCRIPTION

This is the last of several letters dealing with technical metaphysical questions asked by AOH, with answers by Master KH.

As with Letter 66 (ML-14) this letter was copied by APS in his 'copy-book' since the original remained in AOH's possession and is not available. The copy-book is preserved in the British Museum as Folio 6A.

CIRCUMSTANCES

Same as for Letter 66 (ML-14). AOH and APS were both in Simla for the summer.

REFERENCES

As with Letter 66, no attempt is made in the 'Guide' to provide technical commentary on the subject matter of the letter.

p. 90/88: 'See in this connection Subba Row's article ...' This refers to an article by TSR published in the January 1882 issue of *The Theosophist,* pp. 93-8.

p. 98/96: Title of book by Flammarion: *The Resurrection and the End of the Worlds.*

p. 99/97: '...Od force ...' See Alphabetical Notes.

Since the Mahatma uses a number of non-English terms, this may be an appropriate place to give some information which may help the student in understanding them.

In *Transactions of Blavatsky Lodge,* p. 47, HPB is asked a question about the distinction between *Dhyan-Chohans, Planetary Spirits, Builders,* and *Dhyani-Buddhas.* She replies that it would take two more volumes of the SD to explain all the Hierarchies, but that she would try a short definition:

> *Dhyan-Chohan* is a generic term for all Devas, or celestial beings. A *Planetary Spirit* if a Ruler of a planet, a kind of finite or personal god. There is a marked difference, however, between the Rulers of the Sacred Planets and the Rulers of a small 'Chain' of worlds like our own ...
> (p.48): ...the terrestrial spirit of the earth is not of a very high grade. It must be remembered that the planetary spirit has nothing to do with the spiritual man, but with things of matter and cosmic beings. The gods and rulers of our Earth are cosmic Rulers; that is to say they form into shape and fashion cosmic matter, for which they were called *Cosmocratores.* They never had any concern with spirit: the *Dhyani-Buddhas,* belonging to quite a different hierarchy, are especially concerned with the latter...the 'Planetary'—who are not the Dhyani-Buddhas—have everything to do with the earth, physically and morally. It is they who rule its destinies and the fate of men. They are karmic agencies...
> (p.49): The *Dhyani-Buddhas* are concerned with the human higher triad in a mysterious way that need not be explained here. The *'Builders'* are a class called Cosmocratores, or the invisible but intelligent Masons, who fashion matter according to the ideal plan ready for them in that which we call Divine

> and Cosmic ideation. They were called by the early Masons the 'Grand Architect of the Universe' collectively ...they are not an Entity, a kind of personal God, but Forces of Nature acting under one immutable law, on the nature of which it is certainly useless for us to speculate ... The one *Impersonal* Great Architect of the universe is *MAHAT*, Universal Mind.

p. 90/89 ML: *Adi-Buddhi,* the *Glossary* defines as 'Primeval Intelligence or Wisdom; the eternal Buddhi or Universal Mind. Used of *Divine Ideation, "Mahābuddhi"* being synonymous with MAHAT'.

Dharmakāya: The Glossary gives: ' "The glorified spiritual body" called the "Vesture of Bliss". The third, or highest of the *Trikāya* (Three Bodies), the attribute developed by every "Buddha", i.e., every initiate who has crossed or reached the end of what is called the "fourth Path" (in esotericism, the sixth "portal" prior to his entry on the *seventh)*...[it is] represented figuaratively in Buddhist asceticism as a robe or vesture of luminous Spirituality. In popular Northern Buddhism these vestures or *robes* are: 1. Nirmanakāya; 2. Sambhogakāya; and 3. Dharmakāya, the last being the highest and most sublimated of all, as it places the ascetic on the threshold of Nirvāna.'

In *The Voice of the Silence* HPB gives the true esoteric meaning of the three terms:

> The first [Nirmanakāya] is that ethereal form which one would assume, when, leaving his physical, he would appear in his astral body—having in addition all the knowledge of an Adept. The Bodhisattva [one who in another incarnation will become a Buddha] develops it in himself as he proceeds on the Path. Having reached the goal and refused its fruition, he remains on earth, as an Adept; and when he dies, instead of going into Nirvana, he remains in that glorious body he has woven for himself, invisible to uninitiated mankind, to watch over and protect it.
>
> Sambhogakāya is the same but with the additional lustre of

'three perfections', one of which is entire obliteration of all earthly concerns.

The Dharmakāya body is that of a complete Buddha, i.e. no body at all but an ideal breath: consciousness merged in the Universal Consciousness, or Soul devoid of every attribute. Once a Dharmakāya, an Adept or Buddha leaves behind every possible relation with, or thought for, this earth. Thus, to be enabled to help humanity, an Adept who has won the right to Nirvana, 'renounces the Dharmakāya body' in mystic parlance; keeps, of the Sambhogakāya, only the great and complete knowledge, and remains in his Nirmanakāya body.

pravritti; nivritti (ML.p. 90/89): *pravritti* means literally a 'flowing forth', an unfolding of what is within, or evolution. *Nivritti* literally means a 'flowing back' or involving; hence involution in contradistinction to evolution.

... hosts of Dhyan Chohans ...taken collectively. In *The Secret Doctrine* (fn. 2:95, 4th ed.; 1:380 5th ed.) we find the statement: 'In Esoteric Philosophy, the Demiurge, or Logos, regarded as the CREATOR, is simply an abstract term, an idea, like the word "army". As the latter is the all-embracing term for a body of active forces or working units—soldiers—so is the Demiurge the qualitative compound of a multitude of Creators or Builders.' *The Secret Doctrine* states further: 'The whole kosmos is guided, controlled, and animated by almost endless series of Hierarchies of sentient Beings, each having a mission to perform.' (1:318, 4th ed.; 1:274. 5th ed.)

68 (ML-16) Page 99/97 Folio 1 Recd. July, 1882 (after 15th)

DESCRIPTION

This is a 'Question and Answer' letter in which APS asks questions and KH answers them.

APS's questions are on sheets of his usual folded note-paper. The answers, in the KH script, are mostly on separate sheets of fairly heavy bond paper, 8½″ x 10″, in dull black ink on both sides of the paper. In quite a number of instances, APS's questions have been cut out and pasted onto the answer sheet. Reference numbers are in square brackets. The last several sheets are of a different type of paper, and the script is in finer lettering. Some of the footnotes are in red ink. The reference on p. 113/110 indicates that the letter was sent through HPB.

CIRCUMSTANCES

APS and AOH were in Simla. HPB and HSO were in Bombay.

REFERENCES

This letter is often referred to as the 'Devachan Letter', since it is devoted principally to that subject. It is of a technical nature and contains many words and phrases that will be unfamiliar to some students. It is recommended that the *Theosophical Glossary* and other glossaries be consulted, and that use be made of other reference texts which may be available. One should keep in mind the fact that this was all new ground for APS and he often did not know how to frame intelligent questions.

This letter begins with a reference to a letter in 'the last *Theosophist*'. This was the June 1882 issue, pp. 225-6. It was signed 'A Caledonian Theosophist'. This was probably a man by the name of Davidson, or Davison, a scientific ornithologist who at one time worked for Hume in connection with his bird hobby, serving in the capacity of a private secretary. He later left Hume's employment and eventually returned to England. The letter was headed 'Seeming Discrepancies'. The writer was concerned with what he considered were some differences between statements in one of the articles in the series 'Fragments of Occult Truth' written, at that time, by Hume and later by Sinnett, and certain passages in *Isis*

Unveiled, HPB's first book. The so-called discrepancies had to do with spiritualistic phenomena. He also questioned the meaning of the word 'Devachan'.

Generally, the questions and answers in this letter are not difficult to understand. On p. 103/101, the Mahatma lists the principles and describes what happens to them in Devachan. He refers Sinnett to a page number in the current issue of *The Theosophist* in 'Fragments of Occult Truth'. Sinnett lists these in his book, *Esoteric Buddhism,* which was largely developed from the 'Fragments'. They are found on p. 13 of that book, with a commentary. The principles as given are as follows:

1. The Body: *Rupa*
2. Vitality: *Prana,* or *Jiva*
3. Astral Body: *Linga Sharira*
4. Animal Soul: *Kama Rupa*
5. Human Soul: *Manas*
6. Spiritual Soul: *Buddhi*
7. Spirit: *Atma*

It is recommended that the student read the whole chapter on Devachan beginning on page 58 of *Esoteric Buddhism*.

In this same paragraph, the Mahatma has mentioned the 'planet of Death'. This is sometimes confused with *avitchi* but they are not the same. See the definitions of the two in the glossaries. G. de Purucker's *Occult Glossary* gives excellent definitions. The Planet of Death is also called the Eighth Sphere. According to de Purucker, it is an actual planet, while Avitchi is a state which may exist even on this earth. The word is Sanskrit and means 'waveless' suggesting the stagnation of life; 'without happiness'. But it is not without hope, as is the Eighth Sphere.

In his answer to (9) the Mahatma elaborates somewhat on the question of the length of time required for effects to work out. He uses the phrase, '...when you read in the Jats ...' This refers to accounts of the previous lives of the Buddha. In the reference to Mara (Death) (p. 107/104) see the footnote which explains that this is the allegorical image of the 'Planet of Death'.

Three names are listed here: 'Beal, or Burnouf, Rhys Davids ...' Samuel Beal, Émile Louis Burnouf and Thomas William Rhys Davids were well known oriental scholars.

It would be well to consult glossaries for further descriptions of the classes of devas listed on p. 107/104.

On page 108/105-6 mention is made of Sukhavati and Sakwalas. *Sukhavati* is 'the western paradise of the uneducated, where good men and saints revel in physical delights until they are carried once more by karma into the circle of rebirth. This is an exaggerated and mistaken notion of Devachan.' *Sakwalas* refers to 'the infinite number of solar systems in the universe, each containing earths, hells, and heavens (meaning good and evil spheres). When one attains its prime, it falls into decay and is finally destroyed at regularly recurring periods in virtue of one immutable law.'

p.109/106: '*...les Esprits Souffrants'*, the suffering spirits.

p.110/107: *Pisāchas, Incubi, Succubi.* Pisāchas are goblins or demons. In South Indian folklore, ghosts, demons, vampires (generally female) who haunt men. Fading remnants of human beings in Kamaloka, as shells and elementaries. Incubi and succubi are male and female demons.

The key to the philosophical system of the Mahatmas might be thought of as a sentence on p. 110/107: '...you can do nothing better than to study the two doctrines—of *Karma* and *Nirvana*—as profoundly as you can'. They are, says the Mahatma 'the double key to the metaphysics of Abidharma'. Sometimes spelled 'Abidhamma', this is the totality of the psychological and philosophical teachings of Buddhism.

p. 111: *Skandhas:* literally 'bundles' or groups of attributes; everything finite, inapplicable to the eternal and absolute. There are said to be five (esoterically seven) attributes in every human. HPB lists the five which she says are known as *Pancha Skandhas:* 1. form *(rupa);* 2. perception (*vidanā);* 3. consciousness *(saṃjna);* 4. action *(saṃskara);* and 5. knowledge *(vijnāna).* They unite at the birth of a man and constitute his personality. After the maturity of the Skandhas, they begin to weaken and separate, and this is followed by *jaramarana,* or decrepitude and death.

p. 113/110: Here the Mahatma explains that he got himself 'into a scrape' with the Chohan and also with two young men, Scott and Banon. Scott is the Ross Scott who travelled from England to India with the Founders on the *Speke Hall.* He was secretary of the Simla Eclectic Theosophical Society. Banon was Captain A. Banon, Fellow of the Theosophical Society, a British army officer. From the comments made by the Mahatma he had evidently written something severely critical of the Mahatma KH, which the latter says he will ask HPB to send to Sinnett.

'As to the Chohan,' says the Mahatma, 'the matter is more serious ...' This has reference to the Vega incident, when the Mahatma KH 'appeared' to Eglinton on board the *Vega* on which Eglinton was returning to England. This leads into a discussion of Spiritualism, in which the Mahatma states that the Brothers are not against *'true* spiritualism' but against many of the manifestations which so often accompany Spiritualism. And here he discusses the difference between the individuality and the personality.

p. 115/111: The reference to Sinnett's piano playing is interesting. It is understood from other references that the Mahatma KH himself was an accomplished musician. The passage shows how deeply attuned he was to Sinnett.

'...I am far less free to do as I like ...' An indication of the rules under which an Adept must act.

'...the highest *Chutuktus* ...': incarnations of a Buddha or Bodhisattva.

The reference to the 'Pioneer connection' undoubtedly has to do with the difficulties Sinnett was having with the proprietors of the newspaper, *The Pioneer;* it seems to be the first direct reference to it in the Letters. This letter was received sometime in July of 1882, and it was not until December that Sinnett was given his termination notice by the proprietors.

p. 116/112: '...as your lady once kindly remarked ...' another indication that KH was aware of what was going on in the Sinnett home. The Mahatmas seemed to hold Mrs Sinnett in high regard. This comment emphasizes the fact that the Mahatmas are human beings.

p. 116/112: 'H.P.B. is in despair...': HPB was in poor health and spirits and wanted to visit her Master in person. She thought this had been arranged and had packed up to go when permission was refused by the Chohan because of unsettled conditions resulting from hostilities between England and Egypt. She poured out her tale of woe to Sinnett in LBS 15, p. 28. However, she was later permitted to go to Sikkim to see both KH and M.

'Olcott is on his way to Lanka [Ceylon]:...' In ODL 2:368, Olcott says he sailed from Bombay on 15 July 1882. This would date this letter shortly after that date.

Here, too, we have the first intimation that Damodar may be removed from the outer scene.

The reference to the British military operations in Egypt is difficult to point historically, as there were several incidents, any one of which might have been referred to here. It is, however, evident that there was something of considerable urgency in the situation. HPB, in one of her letters to Sinnett, indicated that the Mahatma KH's superiors were unhappy with his refusal to take part in this operation (See LBS, p. 27).

69 (ML-69) Page 373/366 Folio 3 Recd. July 1882 (est.) some time after receipt of 68 (ML-16)

DESCRIPTION: KH to APS

In blue pencil on both sides of a single sheet of thin waxy paper, about 8″ x 10″, unfolded.

CIRCUMSTANCES

Similar to those of Letter 68 (ML-16). This letter appears to be a follow-up to Letter 68 and answers a few questions which arose out of that letter. APS and AOH were both in Simla.

REFERENCES

p. 373/367 (2): It is not clear what 'verse' KH is referring to, but possibly something APS was planning to use in one of his 'Fragments of Occult Truth', which he was now writing for *The Theosophist*.

'Real knowledge': This could be a reference to item No. 1 of M's cosmological notes, where he uses the term 'Dgyu' for 'real knowledge' as contrasted to unreal knowledge (see Appendix II in LBS).

70 A, B, C (ML-20 A,B,C) Pages 123/120, 125/121, 127/123 Folio 1 A and B probably both written in late July, 1882; C received in August (probably early)

DESCRIPTION

70A is from AOH to KH, written on notepaper in black ink. Certain passages have been underlined and reference numbers have been added in blue pencil.

70B is from APS to HPB and is written on small sheets of notepaper. Certain passages have been underlined in blue pencil.

70C is from KH to APS. It is written on the back of 70A, 70B, and on additional sheets of the same size. The writing is in blue pencil and has a 'granular' appearance such as one might produce by writing with a coloured pencil on paper placed on the cover of a cloth-bound book, or similar rough surface. A number of letters dated during the latter half of 1882 have this appearance. How this effect was produced is not known.

In Geoffrey Barborka's book, *The Mahatmas and Their Letters,* pp. 112-118, he describes a process of precipitation and states that this appearance is caused by that process. He gives an illustration from this very letter, a photograph of the original. This is only one interpretation of the process,

CIRCUMSTANCES

These three letters would be confusing without some knowledge of the background. Rather long explanatory notes are therefore essential.

In October 1881, *The Theosophist* published an article by Éliphas Lévi entitled 'Death'. This article may now be found as Appendix I in LBS, beginning on p. 369. Éliphas Lévi and this article are referred to several times in ML; the article became the subject of some controversy or, perhaps more accurately, some discussion and some differences of opinion.

A member of the Theosophical Society by the name of N.D. Khandalawala, wrote to the editor, taking exception to some of the statements in the article. His letter was published in the November 1882 issue of *The Theosophist* more than a year after the article itself appeared. However, as will be seen, it caused a considerable correspondence in the meantime.

N.D. Khandalawala was a provincial judge and a member of the General Council of the Society. He was a sincere and earnest member and a loyal supporter of HPB and Col. Olcott during the disastrous Coulomb affair which developed several years later.

Mr Khandalawala's letter was accompanied by an editor's note which said: 'The following letter states an embarrassment which may very likely have occurred to other readers of the passages quoted.' The letter was followed by a long explanation headed*** which is understood to mean that it was written by the Mahatma KH.

In his letter, Mr Khandalawala quoted from HPB's long editorial comment in which she quoted from the Kiu-Te. He pointed out that, in the same issue of *The Theosophist,* one of the articles in the series, 'Fragments of Occult Truth', seemed to him in direct contradiction to the statements made in the editor's note accompanying Éliphas Lévi's article. 'Evidently,' said Mr Khandalawala, 'there is a gap somewhere.' He asked for clarification.

When HPB received Mr Khandalawala's letter, she sent it to the Mahatma KH. He sent it back to her with a precipitated note as follows:

> Send this to Mr Sinnett. Having now received all the necessary explanations from me, he will not refuse me the personal favour I now ask of him. Let him enlighten his brother theosophists in his turn by writing an answer to this for the next Theos. and sign himself 'A Lay Chela'. (LBS, p. 364.)

HPB forwarded Mr Khandalawala's letter, along with KH's precipitated note, to Sinnett. He went to see Hume (he was in Simla at the time) to discuss the matter. This raised some questions in Hume's mind about an article in the series of 'Fragments' that he was then working on, and he wrote to the Mahatma KH. Hume's letter is 70A (ML-20 A).

Then Sinnett wrote to HPB to try to clarify some of the points in Mr Khandalawala's letter. This is letter 70B (ML-20B). HPB referred this letter to the Mahatma KH, and the Mahatma replied to the letter from both Sinnett and Hume by writing on the back of Sinnett's letter his answers to their questions.

REFERENCES

Discussing the contents of these three letters becomes quite complicated because some of the questions asked in both 70A and 70B are answered in 70C. However, the Mahatma has inserted identifying numbers or letters, and so, by going back and forth between the three letters, some order emerges.

Letter 70A, written by Hume, begins by telling the Mahatma that, in writing this particular article in the 'Fragments' series, he has introduced the views on suicide that the Mahatma had given in his last letter to Sinnett. (This is the Devachan letter.)

He wanted gradually to open the eyes of the Spiritualists. (The Mahatma has inserted a comment to the effect that this is what he finds most unsatisfactory, as it will lead to a number of questions which he will find it puzzling to answer.) The first doctrine presented, says Hume, is that the majority of objective phenomena in spiritualistic seances are due to shells—1½ and 2½ principle shells separated from their 6th and 7th principles.' But as a further development', he says—and here the Mahatma has inserted the number (1), meaning that he is answering this under that same number in his letter which has been numbered 70C.

In Sinnett's letter to HPB (70B), he comments in paragraph 2 that Éliphas Lévi's statements are in direct conflict with KH's teaching. In the Mahatma's opening statement in 70C, KH says: 'Except in so far that he constantly uses the term "God" and "Christ" ...' A clarifying statement follows. Here we come upon one of the very important statements found so frequently—and often unexpectedly—in the letters: '*Love* and *Hatred* are the only *immortal* feelings, the only survivors from the wreck of *Ye-dhamma*, or the phenomenal world.'

To return to some items in the letter, in the last paragraph of 70A, Hume mentions the books of Alan Kardec. He was a French Spiritualist and editor of *Le Revue d'Esprit* or *The*

Spirits' Book, as it came to be known. His real name was Hippolite L.D. Rivail, but he preferred to be known by the names he said he had borne in two previous incarnations—Allan and Kardec.

On p. 130/127 the Mahatma refers to a passage in Isis which, he says, 'was very clumsily expressed' and over which he had to 'exercise my ingenuity'. This passage is found in Vol. 1, p. 352 of *Isis Unveiled.*

On p. 134 (70C) the Mahatma mentions several manuscripts by Éliphas Lévi that have never been published, 'in clear beautiful handwriting with my comments all through'. This raises the question of whether the Mahatma might have known Éliphas Lévi while he was a student in Europe, although this would in no way be essential to his having possession of the manuscripts.

p. 129/125: 'His *Mayavi Rupa* ...' An illusory or projected materialization of a body. See Alphabetical Notes.

p. 130/127. 'I had to "exercise my ingenuity"...' This statement was to cause KH some difficulty with APS and AOH. See pp. 173/169, 182/179 and 280/285.

'...drop into the eighth sphere...' See Alphabetical Notes.

p. 132/129 (middle): '...it is *not* a *felo de se* ...': a suicide.

'A Guiteau will not remain...' Reference to Charles J. Guiteau, assassin of President James A. Garfield, a current event of that time. See Alphabetical Notes.

p. 133/130 [under (4)]:'Allan Kardec was not quite immaculate ...' Kardec was a French Spiritualist. See AOH's reference to his writing, in 70A, which called forth this comment. See also Alphabetical Notes.

'...Bradlaugh ...' Charles Bradlaugh, English social reformer. See Alphabetical Notes.

'Revd H.W. Beecher': Apparently KH had a rather low opinion of the American preacher.

A few passages worth pondering:

p. 127/124: '... we *create* ourselves our *devachan* as our *avitchi* while yet on earth, and mostly during the latter days and even moments of our intellectual, sentient lives. That feeling which is the strongest in us at that supreme hour; when, as in a dream, the events of a long life, to their minutest details, are marshalled in the greatest order in a few seconds in our vision—that feeling will become the fashioner of our bliss or woe, the *life principle* of our future existence.' (It is perhaps from this that the idea of 'death-bed repentance' derives.)

p. 128/125: 'Complete or true immortality—which means an unlimited *sentient* existence, can have no breaks and stoppages, no arrest of *Self*-consciousness.'

p. 131/128: '...the victims whether good or bad sleep, to awake but *at the hour of the last Judgment,* which is that hour of the supreme struggle between the sixth and seventh, and the fifth and fourth at the threshold of the gestation state'.

(The implication of this sentence is that there is a 'last judgement' for every individual.)

p. 132/129: 'Motive is everything and man is punished in a case of *direct* responsibility, never otherwise.'

p. 134/130: 'Nature is too well, too mathematically adjusted to cause mistakes to happen in the exercise of her functions.'

p. 134/131: ' "Nature spews the lukewarm out of her mouth" means only that she annihilates their *personal* Egos (not the shells nor yet the sixth principle) in the Kama Loka and the Devachan.'

(The quoted words are from Revelation 3:16; 'So then because thou art lukewarm, and neither cold nor hot, I will spue thee out of my mouth.')

71 (ML-19) Page 122/119 Folio 1 Recd. Aug. 12, 1882

DESCRIPTION: KH to APS

This letter, as APS comments, consists of two marginal notes attached to proofs of a letter on Theosophy (by APS).

The notes are on odd-sized scraps of paper, in blue pencil, having a grained appearance. The first sheet contains the verse of poetry. The second contains the remainder of the text.

CIRCUMSTANCES

Similar to previous letter, 70 (ML-20).

Sinnett comments, at the head of this letter, that it was attached to proofs of a letter on Theosophy and was received 12 August 1882. In the original in the British Museum, the letter is seen to consist of two notes attached to the proofs. The 'Letter on Theosophy' to which these two notes are attached is to Stainton Moses in London, intended for publication in the magazine, *Light,* a journal of the Spiritualists in that city. Actually the proofs consisted of two letters which were published in the issues of *Light* for September, October, and November 1882 and April 1883. Sinnett had sent the proofs to the Mahatma KH for his comments.

REFERENCES

The first note contains the short verse, which the Mahatma says is 'not for publication' and the second contains the remainder of the text. Since the Mahatma gives no source for the verse, it may perhaps be assumed that it is his own.

The second note obviously is intended as an explanation of the nature of the astral conditions during the earlier stages after physical death.

72 (ML-127) Page 455/447 Folio 6A Recd. Aug. 13, 1882

DESCRIPTION

This letter, as found in the Britisn Museum, is a copy in Sinnett's handwriting of extracts from a letter to him and Hume, and he has noted that the letter was received on 13 August 1882. There is no explanation why it is a copy, but it may be assumed that Sinnett passed the original letter on to Hume, after copying some extracts from it.

CIRCUMSTANCES

APS and AOH were in Simla. HPB was in Bombay and HSO was in Ceylon.

REFERENCES

The opening statement refers to a comment made by the Mahatma in a footnote in the long Devachan letter in connection with a discussion of the Skandhas. In this footnote, the Mahatma—writing of Skandhas—quotes the Abidhamma and several other northern Buddhist texts, which show Gautama Buddha saying that none of these Skandhas is the soul; since the body is constantly changing, and that neither man, animal, nor plant is ever the same for two consecutive days or even minutes. 'Mendicants,' says the Buddha, 'remember that there is within man *no abiding principle* whatever, and that only the *learned* disciple who acquires wisdom in saying "I am"—knows what he is saying.'

This is a very difficult statement to understand, particularly after we are told by the Mahatma that man is the microcosm of the macrocosm—or contains all that is in the universe. We can only assume, perhaps, that the same must be true of the universe itself—that it contains no *abiding principle.* The universe is a manifestation—not the Reality—although it comes from the Reality, the Absolute. As such it is compounded and therefore not ultimately 'abiding' in the sense of being eternal, however inconceivably long it may exist *as* a manifested universe.

The Mahatma refers to Plutarch and Anaxagoras. Plutarch was the great biographer and philosopher of the Neoplatonic School. Plutarch's *Lives* is still a classic textbook even in our times. Anaxagoras was a philosopher and geometrician who, as far back as the 4th century BC, advanced the theory of atoms as a means adopted by an 'all-pervading mind' for holding the physical world together. The word *nous,* used in the next sentence, is generally understood to mean *mind* in the deeper sense; understanding; intelligence. Teilhard de Chardin uses it extensively in his writings to indicate the great reality of universal mind underlying all intelligence.

p. 455/448: '...try to develop lucidity'. In this context KH is apparently indicating that the reasoning mind blocks the ability to 'know directly' the Buddhi or intuition.

(last par.): It is not clear whether this advice is directed to APS or to AOH, but possibly to the latter who, apparently, was a vegetarian.

73 (ML-113) Page 448/441 Folio 3 Recd. Aug. 1882 (est.)

DESCRIPTION: KH to APS

On both sides of a single sheet of rippled white paper, 8″ x 10½″, in blue pencil with grained effect. Large lettering.

CIRCUMSTANCES

APS and AOH were both in Simla.

Edmund W. Fern was serving as a secretary to Hume and probably living in his house. Fern was somewhat of a psychic and the Mahatma considered that he might have some valuable potential for the transmission of messages. He joined the Theosophical Society and was elected secretary of the Simla Eclectic Theosophical Society. The Mahatma M took an interest in him and accepted him as a chela on probation.

Evidently, Fern annoyed Hume and the latter wrote to the Mahatma KH about it and undertook to instruct the Mahatmas as to what they should do about it. His letter to the Mahatma KH put the latter in a somewhat embarrassing position.

Fern, incidentally, failed his probation later on and was expelled from the Theosophical Society. There are two entries about him in Olcott's diaries not included in ODL but noted by C. Jinarajadasa. Evidently these are among the diary entries on file in the archives at the international headquarters of the T.S., Adyar, but not included in Olcott's published books.

REFERENCES

The letter has to do principally with Fern's training and a letter which KH is sending to AOH in reply to a long one from him.

(last par.): KH encloses his reply to AOH along with the letter to APS and asks his advice as to whether or not it should be sent. Apparently this is Letter 74 (ML-30) and was never sent (or passed on) to AOH, as per the request of M. See footnote to Letter 75 (ML-53), p.302/297.

74 (ML-30) ***Page 228/225*** ***Folio 2*** ***Recd. Aug. 1882 (est.)***

DESCRIPTION: KH to AOH

This long letter to AOH is on 13 sheets of 8½″ x 11″ white paper in dark blue ink, in heavy script. The quotation from one of AOH's letters to KH at the bottom of page 226 (3rd ed.) and top of page 227 (pp. 229-30, 1st ed.) is in facsimile of AOH's own handwriting, in which passages have been underlined with what appears to be a blue pencil.

CIRCUMSTANCES

APS and AOH were in Simla. Fern was secretary to AOH. This long letter to AOH is apparently the one enclosed in Letter 73 (ML-113) and was transmitted by some agent in the Central Provinces [see Letter 75 (ML-53)]. At the end of Letter 75, p. 302/297, M appends a note asking APS not to give this letter, Letter 74 (ML-30), to AOH, and apparently APS follows this advice; otherwise the *original* would not be in the British Museum. This is one of the few instances in which we have the original of a letter from KH to Hume.

REFERENCES

The letter deals mostly with the difficulties that the Adepts are having with AOH and particularly those connected with his secretary, Fern. (See Alphabetical Notes on Fern.) This is a long and valuable letter for the serious student, even though it never reached its intended recipient.

p. 229/226 (near bottom): '... an entire ignorance of the *"missing links"* ...' Hume's big problem in connection with Fern was that he was not aware of the fact that the Adepts were attempting to test and train Fern for the purpose of using him as a means for the transmission of their correspondence with the Englishmen. He knew that Fern was somewhat clairvoyant and was having some correspondence with M, but was unaware of what was being undertaken by the Adepts.

M had put Fern on probation and hence KH had little to do with this affair, since it seems a definite rule with the Adepts that they do not intrude into affairs of chelas of another Adept.

Hume became very much annoyed with Fern and wrote a letter to the Mahatma KH complaining that, among all of them, they were spoiling Fern; that Fern's self-conceit was becoming intolerable and that he was becoming a confirmed liar. Hume made other derogatory comments about Fern and blamed the Mahatmas for the whole situation. His letter, as shown on pages 229-30/226-27 is a fascimile rather than a copy. One particularly sharp criticism in it was that Fern had completely 'humbugged' the Mahatma M from the first and that he had convinced Sinnett that M was entrusting him with the most occult secrets, etc.

The Mahatma KH was most reluctant to answer this letter, but the Chohan commanded him to do so, so he wrote this long letter to Hume, but sent it first to Sinnett asking the latter to read it to see whether it fell within the limits of a western code of politeness (See Letter 73). Sinnett was then to decide whether it should be forwarded to Hume.

It probably never was forwarded to Hume. At the end of the next letter in the series, the Mahatma M appends a note asking Sinnett to 'lock the letter into your trunk and leave it there to roost until in demand'. He adds: 'I tell you it will create great *mischief* and no better. KH is too sensitive by far—he is becoming in your Western Society a regular Miss.' Since the original of this letter to Hume is in one of the folios in the British Museum, along with the other letters, it is assumed that Sinnett followed M's advice and laid it aside. In this way, he probably risked the Chohan's displeasure.

p. 231/228: 'You have once upon a time called us Jesuits ...' This was in November 1880, when Hume, in an early letter to KH, said, in speaking of the Mahatma's attitude toward Olcott: '... I cannot but take exception to the terms in which you praise him, the whole burthen of which is that he never questions but always obeys. This is the Jesuit organization over again—and this renunciation of private judgement, this abnegation of one's own personal responsibility, this accepting the dictates of outside voices as a substitute for one's own conscience, is to my mind a *sin* of no ordinary magnitude.' Here the Mahatma takes up the challenge and points out the differences in the motivations, although he agrees that there is a resemblance *externally*.

It will be remembered that the Mahatmas had been

working with Hume's secretary, Edmund Fern, who had great possibilities as a psychic but also apparently an inflated sense of his own importance. He was, of course, being tested by the Mahatma M who had taken him on probation.

p. 232/229 (near top): '... the *Dugpas* at our service ...' There are several references in the letters to the fact that the Adepts sometimes make use of elementals and similar entities to carry out special work for them. Even HPB did this.

p. 233/230 (middle): '... the "Elixir of Life"...' A long article by Moorad Ali Beg, an alias for Godolphin Mitford, published in *The Theosophist.* There are numerous references to this article. It is reprinted as the first article in the book, *Five Years of Theosophy.*

p. 235/232: 'November is fast approaching ...' Again a reference to 17 November 1882, the end of a seven year probation period for the Theosophical Society. (It is worth while noting that the Masters recognized 17 November 1875 as the founding date of the Society.)

Then (p. 236/233) there is a curious statement: 'Apart from this I concede to you the right of feeling angry with M.; for he has done something that though it is in strict accordance with our rules and methods, will, when known, be deeply resented by a Western mind and, had I known of it in time to stop it, I would have certainly prevented it from being done.' And, further, on another page (237/234) '... I will never interfere in his ways of training, however distasteful they may be to me personally'.

Here again is emphasis on the fact that the methods of the two Mahatmas differ considerably.

The Mahatma KH refers again to Fern and says (p. 236/233) '... he is quite welcome to *catch* us and *expose* us [words underlined to show that he is quoting Hume] if it can in any way console him for his failure. And fail he *will,* that's certain, if he goes on it that way playing a double game. The option of receiving him or not as a regular chela [presumably beyond probation] remains with the Chohan.'

A little further on, the Mahatma KH says: 'He was, is, and will be tempted to do all manner of wrong things.' Apparently a probationer is deliberately instructed to do things that are contrary to his own sense of right in order to find out whether he will follow his own moral judgement or obey instructions which he knows to be wrong.

p. 235/232 (near bottom): '... Mussulman menial bent on having his revenge of you ...' There are other references also to how M looked after Hume, all without Hume's being aware of it.

p. 236/233 (top): '... Olcott and a native judge in Baroda ...' This has reference to the time in March 1882 when Olcott and Bhavani Rao went over to Calcutta and visited the Gordons, Watsons, and others.

p. 236/233: '... the trouble of looking back into the past ...' A statement indicating that HPB had the ability to do this sort of thing.

(middle of page): '... very kind of Mr Fern ...' This refers to the attempt to train and test Fern (Hume's secretary) to act as an agent for the transmission of letters.

p. 237/234: This whole page deals with Fern's probation. He failed the test and proved to be of no service of the type hoped for. Some of the correspondence between Fern and the Mahatma M is found in C. Jinarajadasa's little book, *Letters from the Masters of the Wisdom,* Vol. 2, Letter 75.

p. 238/235: 'I have all your letters ...' Presumably he means the ones that Hume had written to M, indicating the closeness of the relationship between the Adepts.

Also, a few lines farther down where KH says, '... that innermost feeling was always detected by the Chohan, etc.' indicates how closely the Mahachohan was following events.

p. 239/236 (middle): Hume is taken to task for his impatience. Both he and Sinnett were counselled often to be more patient regarding the receipt of teachings.

p. 240/236: '... our *Tchutuktus* ...' Same as Chutuktus (see p. 113/110). In LBS, p. 23, HPB calls KH 'The brightest, best, purest of all the Tchutuktus', using the term as for an adept. Apparently the term applies to adepts in general.

On p. 239/236, the Mahatma expresses appreciation for what Hume has done for the work and says: '... you must not think that because we have never shown any knowledge of what you have been doing, nor that, because we have never acknowledged or thanked you for it in our letters — that we are either ungrateful for, or ignore purposely or otherwise what you have done, for it is really not so. For, though no one ought to be expecting thanks for doing his duty by humanity and the cause of truth ... nevertheless, my Brother, I feel deeply grateful to you for what you have done ...'

p. 240/237: '...enclosing here a letter from Subba Row to myself ...' This presumably refers to the attempt by M to have Subba Row give occult instructions to Sinnett and Hume.

75 (ML-53) Page 294/290 Folio 2 Written Aug. 23, 1882 (See p. 301/296, end of par. 2)

DESCRIPTION: KH to APS

On eight full-sized sheets of heavy paper in light blue pencil. The imprint has a grained appearance. The paraphrasings of M's thinking on the lower half of p. 296/292 and top of p. 297/293 are in *red pencil.* In the postscript, the first part is in KH script, but the last paragraph is in M script in red pencil; large, heavy lettering.

CIRCUMSTANCES

APS and AOH were in Simla. HPB was in Bombay and HSO in Ceylon.

This letter is a rather fascinating one, showing as it does both the delightful sense of humour and the great erudition of the Mahatma KH. He seems to have read (whether in books or in the Akashic records) practically everything and to know all kinds of odd facts in many fields—history, geology, etc.

In Letter 75, we take up the next letter which the Mahatma KH wrote to Sinnett on the day following that on which he posted his note enclosing the letter to Hume. From a statement in the letter itself, it seems that this letter was written on 23 August 1882, and it was probably received shortly thereafter.

Letter 74 is the long letter to Hume which, apparently, at M's suggestion, was never sent to Hume.

REFERENCE

p. 294/290: The first sentence refers to Letter 73 (ML-113) and Letter 74 (ML-30).

'Jeremiads': Lamentations or doleful writing (from the Lamentations of Jeremiah in the Old Testament).

'...that bulky brother of mine ...' A light reference to M.

'... instead of tasting in Europe...' Reference to his own education in Europe and England during the 1850's.

p. 294/290: The Mahatma states that he has to reveal a 'dreadful secret' (obviously using the term with his tongue in his cheek). The comment about 'tasting in Europe of the tree of the knowledge of good and evil' is, of course, a reference to the fact that the Mahatma KH was educated in Europe. Indications are that he studied in three universities: the University of Dublin in Ireland, Oxford University in England, and Heidelberg in Germany. He mentions 'the disreputable conduct of my wicked, more than ever laughing Brother', and suggests that he has come to regret that he did not remain in Asia, 'in all the *sancta simplicitas* of ignorance of your ways and manners'. If he had done this, he suggests, he too would be laughing.

The next paragraph shows something of the Mahatma's range of knowledge. Warren Hastings was the first Governor-

General of British India, who began his career as a clerk in the East India Company in the late 1700's. This is the 'Company' referred to in the Mahatma's comment. Hastings's aggressive policy of judicial and financial reform rebuilt British prestige in India but met with opposition when he returned to England. He was charged by Edmund Burke with high crimes and was impeached. Later, however, he was acquitted.

The East India Company was, of course, a British enterprise, chartered by Parliament for the monopoly of trade with India and, later on, in China tea. It became virtually supreme in India for a time. So the Mahatma, in taking on the 'sins' of the Brotherhood, likens himself to Warren Hastings who apparently had to bear the brunt of any abuses committed by the East India Company.

Then we have a paragraph throwing some light on Fern's probation. He himself (the Mahatma KH) had not been at all interested in Fern, but found him to be 'a tavern Pericles with a sweet smile for every street Aspasia'.

p. 295/291: According to the encyclopedia, Pericles was an Athenian statesman who lived about 400 BC, who was determined to make Athens a centre of culture as well as a political power. Aspasia was his mistress. Here the Mahatma calls Fern a 'tavern Pericles' and obviously questions his morals. He had, the Mahatma indicates, suddenly reformed after joining the Theosophical Society.

As previously indicated, Fern had (or claimed to have had) some visions which he was wondering whether or not he should publish. The Mahatma states that it wasn't his business to say how much of Fern's claims were truth, how much hallucination, or even fiction. He had obviously fooled Hume, but here the Mahatma points out that Hume believed him when he was lying and did not believe him when he was telling the truth.

p. 296/291: 'Thus, last year, some of my letters to you were *precipitated*...' This would refer to the year 1881 when the method of precipitation of letters was stopped. It is obvious from this statement that KH then started using a different method which he explains: using Djual Khul to write down his thoughts in his adopted script. It would appear that the reason for the stopping of precipitation was in some measure connected with the formation of the Simla Eclectic TS.

'Anyhow, this year, for reasons we need not mention, I have to do my own work, the whole of it...' The import of this statement is not clear; does he mean the method just described of using DK, or does he mean that he himself is now writing the letters?

p. 296/291: Jean Paul Richter was a pseudonym for Johann Paul Friedrick Richter, 18th & 19th century German author who came into vogue when some of his writings were translated into English.

p. 296/292: Then follows a very long paragraph which explains the situation which brought about writing the letter and the 'tolling of *jeremiads'* mentioned in the first paragraph. The reference to 'D. Kh.' is to Djual Khul, a high chela of the Mahatma KH who, as indicated here, was preparing for initiation. The Mahatma goes on to describe the actions of Fern in connection with a letter occultly delivered.

p. 296/292: In the next paragraph the Mahatma KH becomes a spokesman for the Mahatma M. It has to be remembered that it is the Mahatma KH writing, but he is obviously passing on what the Mahatma M has said to him. Then (p. 297/293) 'owing to the *plants* of that little double-dealing monkey—Fern, I am compelled to disturb you for a friendly advice, since *our* ways are not *your* ways—and vice versa'. Thus reiterating a statement made several times in the letters.

p. 297/293: 'But now see what happened.' The long narrative which follows is most interesting as well as rather amusing at times.

p. 298/293: 'The first letter ... I gave to M ...' This

paragraph contains some very interesting information regarding methods of transmission of letters.

p. 299/295: '... I have the entire picture before me of Fern's brain at the moment...' This is a fascinating comment, implying in what minute detail every thought of ours is impressed on the akashic records.

'Col. Chesney...' Further reference to the photographs mentioned in Letter 76 (ML-21). See also other references given in notes on that letter.

p. 300/295: '... it went the *usual* way, via Djual Khool, Deb and Fern...' An interesting comment indicating how the letters were usually delivered, namely that DK delivered them (somehow) to Bombay (either to HPB, DKM, or Deb, a chela there) and they in turn transmitted the letters to Fern in Simla, probably by post.

p. 301/296: 'Read my letter...' Apparently Letter 74 (ML-30) and the one referred to by M in the PS, p. 302/297.

Then we come to another matter: Col. Chesney. He was a friend of Sinnett's, it seems, an author whom Sinnett was trying to interest in Theosophy. Sinnett had shown him two portraits of the Mahatma KH which had come into his possession in rather unusual circumstances. Fern, however, is also involved. One may feel uncertain why Fern is given so much space and so many explanations, when he simply fades out of the picture. But the subject is still important, showing as it does what a razor-edged path we walk.

p. 301/297: 'Remember, in November comes the great crisis ...' Again a reference to the end of the seven-year probation of the TS.

He closes the letter with a lovely compliment to Patience Sinnett.

PS, p. 302/297: '... your two *Letters* and especially "The Evolution of Man" ...' 'The Evolution of Man' was published in two instalments in *The Theosophist,* as part of the 'Fragments of Occult Truth', Oct. 1882, p. 2, and Nov. 1882, p. 46. A third 'Letter' on 'The Human Life Wave' was published in April 1883, p. 161. See also LBS, p. 365.

The additional note signed by M refers to Letter 74 (ML-30), the long letter to AOH. Apparently APS followed this advice and did not give the letter to AOH. This note is in red pencil.

76 (ML-21) Page 134/131 Written Aug. 12; received back with Mahatma's comments on August 22, 1882

There seems some question whether this letter should not have preceded No. 75, but since that letter concerned the matters discussed in the long letter to Hume sent to Sinnett (No. 74) it seemed better to place it following that letter. Both, however, are during the same period of time.

DESCRIPTION

A letter from APS to KH on two sheets of his usual small notepaper. It was returned by KH with marginal comments and an added note. The answer is on the back of APS's sheets and additional sheets of a different type of paper, in blue pencil, having a grained appearance.

CIRCUMSTANCES

APS and AOH were in Simla. HPB was in Bombay, HSO was in Ceylon.

REFERENCES

p. 135/131: APS refers to two letters which he wrote and sent to Stainton Moses in London for publication in *Light,* the British Spiritualist publication. It appears that he had set up proofs of these letters and had sent one set to KH but, without waiting for his comments (contained in Letter 71 (ML-19); see also LBS-201, p. 365), had sent the proofs to Mr Moses for publication.

'... your long letter about Devachan'. Refers to Letter 68 (ML-16) p. 99/97.

p. 135/132: APS is asking whether he should telegraph Stainton Moses to hold up publication of the letters. KH indicates that he should let them be published.

p. 136/133 (last par.): '... making extracts for Colonel Chesney'. Reference to APS's effort to get Col. Chesney interested in Theosophy. See Letter 77 (ML-50), and Letter 92 (ML-54).

(last sentence): '... Djual Khool's idea and art?' A reference to a portrait of KH precipitated by DK for Col. Chesney, later delivered to him by Fern. See p. 300/295. See also LBS-14, p. 27, in which HPB tries to set APS straight concerning how the pictures were made; and OW, pp. 177, 179.

77 (ML-50) Page 286/282 Folio 2 Recd. Aug. 1882 (est.)

DESCRIPTION: KH to APS

On both sides of a folded sheet, about 5″ x 8″, in blue pencil, with grained effect.

CIRCUMSTANCES

APS and AOH were both in Simla. HPB was in Bombay. HSO was in Ceylon. This very short letter seems to be concerned with Hume's increasing complaints about Fern and his continued efforts to prove the Mahatmas in the wrong in everything they are doing. He is the principal subject of this letter.

Apparently Hume had written another letter about Fern and the Mahatma is sending it to Sinnett. Along with it is the Mahatma's reply, since he tells Sinnett to read the 'two letters' before taking them to Hume; and he asks Sinnett to be present when Hume reads them.

REFERENCES

p. 287/282: The 'tenacious and unreasonable man' is AOH.

p. 287/283: '... lamentations of the "wife"...' Presumably Mrs Hume, but we are left without a clue as to the cause.

p. 287/283: '...what he has written to me of Fern...' Probably the letter in question concerned Fern. See Alphabetical Notes.

'... what can be done for Colonel Chesney ...' Probably APS was desirous of getting the Colonel into the TS. Also, this may concern Col. Chesney's request for a photograph of KH.

'...I would not lose him'. This seems to refer to AOH. Both M and KH had indicated that Hume was valuable to the cause at that time and they hoped to continue his usefulness. However, it did not turn out that way.

Letter 78 (ML-51) ***Page 287/283*** ***Folio 2***
Recd. Aug. 22, 1882.

DESCRIPTION: KH to APS

In blue pencil on small sheets of paper, with a grained appearance.

CIRCUMSTANCES

APS, AOH, and Fern were in Simla. Col. Chesney's residence is not indicated. An attempt was being made to get Col. Chesney interested in Theosophy, and DK had precipitated a portrait of KH to be given to the Colonel. This was to be delivered through the agency of Fern. See references on p. 300/295; also p. 137/133. See also LBS 14, p. 26.

This letter was received on the same day that Sinnett received back his letter of August 12 concerning his two articles, or letters, to Stainton Moses, on which the Mahatma commented and told him to go ahead and have them published. (Letter 76)

REFERENCES

p. 287/283: '... the best of two productions ...' DK had produced a portrait of KH for APS on a previous occasion. KH indicates here that the one for Col. Chesney is the better of the two.

p. 287/283: 'The rest of the performance ...' This would seem to refer to the way in which the picture was delivered to Col. Chesney.

p. 288/283: '... I cannot help thinking that our chiefs and especially M may be after all right'. This is in connection with chela training, which KH indicates is quite severe so that only a few come out victorious. The specific situations to which he refers are not indicated.

It has been mentioned several times that some of the Mahatma M's methods of dealing with chelas were 'distasteful' to KH. The student is reminded that this is only speculation, but from the contents of the rest of the letter it seems that this may have been the point at issue.

Col. Chesney again appears. It is not clear at this point how he is involved, since he is not a member of the Theosophical Society, but it must have had something to do with testing the chelas, and the Mahatma does not want him to be deceived; he has indicated that this testing is so severe that few come out victorious.

79 (ML-116) ***Page 450/443*** ***Folio 3*** ***Recd. Aug. 1882 (est.)***

DESCRIPTION: KH to APS

On the front of an envelope 4″ x 5″ addressed to *A. P. Sinnett,* in blue pencil. The envelope may have enclosed a letter to AOH which KH asked APS to read before sending it on to him.

CIRCUMSTANCES

APS and AOH were in Simla. The correspondence was probably being carried on through the usual channels, via DK to Bombay Hqs., thence to Simla by post.

REFERENCES

KH is evidently getting 'fed up' with AOH.

This letter contains another instance of the Mahatma's ability to turn a phrase. One gathers that the letter from Hume, to which this is probably an answer, must have been filled with 'useless verbiage'.

80 (ML-118) Page 450/443 Folio 3 Recd. Autumn of 1882 (est.)

DESCRIPTION: KH to APS

In blue pencil on a sheet of ochre coloured paper, about 5″ x 9″, which has imprinted on it a Chinese picture in red ink, probably a wood-block print.

CIRCUMSTANCES

The Hume and Sinnett families were spending the summer in Simla. Hume had his large house there called 'Rothney Castle' but the Sinnetts rented a house for this summer season. HPB was in Bombay and HSO in Ceylon.

REFERENCES

The first two paragraphs have to do with Mrs Sinnett's concern for the health of their young son. Apparently Mrs Hume suffered from tuberculosis, and Mrs Sinnett was concerned that she might carry some of the germs home with her after visiting the Humes, or more likely she took little Denny with her when she went up to see Mrs Hume. KH's remark about DK noticing this concern while he 'was on the watch' is one of the several that we find throughout the *Letters* about someone being 'on the watch'. This procedure among the Adepts and their assistants is not explained.

KH, in his kindly sympathy, sent a lock of hair as an amulet for son Denny to wear, since the atmosphere of the Sinnett household made it impossible to do anything directly in person.

At different times he also sent locks of hair to both Mr and Mrs Sinnett to wear as amulets.

The sentence at the end ('Say nothing of this note to anybody') indicates the possibility that if others discovered that the Mahatma had sent a lock of his hair for Denny, they too would want the same. The result can easily be imagined.

81 (ML-52) Page 288/284 Folio 2 Recd. Aug. 1882 (est.)

DESCRIPTION: KH to APS

On both sides of six sheets of thin white paper in dark blue ink. Towards the end, one page is in blue pencil, but the letter is continued in blue ink on the back. Fine lettering.

CIRCUMSTANCES

No changes. AOH and APS were both in Simla. It is evident that the crisis is near at hand when Hume will break with the Adepts and turn against them.

REFERENCES

p. 288/284 (first par.): '... writes out a Hebrew passage ...' See middle of page 291/287.

'... far more an *Adwaitee* ...' Adwaita is a non-dualistic school of Indian speculative philosophy. See LBS, pp. 304-5, for excerpts from letter from AOH to KH, in which KH's added comments are printed in bold type.

'...writes an abusive letter ...' See LBS, p. 29, for HPB's reaction to this letter. The background is as follows: In the June 1882 issue of *The Theosophist,* p. 225, there appeared a letter from 'Caledonian Theosophist' [see Study Notes on Letter 68 (ML-16)], who questioned some things in *Isis.* HPB followed it with an Editor's Note in which she answered some of the comments. C.C. Massey then picked it up and, in the July 8 edition of *Light,* took issue with some of HPB's statements in this 'Editor's Note'. HPB then answered *him* in the August 1882 issue, pp. 288-9, under the heading 'Isis Unveiled and the "Theosophist" on Reincarnation'. Then Hume wrote the letter referred to above as 'an abusive letter' and signed himself 'H.X.' This has become known in Theosophical parlance as the HX letter. In this letter, he took issue with her comments in the August 1882 *Theosophist,* said some things about *Isis,* and criticized the Mahatmas. HPB published this, under protest, in the September 1882 issue, pp. 324-6. She preceded it with a statement that she was publishing it 'under strong personal protest' and only because of 'the express orders received from our great Brothers'. A 'Protest' signed by 12 chelas follows the letter (see references ML, p. 292/288 to this 'Protest'; see also LBS, p. 354-6). Three of the persons signing it are referred to a number of times in ML: TSR, Guala K. Deb, and DKM. See Appendix D.

p. 289/285: ' "... exercising my ingenuity" ? ' See Letter 70C (ML-20C), p. 130/127, where the expression is used. See also pp. 173/169 and 182/179.

p. 289/285: '... *faute de s'entendre* ...' through not understanding each other.

'... the seven principles—constantly referred to in *Isis* as a trinity ...' Information concerning the sevenfold constitution of man was not available until correspondence between the Mahatmas and APS and AOH got under way in 1881 and 1882.

'...Atrya (one whom you do not know)'. One of the Adept Brotherhood. See Alphabetical Notes.

p. 290/286: 'Suttee' An old Hindu custom, long since officially discontinued, in which a widow sacrificed herself to be burned alive on her husband's funeral pyre.

p. 291/286: '... the author of the Review of "The Perfect Way" ...' This review is not signed, but obviously it was written by APS, since HPB refers to this in LBS-14, p. 26, and, in Letter 63 (ML-95). See also Letter 83 (ML-125), p. 453/446. KH comments: 'Your review of the *Perfect Way* ...' The review was published in two instalments, May 1882, p. 207, and June 1882, p. 232.

p. 291/287: '... the great Simla "I am"...' A reference to AOH.

'... the Eclectic has to sink ...' KH indicates on this page that the real reason for Hume's publishing the HX letter was to screen himself in the event of the failure of the Simla Eclectic TS and perhaps also the parent Theosophical Society.

p. 291/287: '... as I see my writing before me ...' An indication that KH was probably writing this letter himself.

'... to add his explanations to mine ...' This refers again to the HX letter. It would seem that KH may have written at least part of the comments attributed to HPB in the August 1882 issue.

p. 292/288: '... I had no right to suppress the "offensive article" '. Reference again to the HX letter.

'The two names that you find heading the signatures of the 12 chelas who protest ...' These names are: Deva Muni.·.·. and Paramahansa Shub-Tung.·.·.

'... the son of Babu Nobin Banerjee...' Babu Nobin Banerjee was one of the signers of the 'Protest'.

p. 293/288: '...I personally am ordered not to break with him until the day of crisis comes'. Perhaps another reference to the seventh anniversary of the TS or to Hume's break.

'... retain his official position in the Eclectic ...' AOH had been President of the Eclectic TS until this time. APS became President on 8 October 1882. See p. 302/298.

p. 293/289: '... the footnote by Djual Khool to be appended to W. Oxley's article ...' (See Study Notes on Letter 49 (ML-48). This refers to the book, *The Philosophy of the Spirit,* by William Oxley, reviewed by DK in the December 1881 issue of *The Theosophist,* p. 62. In the March 1882 issue, p. 150, Oxley replied to the reviewer. The footnote referred to is included in ML as Letter 83 (ML-125). See Study Notes on that letter.

(bottom page): '... experiment *à la* napkin ...' See page 299/294-95.

p. 294/290: 'Buddha Gaya' is a place sacred to Buddhists in North India. See Alphabetical Notes.

82 (ML-32) ***Page 242/239*** ***Folio 2*** ***Recd. Aug. (after 26th) 1882 (est.)***

DESCRIPTION: KH to APS

On both sides of 5″ x 8″ sheets of heavy smooth paper, in blue pencil, with large flowing script.

CIRCUMSTANCES

Same as in Letter 81 (ML-52). APS and AOH were still in Simla.

REFERENCES

p. 242/289: 'Mr Hume has put his foot in a hornet's nest ...' Obviously a reference to the furore over the HX letter.

'... irresponsible "Benefactor"...': AOH.

'I prevented her sending to Hume a worse letter ...' See LBS-16, p. 29.

'... hence the positive order to H.P.B. ...' This is an indication that the Mahachohan ordered the publication of the HX letter over HPB's protest. See Letter 81 (ML-52).

p. 243/240: '... never like to risk myself again with any European ...' From the beginning, the correspondence with APS and AOH had been somewhat reluctantly permitted by the Mahachohan.

'... I hastened to send to you with the letter...' Apparently the chelas attached to an adept are carefully protected from some outside influences.

p. 244/240: 'burking': killing or smothering.

Comment by the compiler: One of the lessons so sharply outlined in this whole situation is the importance of understanding and how much suffering and sorrow are caused by the lack of it. Leaping to conclusions from insufficient evidence, and then—acting on those conclusions—causing pain and distress to oneself and others, is a most regrettable human inclination.

There is a heavy note of sadness in this letter. The Mahatmas had hoped for so much when they undertook the correspondence with the Englishmen—or, at least, the Mahatma KH had. Out of love for humanity and a deep desire to enlighten those who were seeking, he risked the Chohan's displeasure and undertook a very difficult and uncertain task. This made him vulnerable, and his disappointment must have been very heavy at the hovoc wrought by one egotistical and proud man. 'How shall I ever face my Great Master,' he asks, 'who is laughted at, made the object of Mr Hume's wit, called Rameses the Great, and such like indecent remarks?' These particular 'indecent remarks' were not in the HX letter but in a letter which Hume must have sent direct to the Mahatma, since the latter mentions he has sent it on to Sinnett.

83 (ML-125) Page 453/446 Folio 3 Recd. Aug. (near end) 1882 (est.)

DESCRIPTION

Written by DK on thin paper in brown ink. Two corrections have been made in it in blue ink. This is actually not a letter but 'the footnote by Djual Khool' mentioned on p. 293/289, Letter 81 (ML-52). See Study Notes on that letter.

CIRCUMSTANCES

Same as in two immediately preceding letters. APS and AOH were still in Simla. Following the publication of Oxley's reply to DK in the March 1882 issue of *The Theosophist,* Oxley wrote a further article on the same subject, which he sent to HPB. In LBS-14, p. 26, HPB writes to APS about this, calls it 'an interminable article' and says she had intended to reject it but KH 'ordered me not to'. She adds: 'D.K. just brought in a long footnote to be appended to the article which, as it is given to me in double copy, I send to you as ordered. K.H. tells you to make alterations in it if you like it, and send them before the thing is printed.' Apparently APS did make some alterations, as the footnote appended to Oxley's article is very slightly different and is not quite as long as shown here in Letter 83. Oxley's article was published in the September 1882 issue of *The Theosophist,* pp. 298-301. DK's footnote appears at the end, p. 201. Apparently Oxley was under some delusions concerning his supposed contacts with KH, and DK was instructed to issue a denial. (See ML index for other references to Mr Oxley.)

REFERENCES

p. 454/446 (near bottom): '... once honoured him with an autograph letter ...' The letter referred to (not published) is in Folio 6 in the British Museum. It is dated 24/6/81:

p. 454/447 '... THREE SECRET WORDS ...' These three passwords are given in Letter 96 (p. 419/413):

> It may so happen that for purposes of our own, mediums and their spooks will be left undisturbed and free not only to personate the 'Brothers' but even to *forge our handwriting*. Bear this in mind and be prepared for it in London. Unless the message or communication or whatever it may be is *preceded* by the triple words: 'Kin-t-an, Na-lan-da, Dha-ra-ni, *know* it is not me, nor from me.

(See also Letter 118 (ML-96) p. 431/424).

It is interesting, also, that, after all Hume had done, the Mahatma was apparently willing for him to have the passwords. He was still President of the Simla Eclectic Theosophical Society and the Mahatma must have considered that it might still be necessary to communicate with him.

84 (ML-111) Page 446/439 Folio 3 Recd. Sept. 1882 (est.)

DESCRIPTION: KH to APS

On a single sheet of coral coloured paper, about 4″ x 9″, which has a Chinese wood-block print on the back. The writing is in fine lettering in black ink and is continued on the back. The postscript is below the print, in blue pencil.

CIRCUMSTANCES

APS and AOH were still in Simla. The letter was delivered to APS by a couple of KH's chelas, along with Letter 85 (ML-24). This letter 84 (ML-111) is really only a transmittal letter for Letter 85 (ML-24).

REFERENCES

'Dharbagiri Nath': a chela whose identity is shrouded in

some mystery. See Alphabetical Notes. See also Letter 85 (ML-24) p. 190/188 and LMW-II, pp. 156-7. There is also some mention of him in LBS, pp. 167-73 and 338-42.

Dharbagiri Nath was a mystical name for one of the Mahatma KH's chelas, Gwala K. Deb. But there is also a strange connection with another individual—a probationary chela of the Mahatma KH—known in the literature as Babaji, or sometimes Bawajee. This very odd situation is explained by Sven Eek in his book, *Damodar,* beginning on p. 537. The story will be difficult for a Westerner to believe, he says, as it requires a willingness to view man as a composite entity.

Babaji's real name was S. Krishnamachari, or Krishnaswami. He worked at one time in the Collector's office at Nellore, but at the request of the Mahatma KH, he joined the staff at the headquarters of the Theosophical Society in Bombay sometime between 1880 and 1882. At that time he dropped his original name and called himself Babaji. He also came to use the name Dharbagiri Nath, explaining that it was customary among his people to take a new name 'at the time of wearing the Brahmanical thread' and still another one when they became exoteric Sannyasins or mystics, or even pupils of mystics. Babaji's right to this name was questioned by HPB. She called him 'the little pretender'—although this was some time later when he had grievously failed in several ways.

However, at one time—about the time of this letter and probably in connection with it—the Mahatma KH desired to send two chelas to Sinnett, then at Simla. He selected one of his pupils, Gwala K. Deb, who was probably a Tibetan, and R. Keshava Pillai, an inspector of police at Nellore, who had become a probationary lay chela and who was known as Chandra Cusho—a name given him by the Mahatma KH. Deb was in Tibet at the time, undergoing certain occult training, and was unable to go in his physical body. Babaji consented to have Deb use his body for the occasion. This was much to his credit and spiritual benefit. It was, however, *Deb's* mystical name which was Dharbagiri Nath, and it seems that Babaji continued to use the name after the experience was ended. The mix-up is a strange one, and when one meets with the name Dharbagiri Nath, as one does several times in the letters, it is difficult to know whether it is really Gwala K. Deb, as the Tibetan chela, or Babaji. However, when the Mahatma refers to him as 'the little man' or 'my little man' he is probably referring to Babaji (whether as Deb or as himself) as he was of a very small stature.

As mentioned above, Chandra Cusho was a Tibetan name given by the Mahatma to R. Keshava Pillai. He was put on probation by the Mahatma but progressed no further. Later, he lost interest in the Theosophical Society. He received several letters from the Mahatma which, some years later, he gave to Olcott. They are included in LMW, Series 2, pp. 115-119. One letter of the group has some connection with Letter 84. The Mahatma tells him that he is sending 'Deb' to Simla with some letters for Mr Sinnett (whom he calls 'the best of all') and asks whether Brother Keshu (Chandra Cusho) will accompany and help him.

'... deliver into your hands my "answers to the famous contradictions"...' Both APS and AOH had accused KH of contradictions in the teachings. The answers referred to here are found in Letters 85A and 85B (ML-24 A & B).

85A (ML-24A) Page 178/175 Recd. near mid-September 1882

85B (ML-24B) Page 180/177

DESCRIPTION: APS to KH with replies by KH

'The Famous Contradictions.' Letter 85A (ML-24A) is on 7 sheets of thin paper in APS script. Numbers in brackets, 1 to 12B, were added in blue script, as well as underlining of some passages. Under passage numbered (11) is added in red ink: 'See (9) x ante.' Also, added in black ink, is: 'See my notes 10 and 11 about Wagner, etc.' Letter 85B (ML-24B) is on 8 folded sheets about 5″ x 8″, on all sides in KH script and sepia ink.

CIRCUMSTANCES

This two-part letter was enclosed in Letter 84 (see notes) and delivered to Sinnett by two chelas of the Mahatma KH, Dharbagiri Nath (probably Babaji) and Chandra Cusho. It is spoken of as the 'Famous Contradictions' letter.

It will be remembered that both Hume and Sinnett had accused the Mahatmas of contradicting themselves. The Mahatma KH had asked them several times to make a list of the items in question, as he had no time to go searching back through all the letters he had written (an interesting statement, as the search would probably have been through the akasic records). Sinnett finally got around to making the list. He had sent it to KH some time earlier and received it back with the Mahatma's comments (this Letter, 85) sometime in September.

Letter 85A consists of the items listed by Sinnett. Letter 85B contains the Mahatma's answers, plus comments on some other matters. The numbers in brackets in the Mahatma's answers refer to those in Sinnett's letter.

The items mentioned by Sinnett in 85A are not taken up until p. 185/182. The Mahatma's comment under (1) refers to Sinnett's opening statement in which he says that the so-called 'contradictions' did not 'fret' him and so he had delayed acting on the Mahatma's suggestion.

Some of the items in Sinnett's list refer to the Devachan letter and some to comments made by the Mahatma on the margin of the proofs of his two letters to Stainton Moses in London, to be published in *Light*. [See Letters 76 (ML-21) p. 134/131.)]

Before getting into the specific answers, however, the Mahatma mentions several other matters which he asks Sinnett to 'bear in mind'. His discussion of adept use of occult powers fills approximately two pages.

One item of special interest could easily be missed. Earlier letters from the Mahatma were precipitated, and this practice was suddenly stopped. On p. 181/178, the Mahatma mentions 'the unpleasant fact that we are forbidden to use one particle of our powers in connexion with the *Eclectic* (for which you have to thank your President and him alone ...)'. It seems probable that the precipitation of letters was one of these 'powers' and that the practice was forbidden by the Chohan because of some action by Hume. This is supposition, but the comment is as close to a specific statement concerning the reason for the prohibition as can be found in the book.

The reference to 'the exercise of ingenuity' (p. 182/179) refers to the comment of the Mahatma in Letter 70C (p. 130/126) for which the Englishmen rather took the Mahatma to task. This was in connection with the circumstances surrounding the HX letter. Here the Mahatma goes into considerable detail concerning the difference between the Monad and the personal Ego. There is also some discussion of the portrait of the Mahatma KH made by Djual Khool (here G.K.: see notes on Letter 75) and KH says that the account in the OW is not strictly accurate.

REFERENCES

p. 178/175: '... the letter of the 12th of August ...' Refers to Letter 76 (ML-21).

p. 182, 185/179, 180: References to C.C. Massey, HPB, *Isis,* and HX concern the controversy discussed in Letter 81 (ML-52). See Study Notes on that letter. See LBS, p. 26. The reader of this discussion should bear in mind the fact that at that time there was a lot of confusion and misunderstanding of terms being used.

p. 183/180: '...É.Lévi's Fragment on Death!' refers to the article by Éliphas Lévi entitled 'Stray Thoughts on Death and Satan', published in *The Theosophist,* October 1881.

p. 184/181: ' "*Nous verrons,* nous verrons"...' We shall see, we shall see.

'G. Khool says ...' Refers to the portrait of KH in which DK was involved. See Study Notes on Letter 78 (ML-51) and Letter 75 (ML-53).

Djual Khool had, at different times, precipitated two black and white portraits of KH. The first one was for APS and the second one was for Col. Chesney.

p. 186/183 (bottom): '... my early association with Western "Pelings" ...' Another reference to KH's education in Europe in his younger days.

p. 189/187: '... Mr Khandalawala's letter that you had sent back to H.P.B.' See opening sentence of Letter 70B (MI - 20B), p. 121. The reference is to Judge N.D. Khandalawala, a member of the TS who apparently remained loyal throughout.

p. 189/187: the four lines of poetry to which the Mahatma alludes appeared in the note attached to the proofs returned to Sinnett by the Mahatma. They were followed by the words 'Not for publication', which, it was speculated, indicated that they were by the Mahatma. Here the Mahatma calls attention to the fact that they were omitted (presumably from Sinnett's list) along with his (KH's) further explanation which he had given to the proofs. Sinnett's reason for this is not given.

On p. 190/187, the Mahatma quotes a 'Hudibrasian couplet'. This is after the style of Samuel Butler's 'Hudibras' although actually it is from Jonathan Swift's satirical piece of 'poetry':

So, naturalists observe, a flea
Hath smaller fleas that on him prey;
And these have smaller fleas to bite'em,
And so proceed *ad infinitum.*
Thus every poet, in his kind,
Is bit by him that comes behind.

There follow some further derogatory comments about Hume. Then the Mahatma turns to another matter. Sinnett had obviously asked some questions relating to science, which the Mahatma says he will answer 'next week' as he is not at home but in a lamasery near Darjeeling, 'the object of H.P.B.'s longings'. This no doubt refers to her training in Tibet. He had gone there to await HPB's arrival; she was finally to realize her desire to visit her Master, the Mahatma M. While there, the Mahatma KH apparently also had some task to perform in connection with 'Noblin's boy'. It will be remembered that Noblin Banerjee was one of the signers of the PROTEST to the HX letter and that, as a result, his fourteen year-old son was given the privilege of going to a lamasery for training (See ML p. 292/288). The Mahatma closes his letter (85) with 'Do not frighten my little man—only do not forget—he is *but an appearance.*' The 'little man' was undoubtedly Babaji in his capacity as Gwala K. Deb, in which he took Deb's mystic name, Dharbagiri Nath. So the letter closes on a note of puzzlement.

86 (ML-112) Page 447/440 Folio 3 Recd. Sept. (late) 1882 (est.)

DESCRIPTION: KH to APS

On a folded sheet of smooth bluish coloured paper, about 5″ x 8½″, in blue pencil, with grained appearance.

CIRCUMSTANCES

p. 447/440: It seems that Col. Chesney had addressed a latter to the Mahatma KH and the latter had written a reply which he was preparing to have delivered by 'my little man' (Babaji/Dharbagiri Nath) when he received a letter from Sinnett advising him not to correspond with Col. Chesney.

It has been impossible to determine what was behind this, although there is a hint that Col. Chesney had decided that Theosophy was anti-Christian. Sinnett had been very eager to interest the Colonel in Theosophy and had rather pressed the Mahatma to pay some attention to him—even to the extent of sending him a portrait of himself. But Sinnett seemed to have changed his mind completely.

Here the Mahatma implies that the Colonel had lost interest in the Society—and this *may* have been due to Fern since he seems to have had something to do with the situation.

REFERENCES

p. 448/440: 'Phari Jong ...' A large monastery in Tibet just across from the border of Sikkim, on the main road to Lhasa. Apparently KH was at this monastery at the time of writing this letter. APS was in Simla. See Alphabetical Notes.

'Mr W. Oxley ...' Refer to Letter 47 (ML-48), p. 274/270 and Letter 63 (ML-125), p. 453/446. Mr W. Oxley was apparently one of the better English mediums, but believed his guides too implicitly.

87 (ML-34) Page 345/242 Folio 2 Recd. Fall of 1882 (est.)

DESCRIPTION: KH to APS

On a single sheet of glazed paper, about 6″ x 9″, in KH script, in heavy blue pencil.

CIRCUMSTANCES

Since the date is not known very closely, it is difficult to determine the situation. It is probable that APS was still in Simla, and that HPB had just visited M and KH in Sikkim and had returned to Darjeeling for a rest. KH was probably in Sikkim or Phari Jong Monastery.

REFERENCES

p. 245/242: 'Enclosed two letters written and addressed to her with an eye to myself ...' Evidently letters AOH had written to HPB, critical of KH.

It is in this letter that KH makes the statement: 'The Society will never perish as an institution, although branches and individuals in it may.'

He also states that the esoteric doctrines have to be made public gradually.

88 (ML-10) *Page 52* *Folio 1* ***Copied by APS on Sept. 28, 1882.***

DESCRIPTION: KH to AOH

The letter was addressed to AOH. APS copied it for his own reference. His copy is on 38 sheets of small-sized note-paper, in dull black ink.

CIRCUMSTANCES

AOH and APS were in Simla. HPB was perhaps in Darjeeling by this time, following her visit in Sikkim for a few days to see the Mahatmas M and KH.

This is one of the letters most often referred to, sometimes called the 'Letter concerning God'. Some people tend to downgrade it, along with other letters of which the original is missing and only APS's copies remain. While this is a legitimate argument, it seems evident that APS was a responsible and accurate person, and his copies of AOH's letters were generally made soon after their receipt. There seems little reason to doubt their accuracy.

REFERENCES

This is probably the most controversial letter in the volume. Actually, it is not a letter but some notes made by the

Mahatma KH on what Hume called a 'Preliminary Chapter on God', intended as a preface to a book he was writing on occult philosophy. Both Englishmen occasionally submitted their writings to the Mahatma for review and comment, as Sinnett had done with his letter to Stainton Moses (see notes on Letter 76)). It is not known when these notes of Hume's were first sent to the Mahatma. The copy in the British Museum is in Sinnett's handwriting; evidently Hume permitted him to make a copy and, fortunately, Sinnett noted the date.

Not so fortunately, these 'Notes' have caused some people to reject the whole occult philosophy because of the denial of the traditional concept of God. The student is therefore asked to withhold judgement. The Mahatma KH's comments are not expressed in today's language, but in many instances they embody ideas being advanced by some outstanding modern scientists. This is not to say that the ideas are accepted by the entire scientific establishment; the facts presented are undeniable, but interpretations vary. However, the cross-illuminations are extremely interesting.

The letter is a rather long one, but it is one the student must come to grips with if he is to understand the philosophy of the Mahatmas. Some preliminary comments are essential. The student must bear in mind that, in using the word 'God', the Mahatma is dealing with the common concept of a being who, so to speak, sits outside his creation, quite separate from it, but with power over every atom in it. In short, the kind of God in whom many people, and certainly many people in the West, believed implicitly for decades; and of course, many still do. The Mahatma points out that *a* being cannot be other than limited; *a* being cannot be omnipresent. This is underlined by a statement by a modern scientist:

> In a universe which is an inseparable whole and where all forms are fluid and ever-changing, there is no room for any fixed fundamental entity (Fritjof Capra, *The Tao of Physics,* Shamballa 1975, p. 391).

At the risk of making these notes burdensome, the compilers feel impelled to include a number of quotations from various sources which have bearing on the contents of the letter. These may be ignored if the student is already familiar with them or if he is not particularly interested in them.

In an article entitled 'When Man Becomes As God; the Biological Prospect' by Albert Rosenfeld, then Science Editor of *The Saturday Review,* in its issue of 10 December 1977, we find the following:

> As for our genetic inheritance, did it come about through blind chance or as the result of some purposive thrust that pervades the universe? ... In contrast to the vitalists, with whom they have carried on a running philosophical battle, the materialists argue that all life and spirit are made of nothing but inanimate matter from which they derive and the way it is organized. ... But the materialists exult too soon. 'I would say', wrote Loren Eiseley in *The Immense Journey,* 'that if "dead" matter has reared up this curious landscape of fiddling crickets, song sparrows, and wandering men, it must be plain even to the most devoted materialist that the matter of which he speaks contains amazing, if not dreadful, powers and may not impossibly be, as Hardy has suggested, "but one mask of many worn by the Great Face behind".' True enough, the building blocks of living molecules have been produced in the laboratory by subjecting inanimate materials to the simulated conditions presumed to exist in the earth's early atmosphere. And it is freely predicted that one day scientists will go all the way to create life in the laboratory. Would that feat, then, permit the materialists to claim victory? Not at all, for the same reasons implied by Eiseley: If life can be made from non-life, then terms such as 'non-life' and 'inanimate' were inappropriate all along. It would not prove that life and spirit are nothing but matter, but rather that life and spirit inhere in the atoms of bricks and the fires of stars.

Be-ing, by its very nature, means 'in manifestation', and nothing in manifestation can possibly be omnipotent. Nor can it be perfect. As HPB says somewhere, 'Nothing in manifestation is perfect.'

It is probable that the average intelligent Christian's concept of God today does not agree with the concept which the Mahatma is attacking.

In the book, *The Universal Flame,* published by the Theosophical Publishing House, Adyar, 1975, in commemoration of the centenary of the Theosophical Society, there is a very fine article by William J. Ross entitled, 'The Concept of God', which contains some statements of interest in connection with this letter. If the letter itself is approached with some of these ideas in mind, it will be more understandable. The author points out that:

> The history of man shows that the word God was invented to designate the unknown cause of all effects which man either admired or dreaded without understanding them. The storms, the cataclysms, the good or bad crops, were all credited to a force or forces which were anthropomorphized into a god or gods. They were worshipped and sacrificed to, in order that they might be propitiated and act favourably towards their worshippers.

As we know, this attitude has not entirely disappeared from the world.

> Man still makes his God, attributing to him human characteristics and sacrificing or praying to the image he has created to obtain what he wants. Although thinking man has theoretically abandoned anthropomorphism, his God, when he has one, usually has human characteristics and is seen as a superhuman person—masculine—who has power over nature and the fortunes of mankind.

It will be remembered that the Mahatmas were Buddhists. Mr Ross points out that in Buddhism, there is no mention of God.

> One finds in it no mythological vision, no tangible creed. It is, as it were, a therapy, a treatment for those who recognize the pain of the human condition and are strong enough to follow

> the cure which is prescribed. It is not so much a religious philosophy as the advice of a spiritual physician. The Buddha gives the cause of the human condition as ignorant craving. Man suffers because he constantly *wants,* and when he gets what he wants he finds it does not satisfy his craving but only leads to more wants. What is the cure? It is laid down by the Buddha as an operational one, a way of life. ... It involves a commitment to doing things, to living in a certain way, to having certain attitudes towards man and the world. This frees us from our ignorant cravings and helps us to find that sense of identity, that feeling of wholeness, which is the mark of a healthy human being, a being who is at once aware of his own individual uniqueness and of his oneness with the whole of nature.
>
> None of this implies any idea of God. It is a way of life involving a feeling of responsibility, a recognition of man as the agent of his own destiny. It is in the context of this philosophical, Buddhistic point of view that we must see the words, 'We deny God'.

Mr Ross quotes from a statement by HPB in *The Secret Doctrine* (and it is well to remember the Mahatma KH's statement about the authorship of that work—that the SD was '... the triple production of M.·., Upasika, and myself') '... man ought to be ever striving to help the divine evolution of Ideas, by becoming to the best of his ability a co-worker with Nature in the cyclic task'. She continues:

> The ever-unknowable and incognizable *Kārana* alone, the *Causeless Cause* of all causes, should have its shrine and altar on the holy and ever untrodden ground of our heart—invisible, intangible, unmentioned, save through the 'still small voice' of our spiritual consciousness. Those who worship before it, ought to do so in the silence and the sanctified solitude of their Souls; making their spirit the sole mediator between them and the *Universal Spirit,* their good actions the only priests, and their sinful intentions the only visible and objective sacrificial victims to the Presence (SD 1;280, 1978 ed.).

This, says Mr Ross, is the key to the understanding of the

concept of God. It helps to free us from the dichotomy of the religious and the secular, of God and man. It brings us to a sense of wholeness, of unity, to the understanding that the fundamental law of our system is the one homogeneous divine substance-principle (Swabhavat). This is the 'omnipresent Reality; impersonal, because it contains all and everything'.

Now, after that long introduction, it is suggested that the first paragraph of the letter itself be read. The Mahatma's second sentence says, '... Our philosophy falls under the definition of Hobbes'. This refers to Thomas Hobbes (1588-1679) an English philosopher who expounded a rationalist materialism which offended the religious authorities of his day.

Very logically, the Mahatma points out that Hume had already been told that their knowledge was limited to this our solar system and '... ergo as philosophers' they could not either deny or affirm the existence of the being postulated by Hume. The Mahatma denies 'most emphatically' the position of agnosticism. 'Our doctrine knows no compromises. It either affirms or denies, for it never teaches but that which it knows to be the truth.' The rest of the paragraph attempts to explain further why they 'deny God' both as philosophers and Buddhists.

The Mahatma goes on to explain something more of the rationale of their position, and says, 'Pantheistic we may be called—agnostic never.'

Further on, the Mahatma mentions the 'One Life' and says that '... it penetrates, nay is the essence of every atom of matter; and that therefore it not only has correspondence with matter but has all its properties likewise, etc.—hence *is* material, is *matter* itself'. In this connection a former prominent member of the Theosophical Society, Mr F.L. Kunz, commented: 'Matter is a device of Reality.'

It cannot but be noted, as one studies the Letters, that the Masters do not deny the reality of spirit—only spirit as a separate and distinct principle apart from matter. '... It is one of the elementary and fundamental doctrines of Occultism', says the Mahatma KH elsewhere in the letters, 'that the two [spirit and matter] are one, and are distinct but in their respective manifestations, and only in the limited perceptions of the world of senses. ... Spirit is called the ultimate sublimation of matter, and matter the crystallization of spirit ... matter *per se* is indestructible and... coeval with spirit.' (ML p. 141-2/139) Further, 'Bereaved of Prakriti [matter] Purusha [Spirit] is unable to manifest itself, hence ceases to exist—becomes *nihil*. ... Motion is eternal because spirit is eternal. But no modes of motion can ever be conceived unless they be in connection with matter.' (ML p. 142/139)

In the second paragraph of Letter 88 (ML-10) the Mahatma mentions the phenomena which proceed from the infinite and limitless space, duration, and motion. These factors are explained in more detail in *The Secret Doctrine,* where HPB gives the three aspects of the Absolute as Absolute Abstract Space, Absolute Abstract Motion, and (she adds later) Duration. (See p. 14, 1978 ed. for Space and Motion; p. 37, 1978 ed. for Duration.)

Further on in the second paragraph, the Mahatma suggests that if people are willing to accept and to regard as God the One Life, immutable and unconscious in its eternity, they may do so, but he adds 'and thus keep to one more gigantic misnomer'. Then, he says, they will have to say with Spinoza that there is no other substance than God. He quotes Spinoza's 14th proposition which, in Boris de Zirkoff's translation (in a letter to the compilers) 'Beyond (aside from, outside of) God, substance can neither be given nor conceived.'

It might be of interest here to quote some passages from a book mentioned earlier, *The Tao of Physics,* by Fritjof Capra. The author is an eminent physicist. The purpose of the book is to show that 'a consistent view of the world is beginning to emerge from modern physics which accommodates our most advanced theories of the physical world'. Dr Capra writes of the Eastern world view as intrinsically dynamic. 'The cosmos is seen as one separate reality, forever in motion, alive, organic; spiritual and material at the same time.'

> Now, researches into physics are revealing that the forces causing the motion are not outside the objects [comment by compilers: as would be the case if an extraterrestrial God were pulling strings from somewhere outside the universe] but are an intrinsic property of matter ... a principle which controls everything from within. ... The modern physicist, like the Eastern mystic, has come to see the world as a system of inseparable, interacting, and ever-moving components, with man being an integral part of this system.

Another important development in modern physics is that mass is seen to be nothing but a form of energy. We all know of the formula $E=MC^2$ which is the relation between an object at rest and the energy stored in its mass, with C being the speed of light.

'Every time the physicists asked nature a question in an atomic experiment,' says Dr Capra, 'nature answered with a paradox, and the more they tried to clarify the situation, the sharper the paradoxes became.'

The classical concepts of Newtonian physics had to be abandoned – and here there may be a parallel with what we might call the 'classical' or traditional concept of God, as the Mahatma tries to point out in this letter.

'Only when the dynamic, relativistic view is adopted does the paradox disappear,' says Dr Capra. 'The particles are then seen as dynamic patterns, or processes, which involve a certain amount of energy appearing to us as their mass ... the whole universe appears as a dynamic web of inseparable energy patterns.'

Here we have the theosophical concept of the Web of the Universe given in *The Secret Doctrine:* 'Father-Mother spin a Web ...' This concept is beautifully elaborated in the book by E. L. Gardner: *The Web of the Universe* (Theosophical Publishing House, London, 1937).

These quotations show that the whole message of *The Tao of Physics* is really very similar to what the Mahatma is saying in his notes on Hume's chapter, although of course expressed very differently. Just as the classical concept of God was that of an extraterrestrial being who had created and was still managing the universe from outside, so the classical concept of physics was that the world was 'out there' somewhere and totally separate from the observer. One may think, in this connection, of the comment of Dr C.G. Jung, the great Swiss psychologist:

> If I accept the fact that a god is absolute and beyond all human experience, he leaves me cold. I do not affect him, nor does he affect me. But if I know that a god is a powerful impulse in my soul, at once I must concern myself with him, for then he can become important *(Psyche & Symbol,* 1958, Doubleday, pp. 344-5).

Now the dividing lines seem to be disappearing in both science and religion. God is no longer the 'great big man with the long white beard' of a child's conception, but a powerful energy in our own souls; we have identity with that energy; it is the One Life which pulses within every atom. As Dr Jung says in his provocative *Answer to Job* (p. xiii): 'After all, we can imagine God as an eternally flowing current of vital energy that endlessly changes shape just as easily as we can imagine him as an eternally unmoved, unchangeable essence.' So it seems that modern thinkers in several fields are coming to a totally new concept of Deity.

'We are not Adwaitees,' says the Mahatma, at the end of page 53, 'but our teaching respecting the one life is identical with that of the Adwaitees with regard to Parabrahm.'

Subba Row, who *was* an Adwaitee, has given an excellent statement in *The Philosophy of the Bhagavad Gita,* 1912 ed., p. 8 et seq.:

> The first principle ... is the existence of what is called Parabrahman ... the one essence of everything in the cosmos ... Now this Parabrahman which exists before all things in the cosmos is the one essence from which starts into existence a centre of energy which I shall for the present call the Logos. This Logos may be called in the language of old writers either Īśwara or Pratyagatma or Sabda Brahman. It is called the Verbum or the Word by the Christian, and it is the divine Christos who is eternally in the bosom of his Father. It is called Avalokiteśvara by the Buddhists... From its objective standpoint (Logos), Parabrahman appears to it as *Mulaprakriti.* This Mulaprakriti is no more Parabrahman than the bundle of attributes of this pillar is the pillar itself; Parabrahman is an unconditioned and absolute Reality, and Mulaprakriti is a sort of veil thrown over it. Parabrahman by itself cannot be seen as it is. It is seen by the Logos with a veil thrown over it, and that veil is the mighty expanse of cosmic matter. It is the basis of material manifestation in the cosmos ... Creation or evolution is commenced by the intellectual energy of the Logos; this light of the Logos is the link between subjective matter and the subjective thought of Īśvara, usually called Fohat.

The rather long middle paragraph on p. 54 contains a piece of merciless logic and ends with the words: 'Your church is the fabulous Saturn who begets children but to devour them'—a reference, of course, to the Roman myth in which the god Saturn devours his offspring.

On p. 55, the Mahatma makes the statement 'Matter is eternal...' In the section 'Summing Up' in *The Secret Doctrine* (1:280, 1978 ed.) HPB elaborates on this. Matter, she says, is 'the Upadhi (the physical basis) for the one Infinite Universal Mind to build thereon its ideations. Therefore the Esotericists maintain that there is no inorganic or dead matter in nature.'

Another comment from *The Tao of Physics* (pp. 202-3) is in agreement with the Mahatma's statement that 'not an atom is ever in an absolute state of rest ...': 'particles are not seen as consisting of any basic "stuff" but as bundles of energy ...

when we observe them, we see dynamic patterns continually changing into one another — a continuous dance of energy'. This is the Dance of Shiva, 'The whole universe is ... engaged in endless motion and activity, in a continual cosmic dance of energy' '(*The Tao of Physics,* p. 225).

'Intelligence', says the Mahatma (p. 55), 'is a faculty that can appertain but to organized or animated being ... Intelligence requires the necessity of thinking; to think one must have ideas; ideas suppose senses which are physical material, and how can anything material belong to pure spirit?'

Then on p. 56, the Mahatma introduces the term 'phlogiston' without definition. It may have something to do with electromagnetism, since on p. 164/161 the Mahatma mentions 'magneto-electric aura — the phlogiston of the sun'. However, in publishing an article entitled 'What is Matter and What is force? (HPB IV: 208) Boris de Zirkoff, the editor, has added a footnote about phlogiston (p. 218):

> This term is derived from the Greek phlogistos, burnt, inflamable, and phlogizein, to set on fire, to burn. It is a term used for the hypothetical principle of fire, or inflammability, regarded as a material substance. The term was proposed by Stahl who, with J.J. Becher, advanced the phlogiston theory. According to them, every combustible substance is a compound of phlogiston, and the phenomena of combustion are due to the phlogiston leaving the other constituents behind. Similarly, metals are produced from their calces (ashes) by the union of the latter with phlogiston. While abandoned now, the theory is not altogether without worth, and has occult implications.

Matter and fire are discussed extensively in the article referred to above. It was written by the Mahatma KH and published in the September 1882 issue of *The Theosophist*. This is how it came to be written: In a lecture given in Madras on 26 April 1882, Col. Olcott made the statement that electricity, like air and water, is matter. One of his hearers, a member of the

Theosophical Society, took issue with this statement and challenged it in a letter to *The Theosophist*. HPB must have referred this letter to the Mahatma for, on p. 8 of LBS, she comments that, among other things to be published in the September issue of *The Theosophist,* is a criticism of Col. Olcott's lecture entitled, 'Is electricity force or matter?' and an answer by the Mahatma KH who, she says, is becoming a 'true penny-a-liner' (LBS. p. 8). In the article, 'What is Matter and What is Force' the Mahatma confirms Olcott's statement from an occult point of view.

It might be well to give one excerpt from the Mahatma's article which has some bearing on the comment in the ML (p. 55). The Mahatma mentions that three states of matter have been known for ages: solid, liquid, and gas. Then along came Sir William Crookes, English physicist and a member of the Theosophical Society, with his discovery of and experiments in what he called 'radiant matter'. The Mahatma calls this 'one of the grandest [discoveries] in science' (HPB 4:223).

> That the three states of matter—the solid, liquid and the gaseous—are so many stages in an unbroken chain of physical continuity, and that the three correlate, or are transformed one into the other by insensible gradations, needs no further demonstration, we believe. But what is of far greater importance to us, Occultists, is the admission made by several great men of science in various articles upon the discovery of that fourth state of matter. Says one of them in the *Scientific American*: 'There is nothing any more improbable in the supposition that these three states of matter do not exhaust the possibilities of material condition, than in supposing the possibilities of sound to extend to aerial undulations to which our organs of hearing are insensible, or the possibilities of vision to ethereal undulations too rapid or too slow to affect our eyes as sight' (HPB IV: 208).

Then the Mahatma goes on to say that 'if a *fourth* state of matter has been discovered ... and a *fourth* dimension of space [by Prof. Zöllner] ... there is nothing impossible [in the idea that] in time there will be discovered a fifth, sixth, and *seventh* condition of matter, as well as seven senses in man, and that all nature will finally be found septenary. For who can assign limits to the possibilities of the latter?'

The Mahatma ends his article with the statement '... Life, whether in its latent or dynamical form, is everywhere ... it is as infinite and as indestructible as matter itself, since neither can exist without the other, and ... electricity is the very essence and origin of—*Life itself.*'

It might be of interest to compare a few statements of Dr Capra's and some of the Mahatma KH's in Letter No. 88 and elsewhere.

In an article entitled 'Holistic Views of Physicists and Mystics' (*The American Theosophist,* May 1979, p. 138), Dr Capra points out that 'subatomic particles' are not 'things' but interconnections between things, and these 'things' are interconnections between other things, and so on. In atomic physics, he says, you never end up with 'things' at all; you always end up with interconnections. What is more, 'The universal interconnectedness of nature always includes the human observer and his or her consciousness in an essential way ... The crucial feature ... is that the human observer is not only necessary even to bring about these properties ... the electron does not have properties independent of my mind.' This gives a view of interconnectedness in which there is no possible separation but only functional specializations which contribute in myriad ways to the universal dynamics. The Mahatma KH deals with interconnectedness more poetically but just as cogently: 'Nature has linked all parts of her Empire together by subtle threads of magnetic sympathy, and there is a mutual correlation between a star and a man.' (ML p. 267/263)

'... matter is never quiescent, but always in a state of motion,' says Dr Capra in the article mentioned immediately above. 'No atom', says the Mahatma KH in Letter No. 88, 'is ever in an absolute state of rest.'

Again Dr Capra, in the same article: 'The basic equilibrium in nature is not static but a dynamic equilibrium. ... Everything in the universe is connected with everything else and no part is fundamental. The properties of any part are determined by the properties of all parts ... Every particle consists of all other particles.' Could there be a clearer statement of the One Life mentioned by the Mahatma in Letter 88 as the only Reality which might be called God?

The Mahatma KH, commenting elsewhere in the Letters on Avalokitesvara as 'both the unmanifested *Father* and the manifested *Son,* the latter proceeding from, and identical with, the other', equates them with 'Parabrahm and the Jivatman, the Universal and the Individualized Seventh Principle' (ML p. 344/338). In yet another letter, referring to the conclusion of an English member that 'we have no God', the Mahatma says: 'He is right—since he applies the name to an extracosmic anomaly, and ... we, knowing nothing of the latter, find each man is *God*—within himself in his own personal, and at the same time, impersonal Avalokitesvara.' (ML p. 393/387)

Whatever we may choose to call this one Reality, it is clear from Letter No. 88 (ML-10) and from other statements in the letters, that the Mahatmas regard it as inextricably and eternally the very fabric of the universe, dynamically operative at every moment in every atom. However subtle or powerful, however inconceivable to our human brains this Reality may be, we can perhaps catch a distant glimpse of what the Mahatma meant when he made the two statements which have baffled, shocked, and even sometimes repelled students. If one may venture a probable oversimplification, one might say that the God which he denies is the 'extracosmic anomaly' for so long the accepted concept; and the Matter which he affirms is the eternally operative device of Divinity.

The letter then contains a section headed 'Our ideas on Evil'. In this section some quite remarkable statements are made.

It would seem advisable to include some comments regarding these statements, especially the ones in the first paragraph.

p. 56: 'Nature is destitute of goodness or malice; she follows only immutable laws ...' Hence there would seem to be no need to be creating 'gods' that have to be propitiated.

p. 57 (top): 'the butterfly devoured by a bird becomes that bird ...' This, he says, 'cannot be called evil in nature'. A response to the question so often raised by some regarding one species of life subsisting upon another species.

p. 57: '... in man whose intelligence makes him the one free agent in Nature'. This is a most profound statement, indicating the marvellous potential of the human entity as well as its great responsibility.

p. 57 (middle of page): The adept here sets forth the origins and causes of evil.

p. 57 (near bottom): '... the chief cause of nearly two-thirds of the evils that pursue humanity ever since that cause became a power. It is religion under whatever form and in whatsoever nation.' This statement raises the hackles of a great many readers, but one has only to look at the situation honestly, both past and present, to see the truth of the statement. The remainder of this paragraph sets forth in forceful statement instances of how it operates.

p. 58: The letter closes with a reference to 'the chain of causation' (the 13 Nidānas), taught in the Buddhist lamaseries, as a solution of the problem of the origin and destruction of suffering. 'From ignorance spring all the evils,' says the Mahatma. 'From knowledge comes the cessation of the mass of misery.'

89 (ML-46)* *Page 268/264* *Folio 2* *Recd. Sept. 1882 (est.)

DESCRIPTION: M to APS

On both sides of two sheets of heavy paper, in M script in heavy lettering and in bright red ink. Rather blotched in appearance.

CIRCUMSTANCES

APS and AOH were in Simla.

This is a letter from the Mahatma M asking a favour of Sinnett. Mainly this seems to be that he try to get Hume under some control and that he help the Mahatma KH in his efforts to save the Simla Eclectic TS which appears to have been degenerating considerably. At this time Hume was still president of that branch.

The letter must have been written just before HPB left for Sikkim, where the Mahatma M was taking her to restore her health.

The Mahatma M seems to feel that KH is too much of a *'perfect Yogi-Arhat'* to bring Hume to some kind of realization of what he is doing. He himself doesn't want to get involved with corresponding with Hume again since that would 'open the way to an endless correspondence' so he is writing to Sinnett to see if he can do anything to control the situation.

This letter is 'typical Morya' full of metaphors and graphic analogies, forceful, direct and to the point.

REFERENCES

p. 268/264 (first sentence): '... to stop the hand ...' Referring to AOH.

p. 269/265: '...even to us well trained in patience'. Another reference to the need for patience, which even the Adepts have to acquire.

p. 269/265: '... send you a telegram and answer on back

on't...' This refers to a telegram dated Sept. 5, written to HPB. She must have sent it on to M. The telegram and letter are in Folio 5 in the British Museum, and are printed as LBS-157, p. 311. They are as follows:

'To A. O. Hume:
Rothney Castle, Jakko, Simla
'From: H. P. Blavatsky:
Bombay, Byculla

Simla 5.9.82.

'Our ways not their ways. Brothers may not care but dare not go against oldest rules. Two Chohans Chelas protested and ten more signed Subba Row first. Dangerous experiments.'

(This undoubtedly refers to the 'HX Letter' and the famous 'Protest' signed by TSR and others.)

Dear Old Lady,

Just received this—not sure I understand it—if the Brothers understand things so little that they allow not only you, but all their chelas to misconceive wholly alike the purport, spirit and practical bearing of a thing, so that they protest against what they ought to give thanks for—I really think the thing is hopeless—and I give up—no ship can make anything of a voyage unless the captain knows navigation—his being a great chemist will not help the matter and the great powers and virtues of the Brothers will not help the Society, if they, the Captains, are so ignorant as this incident seems to indicate of the navigation of the ocean of worldly life. Ta-ta.

Yours ever,
A.O. HUME

p. 269/265: *ayahs'* are nurses. 'hildagos' are noblemen.

'We have allowed him ... to ventilate his animosity ...' Probably this refers to the 'HX Letter', which they made HPB publish in *The Theosophist,* much against her own wishes.

p. 270/266: '... he will persist in making a fool of himself. ...' This evidently is a statement of his displeasure with KH's efforts to keep Hume from breaking with the TS. Another instance where even adepts can disagree on methods of procedure. The final part of the letter refers to his testing of Fern (Hume's secretary) for use as an intermediary in their correspondence and of Fern's failure to meet the test.

90 (ML-22) Page 137/133 Folio 1 Copied by APS Oct 1882 (est.)

DESCRIPTION: KH to AOH

A copy of a portion of a letter from KH to AOH, made by APS on 20 sheets of his usual notepaper. Date of original unknown.

CIRCUMSTANCES

This is another of KH's long technical discussions with AOH. Other circumstances are not known since the date of the letter is uncertain.

Sinnett makes no comment about how this letter came to be written, but it is the compilers' opinion that, after Hume received the Mahatma's notes on his 'Preliminary Chapter on God' [Letter 88 (ML-10)], he wrote again to the Mahatma to take issue with some of the statements, and that this letter is in response.

REFERENCES

This letter seems to be closely related to Letter 88 (ML-10) in subject matter and should be studied in connection with that letter.

Much of what the Mahatma says about the dual aspects of the brain is well known to present day scientists.

p. 138/134: The cerebellum, says the Mahatma, is 'the fountain of the involuntary nerves' which are 'the agents of the unconscious' which controls the involuntary aspects of the human being, or involuntary bodily processes. He adds: '... And weak and uncertain as may be the control of man over his involuntary [?functions], such as the blood circulation, the throbbings of the heart and respiration, especially during sleep—yet how far more powerful, how much more potential [query: should this word be "potent"?] appears man as master and ruler over the blind molecular motion—the *laws* which govern his body (a proof of this being afforded by the phenomenal powers of the Adept and even the common Yogi) than that which you *will* call God, shows over the immutable laws of Nature.'

p. 137/134: The 'infinite Mind [which the Mahatma says they call 'infinite force'] ... exhibits but the functions of its cerebellum, the existence of its supposed cerebrum being admitted ... but on the inferential hypothesis deduced from the Kabalistic theory (correct in every other relation) of the Macrocosm being the prototype of the Microcosm.'

(*Comment:* might it be assumed that, while no physical brain such as we have in our own heads exists at higher levels—or, as we might say, at finer frequencies—in what we regard as Universal Mind, there is something which corresponds to these functions as they appear in us?)

Science up to that time, the Mahatma suggests, had given little consideration to these theories. But here, again, while the language is different, very similar ideas are being advanced and, in many instances, corroborated today.

Freud's discovery of the 'unconscious' (which, unfortunately, he wanted to reduce to physiological and specifically sexual instincts) and Jung's rejection of that dogma and his further researches into the mysterious realm which he called the 'collective unconscious'—a common ocean of knowledge—have given us greater understanding of its vastness and power.

'... only the unconscious', says Dr Heinrich Zimmer, a prominent Jungian psychologist, 'is equal to every exigency. It is the ageless totality, to which nothing new can happen regardless of the situation, and which watches the movement of the ego as nature calmly watches the flowering and fading of her creatures.' *(Spiritual Disciplines,* Pantheon Books. 1960, p. 10.)

Mircea Eliade, in the same volume, p. xviii, comments that 'The discovery of the unconscious could be compared to the maritime discoveries of the Renaissance and the astronomical discoveries made by the invention of the telescope. For each of these discoveries revealed worlds whose very existence had been previously unsuspected.'

The hidden world of the unconscious obeys its own inner laws. Since the Mahatma has mentioned the Cabbalistic theory, it might be of interest to mention that, in the Jungian sense, 'there is a parallel between the hidden, amorphous, unknowable En Sof and the unconscious'. (See *The Myth of Meaning* by Aniela Jaffe, Putnam, 1971, p. 46.)

p. 138/134: In this Letter 90 (ML-22) the Mahatma quotes a Tibetan proverb: 'Everyone is master of his own wisdom, and he is at liberty either to honour or to degrade his slave.'

p. 138/135: The Mahatma goes on to point out that 'It is the peculiar faculty of the involuntary power of the infinite mind ... to be eternally evolving subjective matter into objective atoms [he calls attention to the fact that he uses the term in its relative sense] ... or cosmic matter to be later developed into form. And it is ... the same involuntary ... power that we see so intensely active in all the fixed laws of nature which govern and control what is called the Universe or the Cosmos.'

p. 138/135: He refers again to eternal motion which goes on even during pralaya—for pralaya is 'only the temporary loss of all forms but by no means the destruction of cosmic matter, which is eternal'.

Some modern thinkers hold a view similar to the Mahatma's statements about law, rather than positing *a* moral Governor—'a Being which at the same time has no form but occupies space'.

On p. 140/136 the Mahatma states: '... there is a force as limitless as thought, as potent as boundless will, as subtle as the essence of life, so inconceivably awful in its rending force as to convulse the universe to its centre were it but used as a lever, but this Force is not *God,* since there are men who have learned the secret of subjecting it to their will when necessary'.

He calls attention to the multiplicity of manifestation and states: 'It is the *motion* with its resulting conflict, neutralization, equilibration, correlation, to which is due the infinite variety which prevails.'

p. 141/137: A little further on, the Mahatma says, '... we recognize but one law in the Universe, the law of harmony, of *perfect* EQUILIBRIUM'.

p. 141/138: '... it is one of the elementary and fundamental doctrines of Occultism that the two [spirit and matter] are one, and are distinct but in their respective manifestations, and only in the limited perceptions of the world of senses'. ... Motion is eternal because spirit is eternal.'

p. 142/139: The Mahatma takes up Hume's startling hypothesis that 'sin and suffering are not the result of matter, but may be perchance the wise scheme of the moral Governor of the Universe'. The idea may be conceivable to Hume, he says, but it is utterly inconceivable to him. He asks, 'Must I repeat again that the best Adepts have searched the universe during millenniums and found nowhere the slightest trace of such a Machiavellian schemer—but throughout, the same immutable, inexorable, law.'

Hume has apparently commented that their differences of opinion should make no difference between them personally. But the Mahatma assures him that it makes 'a world of difference' if Hume expects him to teach and he himself

(Hume) to learn. The Mahatma doesn't see how he can teach Hume anything since Hume invariably (and a priori) contradicts the basic teachings in every respect. In the first place, he asks, what is the use of Hume's learning, since he already knows better? In the second place, why should Hume lose the valuable time involved?

p. 143/140: One of the difficulties, the Mahatma assures him, is that in order to learn to read, we have first to learn our letters, but Hume wants—*at once*—to know a mystery 'that is imparted at one of the last initiations'. He mentions that Hume has accused him of 'dodging' his questions. 'Pardon me for contradicting you,' he says, 'but it is nothing of the kind. There are a thousand questions I will never be permitted to answer, and it would be dodging were I to answer you otherwise than I do.'

p. 143/140: Then he adds some very plain words: 'I tell you plainly you are unfit to learn, for your mind is too full and there is not a corner vacant from whence a previous occupant would not arise, to struggle with and drive away the newcomer...' The newcomer, of course, being an unfamiliar and (to Hume) unacceptable idea.

The Mahatma closes with a paragraph which every aspirant could well take to heart.

91 (ML-110) Page 445/437 Folio 3 Recd. Oct. (mid) 1882 (est.)

DESCRIPTION: KH to APS

In blue pencil on three sheets of paper, two unfolded, the third one folded. They seem to have been written as three separate notes, probably on different days. It is not clear why they were grouped together by Barker as one letter.

CIRCUMSTANCES

Sinnett was still at Simla when his letter was received, and

HPB (who had been taken to Sikkim by the Mahatma M because of her serious illness) was resting in a monastery. She had been in Sikkim only a few days.

The letter begins with a reference to the chela, Dharbagiri Nath, probably Babaji, as this was about the time he had lent his body for the use of the Tibetan chela, Guala K. Deb, who used the mystical name Dharbagiri Nath. It will be remembered that the latter was unable to leave Tibet for certain missions which the Mahatma KH wished carried out, and Babaji took his mystical name and acted for him—actually lent his body for this use—and then continued to use the name.

Here the Mahatma speaks of him as 'the little man' which almost certainly means that it was Babaji—at least the physical body was Babaji's. At the same time, the mystery deepens, as Babaji was a probationary chela and Deb was an accepted chela. It may have been Deb acting *through* Babaji, with a strange blending of identity which is very difficult to comprehend.

REFERENCES

Dharbagiri Nath has got himself into trouble. It seems that while he was travelling from one area to another, he lost money which had been entrusted to him and was afraid to approach the Mahatma about it. Instead, he wired another chela, Ram S. Gargya. The telegram was intercepted by one of the lamas in the monastery where the Mahatma was staying and the lama passed the information on to him.

The Mahatma sends 50 rupees (presumably the amount Dharbagiri Nath had lost) to Sinnett with the request that he give them to this chela the next time he sees him. This, again, indicates that it was the person of Babaji, as Deb was in Tibet and Sinnett would not have seen him.

Then the Mahatma adds: 'My friend, I am afraid you too have again been imprudent. I have a letter from Colonel Chesney—very polite and quite diplomatic. Several such messages may do for an excellent refrigerator.'

Sinnett was not always discreet; he was inclined to be over-eager and impulsive. It will be remembered that the Mahatma had sent Sinnett a letter which he had written to Col. Chesney in response to a letter he had received from him (ML p. 447/440). At the same time the Mahatma received a letter from Sinnett asking him not to correspond with the Colonel. Sinnett had been trying to interest him in the Theosophical Society and had even gone to the length of asking that the Mahatma send him a portrait of himself. At any rate, he seems to have bungled the matter, and the Colonel must have taken offense, with the result mentioned here. It seems that Col. Chesney became alienated because he thought some articles published in *The Theosophist* were anti-Christian and that Theosophy was hostile only to Christianity. (See ML, p. 317/312)

The next segment of this letter contains a reference to a reprint in the *Pioneer* of an article which had appeared in the English magazine, *Vanity Fair.* The Mahatma KH indicates that he had previously asked Sinnett to publish something by this author but that Sinnett had refused, thinking he did not write well enough for the *Pioneer*. Now, his articles had been accepted by a prominent English magazine. The Adept seems to be taking the occasion to 'rub it in' to Sinnett a little.

p. 445/438: Next the Mahatma mentions 'poor Padshah'. We have met him before. The Mahatma had enclosed a poem by him for Sinnett's evaluation. Perhaps Sinnett published it in the *Pioneer,* since here the Mahatma seems rather gratified.

Next the Mahatma says, '... Hume writes to HPB (a most *loving* letter)'. Hume enclosed two copies of a letter of his to the *Pioneer* which he wishes reprinted in *The Theosophist*. The Mahatma believes it is too political.

p. 445/438: The Mahatma then comments briefly on the anniversary of the Eclectic Theosophical Society. About this time, Hume had resigned as President of that group and Sinnett was elected to the office on October 8.

The conclusion to this segment of the letter concerns HPB's visit to Sikkim where she stayed for a few days with M and KH and was restored to better health. She remained in Darjeeling for a period of time resting from the trip.

The last section of this letter has again to do with 'the little man'—although now called 'the little wretch'—Dharbagiri Nath (or Babaji) who was apparently rather irresponsible where money was concerned. This time he had borrowed 30 rupees from Sinnett and the Mahatma KH had just learned of it. He is embarrassed and returns the money to Sinnett, at the same time asking understanding of Babaji.

In closing, the Mahatma tells Sinnett he is writing him a long letter 'by fits and starts' and 'I will send another with answers to your questions'. These will be the next two letters to be considered. He also promises to tell Sinnett 'a ludicrous thing' that happened in connection with a letter from C.C. Massey. This too is related in the next letter, and is usually referred to as the 'Goat Story'.

'Hail and success to the new President at last!' This, of course, is a reference to Sinnett's election as President of the Simla Eclectic, which had just taken place.

Two lines following the signature ask pardon for an 'unavoidable delay', saying that the letter cannot reach Darjeeling before four or five days. The letter was written from the Phari Jong Monastery in Tibet, just across the border from Sikkim, and perhaps was carried by messenger to HPB who was in Darjeeling, so that she could forward it from within the Indian postal service.

92 (ML-54) Page 302/298 Folio 2 Recd. Oct. (mid) 1882 (est.)

DESCRIPTION: KH to APS

This very long letter is in heavy KH script in dark blue ink on 17 full-sized sheets of white paper. The last two sheets are somewhat larger than the others. Some words have been erased, some have been corrected, and others have been scratched out. The writing is somewhat heavier than usual.

CIRCUMSTANCES

APS and AOH were in Simla. HPB had just returned from Sikkim where she had visited her Master and KH, and was resting for a while in Darjeeling near the Sikkim border. KH, according to his statements, was in Phari Jong, a large monastery in Tibet, just across the Sikkim border, on the route to Lhasa.

It seems probable that this letter was dictated mentally to a chela and then precipitated, if the prohibition against this method of communication had by that time been removed. It may have been transported by messenger to Darjeeling so that it could be delivered to Sinnett through the Indian postal service.

REFERENCES

p. 302/298: The opening paragraph concerns Hume's resignation as president of the Simla Eclectic Theosophical Society and the Mahatma confesses that he had something to do with it. Hume has done nothing whatever for the 'hapless "Eclectic" ' and has 'tampered with historical facts'. He encloses Hume's last letter to him (LBS pp. 304-5). Hume is entirely 'under the influence of his new guru—"the good Vedantin Swami"... his argument is ... that with the "good old Swami" he will at any rate learn *something,* while with us it is impossible for him to "ever learn anything" '. There are a few other quoted excerpts from Hume's letter.

The 'good Vedantin Swami' was known as the Swami from Almora—Almora being a hill-station in North India. He had written some articles on Advaitism with which Subba Row had disagreed vigorously. In a letter to Sinnett (LBS, p. 82) HPB mentions this Swami and says he planned to 'expose the Masters as Dugpas'. He died shortly after Hume turned to him for the study which he felt he could not get with the Mahatmas.

The Mahatma goes on to say that he would not like to see Hume sever his connection with the Society. His literary contributions are valuable, but in addition he would be sure to become 'an indefatigable, though *secret* enemy'.

p. 303/298: Then Fern is mentioned: 'One word of advice—an earnest warning from both of us: *trust not little Fern—beware of him.*' It will be remembered that the Mahatma M took some interest in Fern because of his considerable psychic abilities. But he was completely untrustworthy and had eventually to be expelled from the Society —a very rare situation indeed. The Mahatma asks Sinnett to try to save him, but to watch him closely for he could bring the Society to ruin.

p. 304/299: So many subjects are covered in this letter. The next is C.C. Massey, a member of the Society in London but more interested in Spiritualism than in Theosophy. He was, it will be remembered, present at the founding meeting of the Theosophical Society on 17 November 1875 and he was the first president of the British Theosophical Society. The British branch of the Society had lost some momentum and apparently Massey was being instrumental in helping to revive it. The Mahatma says he has no objection to teaching them through Sinnett. Nevertheless, he cannot undertake to furnish either the British TS or Sinnett himself with any *new* facts until what has already been given is put into shape and taught systematically.

p. 304/299: 'Mrs K. and her scribe ...' A reference to Anna Kingsford and Edward Maitland.

p. 304/299: '... such bigots as Wyld'. Dr George Wyld, President of the TS in London, was apparently very orthodox. See M's comments about him on p. 271/267. See Alphabetical Notes.

p. 304/300: '... Typhon and Ahriman ...' Typhon was the dark side of Osiris, i.e. the dark side of Deity. Ahriman was similarly the dark side of Ahura Mazda with the Zoroastrians. Both symbolize generally the spirit of evil.

p. 305/300: 'Let the *Fragments* ...': the series of articles entitled 'Fragments of Occult Truth' published in *The Theosophist*.

p.305/301: One of the places where KH indicates that he does not approve of the publication of his letters without their being properly edited.

'... introduce Eglinton... and to demonstrate + ...' See Alphabetical Notes on Eglinton and Imperator.

p. 306/301: 'Hurrychund Chintamon of Bombay ...' See Alphabetical Notes; ODL-2: Ch. 2; SH, pp. 106, 120, 126.

'Dayanand ...' Swami Dayanand Saraswati, leader of the Arya Samaj Movement. See Alphabetical Notes and App C.

'Dr Billing ...' Dr Hollis-Billing, husband of the well-known American medium. See Alphabetical Notes.

p. 307/303: 'C. Carter Blake ...' See Alphabetical Notes.

'... This made secret enemy—No. 3...' Presumably meaning Blake, Hollis-Billing, and Hurrychund Chintamon.

p. 308/303: '...Swami's unexpected attack...' Swami Dayanand had been an associate of the Founders, but had now turned on them. A sad example of how even a person who has passed the first two initiations can fail.

p. 308/304: 'While in London, at the Billings ...' When HPB and HSO stopped in London in 1879 on their way to India, they stayed at the home of Dr and Mrs Billing. While there, HPB produced some phenomena. See SH, p. 123.

'...the July Supplement...': the Supplement to *The Theosophist* for July 1882. The entire Supplement deals with HSO's answers to charges made by Dayanand. See Appendix C.

'...D. Swami...' Dayanand.

p. 309/304: 'Note the bare-faced lies of India's "great Reformer" ' i.e., Swami Dayanand.

p. 309/304: '...at Badrinath...' A holy place in the Himalayas.

p. 309-10/305: is mainly concerned with conditions of chelaship.

p. 310/305: 'You will perhaps inquire', asks the Mahatma, 'why *we* have not interfered?' He does not believe he can make Sinnett understand, for the explanation obviously involves the rules and disciplines under which the Mahatmas work. It is here that the Mahatma makes that important statement: 'The fact is, that to the last and supreme initiation every chela—(and even some adepts)—is left to his own device and counsel. We have to fight our own battles, and the familiar adage—"the adept *becomes,* he is not *made*" is true to the letter.... Life and the struggle for adeptship would be too easy, had we all scavengers behind us to sweep away the *effects* we have generated through our own rashness and presumption.'

p. 311/306: '...since MOTIVE is everything for us...': an indication of the high value that the Adepts place upon motive.

p. 312/307-8: '... portrait of the "fakir" Tiravalla mentioned in *Hints* ...' See ODL-I, 367-9, for picture mentioned and HSO's account of its production. *Hints* refers to the book, *Hints on Esoteric Theosophy,* consisting of letters from several persons, first published in 1882 and republished in 1909.

'... my portrait by Djual Khool'. See Letter 95 (ML-53) and Letter 78 (ML-51).

p. 315/310-11: '... bid me arrange the "theosophical" marriage...' This has reference to the marriage of Minnie Hume (only daughter of AOH) to Ross Scott (see Alphabetical Notes). The 'arrangement' was a strange incident. See LBS p. 15.

Ross Scott was a young man who came to India on the same boat as the Founders. He had an injured leg. He became interested in Theosophy and took an active part in the work for a few years.

It will be noted that there is no mention of Mrs (Minnie) Hume Scott in the meeting recorded in ODL 5:154. In LBS p. 44, in a letter to Mrs Sinnett, HPB says: 'Poor Minnie Scott is getting blind, she is at the Jhut-Sing's [her father's] paternal residence.' And it will be noted also, from Olcott's mention of meeting her father on their way to England, that she went home with him. Perhaps she and Ross Scott eventually separated. What actually happened is not revealed. She is not mentioned in the item about being entertained in Scott's home (ODL 6: 298). According to Appendix B in the *Guide,* Hume lived in England from 1887 on, but 'for some years nearly every cold season saw him back in India'. It is suggested that he could well have been taking Minnie Hume Scott back to England to live in 1894.

p. 316/311. The Mahatma turns again to the case of Fern and points out that his case affords 'a useful study and a hint' concerning methods adopted in individual cases to test 'the latent moral qualities...' He adds: 'We are no more at liberty to withhold the chance from a postulant than we are to guide and direct him into the proper course. ... We were all so tested; ... there is no such other difficult struggle. If it were not so, adeptship would be but a cheap acquirement.'

p. 315/311 (bottom): '... while a Moorad Ali—*failed* —I, succeeded'. Mizra Moorad Ali Beg—real name Godolphin Mitford. (See Alphabetical Notes.)

p. 320/315: 'I cannot close without telling you ...' See Letter 91 (ML-110), p. 446/439, where KH promises this story. This is one of the most fascinating (and instructive) incidents in ML. It gives an insight into the ways of occultism and the limitations and abilities of adeptship. What KH could not do for himself, he was able to do for the goat, reminding one of the accusation made against Jesus that he was able to help others but could not help himself.

p. 321/316: The Mahatma again refers to 'the little man' and apologizes to Sinnett for his 'several indiscretions'. 'I believe you will not complain of my letter being too short. It is going to be soon followed by another voluminous correspondence, "Answers to your many Questions". H.P.B. is *mended,* if not thoroughly at least for some time to come.'

93 A & B (ML-23 A & B) Pages 145/141 & 149/145
Folio 2 Recd. Oct. 1882.

DESCRIPTION: KH to APS

The first part of this letter consists of a long list of questions from APS to KH, written on notepaper. Some marginal notes and underlinings have been made by KH in blue pencil and some reference numbers inserted. Part B consists of KH's answers to APS's questions, on full-sized sheets of paper, some folded, some single sheets. The first part is on a rippled white paper, and the latter part is on a smooth, bright pink paper. The KH script is in dull black ink through the answer to Q. 5, then changes to pale blue ink. There are a few marks in blue pencil. The letter gives the impression of having been written intermittently. (See p. 446/439 and p. 321/371.)

In the original in the British Museum, the answers by the Mahatma KH to the second series of questions give the impression of having been written intermittently, as the ink is slightly different in various places.

CIRCUMSTANCES

The Mahtama KH mentioned in two previous letters that he would be answering Sinnett's questions in another letter soon. This is that letter.

Fortunately, again we have both sides of the correspondence: both questions and answers. Sinnett's questions seem to be in two sections, and the Mahatma has inserted marginal comments on those questions in the first section; the marginal comments are shown in bold type.

Due to the lack of a specific date, the circumstances are a little uncertain. It may have been that Sinnett was still in Simla and that HPB was still resting in Darjeeling after her trip to Sikkim.

REFERENCES

p. 144/141: '...our "Jakko" friend': A.O. Hume. This is one of several names that the Masters used in referring to Hume. Jakko was the name of the hill in Simla where Hume had his large house called 'Rothney Castle'. It seems that KH had sent Lewis's notes to Hume for translation into English. Apparently Hume was fluent in French also.

p. 145/141: It is interesting that when APS politely requests KH to tell him something regarding his past life, the Master politely declines to do so, only indicating that '...some day I may treat you to a little story... only I promise no details ...and a hint or two to test your intuitional powers'.

One such hint appears in a curious item in the British Museum archives which Barker failed to include in the printed book. This item seems to relate to an incarnation of Sinnett's in Rome in the early days of the Christian Era. It is described in Appendix I attached hereafter entitled 'The Triumph of Germanicus', which see.

p. 149/146: This explanation regarding the cumulative effects of the 'peaking' of several cycles at the same time may have a bearing on the reason for the population explosion of the twentieth century.

p. 150/147: 'Cendrillon' is French for Cinderella.

p. 151/147: '...the Eocene age...' The student is cautioned to exercise care in the consideration of names used in ML and SD for geological periods, as they do not always correspond to today's designations.

It might be well to mention here two valuable books by Elizabeth Preston, *Earth and Its Cycles* and *Life and Its Spirals,* both published by the Theosophical Publishing House.

The first of these books deals with the various Rounds and geological eras, bringing in the subject of the different Root Races. Most theosophical students are familiar with the doctrine of the Rounds and know that we are said to be somewhat past the middle of the Fourth Round in a series of Seven Rounds, which will complete this particular Manvantara, or life wave. It was fairly early in the Fourth Round that our First Root Race appeared, although the first two could hardly 'appear' since they were etheric. This Fourth Round is, of course, our human stage. The Monads (which constitute our true identity) have gone all the Rounds so far: in the first Round brooding over the mineral kingdom, drawing it along in its evolution; in the second, performing the same function in the vegetable kingdom; in the third, the animal kingdom. It was not until the Fourth Round that we reached and incarnated in the human kingdom. Even the first efforts at that were not entirely successful. But finally we had help from more advanced beings. Of course, using the pronoun 'we' is incorrect; it is used for convenience. The reference is actually to the Monads, not to the personalities we now think of as ourselves.

The second book, *Life and Its Spirals,* deals with the Races more in the light of the development of consciousness, or 'history in the light of Theosophy'. The term Root Race is unfortunate; it has nothing to do with ethnic groups but refers to what Geoffrey A. Barborka has termed 'a developmental evolutionary' phase. It is rather startling to see how the doctrine of the Rounds and Races more or less fits into the scientific findings of geological periods.

The 'Sons of Ad'—or the Children of the Fire Mist—were those called the 'Elect' of the Third Root Race, who had learned the secret of immortality; sometimes called the 'Elect Race'. There is quite a bit about them in *The Secret Doctrine* (see index) but the simplest definition to the compilers' knowledge is given by Geoffrey Barborka in *The Divine Plan,* p. 293:

The 'Elect Race' is known by several names, the Sons of Will and Yoga, the Sons of the Fire-Mist, the Sons of Ad, the Hierarchy of the elect. It was produced by Kriyasakti (by will-power and yoga) in the first or earlier portion of the Third Race (before the separation of the sexes) while it was yet in its state of purity.

p. 155/152: '...'Baron d'Holbach...' a French philosopher (1723-89) friend of others who were so influential in the Enlightenment. He is remembered chiefly as a stalwart opponent of all positive religion. Man, he held, is innately moral but perverted by education.

p. 156-7/153: This is an indication that humanity must progress essentially as a mass and that natural law does not allow any group or race to get too far beyond its appointed goal.

There are some very interesting statements made in this section of the discussion regarding the rise and fall of civilizations, especially that pertaining to our fifth root race.

p. 163-4/160: This is the point where the colour of the paper changes to pink for the remainder of the letter.

p. 165/162: *'Maha Yug', Maha Yuga,* the aggregate of four Yugas, or ages, of 4,320,000 years; 1000th part of a Day of Brahma which is 4,320,000,000 years. See calculations in *The Secret Doctrine,* which gives the chronology of the Brahmans.

On p. 169/166, the Mahatma speaks of Edison's tasimeter (an electrical instrument for measuring the expansion of solids) and says that Edison was 'a good deal protected by M'. Edison was a member of the Theosophical Society; his cheque in payment of his first dues is still preserved in the archives at the international headquarters.

p. 173/170: KH here gives an explanation of much of the phenomena connected with mediumship.

p. 175/171: This is perhaps the 'hint' mentioned on page 145/142, regarding a former incarnation of Sinnett. See note above with reference to page 145/142. See Appendix I for details.

p. 176/173: Answer No.23. This statement has caused much controversy among Theosophists.

p. 177/173: Answer No.27. A reference to Guiteau, the assassin of President Garfield. See Alphabetical Notes.

94 (ML-117) Page 443 Folio 3 Recd. Oct. 1882 (est.)

DESCRIPTION: KH to APS

In blue pencil on a postcard cut down to about 2″x5″. Heavy KH script on front and back.

CIRCUMSTANCES

APS was still in Simla. The card was to introduce one of the Indian chelas, Mohini M. Chatterjee (see Alphabetical Notes) to APS, and probably he presented the card when he called.

When Col. Olcott opened the first Theosophical Sunday School in Calcutta on 10 March 1883, almost six months after this card was received by Sinnett, Mohini was the teacher of the 17 boys involved. Later, he travelled about a good deal with the Founders and, at the request of the Mahatma KH, accompanied them to Europe in 1884. He stayed for a while in the home of the Sinnetts who had by then gone to live permanently to England. He will be met frequently in some of the letters still to be studied.

Mohini remained in Europe until 1887, when he returned to India to practise law. The purpose of his trip to Europe was apparently to give the members of the Society there some assistance in understanding the Eastern doctrines. With Mrs Laura C. Holloway, an American widow and clairvoyant, he collaborated in writing *Man, Fragments of Forgotten History*. He failed as a chela and resigned from the Theosophical Society in 1887. He is mentioned a great many times in the

Mahatma Letters and in the letters from HPB to Sinnett. HPB comments in one place that there were some serious errors in the book he and Mrs Holloway wrote (LBS, p. 288). However, the principal difficulty seems to have been that he came under the influence of Babaji (who turned bitterly against HPB while he was in Europe and also succeeded in turning some prominent Theosophists against her), and Mohini himself became involved in some scandals in Paris. At any rate, he seems not to have been able to remain steadfast in his loyalties.

REFERENCES

There is no way of knowing precisely what Mohini's mission to Sinnett was, but that it concerned the end of the cycle referred to several times in these letters in the fall of 1882 seems indicated. This end of a cycle was, of course, the completion of the first seven years of the Theosophical Society. This seven year cycle for the Theosophical Society seems to have been a probationary one for the accomplishment of certain objectives and was considered by the two Adepts to be a critical one.

95 (ML-72) Page 374/368 Folio 3 Recd. Nov. (early) 1882 (est.)

DESCRIPTION: KH to APS

In blue pencil on a single sheet of heavy note paper, about 4″ x 5″.

CIRCUMSTANCES

APS had returned to Allahabad. This letter deals with the problems which MMC (Mohini) and 'the little Doctor' (not otherwise identified) had come to discuss with APS.

REFERENCES

See Letter 94 (ML-117), p. 450/443, introducing MMC and mentioning his purpose in calling on APS. This letter was apparently written in time to reach APS with the arrival of the visitors, or perhaps they delivered the letter personally.

'Before the cycle ends...': refers again to 17 November 1882.

The 'Prayag Fellows' means the TS members in Allahabad. In Letter 36 (ML-36) M calls them 'fools and arrogant men'.

96 (ML-92) Page 419/413 Folio 3 Dated Nov. 23, 1882

DESCRIPTION: KH to APS

On a single sheet of 5" x 7" canary yellow notepaper in KH script, in bright red ink. It is marked 'P.S.' but no indication is given as to which letter it follows.

CIRCUMSTANCES

APS was at home in Allahabad: HPB was in Bombay, having visited the Sinnetts on her return trip from Darjeeling to Bombay.

REFERENCES

This letter gives APS and AOH the 'passwords' which hereafter are to appear on any genuine message from the Adepts coming through mediums. See Letter 83 (ML-125) in which DK announces that these three secret words will be given.

See also Letter 118 (ML-96) to APS in London in which M reminds him of these passwords.

97 (ML-70) Page 373/367 Folio 3 Recd. Dec. 1882 (est.)

DESCRIPTION: KH to APS

This short note is on one side of a half sheet of heavy notepaper, size 5″ x 8″, in blue pencil. On the back side is the ending of another letter signed by a woman. The half sheet was evidently torn from some other letter. Another instance of the fact that the Adepts utilized any type of paper that was readily available.

CIRCUMSTANCES

Since the date is not known with certainty, it is difficult to know the circumstances. It is possible that the letter was received during the summer of 1884.

Perhaps the actual place of this letter in the chronology is less important than the fact that apparently Sinnett was still longing for personal contact with the Mahatma, and the Mahatma had still to say, 'not yet'.

Actually, there is nothing in the letter that indicates with certainty that it was addressed to Sinnett.

98 (ML-105) Page 441/434 Folio 3 Recd. Dec. 1882 (est.)

DESCRIPTION: KH to APS

KH script in black ink, on two sheets of white paper, one folded and the other flat.

CIRCUMSTANCES

Sinnett had just received his notice of termination as editor of *The Pioneer* and had been given a year's salary as severance pay.

It will be remembered that during the Sinnetts' trip to England in 1881, Sinnett had his first book, *The Occult World,* published. The book, familiar to most students of Theosophy, deals largely with phenomena produced by HPB and includes information about the Mahatmas with whom Sinnett had come into correspondence through her. It made a profound impression upon the public at the time, but it earned Sinnett the displeasure of the Anglo-Indian community and alienated the proprietors of *The Pioneer,* of which he was editor. His relations with them from that time on were uneasy. Then there came a change in management: an Englishman by the name of Rattigan purchased the newspaper. He was even less sympathetic with Sinnett and apparently had no reluctance (or perhaps fewer inhibitions) about getting rid of him.

Finally, in November 1882, Sinnett was given notice of the termination of his services as editor of this important newspaper.

REFERENCES

p. 441/434: '...your business letter ...': presumably informing KH that he had just received notice of the termination of his position and possibly suggesting the establishment of another newspaper to promote political freedom in India. While no copy of APS's letter is available, subsequent correspondence indicates that this was its substance.

So we have the inception of what has been called 'The Phoenix Venture'. The letters concerning this matter are grouped together in the book, although, as usual, they concern many other topics.

Since Sinnett's letter is not available it cannot be determined whether he suggested that the Mahatma consult the Mahachohan about the matter. It is probable that he did not, for he would almost certainly have felt that it would be presumptuous to make such a suggestion.

However, the Mahatma begins his reply with the words, 'Before I give you any definite answer to your business letter I desire to consult our venerable Chohan.'

It seems that the Mahatma himself foresaw that this matter might have far-reaching consequences and for that reason he himself wanted to consult the Mahachohan.

p. 442-43/434-35: '...H.P.B. has just quarrelled with Djual Khool...' 'The unpleasant proceeding' mentioned in this paragraph and the next was a meeting of the Eclectic TS in Simla, when HPB and APS were visiting AOH there in 1881, to consider a letter from S.K. Chatterji (not otherwise identified) to AOH in which Chatterji expressed contempt for Theosophy and HPB. Apparently AOH sent this letter to KH to read and KH returned it to him via HPB. The statement at the end of the paragraph that 'D. Khool ...had heard it himself' would indicate that DK was present in his subtle body, as he was not present physically, and was invisible to others except HPB. The difficulty between HPB and DK concerned their differing recollections of this event.

p. 442/435: '..."fertility of resources" at the command of our mutual friend'. A reference to Hume, of course.

'Lord Ripon's high opinion...' Lord Ripon was Viceroy of India at that time.

Apparently KH was much concerned about the damage that Hume might do to their efforts.

99 (ML-78) Page 378/372 Folio 3 Recd. Dec. 1882 (est.)

DESCRIPTION: KH to APS

KH script in black ink, on four sheets of letter-size smooth paper, light in weight and bright pink in colour. Fine lettering on both sides of paper.

CIRCUMSTANCES

The new TS headquarters in Adyar had been purchased and HPB and HSO were in Bombay, getting ready for the move to Adyar. APS was in Allahabad. As noted in Letter 98 (ML-105), he had received notice that his editorship of *The Pioneer* was being terminated. This had come about as the result of a change in management, and probably because of their dissatisfaction with his interest in Theosophy and association with Theosophists. In Study Notes on 98 (ML-105), it was indicated that he had asked the advice of the Mahachohan concerning the possibility of a new newspaper venture. This letter is largely concerned with KH's report of the Mahachohan's ideas on the subject.

REFERENCES

p. 380/374 (following item IX): '...the good and sincere Norendro Babu...': proprietor and editor of the *Indian Mirror* of Calcutta. A pupil of KH. D, pp.147, 185.

p.381/375: '...the 5 lakhs ...' A lakh represents the figure 100,000; in this instance it refers to rupees.

'...over such heads as Rattigan's and Walker's '. These were the new owners of *The Pioneer*.

p. 381/375: 'Our friend foams with rage ...' A reference to AOH presumably, who was apparently writing vitriolic letters about HPB, the Mahatmas, the Theosophial Society, etc., to C.C. Massey and Stainton Moses in London. 'And this is the man who swore his word of honour but the other day that he would *never* injure the Society, whatever may be his opinion of us personally!'

Hume has, he says, placed himself under the influence of the Dugpas.

100 (ML-79) Page 382/376 Folio 3 Recd. mid-Dec. 1882 (est.)

DESCRIPTION: KH to APS

KH script in blue pencil on a sheet of folded heavy notepaper, both sides in heavy lettering.

CIRCUMSTANCES

Similar to previous letter, 99 (ML-78).

REFERENCES

The greater part of this letter deals with the establishment of the new newspaper for Sinnett to edit; i.e., *The Phoenix*.

p. 382/376: (first paragraph): Mr Dare.' This man was proposed as the treasurer and business manager of the new newspaper. While Sinnett was recognized as an outstanding editor, apparently he was not considered to be a very good business executive.

(Third paragraph): There is a hint here, also, that Sinnett was, even this early, thinking of returning to England, perhaps leaving *The Phoenix* (the name selected for the new newspaper) in other hands. It seems that he must have commented in his letter to the Mahatma that he would remain in India for the Mahatma's sake alone. In this, the Mahatma tells him, he is 'wrong...*very* wrong'. He does not feel 'selfish enough to accept the sacrifice ...' In the same paragraph, the Mahatma tells Sinnett why he cannot help the venture occultly: '...the strict law of justice forbids us to do aught to lessen in the slightest degree the merit to which *he who* shall make the dream a reality will be entitled'.

p. 382/376 (last paragraph): The annual convention was held a little early this year due to the impending move of the headquarters from Bombay to Adyar. Sinnett attended this meeting and took an active part in it.

KH thanks APS for attending the December 7 TS Convention in Bombay and taking part in the proceedings.

SH p. 174, says of this convention: 'It was a "grand success". Fifteen delegates from all parts of India were present. Mme Coulomb had made a fine new crimson banner of the Parent Society, and thirty-nine shields were inscribed with the names of Branches. There was a crowded audience, for apparently the public was admitted. Mr Sinnett was in the Chair.'

(bottom): 'The dead-point of the revolving cycle is past...' 17 November 1882, the end of the first seven-year period of the TS, on which the Adepts placed so much importance.

'...a new one begins ...on the 17th of December': the date on which Headquarters was to be moved from Bombay to Adyar.

101 (ML-57) Page 327/322 Folio 2 Recd. Jan. 6, 1883

DESCRIPTION: KH to APS

KH script on 9 small folded sheets of white paper. The type of ink is difficult to describe. Brownish-black in places which often fades into a sort of sepia with great variation in density of colour. Some words have been scratched out, and in one place there is some interlining in *red ink*; on page 3 just following the 'festina lente' motto, the next paragraph is in a dull red ink. The final two pages are on larger-sized paper. On the folded sheet, a portion of the writing is in dull red ink.

CIRCUMSTANCES

The TS Headquarters had just been moved to Adyar on December 17, and the Founders were there. APS was also in Madras, presumably on a business trip in connection with plans for his projected newspaper. The chief theme of the letter is the exposing of some of AOH's machinations—what KH calls (p.335/330) 'an unpleasant and distasteful task'.

To refresh the memory of the student: Massey was a leading member of the Theosophical Society in London. He was also a prominent Spiritualist. His principal weakness seems to have been that he accepted as gospel truth everything derogatory that anyone told him about the Society, HPB, the Mahatmas, etc. Now, it seems that Hume had been writing to him and he had taken his statements as unimpeachable evidence; as a result he wrote to the Mahatma. This is the letter enclosed by the Mahatma in Letter 101. We have to conjecture what was in Massey's letter, although some of it becomes apparent as the Mahatma proceeds.

p. 327/323: '...third on the list of failures...' This refers to C.C. Massey. The other two were AOH and Fern, whom KH discusses at considerable length in this letter. About mid-page 328/323, KH comments: 'Four Europeans were placed on probation twelve months ago; of the four—only one, yourself, was found worthy of our trust.'

'...the proposed new branch in London...' The TS in London had nearly collapsed and was not active. Efforts were being made to rejuvenate it under the leadership of Mrs Anna Kingsford.

Mrs Kingsford was, it will be remembered, an English author and Spiritualist who, with her co-worker and collaborator, Edward Maitland, promoted a Hermetic approach to Christianity and metaphysics. During 1882, they had published the book, *The Perfect Way,* which Sinnett had reviewed in *The Theosophist,* his review being 'more perfect' than the book itself, according to a word of praise from the Mahatma.

In Josephine Ransom's *A Short History of the Theosophical Society* it is stated that Kingsford changed the name of the London 'Branch' to 'Lodge', the first use of that term in connection with theosophical groups.

It seems, according to the Mahatma (p. 328/323) that Mrs Kingsford was claiming that before *The Perfect Way* was published, 'no one "knew what the Oriental school really held about Reincarnation"; and adds that "seeing how much has been told in that book the adepts are hastening to unlock their own treasures ..." ' Massey gave entire credence to this statement and 'blossoms into an adroit compliment to the lady that would not discredit a plenipotentiary'.

p. 329/324 (top): '...a fifth rounder...' A person whose consciousness is far in advance of the mass of humanity, which is said to be in the fourth of seven great cyclic progressions. KH speaks of 'natural clairvoyance' as being one of its characteristics. In SD 3, p. 175 (Adyar ed.), fifth rounders are spoken of as 'prematurely developed intellects'; they represent extreme exceptions.

p. 329/324: 'Better than your Wren...': a reference to Sir Christopher Wren

'...the motto, *festina lente*!' Make haste slowly.

The Mahatma asks Sinnett to write to Massey and disabuse his mind of the idea that it was Mrs Kingsford who first introduced the idea of reincarnation.

A few comments about Mrs Kingsford may be appropriate here. She was a vegetarian and an anti-vivisectionist, and in one place the Mahatma states that for these reasons her phenomena were more reliable than those of most well-known Spiritualists. HPB did not have a very high opinion of Mrs Kingsford, dubbed her 'the Divine Anna', and made several scathing references to her at times. According to one letter from HPB to Sinnett (LBS p.22) it was Massey who first proposed her name as President of the British Theosophical Society.

p. 329/324: Allan Kardec, mentioned here, was a French Spiritualist. His real name was Hippolite L.D. Rivail, but he preferred to be known by the names which he said he had borne in two previous lives—Allan and Kardec. He and HPB disagreed on the constitution of man, Kardec maintaining that man had but two principles—spirit (or soul, which he confused with spirit) and body. Apparently he taught personal rebirth rather than Egoic reincarnation.

p.330/325: '...to bring out their mutual virtues and defects...' It would appear from this that Fern and AOH had served as mutual catalysts in being tested for chelaship.

p.331/326 (near bottom): '...scorched in the candle of Rothney Castle...' AOH's house.

p.331/326: 'That new Avatar does not live at Almorah but on Jakko...' Reference to the fact that AOH considered himself superior to the Swami from Almora in whom he had become interested. As previously noted, 'Jakko' refers to the hill on which the Hume house was situated. See Study Notes on 92 (ML-54).

p.331/326: 'And so the demon—vanity—which has ruined Dayanand...' An interesting comment on what caused the Swami's failure, when it is indicated that he had passed the third Initiation.

p.332/327: 'P. Sreenevas Row, Judge S.C.C....' Judge of the Superior Civil Court.

p. 332/327: '...until the time of Sonkapa...' Son-Kha-Pa or Tsong-kha-pa, Tibetan Buddhist reformer of the 14th century.

'...the HX letter in *The Theosophist* ...' See Study Notes on 81 (ML-52). See Appendix D.

p. 334/329: '...a certain amount of *Pranayam*...' Pranayama—regulation and suppression of the breath, sometimes called the 'practice of the Five Breaths'. According to SD 5, p. 479, (4th ed.) the word means literally the 'death of (vital) breath'. In the same volume, p.486, is the statement that 'it results, for the practiser, in death—in moral death always, and in physical death very frequently'.

p. 336/330: In his final paragraph, the Mahatma makes a surprising suggestion: 'Unless you go to London and with C.C.M.'s help explain the true situation and establish the Society *yourself,* Mr Hume's letter will have done too much harm to undo the mischief.' He suggests that Sinnett might use some of his time while on such a holiday to do some 'theosophical writing'.

The Mahatma seems to have made his suggestion with the thought that Sinnett would return. As will be seen, Sinnett did go back to England with his family, but he did not return to India. He did use his time to write *Esoteric Buddhism*. It was published on 10 June 1883.

102 (ML-56) Page 325/320 Folio 2 Recd. Jan. 1883 (est.)

DESCRIPTION: KH to APS

KH script on two folded sheets of heavy white paper, about 4" x 7", on both sides, fine lettering in dull blue ink.

CIRCUMSTANCES

Similar to previous letter, 101 (ML-57). APS had evidently returned to Allahabad from his Madras trip.

Probably Sinnett had replied to the Mahatma's last letter, in which Hume was painted in rather dark colours. Now the Mahatma asks him to be lenient—or at least, prudent—with Hume because of an element which, while it does not excuse the things he had done, does mitigate the situation somewhat. He is, says the Mahatma, 'pushed on and half maddened by evil powers, which he has attracted to himself'. Near him lives a fakir who has an 'animalizing aura about him'. Also, some parting curses visited on him by Fern when he left Hume's employment are not entirely without effect.

It really appears that Hume must have become, temporarily at least, somewhat unbalanced. He apparently was claiming to be an adept (he had always maintained that he knew more than the Mahatmas did). He had been practising pranayama, a form of regulation and suppression of the breath. According to HPB it is a dangerous practice *(Esoteric Writings of H.P. Blavatsky*, pp. 397-9 and 405); it is believed that she was referring to an extreme form of pranayama.

This paragraph describes the tragic results which may come from dabbling in psychism before one's nature is purified.

Last half of page: KH warns APS against too precipitate a break with AOH because of the damage the latter might do to the TS.

REFERENCES

p. 326/321: '...another vain and ambitious malcontent—Dayanand S...' Swami Dayanand Saraswati was the leader of the reform movement in Hinduism known as the Arya Samaj. See Alphabetical Notes.

The Mahatma has indicated elsewhere that one reason for caution in dealing with Hume is that he could become a dangerous enemy to the cause. Undoubtedly, the Mahatma could foresee coming events.

p. 326/322: Sinnett is advised not to write to Hume but to postpone an open breach until the hour should come when the longer delay would be unpardonable. 'Neither of us', says the Mahatma, 'ought to imperil a cause whose promotion is a duty paramount to consideration of self.' This last statement has some profound implications. Perhaps if more members of the TS would place considerations of the Society before those of the personal self, the work would proceed more swiftly.

p. 327/322 (near top): '...in Madras there are fairer prospects...' This is in connection with procuring funds to finance *The Phoenix* project.

p. 327/322: 'How do you like "Mr Isaacs"? ...(for you must read and review it)...' This was the title of an occult novel (with the subtitle 'A Tale of Modern India') just published by F. Marion Crawford, one time editor of the *Indian Herald* and nephew of Sam Ward (see Alphabetical Notes). See also 105 (ML-25). The book was reviewed in the February 1883 issue of *The Theosophist*. Interestingly enough, a correspondent who signed himself simply 'A***8111' and whose letter was published in the March 1883 issue of *The Theosophist,* took issue with some of the favourable comments in the review, and particularly with the author's attempt to depict KH as Ram Lal the 'adept hero' of the novel. To this letter HPB added a footnote: 'We are sorry to see Mr A***8111 so under-rating—though we may have, in his opinion, *over* rated—Mr Isaacs. There are two of the "grandest occult truths" in it, though neither our critic, nor even the author himself may be aware of them.'

'...the famous "Ski"...' A spirit control of the medium, Mrs Hollis-Billings.

'...the man gave up entirely drinking...' Probably F. Marion Crawford.

'...and even Shere Ali'. Presumably another character in the story.

103A & B (ML-91A & B) Page 415/409 and 416/409 Folio 3 Recd. Jan. 1883 (est.)

DESCRIPTION

103A is in blue pencil on a small sheet of notepaper with rough edges, 5″ x 7″. Heavy KH script.

103B is on three sheets of heavy smooth folded notepaper, in dark blue ink in small script; blotched appearance and a somewhat different calligraphy from early letters.

CIRCUMSTANCES

The Founders were at Adyar. APS was evidently in Allahabad.

The person to whom 103A was addresed is not indicated, but it seems likely that it was HSO in view of the first sentence in 103B. 103B is a commentary on statements made in C.C. Massey's letter, which KH is forwarding to Olcott.

Much of this letter is obscure; there seems to be no further description of the incidents only hinted at by the Mahatma, although they obviously involved, in part at least, the honesty of Mrs Billings. She was the American medium who, with her husband, Dr Billings, went to England and helped with the formation of the London Branch. When the Founders stopped in England en route from the USA to India, they stayed with Dr and Mrs Billings in London and met other Theosophists there.

There seems to be no other reference to the incident mentioned by the Mahatma. In ODL 2:4, Olcott mentions seeing a Master while they were in London, but he does not mention the matter referred to here by KH. This short note, 103A (ML-91A) is simply to transmit a letter from Massey for Olcott to read, with the admonition that it is not to be shown to HPB but to be sent to Sinnett with Olcott's comments. No doubt Olcott did precisely as he had been directed. The opening sentence of 103B relates what the Mahatma himself had done.

It is probable that Massey's letter was one of those which, among other things, attacked HPB. No doubt it was addressed to Sinnett, and Sinnett sent it on to the Mahatma for his comments.

The Mahatma attempts to set the record straight when he points out the error of so many in thinking that 'the selections of members and the actions of Founders and Chelas are controlled by us!' This error persists into the present to some extent. Why, people ask, did the Mahatmas not prevent such and such a thing from happening, since they were supposed to be relatively omniscient and could see into the future? The Mahatma has explained a number of times that they do not and cannot interfere in this manner with the karma of the individuals concerned, be it merit or otherwise.

The Mahatma then proceeds to cite various incidents and situations in support of his statement. We have met some of the persons mentioned in this paragraph: Hurrychund, the treasurer of Arya Samaj, through whom the Founders made their first connections in India, and who later decamped with the funds belonging to that organization, as well as with the fees paid in by the Theosophical Society before the Founders moved to India; Dayanand—the swami at the head of the Arya Samaj who later, through outraged vanity, turned against the Founders and attacked them viciously; and, of course, Hume. This is the first time Edward Wimbridge and Rosa Bates appear in the letters. (See Alphabetical Notes.)

The last named two are rather minor characters in the drama, yet they provide a good example of what the Mahatma has been saying, and they illustrate some of the problems with which the Founders had to deal. They were English, but both were living in New York in the early days of the Theosophical Society. Wimbridge was an artist and architect; Rosa Bates was a teacher. Both accompanied the Founders when they left the United States for India. Olcott indicates that Wimbridge was a decent sort of person, but that he had some reservations about Miss Bates from the beginning (ODL 2:110). He begged HPB not to take these two with them to India, but 'her invariable answer was that the two, being patriotic English in feeling, would afford by their company the best possible guarantee to the Anglo-Indian authorities of [their] innocence of any political designs'. But HPB said she herself would take the consequences, so the two accompanied them.

Difficulties began when the Coulombs arrived and were taken in at Adyar. Olcott describes the situation in ODL 2:207.

REFERENCES

p. 416/410: '...my Darjeeling Letter...' Apparently a reference to 92 (ML-54), which seems to have been sent through HPB while she was resting in Darjeeling. This paragraph contains some interesting statements indicating that the most hostile attitudes and actions may bring about results very different from those intended.

The remainder of the letter is largely a defence of Mrs Billings against a series of accusations apparently made by Massey, mostly on the authority of others. The events involved in these accusations are not at all clear, but the implication is that, in spite of Massey's own sincerity, he has been completely deluded by others who sought to injure Mrs Billings and also HPB. Sinnett may show the letter to Massey. 'Whatever his personal opinion about myself and Brothers can in no way influence the promised "teachings" through your friendly agency.' This refers to the Mahatma's refusal to deal direct with the London Lodge and his promise to work through Sinnett in imparting something of the occult philosophy.

104 (ML-25) Page 191/188 Folio 2 Recd. Feb.2, 1883

DESCRIPTION: KH to APS

KH script in blue ink, mostly on bluish-grey paper. Some white paper, which is stamped with the print of a tree, is used near the end of the letter. The script is large and flowing.

CIRCUMSTANCES

The Founders were in Adyar. APS was probably at home in Allahabad.

Sinnett has headed this letter 'Devachan Notes Latest Addition, Answers to Queries'. The first Devachan letter was 68 (ML-16), p.99/97. Letters 70A, B, and C, (ML-20A, B and C) dealt further with the subject, which continued to raise questions in the minds of the two Englishmen, and they had submitted more questions to the Mahatma KH. This letter is in answer to those questions.

It will be remembered that Sinnett had taken over from Hume the task of writing the series entitled 'Fragments of Occult Truth' which was published in *The Theosophist*. These articles were based on the teachings given by the two Mahatmas, KH and M, through the letters.

For some reason, Sinnett seemed to have difficulty in understanding about Devachan. He did not particularly like the ideas, as a matter of fact. Perhaps his confusion is understandable, for the Mahatma says in this letter, in effect, that he is attempting to describe the indescribable. Sinnett was writing about Devachan in some of his 'Fragments' and he had been attempting to clarify some points that the Mahatma had made earlier. His questions are not really spelled out, although occasionally his comments are quoted. This is one of the few letters from now on devoted to philosophical teachings. He had evidently written that the period in Devachan must be monotonous, and the Mahatma attempts to set him right on this. Earlier the Mahatma had told him, in effect, to image the happiest moment of his life intensified and prolonged and he might have some idea of Devachan.

REFERENCES

The first long paragraph gives a splendid explanation and one is impressed again with the beautiful patience of the Mahatma. The reference to 'the same world as before, or another...' may be confusing, but the meaning is surely another globe in the chain in which our present globe is situated. If the compilers understand the teachings correctly, we can never go outside our own chain of worlds. There is a 'ring-pass-not'. But, conceivably, one could remain in Devachan for such a long time that the life-wave of which one is a part would have moved on to the next globe, or world (p. 192/189; see also p. 101/98-9 in first Devachan letter).

In some earlier comments on Devachan ML (p.127-8/124) the Mahatma had said: 'That feeling which is the strongest in us at that supreme hour [death] — that feeling will become the fashioner of our bliss or woe, the life principle of our future existence.' Undoubtedly this is the occult truth from which the distorted idea of deathbed repentance derives, i.e., in the concept that a man may do evil his whole life and if he repents on his deathbed, he will be 'saved' or 'go to heaven'.

Of course, as the Mahatma has pointed out, Devachan is the state in which moral and spiritual activities find their fruition; it is the 'harvest of earth's sowing', to quote Annie Besant.

p. 193/190: Roden Noel (1834-94), was an English poet, author of 'Behind the Veil' and other poems. Evidently something from his pen, which does not earn praise from the Mahatma, had been published in the Spiritualist magazine, *Light*.

p. 196/193: contains some comments concerning the types of individuals and the consequent types of Devachan, which must be repeated until the end of the seventh round unless the being attains in the meantime to the stature of an Arhat, 'then of a Buddha and thus gets relieved for a round or two'. The colourless personality will have a colourless Devachan, and the 'absolute *nonentities'* go to the eighth sphere. The article 'Death' refers to Éliphas Lévy's article published in *The Theosophist* for October 1891, with marginal comments by the Mahatma KH. It is found as an Appendix in LBS, beginning on p.369. The Mahatma proceeds to clarify some points which Sinnett should use in the 'Fragments'.

p. 195-6/193: KH explains the distinction between the 'eighth sphere' and 'avichi'.

p.200/197: (bottom) ...one who died a *ryot* ...' A peasant.

'...the *skandhas* are the ...' Skandhas literally means bundles, or groups of attributes generally considered as left behind at the end of one incarnation to be picked up at the beginning of the next by the reincarnating ego.

The 'famous contradictions' mentioned by the Mahatma under Query 5 is found in Letter 85A (ML-24A), p. 180/177.

p. 200/197: '...the Dharmakayic ear' refers to one of the so-called Buddhic bodies or vestures which the individual may choose when he has fulfilled his human evolution. The subject is extremly esoteric. We learn from HPB's *Glossary,* and also from her classic, *The Voice of the Silence,* that these vestures are called the Nirmānakāya, the Sambhogakāya, and the Dharmakāya, *kāya* meaning vesture or body.

p. 200/197: The Mahatma comments that there could be no more flagrant misnomer than the phrase 'accidents of birth'. 'When you realize at least the following—that the *skandhas* are the elements of limited existences then will you have realized one of the conditions of Devachan...' Sinnett's inferences that the upper classes have better karma have a 'eudaemonistic ring...' This refers to a philosophy which regards the moral value of actions in terms of their ability to produce happiness, specifically Aristotelian, which the Mahatma says is hardly in keeping with karmic law.

This part of the letter apparently ends the answers to Sinnett's questions. There is reference to the fact that Sinnett plans to write another book based on the series of articles, 'Fragments of Occult Truth', for which he has already selected, or suggested, the title, *Esoteric Buddhism.*

p.201/198: The reference to Sinnett's 'wild scheme' refers to the fact that Sinnett has been trying to devise some plan to see the Mahatma personally before he leaves again for England. He always longed for this and never quite gave up the hope that it would come to pass. Apparently he had some idea of going to Darjeeling, thinking this would facilitate the matter. The Mahatma tells him this is not wild but simply impracticable; he has some encouraging words for Sinnett including the statement: 'Meanwhile be happy in knowing that you have done more real good to your kind within the past two years than in many previous years. And—to yourself also.'

p.202/199: It will be remembered that in a recent letter, the Mahatma had asked Sinnett how he liked the book, *Mr Isaacs,* by F. Marion Crawford. He would like to see the book reviewed by Sinnett before he leaves for England. 'And for the sake of old "Sam Ward" I would like to see it noticed in the "Pioneer".' It is not known whether Sinnett actually reviewed it in that newspaper as well as in *The Theosophist*.

p. 202/200: The last paragraph regarding the initiation of chelas is especially interesting with respect to DK (striving to 'reach the other shore'). This may have been his fifth initiation, as there are indications that he reached adeptship about this time.

The closing sentence is particularly interesting in view of the fact that some writers on occult subjects place Djual Khool's achievement of adeptship much earlier than this. This is in 1883 and the Mahatma says that Djual Khool is 'striving to reach "the other shore".' It is understood that this did take place at some time during this period.

105 (ML-80) Page 383/377 Folio 3 Recd. Jan. or Feb. 1883 (est.)

DESCRIPTION: KH to APS

KH script in blue pencil on both sides of a folded sheet of APS's official paper bearing the *Pioneer* letterhead.

CIRCUMSTANCES

The letter concerns efforts being made to raise capital among the native business community for the venture, *The Phoenix*. APS was probably in Allahabad. HPB was in Adyar. HSO made a trip to Calcutta in late February in an effort to enlist support for the proposed newspaper.

REFERENCES

p. 383/377: 'M's "son"...' Meaning HSO. He was sometimes affectionately called 'Morya Junior'.

The Mahatma mentions the 'malevolent (or if you prefer eccentric) meddling of the Rothney Swedenborg and other artists in calamity'. Rothney Castle was the name Hume had given to his house on Jakko Hill in Simla.

Later in the letter he again refers to A.O. Hume as 'the Simla Yogi' and 'Your Rothney friend'.

p.383/377: '...3 lakhs of rupees...' A lakh in India is 100,000. This was a large sum of money at that time.

(last par.): This deals with APS's proposed trip to England while the newspaper funding was in progress. See 101 (ML-57), last paragraph.

106 (ML-103) Page 440/432 Folio 3 Recd. Feb.1883 (est.)

DESCRIPTION: KH to APS

KH script in blue pencil on a single sheet of canary-yellow paper.

CIRCUMSTANCES

The probable date of this letter is mid-February, since HSO was in Calcutta on Feb. 20. HPB was at Adyar. APS was probably still in Allahabad. Plans were under way to raise money for the projected new paper.

REFERENCES

KH is expressing his dissatisfaction with the way the solicitation for funds for the newspaper was being handled.

Olcott was going about soliciting subscriptions.

The Maharajah of Kashmir was a very important person in India and was also sympathetic to the TS.

Re concluding statement: It is not known precisely what was troubling HPB at the moment, but 'M. will take her in hand'.

107 (ML-77) Page 377/371 Folio 3 Recd. Mar. 1883 (est.)

DESCRIPTION: KH to APS

KH script in blue pencil on all four sides of a sheet of folded notepaper, somewhat cream coloured. It is interesting that the writer ran out of space just before finishing and so completed the letter by turning it upside down and writing at the top of the front page.

CIRCUMSTANCES

The Founders were in Adyar. APS and family had come down to Madràs in connection with plans for their return to England, and probably also in connection with plans for the projected new paper.

REFERENCES

The first long paragraph deals with the formation of another Branch, in Howrah, a major suburb of Calcutta, where the Gordons were living at the time. Calcutta was the capital of India at that time.

KH also indicates that if Col. Gordon should go to Simla (probably for the summer) he might take responsible charge of the Simla Eclectic, since APS would not be there and AOH had lost interest.

Mention is made of the 'Himalayan' for the first time. One can infer from the letter that this was a branch of the 'Eclectic' Society for native Indians.

The first sentence in paragraph 2 refers to a date proposed for APS's sailing for England.

The remainder of the second paragraph deals with the projected new paper.

KH indulges in some rather colourful analogies in the paragraph.

'Zemindars': Indian landed proprietors.

108 (ML-58) Page 336/331 Folio 2 Recd. late Mar. 1883 (est.)

DESCRIPTION: KH to APS

KH script in light blue pencil on two sheets of smooth folded note paper, 5″x 8″, heavy lettering on all four sides.

CIRCUMSTANCES

About the same as the previous letter, 107 (ML-77). APS was still in Madras preparatory to sailing for England.

REFERENCES

p. 336/331: KH indicates that he does not propose to discuss metaphysics any more for the time being, and that what he has already written along that line was as far as he is allowed to go.

This would seem to be the reason why APS was given so little information about the 'Obscurations'.

Paragraph 2 indicates that an attempt had been made by DK to open Sinnett's vision (this may have been before he left Allahabad) but had not been successful. He apparently succeeded in getting Sinnett out of his body but did not succeed in opening his inner vision. This was for reasons 'correctly surmised' by Sinnett himself: hence the Mahatma's answer 'surmise correct—more at Adyar'.

The closing paragraph, while rather long, discusses what the Mahatma will do and will not do for Sinnett personally and in connection with any relations with the London Branch of the TS.

p. 337/332: '... our actual existence be doubted ...' There are several statements in the letters to the effect that the Adepts do not want much information about their existence to be made public.

109 (ML-119) Page 451/444 Folio 3 Recd. Mar. 1883 (est.)

DESCRIPTION: KH to APS

KH script in blue pencil on a sheet of *Pioneer* letterhead, paper size 5″ x 8″. The addressee is not indicated but may have been HPB or Damodar. The second note signed by KH is in blue pencil on a sheet of paper bearing the letterhead of 'Publication Office, The Theosophist, Beach Kandy, Bombay, India'. It is presumably addressed to APS.

A newspaper cutting is pasted on the same sheet of paper, beneath the note.

CIRCUMSTANCES

Similar to previous letters in March. APS was probably still in Madras, preparatory to sailing for England almost immediately.

REFERENCES

1st note: '... time is short ...' A probable reference to the fact that APS would soon be leaving India.

2nd note: The 'obscuration' phase of the doctrine of globes was one that seemed to puzzle APS.

'... Editor of the "Phoenix"'. Anticipating the inauguration of the new paper to be known as *The Phoenix,* a bit of KH's lightness.

The cutting concerns some findings in astronomy, and while the Mahatma, as indicated in letter 108 (ML-58), says that he does not propose to write anything further to Sinnett about stars and obscurations, he suggests that this short article may later on lead to a confirmation of their doctrine on the subject.

Sir John Lubbock, 1834-1913, was an English banker and naturalist. As a member of Parliament, he introduced banking reforms, including bank holidays. Author of *Prehistoric Times*

(1864), he was the first to use the terms Paleolithic and Neolithic Age. Procyon is a bright star in the constellation Canis (the Lesser Dog) east of Orion, near Gemini. Algow (Algol) is a bright variable star in Perseus. It loses most of its brightness when eclipsed by its dark companion. In Greek mythology, Medusa was one of the three Gorgons slain by Perseus.

110 (ML-67) Page 371/364 Folio 3 Mailed from Madras by HSO on 26 May 1883. Recd. by APS in London, June 16-20.

DESCRIPTION: KH to APS (forwarded to APS)

In dark blue ink in heavy KH script on both sides of two sheets of full-sized white paper.

CIRCUMSTANCES

The Founders were apparently in Adyar. The Sinnetts had sailed for London on March 30.

This letter is addressed to Col. Olcott and was received by him when he arrived at Adyar on 26 May 1883 after a long tour on which he had performed many healings. He was greatly depleted in strength and was informed by the Mahatma that he had been ordered home for a rest and was not to do any more healings until he heard from the Mahatma M. Olcott must have sent the letter on to Sinnett the next day, since the Mahatma suggested that he get in touch with Sinnett and that the English mail left on May 27. The Sinnetts had, according to the plan, sailed for England on March 30, and it is probable that he received this letter about the middle of June. So it can be seen that some time had elapsed since he had last heard from the Mahatma KH.

The letter is not actually *to* Sinnett, although it concerns him. No doubt Col. Olcott felt that the simplest thing to do was to forward it to him rather than use the energy (considering his state of exhaustion) to write a letter himself. One wonders a bit why the letter was addressed to Olcott rather than to Sinnett himself, although undoubtedly Olcott also needed to be informed about the situation, and perhaps both energy and time were saved by this method.

REFERENCES

The first two sentences obviously refer to HSO himself. He had been travelling about trying to raise subscriptions for *The Phoenix*.

Apparently Hume (the 'Simla correspondent') had been meddling again. Bishen Lal was one of the chelas who 'failed'—in part perhaps through his own unwise haste, but also through some machinations on Hume's part. Bishen Lal was President of the Bareilly Branch of the Theosophical Society, and was one of those of whom the Mahatmas spoke as having 'intense self-personalities' (ML p. 357/352). The book *Damodar* contains a letter to him outlining the work of a theosophical lodge (p. 175).

Hume had written Olcott a long letter and the Colonel had put it in the bottom of his trunk, not intending that HPB should see it. In it, apparently, Hume attacked almost everyone, including Sinnett who, he said, was a 'credulous imbecile'. The Mahatma had it duplicated by occult means and sent it on to Sinnett, as it was necessary that he be prepared for the mischief which Hume was going to create among the members of the London branch of the Society. Here, he begs Olcott's pardon for 'the bad taste' which compelled him to do this. 'The diabolical malice which breathes thro' [this] letter', says the Mahatma, 'comes straight from the Dugpas who provoke his vanity and blind his reason.' Also, Hume is doing all he can to wreck any chance of success for the *Phoenix* venture.

So the reader can begin to see the doom of the *Phoenix* and the beginning of Sinnett's work in England.

The Mahatma then takes up the matter of chelaship. It may be remembered that, very early on, the Mahatma said, 'Sigh not for chelaship' (LMW 1: Letter 9, p. 31).

Then there is a very curious statement: 'M. sends you thro' me these vases as a home greeting.' This seems a very strange gift for the Mahatma M to be sending to Olcott. The matter comes to light again several years later, in 1886, after the report of the Society for Psychical Research had been published (LBS pp. 139-141). The account is too long to include here but something seems to hinge on whether or not Mme Coulomb did or did not try to trick Olcott and HPB. 'It was done by a chela,' says HPB, 'and for a *certain reason* I need not explain.' In the margin of Mary K. Neff's personal copy of LBS, opposite this sentence, Miss Neff has inserted this comment: 'to expose Mme C'.

The Mahatma closes his letter with the suggestion that Olcott warn Sinnett very plainly.

111 (ML-59) Page 338/333 Folio 2 Recd. July 1883

DESCRIPTION: KH to APS

KH script in blue ink on 20 standard-sized sheets of rippled white paper, on one side only. On page 8 there is a drawing of two interlaced triangles inside a circle, with a dot in the centre.

CIRCUMSTANCES

APS was in London, having arrived there in April. He was busy with the writing and publication of his new book, *Esoteric Buddhism*.

REFERENCES

p. 338/333: '... the Altruist of Rothney ...' AOH.

(middle): '...aiding to build a bridge ...' Perhaps referring to the potential effect of *Esoteric Buddhism* on Western thought.

The second paragraph is a good example of KH's lightness and wit, especially as regards the English climate.

p. 339/333: '...an attempt has been made to dispel some of the great mist that I find in Mr Massey's *Devachan'.* In the August 1883 issue of *The Theosophist* there appears a 'Memorandum' on Devachan which is preceded by an editor's note as follows: 'The memorandum that follows emanates from a British Theosophist. It was sent to "Lay Chela", the author of *Esoteric Buddhism,* in response to whose desire that the objections should be explained away, the three Replies subjoined have been sent. They come from three different sources.' The British Theosophist is obviously Massey. The 'Memorandum', which contains some objections to statements concerning Devachan made in 'Fragments of Occult Truth', is followed by three 'Replies'. There is no indication who the 'three different sources' were, but from the statement herein it would appear that KH may have been one of them. It seems likely that APS had sent the 'Memorandum' to KH and he had sent it on to HPB as Editor.

p. 339/334: '... periodically launched upon by Rahu ...' A mythological demon who made himself immortal by robbing the gods of the elixir of divine life. Vishnu exiled him from the earth and made of him the constellation Draco. During eclipses of the sun and moon, he is said to swallow them (Glossary).

p. 339/334: '... this second one is a dish of cold philosophy ...' Reference to the book, *Esoteric Buddhism,* the writing of which KH seems to have been following at a distance. The first reference is to *The Occult World.*

p. 340/334-35: '...if you could but see the plaint of one of them ...' The description that follows seems to indicate that KH is referring to Moorad Ali Beg (Godolphin Mitford), who wrote the article, 'The Elixir of Life'.

p. 341/335: '...the article "Chelas and Lay Chelas" '. This fine article is to be found in CW IV, p. 606 et seq. See Alphabetical Notes.

p. 342/336 (two line paragraph): This relates to relieving Mrs Kingsford of the presidency of the English Section.

p. 342/336: '... of your locket ...' From this comment, it is evident that APS, as well as the other members of his family, wore a locket containing some of KH's hair. In this paragraph, KH gives some interesting information on healing.

p. 342/337: '... Buddhistic exegesis ...' Interpretation of Buddhist scriptures. Probably meaning that APS was now among some of the western Orientalists, of whom Rhys Davids and Arthur Lillie were noted. See Alphabetical Notes.

p. 344/338: '...far from an inspired "Panini" ...' Panini: a celebrated grammarian; author of the work *Paniniyam* supposed to have been received from the god Siva. Ignorant of the epoch in which he lived, the Orientalists place this between 600 BC and AD 300 (Glossary).

p. 345/340: This contains a profound explanation of the TS Seal.

p. 346/341: '... that remarkable seeress ...' Anna Kingsford, co-author with Edward Maitland of *The Perfect Way*.

p. 348/342: '... criticism of "A Student of Occultism"... and the answer of "S.T.K. .. Chary"...' The story behind this is as follows: The April 1883 issue of *The Theosophist,* p. 161, carried No. VII of 'Fragments of Occult Truth' written by APS as 'A Lay Chela'. In the June 1883 issue, p. 231, there appeared a criticism of this 'Fragment' under the heading 'Cosmical Rings and Rounds' with the byline of 'A student of Occultism'. From KH's comment here—'(whose wits are sharpened by the mountain air of his home)'—this would seem to be AOH. The criticism is followed by an answer signed 'S.T.K. ... Chary' and dated at Pondicherry, May 17. The 'Pondicherry chela' is evidently the writer of this answer. He is not otherwise identified except that he gave some assistance to the Literary Committee at Adyar in 1884. See 128 (ML-63), p. 357/351.

p. 348/343: '... (the Marcus Aurelius of Simla) ...' Further indication that the 'Student of Occultism' mentioned just above was AOH.

112 (ML-81) Page 383/377 Folio 3 Written in mid-June. Recd. July 1883 (est.)

DESCRIPTION: KH to APS

In bright blue ink, on both sides of four full-sized sheets of white paper, in fine KH script.

CIRCUMSTANCES

APS was in London, the Founders in India, and the fund-raising for *The Phoenix* apparently was almost at a standstill.

This is the more private letter which the Mahatma wrote to Sinnett about mid-June and probably sent to him along with 111 (ML-59). It will be noted that the Mahatma has headed it '*Private* but not *very* Confidential'. He explains in his opening paragraph why he is sending it separately.

REFERENCES

The first part of this rather rambling letter tells of the poor progress on the fund-raising for the newspaper and the reasons for it.

p. 385/379: The Mahatma then refers to what he calls Sinnett's 'unfortunate inspiration of the 17th, published in the *Times'*, which obviously injured the cause. This was a letter written by Sinnett, whether to *The Times* of London or *The Times* of India is not specifically indicated. It may have been *The Times* of India, since that is where the disastrous impact was made. Even the nature of the letter is not clear, although the Mahatma calls it 'an untimely confession, *honest as its object may have been'*. He expresses a doubt that Sinnett will ever 'rise above English prejudices and sinful antipathy towards our race and colour'. He adds that ' "Madame" will tell you more'.

The latter part deals mostly with the problems of the London mediums who seemed to be having troubles among themselves.

p. 386/380: 'We, my dear sirs, always judge men by their motives...' This closing sentence is one that students of occultism should keep seriously in mind.

113 (ML-82) Page 387/381 Folio 3 Recd. Aug. 1883 (est.)

DESCRIPTION: KH to APS

In KH script on both sides of six sheets of white paper. The first four lines are in blue ink, which in the course of three lines changes to green.

CIRCUMSTANCES

APS was in London. *Esoteric Buddhism* had been published during the summer. The efforts to subscribe funds in India for *The Phoenix* had all but stopped, nothing substantial having been achieved.

REFERENCES

p. 387/381: The French phrase meaning 'the quarter hour of Rabelais' is probably in connection with the situation existing with respect to *The Phoenix*. Seemingly he is indicating that the moment of decision has arrived. See also p. 38.

(middle): ' "tout chemin est bon qui mène à Rome"...' Every road is good that leads to Rome.

p. 388/382 (top): Ryots are farmers.

This long and complicated letter is KH's final attempt to accomplish something about getting APS's projected newspaper established. The proposition which he suggests is so complicated and so mixed with the tangled political situation then existing in India that it is difficult for the student to make much out of it, especially if he is not acquainted with Indian political history.

The Mahatma several times uses the word 'Races'. This is an incorrect spelling; it should be 'Raises' or landowners.

If Sinnett cannot accept the offer, 'of course the paper scheme is at an end'. This refers to *The Phoenix*.

Evidently, Sinnett did not accept the suggested proposal.

The Zemindars are generally spoken of as 'landlords'. The dictionary gives this definition; 'a collector of the revenue for land, a landowner, esp. one paying revenue'.

p. 392/386: '... the "Morsel" '. Meaning APS's son Denny.

'... your *Esoteric Buddhism*...' An encouraging comment on APS's second book.

'... Mr Hume's theory ... shown by the "Chela" in *The Theosophist'*. Reference to the article by 'A Student of Occultism' and the answer by 'S.K. ... Chary' referred to in 111 (ML-59).

(bottom): 'He was speaking of the *inner*—I, of the *outer* Round '. This has to do with the passage of the Monadic Hosts from globe to globe within a chain and from one planetary chain to another. See *The Divine Plan* by Geoffrey A. Barborka, p. 379 et seq. for explanation.

p. 393/387: The student may be interested to compare this statement about God with 88 (ML-10), p. 52 et seq.

114 (ML-114) Page 393/387 Folio 3 Written Sept. 15, 1883 Recd. Oct. 8, 1883.

DESCRIPTION: KH to APS

In KH script on three sheets of full-sized white paper. The

first page is in blue ink which changes to green on the back. The second page is in green ink and the third page is in green and blue intermingled.

CIRCUMSTANCES

Similar to those described in 113 (ML-82). Mary K. Neff assigns a date of Sept. 11 rather than the date of Oct. 8 as given by APS himself.

Undoubtedly these letters are being sent by surface mail and not being transmitted occultly—except as they came through HPB. It is estimated that between three and four weeks were required for mail to travel between England and India.

REFERENCES

This letter sounds the death knell of the whole venture and closes the discussion concerning it. This is made clear in the first paragraph.

p. 393/387: In Col Olcott's diary entries (not included in ODL but in his original diary in the archives at the international headquarters of the Theosophical Society at Adyar) there is a notation: 'K.H. sent dispatch by cable to Sinnett today, releasing him from his promise and leaving him to act unbiased.'

p. 396/390: Then the Mahatma comes to what he calls a 'pleasanter word' before concluding. He tells Sinnett that his decision to follow his (KH's) lead in *The Phoenix* matter, even in the face of certain social degradation and pecuniary loss, has already earned him good karma.

'Though there was *no test*—(so odious to you)—meant, yet you were as good as tested and you have not quailed. The fiat of contingent non-intercourse between us has been partially revoked. The prohibition with regard to *other Europeans* is as strict as ever, but in *your* case it is removed.' He tells Sinnett that the great sacrifice of his own personal feelings has a direct bearing on the matter.

p. 396/390: Sinnett had rather indiscreetly mentioned the 'eighth sphere' mystery in his book, and this had provoked considerable discussion and curiosity, even ridicule.

p. 396/390 (last sentence): '... the *Replies* to Mr Myers ...' Reference to the long series of articles appearing in *The Theosophist* entitled 'Replies to a British F.T.S.' They were in reply to F.W.H. Myers (See Alphabetical Notes), an English scientist and member of the Society for Psychical Research. M attached considerable importance to these replies and seemingly wrote most of them himself. HPB complained bitterly about using up so much space in her magazine for them. See LBS-23, p. 46.

The postscript indicates that recent letters had been transmitted through HPB but that it was now considered advisable to pass them through HSO or DKM.

115 & 116 (ML-128 & 129) Page 459/449 Folio 3
Dated Nov. 25, 1883

DESCRIPTION: HSO to HPB

Two telegrams from HSO to HPB regarding the disappearance of DKM. The note on No. 116 from KH is in blue pencil, added probably while the telegram was in transit.

CIRCUMSTANCES

In October and November, 1883, HSO, accompanied by DKM and W.T. Brown, was touring about North India. While they were encamped at Jammu, Kashmir, DKM suddenly disappeared, leaving HSO without information of his whereabouts or whether he would return. HPB was in Adyar.

A number of astonishing things happened while Olcott and his associates were on this tour. They are related in detail in chapters 2 through 5 of ODL, volume 3. The student is referred to these chapters.

REFERENCES

How APS came into possession of the telegrams is not explained.

For those who are unable to look up references, the following brief summary is appended:

When Olcott awakened on the morning of November 25 to find Damodar gone—with no clue to where he had gone or when he would return—he searched through the small bungalow in which they were staying, but found no one. When he returned to his own room, however, he found notes from both the Mahatma KH and Damodar on his table. Olcott does not say specifically what was in the notes, but the one from the Mahatma must have been to the effect that they (the Mahatmas) had taken Damodar, for that is the substance of the telegram which the Colonel sent at once to HPB, shown here as being at 10:15. The words at the bottom, in dark print, are important: 'We will send him back. K.H.' Obviously, this was added to the telegram by the Mahatma before HPB received it.

A few hours later, Olcott sent a second telegram explaining in more detail, and including the message from Damodar which he had found along with that of the Mahatmas. Olcott related how, even before he had sent the telegram to HPB, he had a strong impulse to take Damodar's luggage, his trunk and bedding, and pack them away under his own bed.

That evening, he received a telegram in reply from HPB. She told him that a Master had told her (cf. the footnote to the telegram from O.) that Damodar would return, and she added that the Colonel must not let Damodar's luggage, especially his bedding, be touched by anyone else. 'That was strange, was it not,' writes the Colonel, 'that she, at Madras, i.e. some 2,000 miles away—should tell me to do the very thing it had been my first impulse to do on finding out about the lad's departure?' (ODL 3:52)

In ODL 3: p. 54, Olcott makes the following statement:

> It was on the 25th November, at daylight, that Damodar left us: he returned in the evening of the 27th—after an absence of some sixty hours, but how changed! He left, a delicate-framed, pale student-like young man, frail, timid, deferential; he returned with his olive face bronzed several shades darker, seemingly robust, tough, and wiry, bold and energetic in manner: we could scarcely realize that he was the same person.

Damodar describes his experience with considerable restraint, though he was permitted to tell of it. It was first published in *The Theosophist* for Dec.-Jan. 1883-84, pp. 61-2. It is now found in the book, *Damodar,* by Sven Eek, pp. 333-36; and the story is related in Geoffrey Barborka's book MTL, pp. 247-50. Here is the pertinent part:

> ...I had the good fortune of being sent for, and permitted to visit a Sacred *Ashram* where I remained for a few days in the blessed company of several of the much doubted Mahatmas of Himavat and their disciples. There I met not only my beloved Gurudev and Col Olcott's Master (Morya), but several others of the Fraternity, including One of the Highest. I regret [that] the extremely personal nature of my visit to those thrice blessed regions prevents my saying more of it. Suffice it that the place I was permitted to visit is in the Himalayas, not in any fanciful Summer Land, and that I saw Him in my own sthula sarira [physical body] and found my Master identical with the form I had seen in the earlier days of my Chelaship.

117 (ML-93) Page 420/413 Folio 3 Recd. Winter of 1883-4 (est.)

DESCRIPTION: KH to APS

On one side of 19 sheets of white paper, regular size, in medium-sized script. Most of the letter is in medium blue ink. The correct text of the controversial part of the so-called Kiddle Incident is given on pages 12, 13 and 14 of the letter and the parts which were omitted in 12 (ML-60), p. 24, are underlined in bright red ink. The remainder of the letter is in red ink. At the bottom of page 14, a coarser script appears, but the remainder of the letter is in fine script.

CIRCUMSTANCES

APS was living in London and taking an active part in theosophical work there. The Founders were in India. Heretofore KH had not bothered to answer the charge of plagiarism against him because of the passages in Letter 12 (ML-6) attributed to Henry Kiddle. Seeing how much the question troubled APS, he now undertakes a full explanation of the affair. See Appendix E. See Alphabetical Notes on Kiddle.

REFERENCES

p. 420/413: 'Mr Ward ...' Sam Ward, an American businessman. See Alphabetical Notes. 'M.A. Oxon ...' Stainton Moses's pen name.

To understand this letter, it is necessary to go back to page 24 (both editions) of Letter 12 (ML-6). The Sinnetts went to England in 1881, and while they were there *The Occult World* was published. Before leaving India, Sinnett had been told by the Mahatma KH to use anything he wished in his book; the Mahatma had complete confidence in his discretion and judgement. Therefore, Sinnett quoted from one of the letters — the one mentioned immediately above — the passage beginning 'Plato was right, *ideas* rule the world ...' (See p. 24).

After the book's publication, it happened that, in the United States, a Spiritualist by the name of Henry Kiddle read it.

Mr Henry Kiddle had given a lecture at a gathering of Spiritualists at Lake Pleasant, New York. He claimed that the above cited passage from OW plagiarized some comments of his in this lecture.

Mr Kiddle then wrote to Stainton Moses (M.A. Oxon), editor of *Light,* the English Spiritualist organ, claiming that the printed passage in OW was 'taken verbatim' from his address at Lake Pleasant. His letter was published in the 1 September 1883 issue of that journal. At this time, the Sinnetts were permanently in England.

A great deal of correspondence resulted from all this (which came to be called 'The Kiddle Incident'). See Appendix E in the *Guide,* which gives the whole story in some detail.

For some time the Mahatma did not bother to answer the charges of plagiarism, apparently attaching little importance to them. But seeing how distressed Sinnett was over the whole matter, he undertook to explain.

This section is a masterpiece of irony. On p. 421/415, he says: 'The solution is so simple, and the circumstances so amusing, that I confess I laughed when my attention was drawn to it some time since. Nay, it is calculated to make me smile even now, were it not for the knowledge of the pain it gives to some true friends.'

The student is reminded that, at the end of Letter 12 (ML-6) the Mahatma commented that he had not slept for 60 hours. He framed that letter while on a journey on horseback, and had been in the saddle for 48 of those 60 hours, without sleep. The letter was 'dictated mentally, in the direction of and "precipitated" by a young chela not yet expert at this branch of psychic chemistry, and who had to transcribe it from a hardly visible imprint'. (Why 'hardly visible' is not explained.)

The Mahatma gives further explanation and then says that had he dictated his letter in the form in which it appeared in print it would certainly look suspicious. But he did nothing of the kind, 'as the original impression now before me clearly shows'.

This is a provocative statement. Obviously the Mahatma could reproduce at will anything from the akashic records. He feels that he should also make some explanation of this process.

which he does on pp. 422-24/416-17. (This is a somewhat more detailed description than he had previously given.)

The Mahatma proposes to 'transcribe with my own hand this once, whereas the letter in your possession was written by the chela'. He encloses the copy 'verbatim'. He had just referred to the 'palmy days of "impressions" and "precipitations" ' and reminds Sinnett that since those days 'K.H.' has been 'born into a *new* and *higher* light...' but points out that he still has a long way to go before he achieves the 'Light of Omniscience', which shines 'only for the highest Chohan'.

After filling all the omitted portions of the letter, the Mahatma says (p. 426/419) that this 'is the true copy of the original document as now restored—the "Rosetta stone" of the Kiddle incident'.

There follow some semi-serious, semi-humorous comments at which the Mahatma was so facile.

p. 428-9/422: The letter now shifts to other matters. It appears that the matter of the presidency of the London Lodge is arising, and the Mahatma says he would like to see Sinnett have that office. As it turned out, however, another development took place—described in later letters.

A further paragraph contains a word of support for Subba Row. It is probable that the General Cunningham mentioned was Sir Alexander Cunningham (1814-93), English archaeologist and army engineer, who headed some archaeological surveys of India in 1861-65 and 1870-85.

The addendum following the signature relates to a 'plan of a Society within *the* London Society'. Something of this kind, somewhat altered, was later suggested by the Mahatma.

118 (ML-96)   Page 431/424   Folio 3   Recd. Dec. 1883 (est.)

DESCRIPTION: M to APS

The small envelope enclosing this letter is preserved in the British Museum, Folio 3. It is addressed in M's script: 'Sinnett Sahib, Esq. from M'. It has no postmark, the reason being that it was one of several enclosures in a letter from HPB to be explained later.

The first part of the letter is on a folded sheet of smooth notepaper about 5″ x 8″ in size. From the text, we learn that this was a sheet of Sam Ward's monogrammed notepaper. The monogram is a strange one, consisting of a compass face, about ¾ ″ in diameter, printed in red in the upper left-hand corner of the sheet. Outside the circle, in the south-west quadrant, are the letters 'S.W.' (which at first glance one would naturally assume to mean south-west, but apparently in this case stand for Sam Ward). The writing on this sheet is in small script and in bright red ink. The second sheet is a small one, about 4½ ″ x 7″, of extra heavy paper. The script is larger. On this sheet there is considerable unevenness in weight of lines and some smearing of ink.

Equally interesting is its appearance. It is headed, 'Sinnett Sahib, Esq. from M'.

CIRCUMSTANCES

Briefly, as a background which it is hoped will make the Mahatma M's comments a little more intelligible, Sinnett was taking some interest in spiritualistic phenomena, in addition to his theosophical work. He had never entirely released himself from his fascination with Spiritualism. Whether as a rationalization or as a fact, he was convinced that his interest was scientific.

William Eglinton had continued his mediumistic activities after his return to London—in fact he was earning his living in this manner—and this letter (118) is concerned in part with a seance he was holding in the quarters of Sam Ward. These, it seems, were above the Sotheran bookshop in Picadilly, which, the Mahatma M comments, 'is a good place for psychic development'. The Mahatma M's attention was attracted to this seance, he says, by becoming aware that HPB's handwriting was being forged and that a false message purporting to come from him—the Mahatma M—was being produced. He immediately went there in his *mayavi rupa,* or in some way invisibly. In his opening paragraph he describes what happened.

REFERENCES

He begins abruptly, however, by reminding Sinnett that 'Your memory is not good'. Refer to notes on Letter 96 (ML-92) in which the Mahatma KH gave three words which *must* be used in any bona fide communication of this kind, with the warning that if these words were *not* used, 'Know it is not me, nor from me.'

p. 432/425: The bogus message referred to by M ('my message in a feigned hand'), written on Sam Ward's monogrammed paper, is found in Folio 6 in the British Museum, but it has not been published. The 'feigned' handwriting bears no resemblance to the regular M script.

p. 432/425: '... the activity of the Pisachas ...' Ghosts or elementaries, the astral shells of disembodied persons. See *Glossary.*

'...you must not be too hard upon the wretched young fellow'. Referring to the medium, William Eglinton, who was conducting the seance.

The rest of the letter is a sort of defence of Eglinton, who was 'utterly irresponsible' on that night. He is a 'poor epileptic' and 'really honest in his way and to be pitied'. M suggests that Sam Ward get him some other kind of a job 'and thus save him from a life of infamy which kills him'. Also he advises Sinnett to ask Eglinton for the 'card of Upasika with her alleged writing on it'. Apparently Sinnett did ask Eglinton for this fraudulent message. It is in one of the folios in the British Museum but has never been published. 'It is a good thing', says the Mahatma M, 'to keep and show occasionally to the Masseys of the L.L. [London Lodge] who believe pure lies and will suspect fraud where none is meant.'

p. 432/426: '... though I am the first to advise Mrs K[ingsford]'s re-election...' Mrs Kingsford was president of L.L. that year, and the Mahatmas insisted that she be re-elected for another year, much to the dissatisfaction of APS and his followers.

The 'Australian convert' mentioned at the end of the Mahatma M's letter was William H. Terry, an Australian Spiritualist and founder and editor of the magazine *Harbinger of Light* published in Melbourne. Correspondence with him was in part responsible for the series of articles, 'Fragments of Occult Truth'. See also *How Theosophy Came to Australia* by Mary K. Neff.

119 (ML-86) Page 403/396 Folio 3 Recd. London, Jan. 1884. Evidently sent by sea mail along with 120 (ML-85)

DESCRIPTION: KH to APS

KH script in pale blue ink on four full-sized sheets of white paper. Unfortunately three of the sheets are marred by unsightly grease spots.

CIRCUMSTANCES

The Founders were in India; APS was living in London; Mrs Kingsford was President of the London Lodge. The election of officers was soon to take place, and APS, who had the largest following in the Lodge, was interested in becoming President.

In this letter from the Mahatma KH, he reminds Sinnett that he (Sinnett) has indicated to HPB that he will follow the advice of the Mahatma KH 'in almost anything' he may ask of him. And now, the time has come to prove Sinnett's willingness. 'And since', the Mahatma adds, 'I myself am simply carrying out the wishes of my Chohan, I hope you will not experience too much difficulty in sharing my fate by doing—as I do.'

REFERENCES

p. 403/397: Then he practically drops a bombshell in Sinnett's lap. Mrs Kingsford has been President of the London Lodge for about a year. This was really due to the efforts of C.C. Massey, who felt she was the only one who could keep that group from dying. But Sinnett had been back in England for about nine months, and he himself very much wanted to assume that post for the London group. There was considerable division in the lodge as a result.

Now, the Mahatma says that the ' "Fascinating" Mrs K. has to remain President—until the new order'. This must have been difficult for Sinnett to accept. However, the Mahatma explained that he is simply following out the wishes of the Mahachohan—a rather astonishing thing, for up to this time the Mahachohan (while apparently always interested) had never interfered directly in the affairs of the Society or any of its branches.

p. 403/397: Then the Mahatma gives—in part at least—the reason why the Mahachohan approves of her: '... her anti-vivisection struggle and her strict vegetarian diet have won entirely over to her side our stern Master. He cares less than we do for any outward—or even inward—expression of feeling of disrespect to the "Mahatmas".'

p. 403/397: 'Jusqu'au nouvel ordre'—until the new order.

p. 403/397: Then the Mahatma speaks of 'the enclosed paper' which is to be delivered to an officer of the London Lodge—perhaps Mr Massey, who was one of the vice-presidents. That enclosure is the next letter to be considered. Here the Mahatma asks Sinnett to insist that it be read before a general meeting composed of as many Theosophists as can be gathered together, and at the earliest opportunity.

p. 404/398: The Mahatma then deals with some philosophical questions which Sinnett has apparently asked him. Sinnett is still worrying about Devachan, it seems. He never much liked the idea in the first place, it will be remembered.

Apparently Sinnett had wanted to set Massey right on some points, but the Mahatma thinks this would be futile. He adds: 'He is a bit of a misanthrope, your friend.'

p. 405/399: There is a short humorous paragraph concerning the request by a friend of Sam Ward that the Mahatma get him a pair of chamois horns. The Mahatma will try if he can find them without killing.

The next to the last paragraph concerns a pamphlet written by Charles Bradlaugh and Annie Besant entitled *The Fruits of Philosophy.* This was before Mrs Besant had met HPB and had become a member of the Theosophical Society. The pamphlet was one of the first ever published endorsing birth control. HPB was strongly against it, and here the Mahatma speaks scathingly of it. Nothing in the publication changes his respect for the authors, but, he says, the 'advices offered' in it 'are abominable'. It might be worth while to comment that in the latter part of the twentieth century, the contents of the pamphlet would not even raise an eyebrow.

120 (ML-85) Page 398/392 Folio 3 Dated Dec. 7, 1883, Madras. Enclosed with 119 (ML-86), recd. in London in Jan. 1884.

DESCRIPTION: KH to London Lodge Members

In KH script in blue ink, on one side only of ten full-sized sheets of white paper.

CIRCUMSTANCES

This letter is the enclosure mentioned by the Mahatma in his last letter. It is addressed to the members of the London Lodge and is headed, rather whimsically: 'Friends and Opponents'.

This is one of the most important letters in the book so far as the Theosophical Society—especially in the West—is concerned, and it should be read thoughtfully by anyone with that interest in mind.

The Mahatma has just ordered two telegrams to be sent, one to Mrs Kingsford and one to Mr Sinnett, to notify both that Mrs Kingsford should continue as President of the London Lodge. The telegram to Mrs Kingsford is, of course, not available. The telegram to Sinnett is in Folio 6 of the Letters in the British Museum but has not been published. It is short and to the point: 'Kingsford must remain president.'

The London Lodge was badly divided at this time and the Adepts took the rather unusual step of requesting the members to retain Mrs Kingsford as president at the forthcoming election of officers.

REFERENCES

p. 398/392: 'Hermetic philosophy': the school espoused by Mrs Kingsford.

p. 399/393: '... three centres of the Occult Brotherhood ...' A specific statement by KH concerning the widespread nature of the Brotherhood. Also a provocative reference to the fact that there are 'different schools of occult thought' not necessarily in basic conflict.

p. 399/393: Then follows a profound statement which should be taken to heart by all students of occultism. 'The only object to be striven for is the amelioration of the condition of MAN by the spread of truth suited to the various stages of his development and that of the country he inhabits and belongs to. TRUTH has no earmark and does not suffer from the name under which it is promulgated...'

p. 400-401/394-396: At the close of the notes on Letter 117 (ML-93) mention is made of 'a plan of a Society within the London Society'. Now the Mahatma makes a specific suggestion: those who wish to follow the teachings of the Tibetan Brotherhood should be formed into a group under Sinnett's direction and *within* the 'London Lodge T.S.' This is the Mahachohan's desire, and those who belong to this group are urged to observe 'more caution than ever in the exposition of our secret teachings'. The Mahatma then offers advice on how this arrangement can be facilitated.

Although seemingly a rather fragile arrangement, the plan might have worked had it not been for a further complication. Early in December 1883, Mrs Kingsford and the Vice-President of London Lodge, Edward Maitland, issued a circular entitled 'A Letter Addressed to the Fellows of the London Lodge of the Theosophical Society by the President and a Vice-President of the Lodge', which embodied a severe criticism of Sinnett's new book, *Esoteric Buddhism*. Understandably, this did not make for improvement in the harmony of the situation. In late January 1884, Subba Row, in collaboration with 'another still greater scholar' (see ML p. 409) who, it is believed, was the Mahatma M, issued in pamphlet form a 'Reply' to this circular letter entitled 'Observations on "A Letter Addressed..." ' Subba Row sent this to HPB with a covering letter, requesting her to forward it to the London Lodge. She did so on 25 January 1884. The full text can be found in *Esoteric Writings of T. Subba Row,* pp. 393-447.

p. 401/395 (near bottom): Here the Mahatma makes a rather remarkable statement that can give the student something to ponder over: '... though we may not say with the Christians, "return good for evil"—we repeat with Confucius, "return good for good; for evil—JUSTICE" '

121 (ML-84) Page 391 Folio 3 Recd. London Feb. 7, 1884, along with 122 (ML-87), q.v.

DESCRIPTION: KH to APS

KH script in green ink, with heavy lettering on both sides of heavy-folded stationery.

CIRCUMSTANCES

This letter is for the purpose of transmitting a letter addressed to the London Lodge. Sinnett is instructed to present it to the Lodge in his capacity as Vice-President of the parent Society, 'and therefore representative of the President Founder, *not as member of the Branch at London'*. This is an important distinction.

The affairs of the London Lodge were still in somewhat of a turmoil. As a matter of fact, as will be evident in the next letter to be considered, the Mahachohan advised postponement of the election. Apparently the two factions, led by Kingsford and Sinnett, were more or less at loggerheads with each other. Events had not led to the 'magnetic harmony' mentioned by the Mahatma in his former letter to the Lodge [120 (ML-85)].

However, the Mahatma says here, that even this situation is better than the old 'paralytic calm' which had previously existed. An outbreak of fever, he comments, is nature's evidence that she is trying to expel the seeds of disease and perhaps death. The Mahatma indicates that 'Karma has its own'. Presumably this may mean that karma has been satisfied.

REFERENCES

p. 397/391: 'Olcott's forthcoming visit ...' He arrived in London in early April.

p. 398/391: 'He will be accompanied by Mohini ...' Mohini M. Chatterji, one of the chelas of KH. See Alphabetical Notes.

Comments on Olcott's forthcoming visit follow. The Mahatma advises that Olcott divide his time among various members and not stay all the time with the Sinnetts. Nothing is said in this letter about HPB accompanying Olcott, although Mohini is mentioned.

Also, the Mahatma asks Sinnett to do what he can to dignify Olcott's office, 'for he represents the entire Society, and by reason of his official position, if for no other, stands with Upasika [HPB] closest to ourselves in the chain of Theosophical work'.

The closing word 'Asirvadam' is translated by the editors of the third edition as 'Blessings'.

122 (ML-87) Page 406/399 Folio 3 Posted Adyar, Jan. 16, 1884. Recd. London, Feb. 7, 1884. (Apparently sent by sea mail.)

DESCRIPTION: KH to APS

In green ink on both sides of four sheets of full-sized white paper. The script of the letter itself is large, even, copy-book type, and was no doubt written down by the chela from dictation.

The postscript by KH is in green ink. The letter is signed by Bhola Deva Sarma in Devanagari script. The p.ps.

(unsigned) is in KH script, and this is in green, and green and black intermingled. The letter was sent by registered post. The envelope is in the British Museum folio. On the back of it is written, 'From Bhola Deva Sarma'. He was one of the Indian chelas. It seems likely that the letter was written by him under KH's direction. He was living in Mysore in South India.

REFERENCES

APS was in London. The Founders were in India, but planning to go to Europe soon. Mrs Kingsford was President of the London Lodge, but apparently there was considerable dissension within the Lodge. KH had written and telegraphed in Dec. 1883 asking that Mrs Kingsford be re-elected President. This seems to have further complicated the situation, and so on 16 January 1884 (at the time of writing this letter) he sent a second telegram to London, the text of which was 'postpone election, letter follows'. The Letter is of course, 122 (ML-87). The telegram is in Folio 6 of the British Museum (not published).

REFERENCES

First sentence: The telegram mentioned was dated 7 Dec. 1883 and said 'Kingsford must remain President'. The Letter referred to as from Mysore is 120 (ML-85), dated 7 Dec. 1883.

Much of the remainder of the letter is devoted to explaining his position and backing away a bit from the apparently dictatorial statements in his two telegrams, what KH speaks of (p. 406/400) as an 'unusual, not to say arbitrary, action'. Also taking Mrs Kingsford to task a bit for attempting to be dictatorial in her management of the London Lodge.

p. 408/402: 'However little we might care ...' An unequivocal statement concerning the attitude of the Mahatmas towards the relationship between the parent Theosophical Society and its branches.

(near end): '... the President Founder ... is expected to be in England ...' SH p. 197, relates that a new election was held on April 7 with HSO presiding. Mr G.B. Finch (a compromise) was elected President (See also LMW I:18, p. 42).

The closing of the letter indicates that it was written by a chela under the direction of KH.

For an account of the events that ensued after Olcott's arrival in London and on the night of the Lodge election of officers, see ODL 3:90-98. Also see C.W. Leadbeater's description in his book, *How Theosophy Came to Me.*

123 (ML-68) Page 372/366 Folio 3 February 1884 (est.) (Possibly later; see below)

DESCRIPTION: KH to APS

KH script in blue pencil on both sides of a scrap of heavy smooth paper, about 4″ x 10″, folded.

CIRCUMSTANCES

It is probable that Sinnett became a bit discouraged over events in the London Lodge, and he may have written to the Mahatma about this. Letter 123 is a personal note of encouragement and concern. It is impossible to tell precisely when it was written or received, so that it may be incorrectly placed in the chronology. That perhaps does not matter, since no event is mentioned.

There is much in the letter, however, which could be meaningful to every aspirant. The student may therefore find it rewarding to read.

124 (ML-94) Page 429/422 Folio 3 Recd. April 1, 1884 (est.)

DESCRIPTION: KH to APS

KH script, in green ink, on both sides of a single sheet of heavy notepaper. This might indicate that the letter was transmitted through Bhola Deva Sarma.

CIRCUMSTANCES

In the fourth English edition (1884) of OW, Sinnett, in explanation of the Kiddle Incident, mentions several articles recently published in *The Theosophist* and adds: 'A month or two after the appearance of these fragmentary hints, I received a note from the Mahatma relieving me of all restrictions previously imposed on the full letter of explanation he had previously sent me.'

This is the letter removing those restrictions.

REFERENCES

'... forgotten the "Kiddle Incident" '. The charge of plagiarism for using some of Mr Kiddle's phrases. [In No. 11, (ML-6), p. 24.] See Appendix E.

'You have my explanation.' Given in 117 (ML-93).

'...the golden-haired nymph of the Vicarage'. Probably a light reference to Mrs Kingsford.

'The several letters and articles in the last numbers of *The Theosophist* ...' The December 1883 issue of *The Theosophist* carried articles on the subject by General Morgan, Dharani Dhu, and Subba Row which, the Mahatma says in this letter, were published with his permission.

Major-General Henry Rhodes Morgan was a retired British officer who took up residence at Ootacamund in the Nilgiri Hills, South India. He and his wife were close friends of HPB and Olcott. General Morgan joined the Theosophical Society in September 1883.

Dharani Dhu, or Dharani Dhar Kauthami, was a chela of the Mahatma KH.

125 (ML-61) Page 349/344 Folio 3 Recd. April 15 or after, 1884 (est.)

DESCRIPTION: M to APS

In red ink, diagonally on the paper, on a single sheet of smooth, heavy paper of slightly ivory shade, 7" x 9½ ". The script varies in size and is crowded towards the end of the letter. The envelope, bound in the folio, is a long slim one with a Chinese block print on the front. On the back, in red ink and in M script is 'Sinnett Sahib, from M'.

CIRCUMSTANCES

APS was living in London. HSO and MMC had arrived in London and were staying in the APS home. HPB had been in London briefly, but had returned to France. (The chapter in SH entitled 'The Founders Visit Europe', pp. 191/207, gives considerable information on this period.) The Founders were planning to stay in Europe for the summer.

Before they left for Europe, Olcott issued a special order designating certain members of the General Council (the governing body of the Theosophical Society) to act as an Executive Committee during his absence. As a Headquarters Executive Committee, he added Dr Franz Hartmann, St George Lane-Fox, W.T. Brown, and M. Coulomb and named this committee the 'Board of Control'. Subba Row was left in charge of *The Theosophist*. This is mentioned because it was during the absence of Olcott and HPB from the headquarters that the Coulomb Conspiracy took place. That will be dealt with at the proper time. Those who have a copy of Josephine Ransom's *A Short History of the Theosophical Society* will find this period covered very clearly and succinctly on pages 191-207.

Dr Franz Hartmann was a member of the Society from Germany who loyally supported HPB through the Coulomb difficulty. St George Lane-Fox was a newcomer from England who later became somewhat hostile to the Society and more or less followed Hume's lead. W.T. Brown was the young man who was a member of Olcott's company on a tour of some of the northern provinces and who received a note from the Mahatma KH at Lahore [see notes on Letter 115 and 116 (ML-129) and (ML-128)]. M. Coulomb was Mme Emma Coulomb's husband and was in charge of maintenance at headquarters.

REFERENCES

The first part of the letter deals with MMC, and APS is taken to task for having treated him, as well as HSO, in such a poor manner. See pp. 353-4/347-8.

p. 349/344 (first sentence): '... his "Guardian" ...' Obviously KH.

p. 350/344: '... whatever KH may or may not do for him ...' This refers to the repayment of the 125 pound loan which had been made to Mohini to facilitate his trip to Europe for his assignment there. There are a few other references in the Mahatma Letters and other places regarding financial assistance given by the Mahatmas to their chelas in situations of emergency.

p. 350/345: '... his extravagant Asiatic undresses ...' HSO was given to wearing his Indian style clothes in England, which greatly embarrassed APS.

'Arundale Ladies': Mrs A. and Miss F. Arundale.

The last part refers to the situation in the London Lodge. As a result of the election held just a short time previously, a Mr Finch had been elected president, as a compromise, and the two (Sinnett's and Kingsford's) factions in the Lodge were split.

126 (ML-62) Page 351/345 Folio 3 Recd. July 18, 1884

DESCRIPTION: KH to APS

KH script on five sheets, the first three of which are smooth white notepaper, and the last two of a different kind. The script is in blue ink, in small lettering. There are runs and smears in places, giving the impression that the letter was written by hand. The enclosing envelope is attached and is addressed: 'Mr A.P. Sinnett' in KH script in blue pencil. There is no postmark on the envelope.

CIRCUMSTANCES

HPB was still in Europe when this was received. Olcott was in London but had left the Sinnetts' house, in accordance with the Mahatma's suggestion that he divide his time among different members' homes.

REFERENCES

This letter is rather severe. The Mahatma is going to make 'one more effort' he says, to open Sinnett's inner intuition. 'If my voice, the voice of one who was ever friendly to you in the human principle of his being—fails to reach you as it has often before, then our separation in the present and for all time to come—becomes unavoidable.' This, the Mahatma says, is painful to him, but his first duty is to *his* Master. He makes a strong statement about duty and its importance in the Brotherhood.

p. 351/346: 'Patience, patience. A great design has never been snatched at once ...' In Folio 6 in the British Museum, there is a verse from KH, written in blue pencil on a slip of paper. This is printed as a frontispiece in the LBS volume, and reads as follows:

> ...It was thy patience that in the waste Attended Still thy step, and saved MY friend for better days. What cannot patience do

... A great design is seldom snatched at once, 'Tis PATIENCE heaves it on...

Date or circumstance of this communication is not indicated. Apparently Barker did not know what to do with it and so did not include it in the ML. It is impossible to determine whether the line in this letter preceded or followed the receipt of the entire verse.

p. 352/346: 'I had chosen you as the exponent ...' This indicates why correspondence setting forth the occult doctrines was undertaken with APS.

p. 352/347: 'I was tied hand and foot..' KH here explains why he was unable to give more help in establishing a new paper for APS (*The Phoenix*).

p. 353/347: '...the interference in the quarrel ...' A reference to the two telegrams and 120 and 122 (ML-85 and 87) which were sent regarding the presidential election in the L.L.

p. 353/347: 'You simply mistook M's natural brusqueness...' See 125 (ML-61) where M criticizes APS for his treatment of MMC and HSO.

p. 353-4/348: This deals mostly with APS's unfortunate attitude towards the recent events and his resentment against HPB, HSO and Mrs Kingsford and treatment of Mohini.

Mme Gebhard of Elberfeld, Germany, was also visiting the Sinnett home at the time.

p. 355/350: '...what I told you through Mrs H'. A reference to Laura C. Holloway, an American clairvoyant who had come to London to contact APS and the other Theosophists. Seemingly she was a good candidate for development. She worked with MMC for a time, and together they wrote the book, *Man, Fragments of Forgotten History* by 'Two Chelas'. See SH, pp. 199-200. See Alphabetical Notes.

'...the Old Woman's and Mohini's advice...' It is evident from this statement that the Mahatmas had planned to develop Mrs Holloway for use in communicating with APS and perhaps others in London.

p. 356/350 (near end): '... not only to be present at the meeting but also to speak ...' This no doubt refers to the 'Princess Hall' meeting held a few days later (July 21), which was a farewell meeting for the Founders before their return to India. Apparently APS was so irritated that he did not plan to attend. However he did attend the meeting and gave a talk.

127 (ML-133) ***Page 469/453*** ***Folio 3*** ***Recd. July 1884 (est.)***

DESCRIPTION: HPB TO APS

In HPB's handwriting in purplish ink on both sides of a single sheet about 7″ x 8″.

CIRCUMSTANCES

HPB was probably in London. HSO had been there, and perhaps was still there when this letter was written, although he went from England to Elberfeld, Germany, on 23 July 1884 (ODL 3:164). APS was apparently unhappy about the way things were going and about KH's criticism of him.

Apparently Sinnett had written to HPB—or had protested to her in person—following receipt of the letter last considered [126 (ML-62)], in which the Mahatma KH said that he had never approached Sinnett or anyone else through Mrs Holloway. Sinnett felt that the letter could not be genuine, for he believed implicitly that the Mahatma KH *had* spoken through and even possessed Mrs Holloway at a meeting on July 6.

REFERENCES

p. 460/453: 'The *letter is from him* ...' Perhaps meaning 126 (ML-62), in which KH was quite frank in his criticism of APS.

'Olcott has behaved like an ass ...' Probably the reference to Olcott's behaviour is to the unconventional dress in which he appeared and embarrassed everyone when guests were present. Sinnett was inclined to want only the 'elite' as members of the Theosophical Society; both men and women dressed formally for meetings of the London Lodge.

p. 461/454: '...managed to get the Psychic Research Society rid of its nightmare, Olcott...' Probably a reference to the appearance of HSO before the SPR at which he made some foolish and unscientific statements, which were responsible in part for the Hodgson investigation at Adyar. See Alphabetical Notes.

128 (ML-63) Page 356/350 Folio 3 Recd. Summer of 1884 (est.)

DESCRIPTION: KH to APS

KH script in blue pencil on two sheets of paper, one side only.

CIRCUMSTANCES

APS was living in London. Since the date of letter is uncertain, the whereabouts of the Founders is not known. From the contents of this letter, it would appear that APS had asked KH about publishing his letters verbatim as well as those he had received from Master M.

As to whether the letters should have been published (a point still being argued) it seems obvious that they should not have been published at, or near, the time they were written. As it was, almost 50 years passed before they were published; H.P. Blavatsky's great work, *The Secret Doctrine,* written with the help of the authors of the letters and later editorially sharpened by keen and intelligent students, expounded the doctrines and philosophical concepts little more than hinted at in the letters.

Most of the people mentioned or discussed in the letters were no longer living, and there was little risk of unfortunate consequences. At any rate, the letters *have* been published (three editions so far), much to the benefit of the world which has yet to appreciate them at their full value. The letters were not written for public comment, says the Mahatma KH on p. 357, but for private use—and that surely will be where they will continue to have their most profound influence.

REFERENCES

p. 356/351: '...answers were necessarily imperfect, often from different standpoints'. This throws light on some of the seeming discrepancies in the *Letters*.

p. 357/351: '...none but those who have passed at least their third initiation are able to write upon these subjects comprehensively'. A very interesting statement, explaining to some extent why APS's books were rather qualified successes from the standpoint of the Mahatmas.

'Mohini is certainly not quite right ...' A reference to the book written jointly by MMC and Mrs Holloway entitled *Man, Fragments of Forgotten History,* completed in August of that year. See Alphabetical Notes.

p. 357/351: The reference to the *'Secret Doctrine'* on p. 357/351 does not mean HPB's *magnum opus* which was written a bit later. At the time of this letter, the Mahatmas had decided to form a committee of high chelas centred round the Adyar headquarters. This committee, which was more or less secret, was to receive letters and teachings from the Mahatmas and compile them in a systematic way, and this would eventually be issued as a 'secret doctrine'. This group was the Library Committee mentioned in the next paragraph, with a listing of the names of those who composed it. HPB was 'purposely excluded' the Mahatma tells Sinnett, 'to avoid new suspicions and calumnies ...' There is no further reference to this committee in the letter, and it can only be assumed that it did not fulfil its purpose and that the full *Secret Doctrine* awaited HPB's indefatigable efforts.

p. 357/352: Mention is made of Mrs Holloway: 'I am afraid the "poor, dear Mrs Holloway" is showing her white teeth and would hardly be found now "a charming companion" '. Mrs Holloway was, at that time, in danger of losing her sanity, it seems. 'It is Fern, Moorad Ali, Bishen Lal and other wrecks over again,' says the Mahatma. 'Why will "would-be" chelas with such intense self personalities force themselves within the enchanted and dangerous circle of probation!'

This is a hint, surely, concerning the failure of some of these chelas: 'self-personality'. In another letter, a bit further on, the Mahatma has more to say on this theme.

p. 357/352: '...Olcott wrote a letter to Finch...' G.B. Finch was the President of the London Lodge at that particular time, as a compromise between the Sinnett and Holloway factions.

129 (ML-60) Page 349/343 Folio 3 Recd. Sept. 1884 (est.)

DESCRIPTION: KH to APS

KH script in blue pencil on a single sheet of heavy rough paper which looks as though it had been cut by hand. The envelope is preserved in the folio. It is a small white one, bearing only the address 'A.P. Sinnett, Esq.' in blue pencil and KH script. Beneath this are some unrecognizable characters. It bears no stamp or postmark.

CIRCUMSTANCES

HPB was probably in Germany. HSO was in Germany, APS was in London, still in a state of unhappiness. There was an 'Inner Group' of students in London at that time.

The Mahatma appears to be trying to reason with Sinnett and perhaps even to comfort him.

Sinnett had of late been fighting doubts, in part brought about by his conviction that the Mahatma had indeed taken possession of Laura Holloway and spoken through her, and the Mahatma's denial that this had ever taken place. 'When shall you trust *implicitly,*' the Mahatma asks, 'in my heart if not in my wisdom for which I claim no recognition on your part?' This situation has been extremely painful for Sinnett.

REFERENCES

p. 349/343: 'my portrait made by Herr Schmiechen ...' A reference to the oil portrait of KH made by the German painter of that name (See Alphabetical Notes). He came to London in June and July 1884 and painted two portraits, one of KH and one of M, apparently under inspiration. These portraits are now in Adyar. Later, Schmiechen painted duplicates of these portraits and perhaps more.

'...dissatisfied with the one you have ...' This refers to a black and white precipitation of KH made by DK for Sinnett when he was in India.

The Mahatma adds a few lines after his signature asking Sinnett to attend the Wednesday meeting. This is undoubtedly the meeting referred to in letter 126 (ML-62) which Sinnett did not want to attend but finally did. He had been acting as the 'mouthpiece' for the Mahatma KH for this Inner Group.

130 (ML-55) Page 322/317 Folio 2 Recd. Oct. 2, 1884 (est.)

DESCRIPTION: KH to APS

KH script in blue pencil on four small folded sheets of 'L.C. Holloway' notepaper. The envelope in the Folio is addressed in KH script to: 'A.P. Sinnett, Esq., c/o L.C.H.'

This is not really explained, but one may perhaps speculate that the Mahatma had decided to try Mrs Holloway as an intermediary. According to this letter (p. 323/318) she is much improved 'and her whole life hereafter will be benefited by the training she is passing through'.

CIRCUMSTANCES

HSO and HPB were in Germany. The Sinnetts were travelling in Europe at this time (the 'flight from London' mentioned by the Mahatma). While in Switzerland, they received a telegram from Mrs Gebhard inviting them to come to Elberfeld, where HPB and others had been staying. They accepted her invitation. Mrs Holloway was one of the group there. This *may* explain the use of her notepaper in producing this letter, as it seems likely that Sinnett received it after he reached there.

REFERENCES

The first paragraph indicates approval of APS's present trip.

Impending trouble for the TS is indicated.

p. 322/317 (end of first par.): '... represents enormous vested interests ...' Probably meaning the Christian churches and British interests in India. In one of his earlier letters, KH had intimated that the Viceroy of India was under the control of the Vatican.

p. 323/318: '...ready to burst at Adyar ...' A reference to the impending Coulomb-missionary plot, and also perhaps the Hodgson report.

The Mahatma informs Sinnett of an unhealthy situation which has developed in his house ('a colony of Elementaries quartering in it') which was partly responsible for Mrs Holloway's indisposition. The Mahatma gives some advice for ridding the place of these influences (p. 323/318). 'The talismans you have had given you ...' All the Sinnetts had locks of the Mahatma's hair which they wore on their persons: the Mahatma indicates these will help them *'if you keep your confidence in them and in us unbroken'*.

p. 323/318: 'You have heard of the step H.P.B. was permitted to take.' This refers to the fact that she resigned as Corresponding Secretary of the Theosophical Society so as to dissociate herself from the Society. This was a direct result of the Coulomb conspiracy.

Sinnett is gently chided for the touch of hero worship with which he regards the Mahatma. '... learn to be loyal to the idea, rather than to my poor self'. The Mahatma emphatically disclaims infallibility and reminds Sinnett once more that 'an "adept" when acting in his body is not beyond mistakes due to human carelessness'. A further reason is given for the Mahatmas' reluctance to have their letters published at that time. He explains that he has a habit of quoting whatever he sees lying around in the 'Akashic libraries' but he has learned a lesson from the experience with Mr Kiddle. This is a delightful passage, typical of the Mahatma KH's occasional light manner.

p. 324/319 (middle): 'Kiddle incident.' Refer to Letter 12 (ML-6), p. 324/22 and Letter 117 (ML-93), p. 420/413.

p. 324/319: The last half of this page gives some of the reasons why KH did not want his letters published verbatim.

p. 325/320: '..."the Christian-mission-Coulomb" conspiracy...' See Alphabetical Notes on Alexis and Emma Coulomb.

(same paragraph): An interesting statement that the pledges of the London members of the 'Inner Circle' were delivered to the Mahachohan.

p. 325/320: The Mahatma expresses the hope that Sinnett will remain in London during the coming winter and continue to be his mouthpiece for the 'Inner Circle'. He indicates that he can no longer send letters through HPB but must depend upon Damodar. But before anything can be done, the Society will have to pass through 'the coming crisis'. 'The sky is black now,' he says, 'but forget not the hopeful motto *"Post nubila Phoebus!"* ' (After the darkness—the dawn).

131 (ML-66) Page 366/360 Folio 3 Recd. Oct. 10, 1884

DESCRIPTION: KH to APS

KH script in sharp blue pencil on both sides of four sheets of full-sized white paper. The envelope, which is in the British Museum folio, is a plain one addressed in unknown calligraphy:

'A.P. Sinnett, Esq., 7 Ladbroke Gardens, Notting Hill, London.'

It bears a postmark of Bromley, Kent, 9 October 1884. Based upon the statement in the first paragraph, it seems probable that the letter was transmitted through an agent somewhere in England.

CIRCUMSTANCES

APS and HPB had returned to London following their visits to Germany. HSO had returned to India. The Coulomb-missionary plot in India was about to break on the heads of the Theosophists, to be followed soon by the Hodgson investigation and his adverse report.

This is a fairly long letter containing a sharp warning to Sinnett that his attitude is becoming a threat to further communication between them. Sinnett had returned to London from Elberfeld, and HPB had accompanied him to London. Col. Olcott had left England on his return to India. It had become impossible any longer to use HPB as the 'post office' for the letters.

Later on in this letter (p. 369/363) we learn that Sinnett had written to the Mahatma complaining about HPB and delivering what the Mahatma calls an 'ultimatum' paraphrased by him as follows: 'Either Mrs H[olloway] passes a week or so at our house, or I leave the L.L. [London Lodge] to get on as best it can.' It very nearly meant, the Mahatma says, ' "Master" or no Masters to the contrary notwithstanding, I [APS] must and shall show the L.L. that anything they may have heard about this affair was false, and that the "Masters" would never consent to any action hurtful to my pride: that must be protected in any event.' This is 'treading on dangerous ground,' the Mahatma warns him.

Precisely what the situation was is not stated, but there are hints that it may have concerned the Mahatma's denial that he had communicated with Sinnett through Mrs Holloway when Sinnett himself was so convinced that this had taken place, plus perhaps the warning that Sinnett's home had now 'a colony of Elementaries' in it and that it was unwise to bring the sensitive Mrs Holloway there.

REFERENCES

On p. 367/361, the Mahatma gives Sinnett two very sharp pieces of advice: 'Insensibly to yourself, you are encouraging a tendency to dogmatism and unjust misconception of persons and motives.' And: 'Beware then, of an uncharitable spirit, for it will rise up like a hungry wolf in your path, and devour the better qualities of your nature which have been springing into life. Broaden instead of narrowing your sympathies; try to identify yourself with your fellows, rather than to contract your circle of affinities.'

A crisis is taking place, and however it was caused, the whole Society is involved 'and it is rather fanned than weakened from Tchigadze'. Since Tchigadze was the seat of the Brotherhood, this surely indicates that what is involved is something much more serious than a personal affront to Sinnett. The Coulomb-missionary plot in India had broken over the heads of the Society while the group of Theosophists was visiting Elberfeld, and it was to be followed by the Hodgson investigation and adverse report. The fact that it was rather 'fanned' than weakened at Tchigadze inevitably causes speculation that the whole occasion was being used for all sorts of testing of different persons. Sinnett (and certainly Hume, when they were working together) was rather sceptical and scornful of probations, etc. This is no time for such an attitude, the Mahatma warns him. The very writing of such books as *The Occult World* and *Esoteric Buddhism* has aroused the guardians, and 'those who would have that [occult] knowledge should be *thoroughly* tried and tested'. HPB can no longer be used, and Mrs Holloway is 'far from being ready'. The Mahatma seems to feel that attempts to spread the Wisdom in the West have to a large extent failed.

While some are inclined to blame Col. Olcott and HPB entirely for unfortunate developments, they have, the Mahatma insists (p. 370/364) that quality of 'UNSELFISHNESS, and an eager readiness for self-sacrifice for the good of others; what a "multitude of sins" does not this cover!' The Mahatma goes on to say that it is 'real manhood when one boldly accepts one's share of the collective Karma of the group one works with, and does not permit oneself to be embittered, and to see others in blacker colours than reality, or to throw all blame upon some one "black sheep", a victim, specially selected'.

132 (ML-135) Page 464/457 Folio 3 Recd. Oct. 1884 (est.)

DESCRIPTION: HPB to APS

In HPB's handwriting on both sides of a blue card, about 4" x 5".

CIRCUMSTANCES

HSO left for India on October 20, landing in Bombay on

November 10 (ODL 3:183). HPB and APS were in London. In this short letter, HPB tries to put Sinnett right concerning the doctrine of chains and rounds. We do not have Sinnett's letter, to which it was a response, but fortunately another letter from HPB, found in LBS, pp. 91-2, throws some light on the problem.

The Hübbe-Schleiden, to whom HPB refers in 132 (ML-135) was the first President of the Germania Theosophical Society, and Frank Gebhard was a member of the Gebhard family in Elberfeld. There were a number of children, and all but one joined the Theosophical Society.

REFERENCES

The '777' puzzle (to which Sinnett had not the key, as HPB points out) is found in Letter 66 (ML-14), on p. 83 of that letter, in which the Mahatma warns Sinnett that he cannot give complete information. More than one student has cudgelled his wits over this problem, but since there are 'exceptions' it is impossible for anyone who does not have 'the key' to be certain of its full meaning. Yet the Mahatma says, at the end of the paragraph setting forth the problem, 'Try to solve the problem of the 777 incarnations.' Apparently Hübbe-Schleiden and Frank Gebhard had questioned Sinnett's presentation of the whole doctrine of planets and rounds, in which the '777' puzzle is involved.

Turning to the letter in LBS mentioned above, which was written to Sinnett before HPB left England, the pertinent passage is found on p. 92:

> ...You may copy this and send it on to Hübbe-Schleiden and Frank [Gebhard]. I said there were no such garlands of 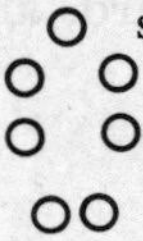
> O sausages as they thought of planets; that this representa-
> O O tion was not even graphical but rather allegorical; that our
> O O seven planets were scattered about; that Rounds meant
> OO what you said, though the explanation was very incomplete, but that the *rings* what you call i.e. the seven root

races and the evolution of man in his eternal septenary generation *was misunderstood,* not only by you but could not be understood by any one uninitiated; and that, even that which *might* have been told by you, you have not told for you misunderstood one of Master's letters.

133 (ML-137) Page 467/459 Folio 3 Recd. Nov. 1884 (est.) Posted from Algiers Nov. 8, 1884

DESCRIPTION: HPB to APS

In HPB's handwriting on both sides of a single sheet.

CIRCUMSTANCES

APS was still in London. HSO was in India. Actually, HPB dated this letter 'Sunday 8th', but Sunday happened to fall on November 9 in 1884. The letter was written from Algiers, while HPB was *en route* from England to India. She returned by way of Egypt.

As an interesting sidelight—not mentioned in this letter—C.W. Leadbeater had received his summons to go to Adyar, but he was unable to leave with HPB, as the decision had been made only about 24 hours earlier. However, he joined her later at Port Said. While they were there, she received instructions from the Mahatma M to go to Cairo, where she would find information that would be of great use to her in dealing with the treacherous Coulombs. She and CWL went to Cairo immediately, along with the Cooper-Oakleys, who were also with her—and it was there that HPB learned the very damaging facts about the Coulombs mentioned in the summary of the 'Coulomb Conspiracy' (See Appendix J).

REFERENCES

The letter to be considered next in these notes was the letter dictated to Djual Khul; it was enclosed in this letter (133).

Letter 133 mainly concerns Mrs Holloway and the 'probation' mentioned here by HPB. Apparently it involved HPB in some way, for she complains that it was done over her 'long-suffering back'.

134 (ML-64) Page 358/352 Folio 3 Recd. November 8, 1884

DESCRIPTION: KH to APS

KH script in blue pencil on folded notepaper. There are variations in the weight of the lines, giving the effect of someone using a soft pencil which had been sharpened a few times during the writing.

CIRCUMSTANCES

Olcott had returned to India. HPB was *en route* to India and was at Algiers at the time of the writing of this letter, which one must conclude is the one written down by DK in her cabin on board ship there [see previous letter 133 (ML-137)].

Sinnett was in London and so were Mohini and Mrs Holloway who were writing, or had completed writing, the book entitled *Man, Fragments of Forgotten History*. APS was apparently quite upset and unhappy at the time.

REFERENCES

p. 358/352: 'F.A.' Miss Francesca Arundale, member of the TS and at one time its Assistant Treasurer. See SH index.

Obviously Sinnett had sent on to the Mahatma a letter which Mrs Holloway had written and sent through Mohini. It must have been rather heavy with self-conceit ('Attavada') but here the Mahatma says that Mohini trusts her implicitly.

Letter 134 (ML-64) mainly concerns Mrs Holloway and deals with the 'probation' about which HPB complained in her covering letter [133 (ML-137)].

p. 358/352: '... a creature of Attavada ...' The sin of self-personality.

p. 359/352 (middle): '...your would-be sibyl'. Mrs Holloway, who seemingly was exercising considerable influence over APS and who was turning against the TS.

p. 359/352: KH discusses Mrs Holloway at considerable length.

p. 359/353: Then, again, the Mahatma speaks regretfully of the failure of chelas.

'...*nothing* short of full confidence in us, in our good motives if not in our wisdom, in our foresight, if not omniscience—which is not to be found on this earth—can help one to cross over from one's land of dream and fiction to our Truth land, the region of stern reality and fact'.

The Mahatma makes some comments about the nature of occult laws and gives what seems a rather curious explanation, including the necessity for the cataclysms of nature. There is reference again to Mrs Holloway and 'those self-opinionated volunteers and candidates for chelaship who will rush under the dark shadow of her wheels' (p. 359/353).

He then explains something about Mrs Holloway's chelaship.

p. 359/353-4: '... the deadly upas-tree of Evil...' The upas tree grows in Java. It is a member of the mulberry family, and its bark yields a poisonous milky substance which the Javanese used for arrow poison. Hence the phrase has come to mean something harmful or deadly in its influence. The Mahatma then explains how karma is, so to speak, concentrated when one becomes a chela.

p. 359/354: Further reference to Fern, Moorad Ali, and Bishen Lal who failed their probationary testing; here KH gives a hint of why probation is so difficult (p. 360/354), then describes some of Mrs Holloway's motivations and the pitfalls into which she walked so blindly—blind, that is to anything 'outside the narrow pathway filled with her own personality'.

He tells how she reached the point of decision and action. She created the 'Student' (a character in the book she wrote with Mohini) in whom she herself believed implicitly. The picture he paints of Mrs Holloway is not, indeed, a very pleasant one.

p. 360/355: 'Dhar[agiri] Nath was despatched and made to impress her thrice ...' This must have been done astrally or in a *mayavi rupa,* for he was in India.

p. 361/355: 'Try to save "Man"...' The book was evidently completed in manuscript but had not yet been published. The book entitled *Man, Fragments of Forgotten History* was finally published in a small edition and has not been reprinted. Copies are very scarce. It is seldom referred to. In Letter 120 of LBS, HPB lists a large number of corrections which she says should be made in the book.

P. 361/355: 'The ice is broken once more,' the Mahatma says in his closing paragraph. Possibly this means that some kind of rapport has been re-established between them.

135 (ML-138) Page 468/460 Dated Adyar, Mar. 17, 1885

DESCRIPTION

In HPB's handwriting on six sheets of blue paper, 7" x 9".

CIRCUMSTANCES

The letter is from HPB to APS. HPB had arrived in Adyar at Christmas time to find the Coulomb conspiracy fully under way. Hodgson from the Society for Psychical Research arrived about the same time and started his investigation. In January, HSO and CWL had gone to Burma on tour. DKM had left in February for Tibet, never to return. HPB was very ill and had to be helped by M again. He also gave her an outline for writing *The Secret Doctrine*. Soon she was sent to Europe to recover and never to return to India.

REFERENCES

p. 468/461: '...from the "brooch" phenomenon ...' Brooch No. 1 (See OW, 9th ed., p. 70 et seq.).

'... The P.R.S. oracle ...' Richard Hodgson, who was making the investigation. See Alphabetical Notes.

'Happy Damodar! He went to ... Tibet ...' DKM had left Adyar for Tibet on February 23 to be with his Master.

'Olcott is returning from Burma in three days ...' HSO and CWL had gone to Burma for an extended tour, but due to HPB's illness, HSO returned to Adyar on March 19.

'Hodgson had *traced* the Brooch!!!' The one mentioned above.

p. 470/462: '... I suddenly got better ...' M had again intervened to save HPB's life.

p. 470/463: 'The shrine was thought of to facilitate the transmission ...' A reference to the portable hanging wall-cabinet in the Headquarters which was used for transmission of letters and became the source of much controversy.

On this page and part of 471/464, HPB describes some of the methods used for occult transmission of letters.

p. 472/464: '... his mission to China...' KH had made a long journey to Burma and south-east Asia during the winter of 1884-5. See 117 (ML-93) and 118 (ML-96).

p. 474/467 (middle): 'This will probably be my last letter to you...' HPB was very ill, and if her Master had not restored her health, it might well have been her last letter to APS.

136 (ML-65) Page 362/356 Folio 3 Recd. probably in April 1885 (est.)

DESCRIPTION: KH to APS

KH script in blue ink on four folded sheets of paper. The long P.S. is in darker ink and finer script.

CIRCUMSTANCES

APS was in London. The Founders were at Adyar. The situation there was very disturbed as the result of the Coulomb affair, the Hodgson investigation, HPB's critical state of health and nerves, and various other attacks from all sides. HPB left for Europe on March 31 never to return to India.

This letter from the Mahatma KH is enclosed in a letter from HPB found in LBS, pp. 75-77. In the postcript to her letter, HPB writes: 'At this very instant I receive a letter for you. I enclose it—pardon me, but I do hope—it is the last, for I have no more strength to suffer.'

REFERENCES

p. 365/356: First two paragraphs—refer to 135 (ML-138).

(middle): '...the centennial attempt made by us ...' The attempt made in the last quarter of each century to further the evolution of mankind. 17 (ML-9). See Alphabetical Notes.

p. 362/356: 'The padris are as busy as bees.' The missionaries in India appeared to be making a united effort to discredit Theosophy.

'The P.R.S. has given them ...' Mr Hodgson's investigation sponsored by the Society for Psychical Research.

(bottom): 'Mr Lane-Fox...' St George Lane-Fox, British electrical engineer who, while at Adyar, was appointed by HSO to the Board of Control, along with Dr Franz Hartmann from the United States and Alexis Coulomb (see Alphabetical Notes on both), when the Founders went to Europe in the summer of 1884.

p.363/357: The Mahatma mentions the 'secret Committee'. This was a committee formed at headquarters for the purpose of receiving letters and teachings from the Mahatmas in the critical year 1884. Dr Franz Hartmann, Chairman of the Board of Control, already mentioned in these Notes, a well-known inventor and scientist, St George Lane-Fox, (both recent arrivals at Headquarters), and A.O. Hume who had not yet resigned from the Society, took it upon themselves to criticize the Society and the Founders with little regard for justice and fairness.

Much of the rest of the letter is composed of examples and illustrations of the statements the Mahatma has made. In his penultimate paragraph, the Mahatma comments: 'Could but your L.L. [London Lodge] understand, or so much as suspect, that the present crisis that is shaking the T.S. to its foundations is a question of perdition or salvation to thousands; a question of the progress of the human race or its retrogression, of its glory or dishonour, and for the majority of this race—*of being or not being,* of annihilation, in fact ...' This is an awe-inspiring statement and one which members of the Society might well think about.

A very long postscript follows the letter proper. The Mahatma has thought of some things which he does not want Sinnett to forget. 'Why is it that doubts and foul suspicions seem to beset every aspirant for chelaship?' he asks. He compares the ancient methods of testings and initiations, but now, he says, 'the aspirant is... assailed entirely on the psychological side of his nature'. Every germ of good and bad in his temperament has to be developed and studied. 'The rule is inflexible, and not one escapes whether he but writes to us a letter, or in the privacy of his own heart's thought formulates a strong desire for occult communication and knowledge.' The teaching 'brings into fierce action every unsuspected potentiality latent in him. Few Europeans have stood this test.' Henceforth 'whatever is imparted will be from individuals to individuals'.

137 (ML-97) Page 433/426 Folio 3 Recd. Fall of 1885 (est.)

DESCRIPTION: M to APS

M script in red ink on a single sheet of folded paper. The sheet is about 7″ x 9″, very rough, and unevenly cut. The writing on the back is diagonally across the page.

CIRCUMSTANCES

HPB had gone to Germany to live and to write *The Secret Doctrine*. Another Indian chela, Babaji, had come over with her from India. MMC apparently had come to meet them. APS had recently published an occult novel, called *Karma,* using HPB as the central character. This letter would seem to be a few words of encouragement to Sinnett at a time when he was not very happy. There had been no letters from KH for some time.

REFERENCES

The question in this letter: 'Are you not man of the world enough to bear the small defects of young disciples?' concerned the behaviour of Babaji and Mohini. Babaji, it developed, was an epileptic and subject to occasional outbursts of erratic and rather wild behaviour which included bitter denunciations of his benefactress, HPB (See letter from HSO to Countess Wachtmeister, LBS, p. 331). Mohini, bound by ties of nationality to the younger chela, was inclined to take his part in several controversies which arose. Moreover, Mohini had met with such adulation on the part of some of the European members that it was beginning to go to his head and he was showing evidence of rather poor judgement in his relations with a number of them.

The last paragraph may refer in part to the financial problems that APS was having; he had lost most of his life savings in some unfortunate business ventures after returning to England, and was no doubt in rather difficult financial circumstances.

138 (ML-145) Page 488/481 Folio 3 Recd. Fall of 1885 (est.)

DESCRIPTION: KH to APS

KH script, written on a card.

CIRCUMSTANCES

Similar to previous letter 137 (ML-97).

REFERENCES

'Courage, patience and *hope,* my brother.' That is all. Perhaps it was prompted by the unhappy frame of mind which was afflicting Sinnett through this period. It is the last letter to be received directly from the Mahatma. A few additional letters from HPB relate to circumstances surrounding the Report of the Society for Psychical Research.

The story of the closing years of Sinnett's life is told in the Epilogue to *Masters and Men,* by Virginia Hanson, beginning on page 380.

139 (ML-140) Page 478/470 Dated Jan. 6, 1886 Würzburg

DESCRIPTION: HPB to APS

In HPB's handwriting on both sides of three sheets of regular notepaper, in black ink.

CIRCUMSTANCES

HPB had gone to Würzburg, Germany, in August of 1885 to live and work on *The Secret Doctrine.* She had been joined in December by Countess Wachtmeister, who looked after her. The official report of the SPR had been issued in December, branding HPB a fraud. HPB had just read it.

REFERENCES

p. 478/470: '...the dear Countess...' The Countess Wachtmeister, who was staying with HPB.

'...to save Hübbe...' Dr William Hübbe-Schleiden, first President of the Germania TS.

The Countess was apparently somewhat clairvoyant.

p. 478/471: '...the *Report* ...' The Hodgson report, just issued by the Society for Psychical Research.

'..in Mah. K.H.'s house'. Said to be in the vicinity of Shigatse in Tibet.

'...with Master, I also used English...' Meaning M.

'...studying in Senzar...' A secret written language of Central Asia.

p. 479/472: This page throws some interesting light on how *Isis Unveiled* was written.

(middle): '...there comes Hübbe-Schleiden's letter to the Countess'. The one mentioned at the start of the letter. See LBS, p. 139 and 140 for explanation.

p. 480/472: This page gives some interesting information on the frequent accusation that HPB wrote that ML.

p. 480/473: This throws more light on the transmission of the Letters.

p. 481/473: '...the Countess for witness...' The Countess Wachtmeister. See Alphabetical Notes.

140 (ML-141) Page 482/471 Folio 3 Dated Mar. 17, 1886.

DESCRIPTION: HPB to APS

In HPB's handwriting, on both sides of three folded sheets of letter paper.

CIRCUMSTANCES

Similar to those of previous letter 139 (ML-140).

REFERENCES

p. 482/474: '... my being Mme Metrovich...' Reference to a story circulated by Mme Coulomb to the effect that HPB had been married to Agardi Metrovitch, a Russian or Hungarian revolutionary whom she saved from death in Turkey and later befriended in Egypt. He died in Egypt and, being unable to find anyone who would bury him, HPB did it herself. LBS, pp. 143-4; D, pp. 577-8; *Personal Memoirs of H.P. Blavatsky* by Mary K. Neff, pp. 170-8.

p. 482/475 (middle): This relates to arrangements to meet APS in Ostend. HPB was arranging to move to Ostend on the Channel on her move from Germany to London.

(bottom): 'Dr Buck, Prof. Coues, Arthur Gebhard...' See Alphabetical Notes.

p. 484/477: 'The first bombshell from the Dugpa world came from America...' This portion relates to Mrs Laura C. Holloway and her testing. She came to London from U.S.A.

p. 484/477 (toward bottom): 'The Oriental Group...' The 'inner group' that had been formed in the LL and was to be instructed by KH through APS.

p. 485/478: This deals with the sad state of affairs in the LL and what could be done to keep it from collapsing. The closing sentence would seem to indicate that part of the letter expressed ideas conveyed from one of the Masters.

141 (ML-139) Page 475/468 Folio 3 Mar. (after 17th) 1886 (est.)

DESCRIPTION: HPB to APS

In HPB's handwriting on both sides of two sheets of letter paper.

CIRCUMSTANCES

Similar to 139 (ML-140) and 140 (ML-141).

REFERENCES

The first sentence refers to the last paragraph of 140 (ML-141).

The 468 (middle): 'Higher Powers.' See middle of p. 484/477. This is probably a portion which was dictated by a Master.

p. 476/469 (top): This is a most interesting description of KH's aura, and gives a clue to how much of the communication at those levels is carried out.

(middle): The 'Princess Hall meeting' to which HPB refers was the one held on 21 July 1884, in London, as a farewell to the Founders before their return to India. See 126 (ML-62), p. 356/350, in which KH asks APS to attend. Apparently he attended, but with little enthusiasm.

p. 476/469 (bottom): HPB is here talking about MMC and Babaji, the Indian chelas who were sent to Europe, and how they are falling by the way.

p. 477/470: 'Before the 15th of April...' This refers to HPB and Countess W. and their crossing over to England to live.

p. 477/470 (last par.): She is here referring to the *Phoenix* newspaper attempt. Gladstone was of course the Prime Minister of England. HPB claimed he was secretly in league with the Roman Catholic Church.

A (ML-33) Page 244/241 Folio 2 Date unknown

DESCRIPTION

In KH script on both sides of a sheet of waxy white paper of figured design. The writing is nearly illegible. APS's notation says the letter was received 'through M'. (presumably MMC) and 'shown to A.B.' (Annie Besant).

CIRCUMSTANCES

The content of the letter indicates that it was received in London sometime after the arrival of MMC in early 1884. The first part of the letter seemingly refers to the metaphysical teachings being given to APS by Morya and KH and the difficulty that Sinnett was having in trying to reconcile the two.

(Last paragraph) The reference to A. Besant would seem to indicate that KH had foreknowledge of her role in theosophical work.

B (ML-75) Page 375/369 Folio 3 Date unknown

DESCRIPTION: KH to APS

KH script in blue pencil on one side of a sheet of heavy note paper, about 5″x7″ in size.

CIRCUMSTANCES

'The right is on her side' would seem to refer to HPB but what and when the difference occurred is difficult to determine. However, it could possibly refer to Anna Kingsford or even to Laura Holloway.

C (ML-124) Page 453/446 Folio 3 Date unknown

DESCRIPTION: KH to APS

KH script in blue ink, on a scrap of folded paper about 3″x9″. The lettering is fine and is written lengthwise on the inside.

CIRCUMSTANCES

Not available, since the date is uncertain. There is no

indication to whom the letter was addressed, but presumably it was to APS. If so, it would seem logical that it was about the time of one of his trips between India and England. This is one of the intriguing little incidents that one finds in the letters for which the compilers have no logical explanation.

D (ML-123) Page 453/446 Folio 3 Date unknown

DESCRIPTION: KH to APS

KH script in blue pencil on the back of a slim Chinese-type envelope about 2½"x5", bearing the imprint of a man and a boy.

CIRCUMSTANCES

The contents of the note are such that a number of different dates could be suggested. It was probably just a note to soothe Sinnett's impatience—a quality which he apparently never quite overcame.

ALPHABETICAL NOTES

ALMORA or ALMORAH, a hill-station in the Himalayas in North India. References in ML to Almora relate to the Swami from Almora, who became AOH's guru for a time. Articles by the Almora Swami, signed 'Paramahamsa Swami' were published in *The Theosophist* in September 1882, February 1883, and March 1883. Notice of his death on 31 December 1883 was published in *The Theosophist* for February 1884. The notice says of him: '...the author of those learned articles on Adwaitism in *The Theosophist* which were opposed by our respected colleague, T. Subba Row'. In Letter 92 (ML-43) he is spoken of as 'the good Vedanta Swami'. (See index.) See also LBS, p. 43, where HPB refers to the Swami as 'Jacolet', and LBS, p. 82, where she comments that he 'was to expose our Masters as Dugpas'. See MATL, p. 351; LBS, 304-5; LMW I, L. 30, p. 66-8.

ARHAT, A Buddhist word used to designate a high degree initiation or one who has reached such an initiation. Cf. Crucifixion, Resurrection. See ML index; also *Glossary*.

ARISTARCHUS SAMIUS (Aristarchus of Samos). Greek astronomer, 3rd century BC. Chief exponent of the heliocentric theory of the universe. Because of this he was accused of heresy. ML. p. 4.

ART MAGIC, See Alphabetical Note on Britten, Emma Hardinge.

ARYA SAMAJ, See Alphabetical Note on Dayanand; also Appendix C.

ATRYA, One of the Adept Brotherhood. He passed through New York in company with the Mahatma Hilarion on their way to the Orient. ML, p. 289/285. BTT, p. 32.

AVICHI, a Sanskrit word, the general meaning of which is 'waveless', suggesting the stagnation of life; it also means 'without happiness'. It is the antithesis of Devachan (q.v.). Not a place of punishment in the Christian sense, but a state where very evil human beings 'die and are reborn without interruption' yet not without hope of final redemption, for there is a possibility of eventual reinsoulment by the ray of the spiritual Monad. Not equivalent to the Eighth Sphere (q.v.). See *Occult Glossary,* G. de Purucker; ML index.

BABAJI or BABAJEE, real name S. Krishnamachari or Krishnaswami. A Brahmin youth who was a probationary chela of KH. He was at one time a clerk in the Collector's office in Nellore. After arrival of the Founders in Bombay, he joined their staff and worked for Damodar. There he assumed the name of 'Babaji' but was also later sometimes called Bawaji' or 'Bowaji'. It is probable that he was the chela who precipitated Letter 12 (ML-6) which caused the 'Kiddle Incident'. See LBS, p. 273. He was present at the time of the Hodgson investigation at Adyar. There is considerable mystery surrounding some phases of his life and the identity of the entity operating through his physical vehicle. It is said that at one time his physical body was 'lent' to another, more advanced, chela, Gwala K. Deb, in order to accomplish certain work and, in doing this, he used the chela's mystical name, 'Dharbagiri Nath', and then continued to use the name subsequently at different times. In March 1885, he accompanied HPB and others to Europe and looked after HPB for some time. There are statements indicating that he was again at one time overshadowed by Gwala K. Deb, and his continued use of the name Dharbagiri Nath caused considerable confusion. Later, he turned against HPB and caused much trouble in theosophical circles in Europe and England, especially at Elberfeld with the Gebhard family. He returned to India and died in obscurity. See references in ML index to Bowaji, Dharbagiri Nath, Gwala K. Deb. See LBS, pp. 170, 286, 331-2, 335, 336, 340; LMW I:132.

BABULA, HPB's personal servant whom she hired in Bombay soon after her arrival there. He was fifteen years of age at that time and is credited with being able to speak six languages. See ML index; ODL, 2:21; LBS, pp. 166-7.

BACON, SIR FRANCIS, first Baron Verulam and Viscount St Albans, 1561-1626. Scientist, philosopher, politician, and member of Parliament. Received many royal favours but was later accused of taking bribes, fined, imprisoned, and banished from Parliament in 1621. He was later released and pardoned but forbidden to re-enter politics. Devoted his later life entirely to scientific and literary endeavours. ML, p. 4. See *Encyclopaedia*.

BANNERJEE, BABU NOBIN K., a prominent Indian Theosophist of the early days of the Society. Magistrate and Deputy Collector at Berhampore, Bengal. One of the signers of the 'Protest' to the 'H.X. Letter'. See Appendix D.

BANON, CAPT. A., Fellow of the Theosophical Society and British Army officer who supported the Founders in the controversy with the Revd Joseph Cook. See ODL 2:329 and SH, p. 167. However, Banon must have written something against KH, since, in Letter 68 (ML-16), p. 113/110, KH speaks of the 'Banon papyrus' which contained 'a severe literary thrashing of my humble self'. See also MATL, p. 271-2.

BATES, MISS ROSA, English schoolteacher who joined the TS while in America in 1878. Returned to England in November of that year and in 1879 went with the Founders to India. For a time she was part of the household at the Bombay headquarters but she and Mrs Coulomb were at odds much of the time. Mr Edward Wimbridge (See Alphabetical Note) took her part. Both left in 1880, and Miss Bates resigned from the TS.

BEATSON, Mr., a young officer of the Bengal Cavalry. He was at Simla in October 1880 at the time of the visit of the Founders, when so many phenomena were produced through HPB. He joined the TS at that time. He is said to have missed advancement in the army due to favouritism. Became much interested in occultism. LBS p. 27

BENJAMIN, one of the nicknames of Djual Khul. Benjamin was the youngest and favourite son of the patriarch Jacob. See Alphabetical Note on Djual Khul.

BENNETT, D.M., an American free-thinker and editor of *The Truthseeker,* who was 'framed' by his enemies and jailed. After his release, his supporters sent him on a world tour during which he visited the Founders in Bombay. APS took a dislike to him because of his somewhat uncouth appearance and was reproved by the Mahatmas. See ML index; ODL 2:328; D, p. 521; SH, pp. 165-6; HPB X: 141.

BHAVANI RAO or BHAVANI SHANKER, a chela who lived for a while at the headquarters of the TS in Bombay. He was present there with HPB and others at the time of the 'Vega Incident' connected with the medium Eglinton (See Alphabetical Note). He travelled at times with HSO about India and was with him at Allahabad at the APS home at the time of the plaster cast phenomenon on 11 March 1881. Probably he is the person referred to by APS on p. 222 of OW, who transmitted some messages for him at Allahabad. According to SH, p. 165, he was one of a group at the headquarters of the TS (then in Bombay) in January 1882, to whom M. appeared. Ross Scott, Damodar, 'and others' were in the group. ML index; OW, pp. 130, 222; D, pp. 191, 331, SH index. In later years he transferred his activities to the ULT organization.

BHOOT or BHUT, a Sanskrit term meaning a 'has been'. In ML it seems to be used as applying to elementaries of an earth-bound and generally low type. Their habitat is determined by their affinities and they can be evoked by living persons who are sorcerers. In Letter 118 (ML-96), p. 431/424, M speaks of 'Bhoot-daks' (see DAK), or communication through a medium.

BILLING or BILLINGS, MRS M. HOLLIS, a prominent American medium. Mrs Billing was active in the formation of the London Lodge but did not join it, preferring to retain her membership in the Parent Society. At that time (1877), if a member of the Parent Society joined a branch, membership in the former was forfeited (SH, p. 103). When HSO composed his first circular explaining the origin and plan of the TS and the aims for which it stood, Mrs Billing took a packet of these circulars to London (SH, pp. 104-5). When the Founders went to England in 1879 *en route* to India, they stayed with Dr and Mrs Billing for a time (SH, p. 123). At the election of officers in London Lodge on 5 January 1879, Dr Billing was elected one of the two Vice-Presidents (SH, p. 124). Of Dr Billing, Letter 92 (ML-54), pp. 306/301-2, has some rather severe things to say.

BISHEN LAL or LALLA, President of Rohitcund TS in Bareilly. One of the chelas who apparently failed. ML, p. 357/352; D, pp. 150, 175; BTT, p. 175

BLACK, or BLAKE, CARTER, present at the organization of the British TS on 27 June 1878. He was expelled from the TS for slandering other members, but later rejoined. See ML index; SH, pp. 107, 120.

BOD, a Tibetan name for Tibet. It is often used in conjunction with other terms, as Bod-pa (a man of Tibet), Letter 33 (ML-38), p. 251/247; or Bod-Lhas (Divine Rulers of Tibet), Letter 21 (ML-26), p. 203/201.

BON-PO, the original animistic religion of Tibet prior to the entry of Buddhism into that area. The first attempts to bring Buddhism there resulted in a considerable mixture of the two and gave rise to the Tantric form of Buddhism sometimes referred to as the 'Red Cap' sect. The reformation of Tibetan Buddhism in the fourteenth century by Tsong-kha-pa resulted in the sect now known as the 'Yellow Caps'. See *Glossary;* also *Buddhism* by Edward Conze.

BOWAJI, see Babaji.

BRADLAUGH, CHARLES, noted English social reformer with whom Annie Besant was associated before she joined the TS. See ML index; SH, pp. 20, 257, 261.

BRITTEN, EMMA HARDINGE, a well-known Spiritualist in America, elected one of the counsellors of the TS at the organizing meeting in New York on 7 September 1875 (SH, p. 82). Some of the early meetings of the TS were held in her house (SH, p. 100). Author of the book, *Art Magic,* which she announced was written by 'an adept' of her acquaintance, Louis Constant (apparently not the one who used the pseudonym of Éliphas Lévi) for whom she was 'acting as translator and secretary'. She left the TS fairly soon, however, became hostile, and joined with Prof. Coues and others in spreading calumny about HPB. See biography, HPB I: 466-7; ML, p. 50; SH, pp. 111, 275; See also HPB VI, p. 466.

BROTHERS OF THE SHADOW: A term given to those who follow the 'left-hand path', or the 'path of the shadows'—meaning the path of matter. Their existence and aims are essentially selfish opposed to evolution and to the spiritualizing aims of the 'Sons of Light' who follow the pathway of self-renunciation, self-sacrifice, self-conquest, and an expansion of the heart and mind in love and service to all that lives. The Brothers of the Shadow are called 'Chohans of Darkness' in ML, p. 462/455, which implies that they are initiates and adepts of the left-hand path. *Occult Glossary,* G. de Purucker; ML index.

BROWN, ELDRIDGE GERRY, editor of the magazine *Spiritual Scientist* in Boston. Referred to in ODL and early letters from the Egyptian Adepts to HSO. Apparently he was one of the three selected by the Brotherhood to start the TS movement through an interest in Spiritualism. 'Educated but very poor; for, to become a Spiritualist and editor of a spiritualistic paper, he had quarrelled with his family' (SH, p. 68). Later, when HPB and HSO were trying to wean the public mind away from Spiritualism, Brown decided to go his own way and keep his belief in 'spirits'. HPB said 'he might have become a *Power'* but prefered otherwise (SH, p. 71).

BROWN, WILLIAM TOURNAY, a young Scotsman who had been educated as a lawyer. He joined the TS in London while APS was there and sailed for India in 1883. Apparently he was a man of nervous temperament but of considerable promise. HPB sent him to join HSO and DKM, who were on tour in North India (LBS, p. 62). In Lahore he was visited by KH (LBS, p. 68). During the absence of the Founders from Adyar, he served on the Board of Control appointed by HSO and was present at the time of the Hodgson investigation. He left India in 1885 and travelled for most of the rest of his life, principally in the USA and Europe. ML, p. 428/421, SH, pp. 184, 185, 192; D, p. 570; HPB, VI: 31, 429; ODl 3: 23, 42; LMW 1:28. See Chronology for October and November 1883.

BUCK, DR JIRAH DEWEY, 1838-1916. A medical doctor and prominent member of the TS in Cincinnati, Ohio. Appointed by HSO as a member of the Board of Control of the TS in America, 13 May 1884. He remained loyal to the Society throughout. ML, p. 483/475; D, p. 184; SH index (many references).

BUDDHA GAYA, a place just east of Benares (Varanasi) where the Buddha received his enlightenment and preached some of his sermons. ML, p. 294/290. See account by Dharmapala in BTT, p. 65.

BULWER-LYTTON, EDWARD GEORGE EARLE, (1803-73), first Baron Lytton of Knebworth. English novelist and prolific writer. Member of Parliament as a Liberal from 1831-41; in 1852 returned to Parliament as a Conservative. Of all his works, those most pertinent to the study of ML are *Zanoni,* an occult novel published in 1842, and *The Coming Race,* published in 1871, based on speculation about the future of electricity. His son, Lord Lytton, was at one time Viceroy of India.

CENTENNIAL ATTEMPT, an attempt made by the Adept Brotherhood during the last quarter of each century to enlighten mankind (ML, p. 51). It is stated in SD 5:396 that this effort was first advocated by Tsong-Kha-Pa (see Alphabetical Note) in the 14th century. The latest effort, made through the TS, nearly failed due principally to the Coulomb-Hodgson affair (ML, p. 362/356).

CHATTERJEE, MOHINI MOHUN (usually referred to simply as Mohini), 1858-1936. A chela of KH, native of Calcutta, of Brahmin caste, and a descendant of Ram Roy, a well-known reformer of Hinduism. When HSO opened the first Theosophical Sunday School in Calcutta on 10 March 1883, with 17 boys, Mohini was appointed their teacher. Later he travelled about considerably with the Founders and, at the request of KH, accompanied them to Europe in 1884 and stayed in the home of APS for a time. He remained in Europe until 1887 when he returned to India to practise law. The purpose of his trip to Europe was seemingly to give the members there some assistance in understanding the Eastern doctrines which had been brought into prominence by APS in his book *Esoteric Buddhism.* With Mrs Laura C. Hollaway (see Alphabetical Note) he wrote the book, *Man, Fragments of Forgotten History.* He failed as a chela and resigned from the TS in 1887. See ML index, references to Mohini; also in LBS and SH.

CHELAS AND LAY CHELAS, an important article which appeared in *The Theosophist* for July 1883; reprinted in HPB IV: 354 *et seq*. It deals with the subject of selection and training of chelas by the Adepts. ML, p. 341/335.

CHINTAMON, HURRYCHUND, a chela of Dayanand of the Arya Samaj movement (see Alphabetical Note on Dayanand and Appendix C). While HPB and HSO were still in the USA they had correspondence with him and sent fees to the Arya Samaj through him. It was discovered that he had diverted these funds, amounting to about Rs. 600, to his own pocket. Later he attempted to arouse suspicion of HPB as a 'Russian spy'. He was expelled from both the TS and the Arya Samaj and decamped to England with Rs. 4,000 belonging to the latter body. He was the originator of the 'Hermetic Brotherhood of Luxor'. He was forced to leave England and seems to have disappeared in the USA. See ML index; ODL 2; SH, index.

COOK, REVD JOSEPH, a Boston preacher who at one time supported the idea of Spiritualism, but when he went to India in 1882, he denounced both Spiritualism and Theosophy. Damodar countered his accusations in the press. M. calls him 'a pump of filth' (ML, p. 271/267). There is a newspaper cutting about him in HPB's scrap-book. ODL 2:329; D pp. 178-80; SH index.

COOPER-OAKLEY, A.J., an English Theosophist who, with his wife Isabelle (Cooper), went to India with HPB in 1884 and served for a time as one of the Recording Secretaries of the TS. (Mrs Cooper-Oakley returned to England in 1885.) He became a pupil of T. Subba Row and left the TS when his teacher died. He settled in India and became a schoolteacher. ML, pp. 469/462; 473-5/466-7; LMW I:113-16; D, p. 566; SH index.

COPERNICAN OPINION, the Copernican System devised by Nicolaus Copernicus (Polish astronomer 1473-1543) which explains the apparent motions of the heavenly bodies as due to the diurnal rotation of the earth on its axis and its annual revolution around the sun. ML, p. 4. See *Encyclopedia*. See also MATL, p. 143.

COSMOLOGICAL NOTES. See ML, p. 70.

COUES, PROFESSOR ELLIOT F., employed by the Smithsonian Institution, Washington, D.C., for many years a loyal and active member of the TS. Later he turned hostile and, in 1880, published an article in the *New York Sun* in which he made an outrageous attack upon the Founders, particularly HPB. She could not let this stand and sued Professor Coues for $50,000, but died before the suit was finally settled. However, the *Sun* published a retraction and, when the suit reached the Supreme Court, the attorney for that newspaper confessed complete inability to prove the charges. In 1889, Professor Coues was expelled from the TS for 'untheosophical conduct'. ML, p. 483/475. SH index.

COULOMB, ALEXIS and EMMA, residents and staff members at the headquarters of the TS. In 1880, the two appeared, penniless, at the headquarters of the TS in Bombay and asked for shelter. HPB had known Mme Coulomb slightly as Miss Emma Cutting in Cairo, Egypt, in 1871. The Coulombs were given a home with the Founders, and Mme Coulomb assumed the duties of housekeeper, with the freedom of HPB's purse. Mr Coulomb was a carpenter and draftsman who made himself useful as a handyman. He was appointed by HSO to the Board of Control when the Founders went to Europe in 1884. This appointment was made because Mme Coulomb insisted to HSO that her husband was a proud man and his feelings would be hurt if he were left out. In ODL 3: 74, HSO comments: 'If I had had even an inkling of her real character, instead of making her husband ... a Committee man, I should have had our servants chase both of them out of our compound with bamboo switches.' The story of how these two, particularly Mme Coulomb, conspired with Christian missionaries to discredit HPB and furnished false 'evidence' to Richard Hodgson (see Alphabetical Note) is told in numerous places—in greatest detail in *Obituary—'The Hodgson Report' on Madame Blavatsky* by Adlai E. Waterman. ML index; D, pp. 450, 573. Also MATL, p. 271.

CRAWFORD, F. MARION, author and ex-editor of the *Indian Herald*. Wrote an occult novel entitled *Mr Isaacs,* which is commented on by KH at the end of Letter 102 (ML-56).

CRAWFORD, LORD, JAMES LUDOVIC LINDSAY, 1847-1913, twenty-sixth Earl of Crawford and ninth Earl of Balcarres. A prominent British astronomer and man of note. He was interested in occultism and had been in touch with APS and HPB. He was for a time a councillor of the TS. KH speaks very highly of him (ML, pp. 26-7). He was reputed to have had one of the largest private libraries in England. At the time of his death, he had in his possession some letters from HPB and other interesting material. These were retrieved by Mrs Doris Groves, of the TS in England, for the Society, See ML index; D, p. 635; HPB II:554.

CROOKS, SIR WILLIAM, 1832-1919. English physicist and scientist of note. Member of the Royal Society. He achieved some remarkable results with experiments in 'Radiant Matter'. He was one of the 'highest minds' whom the Adept Founders had hoped to interest in Theosophy. He became a member of the TS and one of the five counsellors of the Society. HPB states (LBS, pp. 224-5) that he was teaching a very occult doctrine and that the Mahatmas intended to help him. See ML index.

DAK, an Indian word for postal or mail service, but often used in a combining form as dak-bungalow or pillow-dak, as in ML, p. 11, referring to the phenomenon at Simla in which a brooch was transported phenomenally and placed inside a pillow. See also BHOOT.

DALAI LAMA, also TALEY LAMA: literally, 'the Ocean'; before the Chinese invasion the temporal ruler of Tibet with headquarters at Lhasa. According to popular belief, the Dalai Lama is an incarnation of Chen-Re-Zi, or Avalokitesvara (see *Glossary*). Called 'our Priestly King' in ML, p. 443/436. ML index; HPB III:179-85.

DAMODAR K. MAVALANKAR, born in September 1857 at Ahmedabad, Gujarat State, India. For a biographical sketch see *Damodar and the Pioneers of the Theosophical Movement* by Sven Eek, p. 1 *et seq.* Lived at TS headquarters and was of invaluable assistance to the Founders; at one time served as Assistant Recording Secretary. He testified to the existence of the Adept Brotherhood in defense of APS's *The Occult World* (D, p. 167; also *The Theosophist,* August 1881). A letter from HPB to Franz Hartmann also contains some interesting material about him (D, p. 532 *et seq*). His personal account of his visit to his Master's retreat while on a trip to Jammu with HSO and Brown (D, pp. 335-7). While in North India with HSO, tried to materialize at Adyar in presence of HPB (Moradabad incident, D, pp. 344-5). Account of disappearance at Jammu (D, pp. 350-1). Final disappearance—sailed from Madras 23 February 1885, for Calcutta, thence to Darjeeling and on into the Himalayas to join his Master (ODL 3:259; D, p. 12). Often referred to by the Mahatma as 'the Maratha Boy'. Account of his joining the TS ODL 2:102. His early life ODL 2:292. Damodar's fall, LMW, 1: 71-2. See ML index and many references LBS and SH, indexes. See also MATL.

DARJEELING, a city in India near the border of Sikkim and on the main route through Sikkim to Tibet. In 1882, HPB visited the Mahatmas 23 miles north of Darjeeling. ML index; LBS, pp. 34, 38; BTT, p. 36.

DAVIDS, THOMAS WILLIAM RHYS, English Oriental scholar, 1843-1922. Filled judicial positions in Ceylon after 1866. Professor of Pali and Buddhist literature at University College, London, 1882-1912, and professor of comparative religions, Manchester, 1912-15. Among his works are *Buddhist Suttas* and *Vinaya Texts* (Sacred Books of East Series 11, 13, 17, 20) and *Dialogues of the Buddha* (Sacred Books of the Buddhists Series 2-4), etc. In 1894 he married Caroline Augusta Foley, an authority on Buddhism. ML index.

DAVISON, MR (sometimes DAVIDSON), a scientific ornithologist who at one time worked for AOH at Simla in connection with the latter's bird hobby. He served in the capacity of a private secretary. He was there at the time of the first visit of the Founders in 1880. Later he became quite disgusted with AOH and left his employment. He went back to England and is reported to have become associated with the Hermetic Brotherhood of Luxor (see Alphabetical Note on Hurrychund Chintamon). ML index.

DAYANAND, SWAMI SARASWATI, leader of a reform movement in Hinduism known as Arya Samaj. The Founders temporarily associated the TS with this movement just before and after they went to India. Soon they became dissatisfied with Dayanand and he, in turn, became antagonistic towards the TS. He is credited with being a high chela, but seemingly failed because of pride and ambition. Notice of his death on 30 October 1883 appeared in *The Theosophist,* February 1884. ML index; Appendix C.

DEB, GWALA or GUALA K., a chela of KH. He was 30 years of age in 1882. See ML index; also ML index under Babaji and Dharbagiri Nath. See also LBS, pp. 10, 14, 16 and MATL, p. 273.

DEE, JOHN, English mathematician and astrologer, 1527-1608. Suspected of sorcery and imprisoned by Queen Mary I on charge of practising magic. Later freed and was held in high regard by Queen Elizabeth I. He was the author of 79 works in his field. ML, p. 4; HPB IV: 642. See also *John Dee, the World of an Elizabethan Magus,* by Peter J. French, Routledge & Kegan Paul, London 1972.

DEN, DENNIE or DENNY SINNETT, only son of APS and Patience Sinnett. Born in 1877. C.W. Leadbeater was his tutor in England in 1889. ML Index.

DEVACHAN, a Sanskrit-Tibetan compound word: deva, a 'god'; chan, 'land' or region. Not a locality but the state between earth lives into which the human Monad enters and there rests in bliss and repose. Devachan is the completion of all the unfulfilled spiritual hopes of the past incarnation, an efflorescence of all the spiritual and intellectual yearnings which, in that past incarnation, had no opportunity for fulfilment. It is a period of unspeakable bliss and peace for the human soul, until it has finished its rest time and the stage of recuperation of its own energies. *Occult Glossary,* G. de Purucker. ML Index.

DHARBAGIRI NATH, apparently the mystical name for a chela of KH whose real name may have been Gwala K. Deb (see Alphabetical Note). A brother chela of Chandra Cusho. There is much mystery connected with the relationship between this chela and a younger one by the name of Babaji, or Bawaji, who is supposed to have lent his body at various times to Dharbagiri Nath. The real Dharbagiri Nath was a chela of some 14 years standing, whereas Babaji was only a probationary chela. ML index; OW, p. 222; LMW I: 132; LBS, pp. 166-73, 338, 342. MATL, p. 240.

DIKSHITA, one who is initiated, ML, pp. 218/216, 97/95.

DISINHERITED, THE, see Djual Khul.

DJUAL KHUL (various spellings such as Djual Khool, Gjual Khool, sometimes simply DK or GK). Frequently called 'the Disinherited' because he had been disinherited by his family when he became a chela. He was a first degree chela who later became an Adept. KH refers to him as his 'alter ego'. He precipitated some pictures of the Mahatmas for APS and others, but he did not possess the artistic ability of HPB. See LBS, p. 12 for account of how the Dugpas once caught him off guard and he fell down a cliff. See many index references ML, LBS, SH.

DONDOUKOFF-KORSAKOFF, PRINCE (also spelled Dondukev-Korsakev), a Russian prince and friend of HPB who furnished her with credentials for use in India. ML, pp. 463/456, 255/251; HPB X:293.

DUGPA, generally referring to a magician of the left-hand path, as opposed to the Gelukpas, the 'virtuous ones'. *Glossary;* ML index.

DURBAR, in India, an official reception or audience held by a British ruler or by an Indian prince or rajah. BTT, p. 252.

DWELLER ON THE THRESHOLD, a term used by Bulwer-Lytton in his occult novel *Zanoni.* The concept is a subtle and elusive one. See article by HPB in *Lucifer,* September 1893 entitled 'Elementals'. See also 'The Dweller on the Threshold' by Hugh Shearman, *The Theosophist,* September 1956, in which he comments: 'At the gateway of each new advance towards a better life, there is ... a dweller on the threshold. He is a very subtle adversary who strikes indeed 'below the belt' and never plays fair or fights cleanly...and the reason why he is such a subtle enemy and strikes so cleverly at our weakness or unpreparedness is that we ourselves have put him there, having created him out of the very life-stuff of our past everyday selves.' For those familiar with Jungian psychology, 'the Dweller' can be equated with 'the Shadow', perhaps more clearly explained in *The 'I' and the 'Not-I'* by M. Esther Harding. ML, pp. 42-3. See also *Occult Glossary* by G. de Purucker.

ECLECTIC, by definition, not exclusive; selected from every school. Hence, as applied to philosophy, embracing all approaches. Simla Eclectic Theosophical Society was organized by APS and AOH, together with Ross Scott (see Alphabetical Note) and a few other Europeans at Simla. Meetings were apparently held at the home of AOH. AOH was the first president, and later APS filled that post. Nothing seems to have been heard about this group after APS went to England to live.

EGLINTON, WILLIAM, a popular medium who came to India and spent the spring of 1882 in Calcutta. His principal guide was known as 'Ernest'. Apparently he was an excellent medium but had a number of personal weaknesses. There are indications that KH intended to bring him to Simla for a period of training so that he could be used in their work, but that after his arrival in Calcutta, KH decided against this and left him there. After a while, Eglinton became disappointed and returned to England in mid-March of 1882, aboard the ship *Vega*. while he was at sea, KH appeared to him in what is generally referred to as the 'Vega Incident'. The Mahatmas did not let him join the TS. ML index; D, pp. 185, 199-200; OW, pp. 192-95; LBS, pp. 3, 21, 23, 24, 361.

EIGHTH SPHERE, frequently, but incorrectly, confused with Avichi (q.v.) it represents a degree of psychomental degeneration even more advanced than Avichi. The possibility of reinsoulment vanishes, as the entity becomes separated from its sixth and seventh principles (Buddhi and Atma). The Eighth Sphere, or 'Planet of Death' is said to be an actual globe, but also a state or condition in which an entity may find itself. Here the 'lost souls' are 'ground over and over in Nature's laboratory, and are finally dissipated into their component psycho-astral elements or life atoms'. *Occult Glossary,* G. de Purucker; ML index; D, p. 438.

ELEMENTALS and ELEMENTARIES. The former are said to be creatures evolving in the four kingdoms or elements—earth, air, fire, and water. They are called respectively gnomes, sylphs, salamanders, and undines. They are rather forces of nature than ethereal men and women. Elementaries are the disembodied souls of persons (often of the depraved) whose temporary habitation is the Kama Loka (see Alphabetical Notes). ML index; LBS, p. 204. See also article by HPB in *Lucifer,* August to October 1893, in which she describes the various types, including Elementaries. Of the Nature Spirits, she says they have no form, being really centres of force having instinctive desires, but no consciousness as we understand it, hence their acts are without sense of good or evil. They have etheric vehicles and can mould matter and condense it into visible forms and can readily assume any form. In the seance room, they can assume any likeness they find stamped in the memory of the sitter. It is not necessary that the sitter be consciously thinking about it at the time; they can pick it up from the forgotten recesses of memory. See Glossaries.

ELIXIR OF LIFE, a long article published in *The Theosophist* of March and April 1882, written by Godolphin Mitford (see Alphabetical Note) under the pseudonym of Murad Ali Beg. Considerable importance seems to have been attached to this article and there are several references to it. There are hints that the author may have been inspired by some more advanced being. ML index.

ESOTERIC BUDDHISM, the title of a book by APS published in London 11 June 1883. It followed the first book, *The Occult World,* by about two years and was the first technical exposition of Theosophy to appear in the western world written in a clear, concise form. It was based essentially on the information contained in the letters from the Mahatmas. ML index; BTT, p. 269.

FAKIR, a Moslem ascetic in India; a Moslem 'yogi'. Sometimes used erroneously for Hindu ascetics. ML index.

FECHNER, G.T. (Gustav Theodor, 1801-1887), German experimental psychologist, professor of physics at University of Leipzig. The reference in ML, p. 44, relates to KH's education in Europe. An inquiry from C.C. Massey, who was sceptical of KH's existence, addressed to Dr Werneke at Weimar, brought information from Prof. Fechner that KH's real name was Nisi Kanta Chattopadhyaya (see MATL, p. 315). Subsequent research has led students to question this statement; it was apparently a matter of wrong identification. Prof. Fechner was the author of many books, his best known being *The Elements of Psycho-physics* (1862). See HPB III:508.

FERN, EDMUND W., a young Englishman born in India. At the time the letters were being written, he was apparently serving as some kind of secretary to AOH at Simla and may have been living in the Hume residence. Apparently he was something of a psychic and the Mahatmas considered that he might have valuable potential for the transmission of messages, etc. He joined the TS and was placed on probation under the supervision of M. It appears that he failed to pass the probationary tests. ML index; LMW; D, p. 524.

FINCH, G.B., an English Theosophist who was elected president of the London Lodge in 1884 as a compromise between the APS and Kingsford factions in the Lodge. SH, pp. 197, 230.

GALILEO (Galileo Galilei) 1564-1642. Italian astronomer, mathematician, and physicist whose investigations of natural laws laid the foundation of modern experimental science. He espoused the Copernican system and is credited with conclusions foreshadowing Newton's laws of motion. He constructed the first complete astronomical telescope. ML, p. 4.

GEBHARD FAMILY, a German family living in Elberfeld, quite prominent in the early history of the TS in Europe. The family consisted of Gustav Gebhard and sons Franz and Arthur. For a full description see biographical sketch by Boris de Zirkoff in HPB VI:434 and D, p. 592. See ML index,

GELUKPAS (or GELUG-PAS), the virtuous ones. A sect of Tibetan Buddhists generally referred to as the 'Yellow Caps'. The sect originated as a result of the purification of Tibetan Buddhism in the 14th century by Tsong-Kha-Pa. ML, p. 272/268.

GILBERT, WILLIAM, 1544-1603. The most distinguished man of science in England during the reign of Queen Elizabeth I. Practised as a physician in London and, in 1601, was appointed physician to the Queen. He was the first English advocate of Copernican views. His principal work was a treatise on magnetism, outstanding because of its strict adherence to the scientific method of investigation and experiment, as well as originality of subject matter. ML, p.4.

GITEAU or GUITEAU, CHARLES JULIUS, 1840-82. Assassin of James A. Garfield, 20th President of the United States, on 2 July 1881, hence the current interest around the world at the time of the writing of the ML. Giteau was an erratic lawyer who wanted a consular appointment from the Government; when this was not given him, he became so furious that he assassinated the President. ML, pp. 132/129 and 148/145.

GORDON, LT. COL. W., and MRS ALICE, members of the TS, residents of Calcutta and friends of APS, AOH, and the Founders. They were primarily interested in Spiritualism. Mrs Gordon accompanied the Founders on their first trip to Simla in 1880. The Gordons were hosts to the medium, William Eglinton, in Calcutta, in the spring of 1882, after his original host, Mr Meugens, had left Calcutta. The Gordons were involved in the *Vega* phenomenon connected with Eglinton's return trip to England. ML index; LBS, p. 16.

HARTMANN, DR FRANZ, 1838-1912, native of Bavaria. After serving in the war between Austria and Italy in 1859, he took up the study of medicine and graduated as a physician in 1865. He went to the United States the same year, built up a lucrative practice, and became an American citizen in 1867. Deeply interested in philosophy and the esoteric aspects of the different religions, he travelled about considerably; he lived for a while in Mexico, studying the Indians; later he returned to the United States and explored both Judaism and the Mormon religion. In 1879, he took up a gold and silver mining claim in Colorado. Shortly thereafter, he came upon a copy of *The*

Occult World by APS; this led to corespondence with HSO and he was invited to join the headquarters staff at Adyar. He arrived there on 4 December 1883. In February 1884, when the Founders left for Europe, HSO appointed him chairman of the newly created Board of Control to manage the affairs at headquarters during their absence. The 'Coulomb conspiracy' came to a head while he was serving in that capacity, but he remained loyal to the TS and the Founders throughout. Later he published a *Report of Observations Made During a Nine Months' Stay at the Headquarters of the Theosophical Society,* which is said to be unsurpassed historically because of its objectivity and honesty. He is reported to have received at least ten letters from the Mahatmas. In the late 1880's he helped to organize the TS in Germany. One of the most prolific and learned writers in the theosophical movement, he collaborated with Dr Robert Froebe of Germany in translating *The Secret Doctrine* into German; this was published in 1899. See biographical sketch HPB VIII: 439 and D, pp. 596-612; ML index; LBS, pp. 118, 121. See also MATL, p. 269 et seq.

HENDERSON, MAJOR PHILIP D., British Chief of Police who was a member of the party ('Mr X') at the picnic at Simla at which HPB produced the cup and saucer phenomenon. He joined the TS that day and his membership certificate was produced phenomenally on the spot. The next day he became suspicious and resigned. He may have been the person referred to by KH in ML 3-C, p.11, SH, pp. 146, 148.

HILARION, MASTER, a Greek member of the occult Brotherhood who was closely associated with the founding of the TS in New York and with the early training of HSO. He is supposed to have passed through New York and Boston on 27 May 1875 in company with the Master Atrya on their way to the East. BTT, p. 32.

HOBILGAN or HUBILHAN, a Mongolian term with various shades of meaning ranging from that of a superior adept to a reincarnation of a Buddha or an Avatara. In the lower range, it may be similar in meaning to that of Shaberon; may also be equivalent to 'Chutuktu'. HPB III:22 states that the Hobilgans are five in number and that they are interpreters of the Supreme Wisdom.

HODGSON, RICHARD (1855-1905). Member of the British Society for Psychical Research who was sent by that organization to Adyar in 1884 to investigate and report on the phenomena occurring there. His report was released by the SPR while HPB was in Germany in 1885. According to some, the real cause of the investigation was an unfortunate appearance before the SPR by HSO while he was in London, when he gave some data of an unscientific nature and showed M's turban which he had received in New York as proof of certain of his statements. ML index; LBS, p. 113; D, p. 612 for biography. See also the book, *Obituary: The 'Hodgson Report' on Madame Blavatsky* by Adlai E. Waterman, Theosophical Publishing House, Adyar, 1963. Two developments during recent years have considerable bearing on the validity of this report. On 19 July 1968, *Time* magazine published a defamatory article about HPB in which the whole situation was resurrected. The then secretary of the Society for Psychical Research wrote to the editor of *Time* disclaiming responsibility of the SPR for the report of this investigation, saying that it was entirely the responsibility of the author of the report, Richard Hodgson. *Time* did not publish this letter, or any of the letters written in protest at the article, although many copies of them were received at the headquarters of the American Section of the Theosophical Society, including a copy of the letter from the secretary of the SPR. The second development occurred when the SPR *Journal* for April 1986 published a forceful critique of Hodgson's 1885 Report. The case was re-examined by Dr Vernon Harrison, past president of the Royal Photographic Society and formerly research manager to Thomas De La Rue, an expert on forgery. *The American Theosophist* for July 1986 carries pertinent excerpts from this report:

'The "exposure" of the Russian-born occultist, Madame H.P. Blavatsky, by the SPR in 1885 is in serious doubt with the publication in the SPR *Journal* (Volume 53, April 1986) of a forceful critique of the 1885 report...

'Central to the case were two sets of disputed letters. One set, provided by two dismissed employees of the Theosophical Society at its headquarters in India, was apparently in the handwriting of Madame Blavatsky, and implicated her in fraudulent psychic phenomena. The other set was ostensibly written in support of the Theosophical Society by members of an oriental fraternity, popularly called the Mahatmas. Dr Hodgson accepted the genuineness of the first set. He argued that the Mahatma Letters were spurious productions by Madame Blavatsky and occasional confederates.

'Dr Harrison, on the contrary, suggests that it is the incriminating letters that are forgeries, concocted by the ex-employees for revenge; while the bulk of the Mahatma Letters, now preserved in the British Museum, are not in Madame Blavatsky's handwriting, disguised or otherwise, Dr Harrison concluded:

"As detailed examination of this Report proceeds, one becomes more and more aware that, whereas Hodgson was prepared to use any evidence, however trivial or questionable, to implicate HPB, he ignored all evidence that could be used in her favour. His report is riddled with slanted statements, conjecture advanced as fact or probable fact, uncorroborated testimony of unnamed witnesses, selection of evidence, and downright falsity. As an investigator, Hodgson is weighed in the balance and found wanting. His case against Madame H.P. Blavatsky is not proven." '

It should be noted that Dr Harrison is not a member of the Theosophical Society and therefore presumably not prejudiced in its favour.

HOLLOWAY, LAURA C., an American widow who went to London in 1884 and worked for a time with APS and MMC. She had some natural clairvoyance. Seemingly it was the intention of the Adepts to use her in connection with the work in London. This did not work out, however, and KH seems to lay most of the blame on Sinnett. See Letter 128 (ML-62) and end of Letter 127 (ML-63). She collaborated with MMC in writing a book entitled *Man, Fragments of Forgotten History*. She later married a Colonel Langford. She did some writing for theosophical journals and signed her initials variously LCL and LCH. She returned later to the United States and left the TS. ML index; for biography see D, p. 626; HPB VII:350;

LMW 1—end of book. See *The Theosophist,* November 1931, p. 201.

HOME, DANIEL D., an American medium of unsavory reputation but with considerable ability as a medium. HPB denounced him in strong terms (See HPB I index). See also *Sense and Nonsense in Prophecy* by Eileen Garrett. ML, p. 37.

HOOKE, ROBERT, English scientist (1635-1702). First European to formulate the theory of planetary movements as a mechanical problem. He also devised or improved a number of inventions and was the author of Hooke's Law of elasticity which states that within the elastic limits of a material, stress divided by strain equals a constant, viz., that the distortion of an object is proportional to the stress placed upon it.

HÜBBE-SCHLEIDEN, DR WILLIAM, Doctor of Jurisprudence and Political Economy, born in Hamburg, Germany. He was the first president of the Germania TS in Elberfeld and was in touch with HPB during her stay there. See biography HPB VII:375-77; ML index.

IMPERATOR, the name of the principal spirit guide of the English medium, Stainton Moses. The identity of the guide was something of a mystery. It is intimated that originally it was one of the 'Brothers', identity not disclosed. Later it appears to have been some other entity, or possibly SM's own Higher Self (LBS, p. 22). This guide is frequently designated in the Letters by a plus sign (+). See ML index; HPB IV: 128, 131. See also ML, p. 43.

ISIS UNVEILED, HPB's first published book. Published 29 September 1877 by J.W. Bouton, New York. It was intended that the title should be *The Veil of Isis,* but this was changed at the request of the publisher because a book of similar title had been published in England regarding the mysteries of the Druids. According to KH the book was intended only to be an opening wedge in the Western world for later specific information on occultism. ML index.

KALKI AVATAR (or AVATARA), the last incarnation of Vishnu, according to the Hindus, to take place at the end of the Kali Yuga, 427,000 tears hence; according to Northern Buddhism, the last manvantaric appearance of Maitreya Buddha; according to the Zoroastrians, the appearance of Saoshyant, their last hero and Saviour; the 'White Horse Avatar' of Rev. 19:2. ML, p. 26.

KAMA, Sanskrit word meaning 'desire' or clinging to existence. See *Glossary*.

KAMA LOKA, the semi-material plane, to us subjective and invisible, where the disembodied 'personalities', the astral forms called *Kamarupa* remain until they disintegrate. It is the Hades of the ancient Greeks and the Amenti of the Egyptians.

KAMARUPA, metaphysically, the subjective form created through the mental and physical desires and thoughts in connection with things of matter, which survives the death of the physical body. See *Glossary*. ML index.

KARDEC or KARDEK, ALAN, a French Spiritualist and editor of *La Revue Spirite*. His real name was Hippolite L.D. Ravail, but he preferred to be known by the names he said he had borne in two previous lives—Allan (Alan) and Kardec. HPB did not agree with his theories on the constitution of man. ML index; SH, pp. 14, 16.

KHANDALAWALA, N.D., a provincial judge, member of the TS from its early days in India. A loyal supporter of HSO and HPB in the Coulomb affair which developed in 1884. ML p. 187.

KIDDLE, HENRY, an American Spiritualist who gave a lecture at Lake Pleasant, New York convention, on 15 August 1880, entitled 'The Present Outlook of Spiritualism', which was published in *The Banner of Light* in Boston the same month. Certain passages from this talk appeared in Letter 11 (ML-6) from KH to APS. APS published much of this letter verbatim in his book, *The Occult World,* and this resulted in a claim of plagiarism by Mr Kidddle. The incident became known in TS circles as 'The Kiddle Incident'. KH did not give APS an explanation of the matter until two years later (ML, p. 421/415). See Appendix E.

KING, JOHN, a well-known materialization in Spiritualist circles in the 1870's. Somewhat mysterious in character and generally claiming to be the spirit of the pirate, Henry Morgan. There are several references in occult literature to the employment by adepts and other proficients in the occult arts of elementals and elementaries for accomplishing work which they wish to have done. HPB apparently used John King in this manner for some time while in the USA. A picture of him produced jointly by him and HPB is at the Adyar Headquarters. HPB VI:270-71; *HPB Speaks,* 1:83, *et seq.*

KINGSFORD, ANNA BONUS, 1846-88. English author and Spiritualist who, with her co-worker, Edward Maitland, promoted a Hermetic approach to Christianity and metaphysics. She is best known for her book, *The Perfect Way,* published in 1882. She was a strict vegetarian and antivivisectionist, and KH states that on this account her phenomena were more accurate and reliable than most. He was instrumental in having her elected President of London Lodge. In October 1883, she wrote to HPB sending her photograph and asking that it be forwarded to KH. HPB's reply to her was torn up by M and she complained bitterly about it to APS (LBS pp. 30, 69, 73). HPB also complained about Mrs Kingsford's being kept in the presidency of London Lodge, telling APS that it was due to a request of the Maha Chohan (LBS, pp. 82, 90). HPB sometimes called her the 'Divine Anna' and asked Mrs Sinnett to get a picture of her and send it to her at Adyar. In 1883, Mrs Kingsford issued a circular letter to the London Lodge members which was critical of APS's book, *Esoteric Buddhism.* TSR issued a reply in pamphlet form in January 1884. See biography HPB X: 438-40; ML index.

KIU-TE OR KIU-TI (various spellings, such as Keu-Ti, Khai-Ti, Khin-Ti), a series of Tibetan occult works said to consist of 35 volumes of popular writings and 7 volumes of esoteric writings; also 14 volumes of commentaries. Some of these, at least, are supposed to be in Senzar, a type of writing yet unknown to the outer world. The Stanzas of Dzyan (see SD) are said to be a part of this series, as are also the *Book of the Golden Precepts* and *The Voice of the Silence.* ML index; HPB VI: 425; LBS, p. 63.

LÉVI, ÉLIPHAS, 1810-75. A pseudonym for Louis Constant, a French abbé, who became interested in occultism and the Cabbala and wrote extensively on these subjects. M and KH frequently referred to his writings and indicated that there was much of value in them if one had the right key to understanding. He was at one time a member of Bulwer-Lytton's club for the study of practical magic. ML index; LBS, Appendix 1; *The Theosophist,* January 1886; HPB IV:136, 238, 439.

LHAS, spirits of the highest spheres. Tibetan equivalent of Divine Rulers or Kings. Also synonymous with Dhyanis or Planetary Logoi *(Glossary)*. ML, p. 285/281. See *The Divine Plan* by Geoffrey A. Barborka under 'The Doctrine of the Spheres'.

LINDSAY, EDWARD GEORGE BULWER, see Bulwer Lytton.

MAHA-CHOHAN, an adept of a grade higher than that of Chohan. The designation is usually reserved for that of the office of the superior Adept who supervises the activities of most of the Adepts. Often referred to by KH as the 'Hobilgan'. HPB describes him as 'stern and impassionate as death itself' (LBS, p. 25). ML index.

MAN, FRAGMENTS OF FORGOTTEN HISTORY, a book published in 1885 by Mohini Chatterji and Laura C. Holloway. It was an attempt to expand some of the ideas presented in *Esoteric Buddhism*. However, it was so full of errors that HPB insisted that it be rewritten, and she wrote up a long list of corrections (LBS, pp. 255-61). It was republished later, but HPB's corrections were apparently ignored. Copies of the book are now very difficult to find. ML, pp. 357/351 and 361/355.

MARCUS AURELIUS, A.D. 120-80 Emperor of Rome for 20 years, a benevolent ruler who instigated many social reforms, including a merit system in government. His best known book, *Meditations,* is a literary classic. ML, p. 12.

MASSEY, CHARLES CARLTON, an English lawyer much interested in Spiritualism. He went to the USA in 1875 to visit Chittenden, Vermont, to verify for himself HSO's accounts of the Eddy phenomena (See ODL I) and became a life-long friend of HSO. He was one of the first members of the TS and later a founder and first president of the TS in England. He was also one of the founders of the Society for Psychical Research. After the Hodgson Report was issued, he resigned from the TS. HPB tried hard to get the Mahatmas to teach him but they refused

(ML, pp. 417-18/411-12). See SH, p. 112 for a brief résumé of his career. ML index.

MAYAVI RUPA, illusory form used for the projection of consciousness. Its method of production is not specifically explained, but may be mostly at the etheric level. The Adepts are said to be able to project these illusory appearances at will, and most of their appearances to people seem to be of this type. Damodar describes a visit by M to HPB in April 1883 in her room at the Adyar Headquarters (D, pp. 307-8). ML index.

MITFORD, GODOLPHUS, born in Madras, scion of the English family of that name; author of a long article appearing in the March and April 1882 issues of *The Theosophist* under the pseudonym of Moorad Ali Beg—also referred to as Mirza Murad Ali Beg—entitled 'Elixir of Life'. This article is mentioned several times in the Letters. There are indications that he was inspired to write much of it. However, he was a strange character, who took up Eastern ways of dress and dabbled in black magic until his health was ruined. He came to the Headquarters of the TS at one time and HSO tried to help him with mesmeric healing, but in the end he could not be helped and died insane in 1884 or 1885. See ML index under Moorad Ali Beg. LBS, pp. 161, 165; HPB IV:241; HPB VII:350; ODL, 2:289; MATL, pp. 268-70.

MONIER-WILLIAMS, SIR MONIER. 1819-99, a famous English Sanskrit scholar. He became professor of Sanskrit at Oxford in 1860 and continued in that position until 1899. He travelled extensively in India in connection with his translations of Indian writings. ML, p. 241/238.

MOHINI, see CHATTERJEE, Mohini Mohun.

MORAD ALI BEG, See MITFORD, Godolphin.

MOSES (or MOSEYN), WILLIAM STAINTON, 1839-92, an English Spiritualist and one of the leaders of that movement in England. He had a guide called 'Imperator' (usually designated in ML as +). There is considerable speculation as to the identity of this control, and it is intimated that at one time it was one of the Brothers, and at other times some other entity, and again perhaps the Higher Self of Moses. He sometimes used the pen-name of 'M.A. Oxon'. ML index; LBS, p. 22; ODL I:365 (photograph); ODL I:300, 303; HPB X: 177-8.

MÜLLER, MAX, 1823-1900, a German born and educated philologist and famous Sanskrit scholar. He translated many oriental works for European readers, his major works appearing in the series entitled 'Sacred Books of the East'. KH indicated (ML, p. 241/238) that he was not sufficiently conversant with Indian thought to interpret properly some of the books he translated.

MYERS, FREDERICK W.H., an English FTS of note. A number of questions raised by him in regard to some of the material that was appearing at that time in TS literature were answered at length in *The Theosophist*. It is intimated that some of these answers were dictated by the Adepts and that they seemed very anxious to answer his questions satisfactorily. Later he published a monumental work entitled *The Human Personality and Its Survival of Physical Death,* which is still referred to as a comprehensive study of the subject. ML index.

NOEL, RHODEN, 1834-94, an English poet, author of 'Behind the Veil' and other poems, ML index.

OAKLEY, see COOPER OAKLEY

O'CONOR, J.E., a Theosophist who was *en route* to England aboard the ship *Vega* with William Eglinton, the prominent medium, at the time of the well-known 'Vega Incident'. He wrote a letter to HPB which was transmitted to her at the same time as Eglinton's (see account in D, pp. 188-9). He was a friend of Mrs Minnie Scott (see Hume). LBS, Letters X and XI, pp. 13-21.

OCCULT WORLD, THE dedicated to the Mahatma KH. See KH's comments in Letter 18 (ML-9), p. 38. (See p. 50).

OD (derivatives odic, odylized), a term appearing in some of the early TS literature. The exact meaning is somewhat vague. In the Cosmological Notes it is spoken of as 'the fourth universal principla...shining active astral light'. It is also equated with *vach* (voice) or Cosmic Will. Again, it is spoken of as the sixth principle of elemental fire (LBS, pp. 378-9). ML pp. 99/97; 140/137; 144/140; 384/378.

OXLEY, WILLIAM, a British Spiritualist. KH refused to let him join the Simla Eclectic TS (ML 448/440). He wrote a long letter to KH on 24 June 1881, telling him about his spiritualistic contacts (see ML, p. 453/446). KH was apparently rather amused by it and made some marginal notes on it in a lighter vein and sent it to APS. It is in Folio 6 in the British Museum. Author of the book, *Philosophy of the Spirit*. This was reviewed in *The Theosophist* by DK, and Oxley took some exceptions to the review. See *The Theosophist* for April 1882. HPB IV: 69-70, 320.

OXON M.A., See Stainton Moses (Master of Arts, Oxford).

PADSHAH, SORAB JAMALP, a Parsee and early TS member. He was at one time on the General Council of the TS. One of the joint signers of the testimonial sent to the *Spiritualist Magazine* in London 19 August 1881, affirming belief in the existence of the Adepts (D, p. 169). He sent KH a poem which he had written and which KH sent on to APS for appraisal (ML, p. 207/205). He was said to be one of the cleverest Parsee graduates of Bombay University. Later, he became obstreperous due to over-development of his fifth principle (LBS, pp. 40, 120). ML index; MATL, p. 271.

PARACELSUS, PHILIPPUS AUREOLUS, real name Theophrastus Bombastus von Hohenheim, a great Swiss physician and alchemist, 1493-1541. He spent much of his life searching for a universal specific and the philosopher's stone. In his wide travels, which extended to the East, he acquired (in addition to the arts of alchemy and magic) a knowledge of certain remedies not then familiar to continental physicians and effected many cures which brought him considerable prestige. He drew about him a school known as the Paracelcists. ML, p. 4.

PHARI JONG (or DZONG), a large monastery in Sikkim about 100 miles north of Darjeeling on the main road to Lhasa. It was the locale of the 'goat story' related in ML, on p. 320/315. See also ML,p. 448/440.

PHILOSOPHY OF THE SPIRIT, book by William Oxley (see Alphabetical Note).

PHOENIX, THE: Following Sinnett's dismissal as editor of *The Pioneer*, an effort was made to establish another journal with

Sinnett as editor. This effort was aided to some extent by the Mahatma KH; at least he took a definite interest in it but could not use any special powers. Efforts to raise the necessary funds were not successful and the project failed. Sinnett is advised (ML, p. 353/347) of the real reason for the failure of the venture. A section of ML is under the heading 'The Phoenix Venture and the Condition of India' (pp. 377/371, 396/390).

PUKKA, or PUCKA, a word in common usage in India which seems to have a rather loose definition but generally is used to denote a thing of good quality. Applied personally, it indicates that a person is of high quality or good character. It can also mean genuine, as contrasted with spurious.

RAMASWAMIER, S (Ramabadra), a prominent South Indian who joined the TS in 1881 and became a chela of M. He died in 1893. Best known in TS literature for his account of his trip to Sikkim 5-7 October 1882, to visit M and KH in person which was a very special occasion for a chela of such short training. He wrote to DKM about the trip (D, p. 289), ML, p. 444/437; BTT, p. 405; OW, p. 221; HPB VI:21; MATL, p. 320.

RATTINGAN, apparently an Englishman who became owner of the newspaper, *The Pioneer,* about 1882. He relieved APS of his job as editor and gave him a year's salary in compensation.

RAVAN, DREAM OF, an anonymous essay published in several instalments in the Dublin University magazine during 1853-54. Its authorship has never been established. It was published in book form in 1895 by the Theosophical Publishing House, London, with a preface by G.R.S. Mead. The story is based principally on incidents taken from the *Rāmāyana* of the Hindus. See *The Theosophist* for May 1951.

RECORDE, ROBERT, 1510-58, English mathematician. Became physician to Edward VI and Queen Mary. For over a century his works on mathematics were used as textbooks in English schools. He was the first to use the sign = for 'equal'. Considered a skilful physician, an able lawyer, and outstanding philosopher. ML, p. 4.

ROTHNEY CASTLE, AOH's large house on Jakko Hill in Simla. Reputed to have cost nearly a quarter of a million dollars to build in 1880. His large bird museum was connected with it. It was the frequent practice of the British in India to give their homes names, often after some mansion in England. According to a large map of Simla made in the 1870's, most of the houses there had individual names.

ROW, T. SUBBA, also RAO, a Brahmin who was initiated privately into the TS by HPB and HSO on 25 April 1882. Later, during HPB's absence from headquarters, he was in charge of *The Theosophist*. At the time of the Coulomb affair, several years later, he at first supported HPB, but after her resignation he changed and opposed her recall (SH, p. 232). He always opposed giving out the secrets of occultism, particularly to Westerners. He died in June 1890 'in great physical misery' which HSO tried to alleviate mesmerically (SH, p. 246). ML index under Subba Row; HPB III, 399 *et seq*.

ROYAL SOCIETY, a British scientific society founded about 1660 by Boyle, Hooke, Wren, and others. It was chartered in 1662 by Charles II. Its organization was perhaps influenced by the ideas of Francis Bacon as expressed in his book, *The New Atlantis*. See *The Royal Society* by H. Hartley, 1960, ML index.

SADHU or SADDHU, a saint or sage. ML, p. 462/455.

SANG-GYAS or SANG-GUAS, a Tibetan term meaning perfect, holy; used for Gautama Buddha. ML, pp. 254/251, 462/455.

SANNYASI, a Hindu ascetic who has reached the highest mystic knowledge and has renounced worldly concerns. ML, p. 462/455.

SCHMIECHEN, HERMANN, a German portrait painter of note. While the Founders were in England during the summer of 1884, he went to London to paint the portraits of M and KH under the inspiration of HPB. He began these on June 19 and completed them on July 9. After completing them, he painted duplicates of each, probably two. The two original portraits of M and KH were taken to Adyar in October of 1884 and displayed there for some time. They are now in the Shrine Room in the Headquarters Building. He also painted two portraits of HPB, the first in Elberfeld, Germany, in the fall of 1884 and the second in London in 1885. The first one is now in London and the second is at the Headquarters of the Indian Section of the

TS in Varanasi (Benares), India. ML index; ODL 3:156; LMW 1:214; HPB VI (chronology); D, p. 338; *The Theosophist* for September 1948, article by LCL.

SCOTT, ROSS, a young Irishman and British civil servant who was on his way to his post in North India when he met the Founders aboard ship in February 1879, as they were sailing to Bombay (ODL 2:16-17). KH asked APS to make friends with him (ML, p. 286/282). Ross received a letter from M in the late fall of 1881 (LBS x-c). He became a first secretary of the Simla Eclectic TS on 21 August 1881. M asked APS to discuss certain things with Scott. Apparently he had an injured leg which the Mahatmas promised HPB they would cure if Scott passed the six months probation on which he had been placed. HPB was told by the Mahatmas to try to find a suitable wife for him—certainly one of the strangest things in the Letters. He married Minnie Hume, only daughter of AOH, on 8 December 1881 (LBS, pp. 15-18). It appears that he failed his probation, partially because of his wife's attitude toward the Adepts. Later, he became a magistrate in the Central Provinces. ML index; D, p. 645; LBS, p. 44. Apparently he did not leave the TS (ODL 3, p. 434, and ODL 6, p. 298).

SINNETT, ALFRED PERCY, See Appendix A.

SLADE, DR HENRY, an American medium of exceptional talents. He was thoroughly tested by HPB and HSO and was picked by HSO and others to go to Russia for scientific tests of his phenomena. At one time he gave special courses to professors of Leipzig University in Germany, and, as a result, Prof. Zöllner published a book *Transcendental Physics* in which he challenged the world to account for Slade's phenomena save by a 'spiritual' hypothesis. The book was translated into English by C.C. Massey (see Alphabetical Note). See biography HPB I:525; ML index; ODL I:101; SH, pp. 13, 18, 74, 166.

SUBBA ROW, T (See Row, T. Subba.)

SWAMI from ALMORA, see Alphabetical note on ALMORA.

TERRY, WILLIAM H. 1836-1913. An Australian Spiritualist and founder and editor of the magazine, *Harbinger of Light,* published in Melbourne. He joined the TS in March 1880. He made a number of inquiries concerning theosophical ideas and these were considered sufficiently important that APS and AOH were persuaded to answer them at length. Out of this grew the series of articles. 'Fragments of Occult Truth'. ML, p. 250/246; LMW II:80; BTT, p. 259; D, pp. 164-5. See also *How Theosophy Came to Australia* by Mary K. Neff.

THAUMATURGY, wonder or 'miracle-working'; power of working wonders with the help of the gods. From the Greek *thauma* (wonder) and *theurgia* (divine work), *Glossary*. ML, pp. 35, 262/258.

TSONG-KHA-PA, 14th century reformer of Buddhism, 1358-1419. ML, pp. 44, 332/327. See also SD index.

VRIL, a term used by Bulwer-Lytton in his occult novel, *The Coming Race,* to denote a mysterious electric type of force used by some of the characters in the story. See pp. 37-8 of the novel for a description. For lack of a better word the Mahatmas sometimes used it to describe forces for which there were no scientific equivalents in English. ML index.

WACHTMEISTER, COUNTESS CONSTANCE, companion of HPB and co-worker after HPB's return to Europe in 1885. Shortly after HPB's death, the Countess wrote a small book entitled *Reminiscences of H.P. Blavatsky and 'The Secret Doctrine'* in which she told of her life with HPB from 1885 until the latter's death. ML index; HPB VI: 448; D, p. 562 *et seq.;* MATL, p. 305.

WALLACE, PROFESSOR ARTHUR RUSSELL, 1823-1913. Prominent English naturalist, much interested in spiritualist phenomena. He was one of a group which met the Founders in London when they stopped there *en route* from New York to India. Prof. Wallace was a world traveller and collector of specimens. He originated the theory of natural selection although he differed somewhat from Darwin on some points. In 1868 he received the Royal Medal; in 1890 he received the first Darwin Medal of the Royal Society; in 1910 he received the Order of Merit. In 1875 he published *Miracles and Modern Spiritualism*. ML index.

WARD, SAM, sometimes called 'Uncle Sam' in the Letters. An American businessman who was in London at the time some of the Letters were received by APS. It appears that he visited India at one time. He was an uncle of F. Marion Crawford who wrote the occult novel, *Mr Isaacs.* He used a monogram on his personal stationery which consisted of a compass face with the letters 'SW' appearing in the south-west quadrant. Two of these letterheads appear in the Folios in the British Museum, one a bogus spiritualistic note to APS from M, and another used by M to write APS and warn him of the fraud (ML, pp. 432/425). Reference in ML, p. 202/199-200 indicates that KH held him in some affection and regard. He gave away 250 copies of *The Occult World* to friends. ML index; D, pp. 523, 530; LBS index; ODL, 2:394.

WILDER, PROFESSOR ALEXANDER, early member of the TS in New York and staunch friend of the Founders. In ODL I:413, HSO describes him as having 'a head full of knowledge' although 'not a college-bred man'. He was, according to HSO, 'a tall, lank man of the Lincoln type, with a noble, dome-like head, thin jaws, grey hair, and language filled with quaint Saxon-Americanisms'. He spent much time with HPB when she was writing *Isis* and 'She got him to write out many of his ideas which she quoted.' HSO says Prof. Wilder cared little about the phenomena HPB was able to produce, although he believed in their scientific possibility. He was principally interested in the philosophy. ML index.

WILLIAMS, SIR MONIER—see Monier-Williams.

WIMBRIDGE, EDWARD, an early member of the TS in New York, an architect by profession. He, together with another member, Miss Rosa Bates, accompanied the Founders first to England and then to India in 1879. He designed the first cover for *The Theosophist*. Due to difficulties at the Bombay Headquarters, he left there and set himself up in the furniture and decorating business in Bombay (ODL 2:210). In ML, p. 416/410, KH comments on the purpose and results of these persons in coming to India.

WYLD, DR GEORGE, a homeopathic doctor in London who became

the first president of the London Lodge. He seemed to have had strong orthodox leanings, and his severe criticism of *Esoteric Buddhism* caused a storm of protest. ML index; D, pp. 328-9; HPB I:409, 436.

YUGA, a cycle, age, or period of mundane time in a recurring sequence during manifestation. There are greater and smaller cycles. Usually a yuga consists of four smaller cycles on a ratio of 4, 3, 2, and 1 (= 10). The four yugas comprising our present age are:

Krita, or Satya, Yuga (gold)	...	1,728,000 years
Treta Yuga (silver)	...	1,296,000 years
Dvāpara Yuga (bronze)	...	864,000 years
Kali Yuga (iron)	...	432,000 years
Total	...	4,320,000 years

We are said at the present time to be in the early part of the Kali Yuga. It is also considered that the yugas are related to the outward forms of the earth, i.e., the changing of continents, etc. *The Secret Doctrine*; ML index.

ZANONI, see Bulwer-Lytton.

ZÖLLNER, PROFESSOR, a famous German astronomer and scientist who died in 1882. He published a work entitled *Transcendental Physics* which C.C. Massey translated into English. He conducted an investigation of the American medium, Dr Henry Slade. ML, p. 174/170; ODL I:101; HPB I (see ref.)

APPENDIX A

Article published in *The American Theosophist,* July 1966

ALFRED PERCY SINNETT
(1840-1921)

SVEN EEK

ALFRED PERCY SINNETT achieved fame as the recipient of *The Mahatma Letters* and *The Letters of H.P. Blavatsky to A.P. Sinnett,* upon which much of the authentic history and philosophy of the early Theosophical Society are based. He was a journalist and his providential meeting in India, in 1882, with Madame Blavatsky and Colonel Henry Steel Olcott, two of the chief Founders of the Society, was in the nature of a scoop, without the overtones of spiritual exaltation which we find in a similar meeting between H.P. Blavatsky and Henry S. Olcott on the one hand and Damodar K. Mavalankar on the other, which was just as fateful as the Sinnett encounter.

Sinnett became attached to the theosophical movement for the rest of his life and rendered outstanding service to its promotion, but his theosophical career reflects the uncertainties which accompany the lives of many unsuccessful men.

Alfred Percy's entire childhood was marked by an almost unbroken series of deprivations; his widowed mother had to provide for the entire family through the writing of newspaper articles and translations. His father died penniless when the boy was only five years of age. There were three sisters and two brothers, none of whom did well, except a sister, Ellen, who married the prominent philanthropist, William Ellis.

The lad did poorly in school and left it without finishing his studies. He took up mechanical drawing and became a skilled draftsman and was able to support himself and contribute to the meagre earnings of his mother. Eventually, however, he obtained a position as assistant and sub-editor of *The Globe,* an evening newspaper.

He fell in love with a German girl who evidently did not consider his prospects good, so returned to her native country. This so upset the young swain that he neglected his work on the newspaper and lost his job. There followed a period of intermittent employment on various newspapers, but finally, in 1865, he was offered the editorship of *The Hong Kong Daily Press.* Sinnett accepted this position and remained in Hong Kong for three years. He returned with 800 pounds in savings and a knowledge of the game of poker which he later introduced into England.

On his return journey to England he travelled via America, where he visited the Mormon colony in Utah. He had an interview with Brigham Young, who impressed him very favourably, as did the Mormons, who numbered 100,000 people.

Shortly after his arrival in England he was introduced to a young lady, Patience Edensor, whom he married on the sixth of April 1870. He had become an editorial writer for *The Evening Standard,* which assured him of an adequate income.

Mrs Sinnett very soon began to keep a diary which, on her death, consisted of 31 copybook volumes. Sinnett used this diary to compile his own autobiographical sketch which has been largely used in writing this article. Strenuous efforts have been made to locate these papers, but they were evidently turned over to Miss Maud Hoffman, Sinnett's executrix, who presumably gave them to some-one connected with the London Headquarters of the Theosophical Society and they were lost in the confusion of World War II.

Their historical value can hardly be overestimated, as they cover the entire period of Madame Blavatsky's public life in India and Europe, her passing, and the years to 1908. As Mrs Sinnett died in 1908, they also cover the critical years following H.P.B.'s death.

In 1872, Sinnett had his great opportunity when Mr George Allen, the proprietor of *The Pioneer,* an Anglo-Indian newspaper, offered him the editorship. He resigned his position on *The Standard* and set out for Allahabad, India, where he arrived towards the end of the year. The following years were probably the happiest in his life; a good income, social position, and professional recognition combined to make life agreeable for the Sinnetts.

In 1875 Sinnett went to England for a three months' holiday. During this visit he attended a spiritualist seance at the house of the celebrated medium, Mrs Guppy. This was a fateful experience, as it seemed to obscure Sinnett's perception of the reality of supernatural phenomena, as the Mahatmas M. and K.H. later were to demonstrate to him and others through H.P. Blavatsky. Sinnett writes in his diary:

> The physical phenomena were overwhelming and precluded any conceivable theory of imposture. My conviction concerning the reality of spiritualistic phenomena was then firmly established and never shaken.

In May 1877 Mrs Sinnett gave birth to a son, Denny, whom H.P. Blavatsky at one time thought could become a powerful influence for good, but he died from tuberculosis in 1908 after a short life of unbroken failure.

Sinnett writes in his *Autobiography:*

> Now I approach the period of the great and momentous change in my life arising from my acquaintance with Madame Blavatsky and my introduction to occultism.
>
> Someone—Herbert Stack I think—had told me about Madame Blavatsky's book *Isis Unveiled* as opening up a new idea in advance of spiritualism, the actual reality of magic. Then I saw a statement in the Bombay papers that she and Colonel Olcott had arrived in Bombay, and I wrote a note about them in *The Pioneer* assuming that they were spiritualists coming to India in search of a new variety of mediumship. Apropos of this note Colonel Olcott wrote to me and we somehow made acquaintance by letter. We thought they would be interesting people and decided to ask them to pay us a visit if they were—as I gathered that they intended—about to come up country. They came on the 4th December 1879.

This was the beginning of a lifelong association between Madame Blavatsky and Colonel Olcott on the one hand and the Sinnetts on the other. A British Civil Servant and an ardent ornithologist, who was to write an important chapter in the history of India, Mr A.O. Hume, was at Allahabad at the time and took a lively interest in the ideas and lives of the two Theosophists. He became closely associated with A.P. Sinnett and joined with him later in a somewhat critical conspiracy against the chief founders of the Theosophical Society.

While spending the hot weather at Simla in 1880, the Sinnetts received a second visit from H.P.B. and Olcott. It was during this visit that the correspondence between the Mahatma K.H. and Sinnett began. It seems that during a conversation between Madame Blavatsky and Sinnett, the latter, having expressed himself critically concerning H.P.B.'s conduct of the Society's affairs, had suggested that if he could get in direct touch with the 'Brothers', they would show more common sense. H.P.B. was agreeable and the Mahatmas consented to try it as an experiment. The messages would be transmitted psychically, but since Sinnett himself lacked psychic powers, the process had to be done through mediators such as H.P. Blavatsky, Damodar K. Mavalankar, and other chelas. The exchange of letters continued for several years until 1885, when Sinnett's attitude had become offensive not only to the Mahatmas but to the chelas also.

In March 1881 the Sinnetts went to England for a holiday. During the trip Sinnett wrote his first theosophical book, *The Occult World*. It described occult phenomena which had been produced by Madame Blavatsky in India, with the Sinnetts and friends as witnesses. It made a profound impression upon the public at the time, but earned Sinnett the displeasure of the Anglo-Indian community; it alienated the proprietors of *The Pioneer* and cost him their friendship. They now desired to get rid of him because he had broken the canon of Anglo-Indian behaviour. The publisher gave Sinnett notice that he wished to terminate his editorial contract.

This was an occasion when the Mahatmas actively tried to help a Theosophist in his affairs. They endeavoured to raise the necessary capital for a new paper under the name of *Phoenix*. Public apathy and the fact that Sinnett himself sat back and did not use his own initiative caused the effort to fail.

Sinnett received quite a generous settlement from the publisher, Mr Rattigan, and the money he had accumulated in India totalled 8,000 pounds. He was anxious to return to England where he felt sure he would be able to earn his living and particularly so with the aid of the interest on his accumulated capital. He left Simla early in 1883 via Adyar where he visited Madame Blavatsky.

On his arrival in England, he soon attracted interest and a number of important people were drawn to him, such as Mrs and

Miss Arundale, Dr Anna Kingsford, and also C.C. Massey, one of the seventeen co-founders of the original Society in New York. He also attracted some leading members of the Society for Psychical Research, such as Frederick Myers, Gurney, Professor Sidgwick, and others.

Sinnett made friends with the Gebhard family of Elberfeld, Germany, who played an important role in the early Theosophical Movement.[1]

Sinnett's idea had been to invest his money in some newspaper and thereby secure an editorial position as well as interest on his capital. He put an advertisement in the *Athenaeum* to this effect. He received one reply only, from a rogue, a Mr Bottomley, who succeeded in separating Sinnett from his Indian savings.

In January 1884, the Sinnetts moved to new quarters which soon became the centre of theosophical activities. He writes in his *Autobiography,* p.40, as follows:

> At this time interest in the subject [Theosophy] was spreading rapidly in the upper levels of society and news of this development induced Madame Blavatsky to abandon her intention—very definitely expressed to us when we stayed with her at Adyar on our way home—of remaining there for the rest of her life. She arranged to come to Europe, accompanied by Colonel Olcott—much to my regret as I foresaw trouble in connection with their presence in London.

Trouble did start, but that was hardly sufficient reason why Madame Blavatsky should be prohibited from visiting England, where eventually her most important literary work was performed.

Colonel Olcott did commit a *faux pas* on the 30th of June, when at a meeting of the Society for Psychical Research he rose uninvited and made a most injudicious speech which was to create very unfortunate repercussions. As a result the Society for Psychical Research decided to investigate the matter on the spot, i.e. Adyar.

They assigned a young man by the name of Richard Hodgson, whose subsequent report all but wrecked the Theosophical Society.

Referring to Colonel Olcott's unfortunate speech, Sinnett comments:

[1] See Sven Eek, *Damodar and the Pioneers of the Theosophical Movement.*

> The catastrophe, in my opinion, justified the regret I had freely expressed when Madame Blavatsky announced her change of plans and intention of coming to Europe, to play a part in the unexpected enthusiasm which *Esoteric Buddhism* had excited.

Sinnett's catastrophe was that he never understood his place in the theosophical movement. No matter what error of policy H.P. Blavatsky may have committed, she was the direct agent of the Mahatmas who had inaugurated the Theosophical Society. He was a professional journalist; she was an occultist; he was an excellent observer of the many phenomena which H.P.B. produced and has preserved an account of them for later generations, but H.P.B. was the one who produced them.

Madame Blavatsky, Damodar, and other chelas had become less and less inclined to act as a 'post office' for Sinnett's correspondence with the Mahatmas. His grasp of Theosophy lacked the depth which comes not merely from intellectual penetration but also from a spiritual identification of one's personal life with the philosophy.

On the 26th of April 1886, Sinnett was introduced to a lady whom he later called 'Mary'. She possessed remarkable mesmeric powers and Sinnett hoped that she would put him in touch with the Mahatmas again and also help him with his psychic experiments. She belonged to the London Lodge, whereas Madame Blavatsky founded the famous 'Blavatsky Lodge' to which many of the best members of Sinnett's lodge transferred their membership, not without a great deal of bad feelings on Sinnett's part.

It was at this time that Sinnett wrote his book entitled *Incidents in the Life of Madame Blavatsky*. She helped him with information, as she was anxious to clear her name from the scandals which had been created by the Coulomb's trouble and the subsequent Hodgson report. Mr and Mrs A. Coulomb had been members of the Adyar household, but on being disaffected, accused Madame Blavatsky of faking occult phenomena. The book is very valuable, but it contains many inaccuracies, which have been corrected by later writers.

At this time the proprietors of *The Pioneer* decided to establish a London office of *The Civil and Military Gazette* and *The Pioneer*. The task was entrusted to Sinnett who succeeded in establishing such an office, of which he was in charge for a couple of years with a salary of 500 pounds, which was a godsend, as he was at this time almost completely without funds. However, the former owner of *The Pioneer,* now Sir George Allen, had bought back a number of shares in this journal and, having returned to England, decided to take over the office himself. Sinnett thus found himself again in a precarious financial situation.

In 1888, Sinnett became associated with the publisher G.W. Redway, who first printed H.P.B.'s magazine *Lucifer.* H.P.B. brought an action in a county court against him for allegedly having overcharged her some thirty pounds. Sinnett was Redway's partner, and the action therefore indirectly involved him as well. Redway won the case, but it did little to promote the friendship between H.P.B. and Sinnett.

Sinnett's medium Mary wrote to him in October 1888 to make friends with H.P.B. again, which he did. But soon the final break came. The publication of *The Secret Doctrine,* H.P.B.'s *magnum opus,* in 1888 definitely contradicted many of the views expressed in Sinnett's *Esoteric Buddhism.* This Sinnett could not tolerate and he virtually made himself an outcast from the brilliant coterie which now surrounded Madame Blavatsky: Bertram and his uncle Dr Archibald Keightly; Annie Besant; George Mead, the writer of mystic lore; Walter R. Old, the astrologer; Mrs Cooper-Oakley and her sister Laura Cooper who married George Mead; Emily Kislingbury, and many others. He sulked in his tent and claimed that the *Transactions of the London Lodge* were the result of his conversations with K.H. through Mary's mediumship.

In 1889 Sinnett became instrumental in bringing Mr Leadbeater from Ceylon to instruct his son Denny, then twelve years of age. Mr Leadbeater brought with him a boy by the name of C. Jinarājadāsa who many years later became the President of the Theosophical Society.

On 8 May 1891, H.P. Blavatsky passed away, and about this event Sinnett writes:

> We were not in close touch with the household at the Avenue Road [H.P.B.'s residence] and I find a record in the *Diary* for the 9th of May, that we heard then of the death of Madame Blavatsky which had taken place the previous day.

This is a rather sad obituary from the man to whom H.P.B. had introduced the Masters and had permitted to participate in her life's work. Sinnett did attend the cremation at Woking on the 11th, but there are no further remarks in his *Autobiography* about her.

Sinnett devoted himself to the work of the London Lodge, but Mary married one of the members and drifted away from her erstwhile collaborator. He experimented with another medium called King.

Colonel Olcott died in 1907 and, by that time, Sinnett had become the Vice-President of the Society. Pending the election of a new President, Sinnett became Acting President for six months. Mrs Annie Besant was at that time at Adyar and wired Sinnett, suggesting that she become his deputy at Headquarters. This he refused, but appointed instead the then Treasurer, Mr Frank Davidson, on his behalf. This did not sit well with the Council and friction was thus created.

Sinnett toyed with the idea of himself becoming President for the West, but the Society was not interested. Annie Besant became the only candidate and was elected President.

In July of the same year, in his little magazine *Broad Views,* Sinnett published an article entitled 'The Vicissitudes of Theosophy' in which he criticized Mrs Besant and also challenged the generally accepted idea that H.P. Blavatsky had been especially sent by the Masters to found the Theosophical Society. Mrs Besant felt that these views were not compatible with the office of Vice-President and asked for his resignation. In 1911 she and Sinnett composed their differences and he was reinstated.

On the 19 October 1910, Sinnett had a private seance with his friend King. Damodar allegedly appeared on this occasion. Later, Sinnett avers that he saw Damodar who gave him an account of Colonel Olcott's death at which the Mahatmas appeared. In this same year, Sinnett made the acquaintance of an American actress, Maud Hoffman, who later became the executrix of his estate, which included the important letters from the Masters and H.P.B.

Mrs Besant initiated the raising of a fund to assist Sinnett in his old age. Five thousand pounds were turned over to him, but he did not live long to enjoy his surcease from want. He passed away on 27 June 1921, at the age of 81.

[For a full account see Sven Eek, *Damodar and the Pioneers of the Theosophical Movement*.]

APPENDIX B

Article published in *The Theosophist,* October 1912

MR A.O. HUME, C.B.
Founder of the Indian National Congress

BY C.S. BREMNER

To all who know and love India, the passing of Mr A.O. Hume is an event of no mean importance. As founder of the Indian National Congress his name is known and honoured in that vast continent from the Himalayas to Cape Comorin, from Sindh to Assam, as the 'Friend of India'. He inherited the will and capacity of the reformer, the statesman and economist who led the Radical party for thirty years during the earlier half of the nineteenth century. It is an interesting coincidence that this year marks the centenary of the connection of father and son with English public life, for in 1812 Joseph Hume purchased the right to represent Weymouth in Parliament. Students of history are aware how great were his services to his country. He worked for parliamentary reform, the repeal of Catholic disabilities, and of those that pressed on Nonconformists in the Corporation and Test Acts, the repeal of the Corn Laws, the satisfaction of Ireland's claims, the abolition of severe laws pressing on labour, of flogging in the army and impressment in the navy; no measure that aimed at greater justice and equity in our social relations but found a friend, a determined supporter, in Joseph Hume. He caused Retrenchment to be added to the Liberal watchword 'Peace and Reform'; the self-elected guardian of the public exchequer, during most of his life he questioned every item of public expenditure, and condemned the wasteful system by which the taxes were collected. He died in 1855, he and his gifted son having served the State contemporaneously for six years.

Mr A.O. Hume was born in 1829, educated at Haileybury and London University, and in 1849 entered the service of the East India Company in Bengal. The theatre of the father's labours had been the British Parliament; that of the son was India. At an early age he showed seriousness and earnestness of purpose, mastering the languages which were necessary for a successful administrator, entering into friendly relations with the people among whom he dwelt. He had the qualities of a ruler and organizer, the determination not only to deal with difficulties when they arose —such as at recurring famines—but to search out their causes and if possible prevent their repetition. During the Indian Mutiny, when he was at Etawah, Uttar Pradesh, he raised and drilled a local force and rendered such service that he was made a C.B. and received the medal and clasp. His rise was fairly rapid, for he became Magistrate and Collector in the N.W. Provinces (now the U.P.); Commissioner of Customs; Secretary to the Government of India. Whilst recognizing and appreciating the essential greatness, the purity of aim, the solid achievements of our rule in Inda, Mr Hume was one of that small band of men within the Civil Service who considered that things might be even better and that we had not yet attained absolute perfection. Perhaps the continuance of our empire in India depends more on our capacity to furnish men of this stamp than on any other factor whatever. Reformers are always the men who see life in its true perspective, who are eternally trying the present not at the bar of the Past, but of a Future yet to come where greater justice and freedom shall distinguish our mutual relations.

When Mr Hume retired from the Indian Civil Service in 1882, he devoted himself more than ever to the welfare of India, to the study of grave questions such as the increasing poverty of her peasantry, her social and political difficulties, the increase of centralization, the atrophy of such ancient local government as existed in villages and towns, which in the nature of things must suffer under a foreign rule, the disorganization of her ancient industries, which resulted from her connection with a country where capitalism is supreme. He attracted to himself men of like mind and capacity, such as Sir William Wedderburn, George Yule, Sir Henry Cotton, Garth; Indian leaders and thinkers like Messrs. W. Bonnerjee, Ghose, Dadabhai Naoroji. In 1885 Mr Hume founded the Indian National Congress, which ever since has met yearly, with the exception of 1907, in some large town.

The Congress deals with the hardships, which are to some extent inevitable, bound to arise where one nation governs another, with the incidence of taxation, reform in the land laws, the separation of judicial from executive functions in the same individual, the reform of the police and the liquor-laws; with the introduction of a representative element into the Provincial Councils; with the employment of Indians in government posts; in a word it exercises that kind of control over the administration that the representatives of the people exercise over government at home by means of questions in the House of Commons. Mr Hume, who ever since the Congress was founded, had been one of its two Secretaries, explained at a great meeting at Allahabad in 1888, that it was only one outcome, though at the moment the most prominent and tangible one, of the labours of a body of cultured men, mostly Indians, who some years ago bound themselves together to labour silently for the good of India. That Association had three main objects: the fusion into one national whole of all the different and, until recently, discordant elements that constitute the population of India; second, the gradual regeneration along all lines, spiritual, moral, social and political, of the nation thus evolved; and third, the consolidation of the union between England and India.

To this immense undertaking Mr Hume brought no mean gifts. He was a born ruler and organizer, skilled in the management of men, ready to spend himself in India's service, devoted to her people whom he knew and loved and who reverenced him in return, as they always have reverenced a small minority of the Civil Service, even to the point of worship among the humbler classes. An educated Indian only a year or two since, alluded to Sir William Wedderburn, a life-long friend and fellow-worker of Mr Hume, as one of the 'rishis vouchsafed to us from on High'. And Mr Hume too was counted among these elect ones who laboured for India's good in season and out, who, when they had retired from the Service, and might have lived easily and softly to the close of their days, redoubled their energies, toiled as they had never done before, and reaped from their own nation little but obloquy, blame, detraction, at times, downright scurrility. 'To Mr Hume', said one of the minor press of a great city in the north of England, 'belongs the dubious honour of having initiated the Congress movement.' And yet when Lord Macaulay introduced the entire system of western education into our great Empire, using the English language as the vehicle, he foresaw that Indians would one day claim a share in the government of their country and declared that such a demand would be 'a title to glory all our own'. The founding of the Congress raised a storm of violent opposition and vituperation among the men who had not foreseen that its coming was a mere question of time. The Englishmen who assisted the movement were treated pretty much as deserters to the common enemy. Yet the whole course of reform in India proceeds along the lines the Congress laid down. During the Viceroyalty of Lord Minto and with the hearty cooperation of Lord Morley as Secretary of India—merely to cite one reform among many—was passed the India Councils Act, 1909, reconstituting the Provincial Legislative Councils, conferring on them wide powers of discussion, and providing for an elaborate system of election of their members on a representative basis, or of nomination wherever election was impossible.

It is in fact the beginning of representative government for India. Whilst this Act was on the stocks, India celebrated the fiftieth year of government by the Crown, and the King Emperor sent a message to the princes and peoples of India. They were reminded how, from the first, representative institutions had been gradually introduced, how important classes were claiming equality of citizenship and a greater share in legislation and government. 'The politic satisfaction of such a claim'—so the Message runs—'will strengthen, not impair existing authority and power. Administration will be all the more efficient if the officers who conduct it have greater opportunities of regular contact with those whom it affects and with those who influence and reflect common opinion about it.' These wise and weighty words form the complete justification of the Congress movement, nor will those who realize the unparalleled difficulty of a mere handful of foreigners ruling 315,000,000 of people do aught but admire the acumen and foresight of those Englishmen who helped to voice the national aspirations, and who voluntarily associated themselves with their fellow-subjects in India to adapt the British Raj to the needs of India. The Councils Act came into force when Mr Hume attained his eightieth year, so that he 'saw of the travail of his soul and was satisfied'.

From 1887 onwards Mr Hume lived in Upper Norwood, but for some years nearly every cold season saw him back in India, organizing and extending the work, finding funds, making programmes, sifting and collecting evidence of grievances. He was the author of several well-known pamphlets, such as *Audi Alteram Partem, The Old Man's Hope, The Star of India.* On the occasion of his last visit to India, his farewell speech was reprinted as *Mr Hume's Farewell to India.* It can never be said that Indians idolized him because he flattered them, for in this farewell speech he reminded them how dear are truth and straight dealing to the British people and how necessary it is for the sake of their great cause to allay those jealousies which spring up and rob men of the fruit of their labours and mar its achievement.

Mr Hume's was a many-sided nature; more than most men he reminded one of the fact that Life has many Mansions. In his day he had been a great *shikari,* and the walls of his library at Norwood were covered with the heads and horns of the ibex, Himalayan sheep, and big Indian game, which bore witness to the prowess of himself and his friends. He had become a Theosophist, and in his later years, a vegetarian and anti-vivisectionist. He was a great authority on Indian ornithology, and joint author with Col. C.H.T. Marshall, of a classic work on the subject; his magnificent collection of specimens, said to number 70,000, was bequeathed to the nation many years ago.

At the age of seventy, his untiring energy, which Sir William Wedderburn characterized as the cause of admiring despair among his colleagues, was diverted to the gentler study of botany, and the last years of his life were devoted to, and it may have been too much consumed by, its pursuit. He started another enormous collection; no outing but had a botanical end in view. Gradually his house became more and more encumbered with huge metal cases of the latest pattern; between 30,000 and 40,000 specimens were collected, many of them gathered by his own hands, and all mounted, arranged and classified under his personal supervision. He was involved in a considerable correspondence with other botanists. A house was taken at 323 Norwood Road, and only a few months ago the collection was removed there. It was informally opened to the public last February by means of a lecture. It was presented to the enormous population south of the Thames as the South London Botanical Institute, and its permanent endowment arranged for by the generous founder, so that its facilities might be offered gratis to students. Mr Hume was unable to be present at the opening, his health having failed during the last years of his life. For many years he was President of the Dulwich Liberal and Radical Association, nor would the executive ever consent to accept the resignation which he tendered more than once. Mr Hume led many a good fight in the Liberal interest in his constituency, but always without success, Dulwich being a Unionist stronghold. Had Mr Hume consented to stand for Parliament himself, as he was several times requested to do, the result might have been different. It was thought that he, Sir W. Wedderburn, and Mr D. Naoroji would have made a particularly capable trio of Friends and Representatives of India, whilst ably and earnestly upholding the cause of social reform at home. As is well known, his colleagues entered Parliament and Mr Hume rendered them valuable aid outside, keeping in touch with the Indian movement to the end of his life.

Mr Hume was a man of very distinguished presence, tall, well built, and exceptionally handsome. His manners were a blend of dignity, old fashioned courtesy, kindliness and benevolence. The keen eye of a life-long naturalist served him well in the management of men. As Chairman of Committee he insisted on a hearing for every objector, and from opposition extracted an elixir which allowed him a great deal of his own way, whilst persuading his colleagues, and sometimes his opponents, that it was wisest and best.

APPENDIX C

SWAMI DAYANAND SARASVATI (1824-1883)

SWAMI DAYANAND played an important role in the early days of the Society in India until his break with the Founders in 1882. He is referred to a number of times in the *Letters* and it may be of interest to the student to know something of his background. See ML-54 (92), p. 302/298, a long letter in which he is discussed a number of times; ML-56 (102), p. 325/320; ML-57 (101) 327/322 and ML-91B (103B), p. 416/409. The numbers in parentheses are, in these instances, chronological.

In *A Short History of the Theosophical Society,* Josephine Ransom gives the story from the time the Founders came in contact with him before leaving the United States. (See index for page numbers.) The following is in part summarized from that account.

As the dream of the Founders of the Theosophical Society was to go to India and to form connections with Asiatic people, they welcomed eagerly any opportunity of knowing more about them. An American who had been in India called upon them, and Col. Olcott showed him the photograph of the two Hindus who had been fellow-passengers with him on the same ship from England to America in 1870. They were on a mission to the West to see what could be done to introduce Eastern spiritual and philosophic ideas. The traveller had met one of them, Mulji Thackersey, in Bombay, and gave Col. Olcott his address. He wrote at once and told Mulji about the Society, of their love for India and the reason for it. Mulji enthusiastically accepted the diploma of membership offered to him and, in return, informed the Colonel about a Hindu Pandit and reformer, Swami Dayananda Sarasvati, who had begun a powerful movement, called the Arya Samaj, for the revival of the pure Vedic religion. He introduced also Hurrychand (usually spelled Hurrychund in the *Letters*) Chintamon, President of the Bombay group of the Arya Samaj, with whom Col. Olcott then corresponded. Hurrychund, too, spoke highly of Swami Dayanand. He put the Colonel into touch with him, and they exchanged letters... 'It [the Arya Samaj] seemed like a Hindu Theosophical Society to Col. Olcott, and he decided at once [in 1877] to make an alliance with it.'

In 1878 Col. Olcott sent, in February, a diploma to Hurrychand and a Charter for Mulji Thackersey to form a Bombay Branch of the Theosophical Society. Swami Dayanand accepted a diploma. Hurrychand presently suggested that there was no need to have two Societies with the same objects, and an amalgamation was agreed upon. In May, Col. Olcott wrote to Dayanand:

> A number of American and other students who earnestly seek after spiritual knowledge, place themselves at your feet, and pray you to enlighten them...

Later in May, Augustus Gustam, the Recording Secretary of the Theosophical Society, wrote to the chiefs of the Arya Samaj:

> You are respectfully informed that at a meeting of the Council of the Theosophical Society, held at New York on 22 May 1878 ... it was unanimously resolved that the Society accept the proposal of the Arya Samaj to unite with itself, and that the title of this Society be changed to 'The Theosophical Society of the Arya Samaj of India'.

Dayanand was recognized as the 'lawful Director and Chief'.

On the same date, Col. Olcott wrote to Hurrychand in most enthusiastic terms, and on May 30, HPB wrote to Hurrychand that she was '*officially* and *personally* subject to the Swami's wishes'.

At one time consideration was given to the purchase of land in Brooklyn for the purpose of building a temple for 'the native members of the Hindu Arya Samaj of the Theosophical Society'. Apparently throughout all this time the Founders were most enthusiastic about and cordial to Dayanand.

Many plans were afoot to promote the movement, but they were upset when the full 'Rules of the Arya Samaj' were received in August of 1878. It was seen that the views of the Samaj were too sectarian for the Theosophical Society to approve. The situation was hastily revised.

Out of the revision emerged three organizations: (1) The Theosophical Society—the Parent Society; (2) The Arya Samaj;

(3) the 'link-Society' between them. This 'link-Society' had few members and by about 1880 had died out as futile.

In 1879, after the Founders had gone to India, they met the Swami and discussed matters with him, especially the rituals they were still thinking of introducing. The Swami wrote to Gen Doubleday, a member of the Society in New York, that he would send these rituals, basing them on Aryan Masonry. As time went on, the Swami became more sectarian, and to this neither Col. Olcott nor Madame Blavatsky could agree. He threatened withdrawal.

In May of 1882, the Swami suddenly and openly attacked the Founders of the Theosophical Society, charging them with being converts to Buddhism, and not to the Vedas. He denied having been a Fellow of the Society, said he had never had other connection with Theosophists than to consent to be their instructor in the Vedas—though he had never taught them anything and that the Society had not laid out one pie (about 1/12 of a cent) in the furtherance of the Vedic cause—and this in spite of the monies sent to him from initiation fees, etc. He announced that neither Col. Olcott nor Madame Blavatsky knew anything of Yoga Vidya, though they might know a little mesmerism and the art of clever conjuring. He had earlier affirmed HPB's yogic power. He issued a handbill to warn all Arya Samaj members against any relationship with such 'atheists, liars and selfish persons'. A careful analysis of the Swami's charges was given in *The Theosophist* by 'one of the Hindu Founders of the Parent Society (The Master Jupiter); also Col. Olcott's exhaustive reply giving a full account of what had actually occurred. The outcome was a total severance of the two organizations.'

Swami Dayanand died on 30 October 1883 (See *The Theosophist* for December 1883, p. 105). In connection with his death, an interesting passage is found on pages 184-5 in the *Short History*: On 19 November 1883, Col. Olcott with several others was at Lahore. That night, as Olcott lay asleep, 'he was aroused by a touch and, starting awake, grasped the visitor, only to hear a voice of great sweetness ask: "Do you not know me?" He saluted reverently and wished to jump out of bed to bow in respect, but the Master restrained him, left a note and laid a hand on his forehead in blessing. ... The note contained counsel to the Colonel and the prophecy of the deaths of two people then active opponents of the

Society—Swami Dayanand and Keshub Chandra Sen.' It would seem that the identity of the two persons was an assumption on the part of the Colonel, since he states in ODL 3:36 that the letter contained 'prophecies of the death of two undesignated, then active, opponents of the Society, which were realized in the passing away of the Swami Dayanand Sarasvati and Baba Keshab Chandra Sen'. As noted above, Dayanand had died more than two weeks earlier, although this fact was unknown to Olcott at the time he received the letter.

The Mahatma Letters contain several references to Swami Dayanand. In Letter 57 (p. 331/326, bottom) the Mahatma KH indicates that Dayanand's downfall was due to vanity. In Letter 56, he describes the actions taken to prevent Dayanand from wrecking the Theosophical Society.

APPENDIX D

THE H.X. (HUME) LETTER

IN the Study Notes on ML-52 (81), p. 288/284, mention is made of a letter sent to HPB by AOH in which he signed himself 'H.X.' The sequence of communications which led up to this and the protest by the Chelas which followed are given below.

In the June 1882 issue of *The Theosophist,* page 225, the following letter was published under the title of 'Seeming Discrepancies':

> To the Editor of 'The Theosophist'
>
> I have lately been engaged in devoting a few evenings' study to your admirable article, 'Fragments of Occult Truth', which deserves far more attention than a mere casual reading. It is therein stated that the translated *Ego cannot* span the abyss separating its state from ours, or that it cannot descend into our atmosphere and reach us; that it attracts but cannot be attracted, or, in short, that no departed Spirit can visit us.
>
> In Vol. 1, page 67, of *Isis* I find it said that many of the *spirits,* subjectively controlling mediums, are human disembodied *spirits,* that their being benevolent or wicked in quality largely depends upon the medium's private morality, that 'they cannot materialize, but only project their aetherial reflections on the atmospheric waves'. On page 69: 'Not every one can attract *human spirits,* who likes. One of the most powerful attractions of our departed ones is their strong affection for those whom they have left on earth. It draws them irresistibly, by degrees, into the current of the astral light vibrating between the person sympathetic to them and the universal soul.' On page 325: 'Sometimes, but rarely, the planetary spirits...produce them [subjective manifestations]: sometimes the spirits of our translated and beloved friends.'

From the foregoing it would appear as if both teachings were not uniform, but it may be that *souls,* instead of *spirits,* are implied, or that I misunderstood the meaning. Such difficult subjects are rather puzzling to Western students, especially to one who, like myself, is a mere tyro, though always grateful to receive knowledge from those who are in a position to impart such..

Yours &c

9 January 1882. Caledonian Theosophist

To this letter, HPB appended an Editor's Note:

It is to be feared that our valued Brother has both misunderstood our meaning in 'Isis' and that of the 'Fragments of Occult Truth'. Read in their correct sense, the statements in the latter do not offer the slightest discrepancy with the passages quoted from 'Isis' but both teachings are uniform.

Our 'Caledonian' Brother believes that, because it is stated in 'Isis' that 'Many, among those who control the medium *subjectively, are human disembodied spirits',* and in the 'Fragments', in the words of our critic, that 'the Ego cannot span the abyss separating its state from ours ... cannot descend into our atmosphere ... or, in short, that no departed SPIRIT can visit us '—there is a contradiction between the two teachings. We answer ... 'None at all'. We reiterate both statements, and will defend the proposition. Throughout 'Isis' although an attempt was made in the Introductory Chapter to show the great difference that exists between the terms 'soul' and 'spirit'—one the reliquiae of the *personal* Ego, the other the pure essence of the spiritual INDIVIDUALITY the term 'spirit' had to be often used in the sense given to it by the Spiritualists, as well as other similar conventional terms, as, otherwise, a still greater confusion would have been caused. Therefore, the meaning of the three sentences, cited by our friend, should be understood:-

On page 67 wherein it is stated that many of the spirits, subjectively controlling mediums, are 'human disembodied spirits', &c, the word 'controlling' must not be understood in the sense of a 'spirit' possessing himself of the organism of a medium; nor that, in each case, it is a 'spirit'; for often it is but a *shell* in its preliminary state of dissolution, when most of the physical intelligence and faculties are yet fresh and have not begun to disintegrate, or *fade out*. A 'spirit' or the spiritual Ego, cannot *descend* to the medium, but it can *attract* the spirit of the latter to itself, and it can do this only during the two intervals—before and after its 'gestation period'. Interval the first is that period between the physical death and the merging of the spiritual Ego into that state which is known in the Arhat esoteric doctrine as 'Bar-do'. We have translated this as the 'gestation' period, and it lasts from a few days to several years, according to the evidence of the Adepts. Interval the second lasts so long as the merits of the old *Ego* entitle the being to reap the fruit of its reward in its new regenerated Egoship. It occurs after the gestation period is over, and the new spiritual Ego is reborn—like the fabled Phoenix from its ashes—from the old one. The locality, which the former inhabits, is called by the northern Buddhist Occultists 'Deva-chan', the word answering, perhaps, to Paradise or the Kingdom of Heaven of the Christian elect. Having enjoyed a time of bliss proportionate to his deserts the new *pesonal* Ego gets reincarnated into a *personality* when the remembrance of his previous egoship, of course, fades out, and he can 'communicate' no longer with his fellow-men on the planet he has left forever, as the individual he was there known to be. After numberless reincarnations, and on numerous planets and in various spheres, a time will come, at the end of the Maha-Yug or great cycle, when each individuality will have become so spiritualized that, before its final absorption into the One All, its series of past *personal* existences will marshal themselves before him in a retrospective order like the many days of some one period of man's existence.

The words—'their being benevolent or wicked in quality largely depends upon the medium's private morality'—which conclude the first quoted sentence mean simply this: a pure medium's Ego can be drawn to and made, for an instant, to unite in a magnetic relation with a real disembodied spirit, whereas the soul of an *impure* medium can only confabulate with the *astral* soul, or 'shell' of the deceased. The former possibility explains those extremely rare cases of direct writing in recognized autographs, and of messages from the higher class of disembodied intelligences. We should say that the personal morality of the medium would be a fair test of the genuineness of the manifestation. As quoted by our friend, 'affection to those whom they have left on earth' is 'one of the most powerful attractions' between two loving spirits—the embodied and the disembodied ones.

Whence the idea, then, that the two teachings are 'not uniform'? We may well be taxed with too loose and careless a mode of expression, with a misuse of the foreign language in which we write, with leaving too much unsaid and depending unwarrantably upon the imperfectly developed intuition of the reader. But there never was, nor can there be, any radical discrepancy between the teachings in 'Isis' and those of this later period, as both proceed from one and the same source—the ADEPT BROTHERS.

In the 8 July 1882, issue of *Light,* the British Spiritualist publication, C.C. Massey took exception to some of the comments in this Editor's Note. The issue of *Light* is not available, but some of Mr Massey's comments are included in an article published in the August 1882 issue of *The Theosophist,* in which H.P.B. answers him. This article follows:

'ISIS UNVEILED' AND 'THE THEOSOPHIST' ON REINCARNATION

In *Light* (July 8) C.C.M. quotes from *The Theosophist* (June 1882) a sentence which appeared in the Editor's Note at the foot of an article headed 'Seeming Discrepancies'. Then, turning to the review of *The Perfect Way* in the same number, he quotes at length from 'an authoritative teaching *of the later period',* as he adds rather sarcastically. Then, again, a long paragraph from *Isis.* The three quotations and the remarks of our friend run thus:-

'There never was, nor can there be, any radical discrepancy between the teachings in 'Isis' [*Isis Unveiled*] and those of this later period, as both proceed from one and the same source—the ADEPT BROTHERS'. (*Editor's Note* in 'Seeming Discrepancies')

Having drawn the attention of his readers to the above assertion, C.C.M. proceeds to show—as he thinks—its fallacy:—

'To begin with, reincarnation—if other worlds besides this are taken into account—is the regular routine of nature. But reincarnation in the next higher objective world is one thing: reincarnation on this earth is another. *Even that takes place over and over again till the highest condition of humanity, as known on this earth, is attained, but not afterwards,* and here is the clue to the mystery.*** But once let a man be as far perfected by *successive reincarnations* as the present race will permit, and then this *next* reincarnation will be among the early growths of the next higher world, where the earliest growths are far higher than the highest here. *The ghastly mistake that the modern reincarnationists make is in supposing that there can be a return to this earth to lower bodily forms;*—not, therefore, that man is reincarnated as man again and again upon this earth, for that is laid down as truth in the above cited passages in the most positive and explicit form.' (Review of *T.P.W.* [*The Perfect Way*] in *The Theosophist.*)

And now for 'Isis': —

'We will now present a few fragments of this mysterious doctrine of reincarnation — as distinct from metempsychosis — which we have from an authority. Reincarnation, i.e. the appearance of the same individual — or rather, of his astral monad — twice on the same planet is not a rule of nature; it is an exception, like the teratological phenomenon of a two-headed infant. It is preceded by a violation of the laws of harmony of nature and happens only when the latter, seeking to restore its disturbed equilibrium, violently throws back into earth-life the astral monad, which has been tossed out of the circle of necessity by crime or accident. Thus in cases of abortion, of infants dying before a certain age, and of congenital and incurable idiocy, nature's original design to produce a perfect human being has been interrupted. Therefore, while the gross matter of each of these several entities is suffered to disperse itself at death through the vast realm of being, the immortal Spirit and astral monad of the individual — the latter having been set apart to animate a frame and the former to shed its divine light on the corporeal organization — must try a second time to carry out the purpose of the creative intelligence. *If reason has been so far developed as to become active and discriminative, there is no reincarnation on this earth,* for the three parts of the triune man have been united together, and he is capable of running the race. But when the new being has not passed beyond the condition of monad, or when, as in the idiot, the trinity has not been completed, the immortal spark which illuminates it has to re-enter on the earthly planet, as it was frustrated in its first attempt... Further, the same occult doctrine recognized another possibility, albeit so rare and so vague that it is really useless to mention it. Even the modern Occidental Occultists deny it, though it is universally accepted in Eastern countries. This is the occasional return of the terribly depraved human Spirits which have fallen to the eighth sphere — it is unnecessary to quote the passage at length. Exclusive of that rare and doubtful possibility, then, "Isis" — I have quoted from volume 1, pp. 451-2 — allows only three cases — abortion, very early death, and idiocy — in which reincarnation on this earth occurs.

'I am a long-suffering student of the mysteries, more apt to accuse my own stupidity than to make "seeming discrepancies" an occasion for scoffing. But after all, two and three will not make just four; black is not white, nor, in reference to plain and definite statements, is "Yes" equivalent to "No". If there is one thing which I ardently desire to be taught, it is the truth about this same question of reincarnation. I hope I am not, as a dutiful Theosophist, expected to reconcile the statement of "Isis" with that of this authoritative Reviewer. But there is one consolation. The accomplished authoress of "Isis" cannot have totally forgotten the teaching on this subject therein contained. She, therefore, certainly did not dictate the statements of the Reviewer. If I may conjecture that Koot Hoomi stands close behind the latter, then assuredly Koot Hoomi is not, as has been maliciously suggested, an alias for Madame Blavatsky.

'C.C.M.'

We hope not—for Koot Hoomi's sake. Mme B. would become too vain and too proud, could she but dream of such an honour. But how true the remark of the French classic: *La critique est aisée, mais l'art est difficile*—though we feel more inclined to hang our diminished head in sincere sorrow and exclaim: *Et tu Brute!* than to quote old truisms. Only, where that (even) 'seeming discrepancy' is to be found between the two passages—except by those who are entirely ignorant of the occult doctrine—will be certainly a mystery to every Eastern Occultist who reads the above and who studied at the same school as the reviewer of 'The Perfect Way'. Nevertheless the letter is chosen as the weapon to break our head with. It is sufficient to read No.1 of the *Fragments of Occult Truth,* and ponder over the septenary constitution of man into which the triple human entity is divided by the occultists, to perceive that the 'astral' monad is not the 'Spiritual' monad and vice versa. That there is no discrepancy whatsoever between the two statements, may be easily shown, and we hope will be shown, by our friend, the 'reviewer'. The most that can be said of the passage quoted from *Isis* is that it is incomplete, chaotic, vague, perhaps—clumsy, as many more passages in that work, the first literary production of a foreigner, who even now can hardly boast of her knowledge of the English language. Therefore, in the face of the statement from the very correct and excellent review of 'The Perfect Way'—we say again that 'Reincarnation, i.e. the appearance of the same individual—or rather, of his *astral* monad (or the *personality* as claimed by the modern Reincarnationists)—twice on the same planet is not a rule in nature and that it *is* an exception.' Let us try once more to explain our meaning. The reviewer speaks of the 'Spiritual Individuality' or the *Immortal Monad* as it is called, i.e. the 7th and 6th Principles in the *Fragments*. In *Isis* we refer to the *personality* or the *finite* astral monad, a compound of imponderable elements composed of the 5th and 4th principles. The former as an emanation of the One absolute is indestructible; the latter as an elementary compound is finite and doomed sooner or later to destruction with the exception of the more spiritualized portions of the 5th principle (the *Manas* or mind) which are assimilated by the 6th principle when it follows the 7th to its 'gestation state' to be reborn or not reborn as the case may be, in the *Arupa Loka* (the Formless World). The seven principles, forming, so to say, a *triad* and a *quaternary*, or, as some have it a 'Compound Trinity' sub-divided into a triad and two duads may be better understood in the following groups of Principles:

GROUP I 7. *Atma*—'Pure Spirit'. 6. *Buddhi*—Spiritual Soul or Intelligence.	SPIRIT *Spiritual Monad or* 'Individuality' and its *vehicle*. Eternal and indestructible.
GROUP II 5. *Manas*—'Mind or Animal Soul' 4. *Kama-Rupa*—'Desire' or 'Passion' Form	SOUL *Astral Monad* or the *personal Ego* and its vehicle. Survives Group III and is destroyed after a time, unless *reincarnated* as said under exceptional circumstances.
GROUP III 3. *Linga-sarira*—'Astral or Vital Body'. 2. *Jiva*—'Life Principle' 1. *Sthula Sarira*—'Body'	BODY Compound Physical, or the '*Earthly Ego*.' The three die together *invariably*.

And now we ask—where is the discrepency or contradiction? Whether man was good, bad, or indifferent, Group II has to become either a 'shell' or be once or several more times reincarnated under 'exceptional circumstances'. There is a mighty difference in our Occult doctrine between an *impersonal* Individuality, and an individual *Personality.* C.C.M. will not be reincarnated; nor will be in his next rebirth C.C.M. but quite a new being, born of the thoughts and deeds of C.C.M.: his own creation, the child and fruit of his present life, the effect of the causes he is now producing. Shall we say then with the Spiritists that C.C.M., the man we know, will be reborn again? No; but that his divine Monad will be clothed thousands of times yet before the end of the Grand Cycle, in various human forms, every one of them a *new* personality. Like a mighty tree that clothes itself every spring with a new foliage, to see it wither and die towards autumn, so the eternal Monad prevails through these series of smaller cycles, ever the same, yet ever changing and putting on, at each birth, a new garment. The bud, that failed to open one year, will reappear in the next; the leaf that reached its maturity and died a natural death—can never be reborn on the same tree again. While writing *Isis,* we were not permitted to enter into details: hence—the vague generalities. We are told to do so now—and we do as we are commanded.

And thus, it seems, after all, that 'two and three' will 'make just four' if the 'three' was only *mistaken* for that number. And, we have heard of cases when that, which was universally regarded and denounced as something *very* 'black'—shockingly so—suddenly became 'white', as soon as an additional light was permitted to shine upon it. Well, the day may yet come when even the much misunderstood occultists will appear in such a light. *Vaut mieux tard que jamais* !

Meanwhile, we will wait and see whether C.C.M. will quote again from our present answer—in *Light*.

Then came the following letter from AOH, which he signed 'H.X.' It was published in *The Theosophist* for September 1882, pp. 324-6, and was preceded by a long Editor's Note, also included.

'C.C.M.' AND ISIS 'UNVEILED'

(We publish the following letter from 'H.X.' under a strong personal protest. Another paper signed by several Chelas—all accepted pupils and disciples of our Masters—that immediately follows it, will show to our readers that we are not alone in feeling pain for such an ungenerous and uncalled-for criticism, which we have every right to consider as a very one-sided expression of a merely personal opinion. If it is never fair or just in a European to judge an Asiatic according to his own Western code and criterion, how much more unfair it becomes when that same standard is applied by him to an exceptional class of people who are—owing to their great purity of life—exempted from judgment even by their own people—the teeming millions of Asia, of whatever nation, religion or caste. Our correspondent must surely be aware of the fact known to every child in India, namely that they, whom the numberless masses of Asiatics call *Mahatmas*—'great souls'—and reverentially bow to, are subject to neither the tyranny of caste, nor to that of social or religious laws. That so holy are they in the eyes of even the most bigoted, that for long ages they have been regarded as a law within the law, every ordinary and other law losing its rights over such exceptional men. *Vox populi, vox Dei,* is an old proverb showing that the intuitions of the masses can rarely fail to instinctively perceive great truths. Nor can we really see any reason why, a hitherto unknown and profoundly secret Fraternity, a handful of men who have strenuously avoided coming in contact with the outside world, who neither force themselves upon, nor even volunteer the first their teachings to any one—least of all Europeans—why, we say, they should be so unceremoniously dragged out before the gaze of a perfectly indifferent public (that is neither interested, nor does it generally believe in their existence), only to be placed in a false light (false because of its great incompleteness) and then cut up piecemeal by one dissatisfied student for the supposed benefit of a few who are not even lay-chelas. However, since it is the pleasure of our MASTERS themselves, that the above criticism should be placed before the Areopagus of a public, for whose opinion they must care as much as the great Pyramid does for the hot wind of the desert sweeping over its hoary top—we must obey. Yet, we repeat most emphatically, that had it not been for the express orders received from the Brothers we should have never consented to publish such a—to say the least—*ungenerous* document. Perchance, it may do good in one direction: it gives the key, we think, to the true reason why our

Brothers feel so reluctant to show favours even to the most intellectual among the European 'would-be' mystics.—Ed.)

TO THE EDITOR OF THE THEOSOPHIST

Dear Madame,

I cannot say that, to me, the explanation furnished at page 288 of the last number of THE THEOSOPHIST of our friend 'C.C.M.s' difficulties seems altogether satisfactory, or sufficient—not to the uninitiated, at least.

In the first place, I think it a pity that it is not plainly said that ISIS UNVEILED for all but the adepts and chelas—*teems* with what are practically errors. Passages on passages convey, and *must* convey to every ordinary reader, wholly erroneous conceptions. No uninitiate can take any single passage in this work, relating to occult mysteries, and construing this as he would an ordinary work, infer therefrom that he understands the real meaning.

The fact is, 'Isis' never has been, and never will be, unveiled to any outsiders—all that can be said is that in 'Isis Unveiled' a few rents were torn[1] in the veil, through which *those knowing how to look* can obtain glimpses of the Goddess.

The work was essentially destructive in its character; it never seriously aimed at reconstruction, but only at clearing the way for this. Its mission was, as it were, to clear the site for future building operations.

Hence all that it contains, touching occult mysteries, was purposely so written as *not* to convey correct ideas to outsiders, while, at the same time, the correct ideas *were* given sufficiently plainly to permit of their recognition by initiates.

But besides this, the text, written much of it by different adepts imperfectly acquainted with English, had to be put into shape by yourself (necessarily in those days no great English scholar) and Colonel Olcott, who was quite ignorant at that time of occult philosophy.

[1] That is just what we had the honour of repeating more than once, privately and in print. We have repeatedly stated that the title was a misnomer and through no fault of ours. Therefore the charge that precedes, is quite uncalled for.—Ed.

The result was that, into sayings purposely dark and misleading to all outsiders, a number of distinct errors were introduced in the process of putting those sayings into English.

Surely, if I am correct in the above, it is best to say so plainly, once for all, and avoid what may otherwise become a perpetually recurrent demand for the reconciliation of apparent discrepancies between passages in 'Isis' and passages in articles in THE THEOSOPHIST.

In the second place it seems to me that it should be clearly understood that what we, LAY DISCIPLES, write on the subject of Occult Philosophy is not to be taken as exhaustive, or as necessarily correct to the letter, in every detail. We receive certain instructions, and portions of what we are taught we reproduce as occasion demands; doubtless our contributions are looked at, and any glaring errors, should such find a place there, are eliminated, but it is not pretended that papers like the FRAGMENTS or the Review of THE PERFECT WAY, are to be considered as authoritative or final—correct, in the main, of course they are and must be, or they would not be allowed to appear, but for all that no 'verbal inspiration' is claimed for them; and while they will necessarily *always* be imperfect (for how can such questions be exhaustively dealt with in a few pages?) they will very often fall short of perfect accuracy in regard to even those points with which they do deal.

Hereafter, a more or less comprehensive and complete sketch of the whole system will perhaps be given. At present the object of all these detached papers merely is to familiarize readers with the barest outlines of some of the more salient of its features. We do not pretend to furnish pictures, much less photographs, only the roughest possible sketches.

If 'C.C.M.' wants to know why he and others like himself, honestly anxious to learn the whole truth, cannot get this at once *totus, teres, atque rotundus,* the reply is that those who presumably know best, and who, be this as it may, hold the keys of the position, declare that the time has not come for giving more than stray glimpses of that truth to the world.

It would be well too for 'C.C.M.' and other worthy Brothers, unacquainted with the East, to remember that the Adepts (with whom it rests to give to us little or much and to give what they do give slowly or promptly, grudgingly or freely) differ intellectually in many respects from ourselves. I, for instance, distinctly hold that knowing what they do, it is a *sin* on their part not to communicate to the world all the knowledge they possess, which would not involve conferring on people unworthy, probably, to exercise them, occult powers. I hold that, be a man an adept or what not, all the knowledge he possesses, he holds, simply, in trust for his fellows, but the rest he is *bound* to give. But they scout any such idea, and hold that the knowledge they possess is their own special property, to communicate or not to others as they please and they consider this communication, which I hold to be a simple *duty,* the greatest possible favour and one which must be worked for.

Again, even when disposed to teach, their ideas of doing this differ *toto caelo* from ours. If we wanted to teach anything, we should teach it piece by piece, and each branch with perfect accuracy. They on the contrary seem to care nothing about complete accuracy. All they appear to desire to convey, is a sort of general conception of the outline. They do not seem to wish, that any one, not bound to them by obligations rendering them practically their slaves, should learn even their philosophy, *thoroughly.* It suits them now to have some general conception of their views disseminated and they therefore condescend to vouchsafe stray scraps of information sufficient to enable us to put forth now and again feeble sketches of their views on this or that point. But, certainly, in one week I could teach any ordinarily intelligent man, all, that in eighteen months, we all of us have succeeded in extracting from them.[1]

From my point of view, from the point of view, I believe, I may say, of every educated European gentleman, nothing can, in certain respects, be more unreasonable and unsatisfactory than the position they take up; but, from an Oriental point of view this position so repulsive to me that I have more than once been on the point of closing my connection with them for good, this position I say, would seem to wear no such aspect, since many of my native friends seem to look upon it as not only natural and what was to be expected, but as actually reasonable and right.

[1] No doubt, no doubt. Any 'ordinary intelligent man' may learn in an hour, or perhaps less, to speak through a telephone, or a phonograph. But how many years were required to first discover the secret force, then apply it, invent and perfect the two wonderful instruments?—Ed.

European Theosophists should realize this feature of the case, and further that one might as well try to argue with a brick wall as with the fraternity, since when unable to answer your arguments[1] they calmly reply that their rules do not admit of this or that.

To me personally it appears very far from a hopeful business this dealing with the BROTHERS—one may respect *all,* for the great knowledge, in certain lines, that they possess, and for the extremely pure and self-denying lives that they have led and do lead, and one may even heartily love, some if not all of them for their geniality and kindly natures; but their system and their traditions are opposed to our ideas of right and wrong and it is, to me, still doubtful whether we shall ever be able to get any good out of their teaching at all commensurate with the expenditure of time and energy that this involves. At the same time it is to be borne in mind, that they, and they only, possess the highest knowledge; they are not to be reasoned with, nor persuaded; they are neither, according to our European views, altogether just, nor generous; in a dozen different ways they fall short of the European ideal of what men so elevated in learning and so pure in personal life should be, but for all that they alone hold the keys that unlock the secrets of the unseen world, and you must either accept them, as they are, in the hope that in doing their work you may be able to do some little good to others, or give them up altogether and devote your energies to the service of your fellows in *perhaps* a lower, but *certainly* a more promising field of action.

It is absolutely certain that the BROTHERS honestly believe themselves to be entirely right in their ways and in all they do and say; it is qually certain that no educated European will altogether concur with them. But then they do unquestionably possess knowledge entirely hidden from us and which if known to us might wholly change our verdict and so it may well be that they *are* right, despite the look matters bear to us, and we *wrong.*[2] *But,* without this knowledge (and not the slightest hopes of our ever acquiring it is held out to us), *no* European will see it in this light (Asiatics see it as the Brothers do) and so C.C.M. and other British Theosophists, must be

[1] Our esteemed Brother and correspondent would, perhaps, do well to first make himself sure that our Masters 'are unable to reply' before venturing such a bold assertion.

[2] With such a possibility in view, it would have been perhaps wiser to abstain from such premature and wholesale denunciation. — Ed.

prepapred to meet constantly with all kinds of things in connection with the alleged sayings and doings of the Brothers which to them seem quite inconsistent with such being as adepts, or more properly with *their* Ideals of what these OUGHT to be. We have to deal with a set of men almost exclusively Orientals; very learned in some matters, learned beyond the conception of most Westerns, very pure in life, very jealous of their treasured knowledge, brought up and petrified in a system that can only recommend itself to Eastern minds, and saturated with a stream of thought flowing directly at right angles to that in which runs all the highest and brightest modern Western Thought. Their aims, their objects, their habits of thought, their *modi operandi,* even their standards of right and wrong, where many questions are concerned, differ entirely from ours; and the sooner European Theosophists understand all this and square their expectations and demands accordingly, the better it will be for all.

To use Mr Gladstone's now traditional formula three courses are open to us:

1. To accept the Brothers as they are—make the best we can of them, accept gratefully such small crumbs as fall from our Masters' tables and admit once and for all that there is at present no possibility of any such explanation of their policy and system as can be wholly satisfactory to our European (and *perhaps* as they would tell us, warped and *demoralized*) minds.

2. To give up the Brothers and their painfully doled out glimpses of the hidden higher knowledge altogether, but to work on in the practical groove indicated by them, labouring to unite all we can in bonds of brotherly love and mutual forbearance and regard.

3. To cut the concern altogether as affording no prospects of any practical results at all commensurate with the time and energy demanded from all who are to be more than nominal members of the Society.

I, at any rate, as at present advised, prefer the first alternative—but I do think that every Theosophist should clearly realize that these are the only three courses logically open to him, and decidedly to adopt one or the other of them.

And now before closing I venture to suggest that it might be well to make clear to C.C.M. *why* it is that what we call the personality *can* reappear in the case of idiots and children dying before the time of responsibility arrives. Otherwise looking at the Personality in its literal sense, derived from *persona* or mask, he will possibly be disposed to think that as the mask, the body, dies in those two cases as well as in all others, rebirths in these cases must as in others be accompanied by new personalities. Of course the fact that with us the *personality* stands not for the fleshy masks of the higher duads but for the lower of these two latter, which even to the man himself in most cases, is a very iron mask to the higher one.

Now to evolve a new personality, in our application of this term, there must be some new materials to melt up with the old, and those materials can only be KARMA, i.e. responsible deeds, words or thoughts—but where there has never been responsibility, there then can be no KARMA, and therefore no new materials; therefore, perforce, no new personality despite the new birth. So too in our sense of the word there is no change, only development in the personality, right through the lower kingdom, up to that man-life when as a sequence of multitudinous men-ape, ape-men and physical men lives, the fully responsible man appears and KARMA begins to attend each life. Up to that time there has been evolution, but no recast; from that time save in exceptional cases (two classes of which are above referred to) there is a recast and therefore a change in personality after every life, and with this change (not a mere forgetting but) a *loss* of all memory, the experiences which constituted this, having been melted up into the body of the new personality.

The *perfect* adept, of course, claims to be able to avert this change of personality and so through thousands of births and through millions on millions of years to preserve his personality and not merely his individuality, unchanged. But he must be a *perfect* adept[1] which our immediate adept masters cannot, they tell us, claim to be.[2] The Perfect Sorcerer can similarly secure a personal

[1] One who has successfully passed the highest degree of initiation beyond which is *perfect* Adi-Buddhaship, than which there is no higher on this earth.—Ed.

[2] May not this confession of our Brothers be partially due to one more attribute they are found to share so 'grudgingly' and rarely with the too 'educated Europeans', namely 'modesty'?—Ed.

immortality through millions of years, but it is an immortality of misery.

Yours obediently,
H.X.

The letter from 'H.X.' was followed in the same issue by a protest from a number of chelas:

A PROTEST

We, the undersigned, the 'Accepted' and 'Probationary' Hindu *Chelas* of the HIMALAYAN BROTHERS, their disciples in India, and Northern Cashmere, respectfully claim our right to protest against the tone used in the above article, and the bold criticisms of H.X. — a lay chela. No one who has once offered himself as a pupil has any right to openly criticize and blame our Masters simply upon his own unverified hypotheses, and thus to prejudge the situation. And, we respectfully maintain that it ill befits one, to whom positively *exceptional* favours were shown, to drag their personalities as unceremoniously before the public as he would any other class of men.

Belonging, as we do, to the so-called 'inferior' Asiatic race, we cannot help having for our Masters that boundless devotion which the European condemns as *slavish*. The Western races would however, do well to remember that if some of the poor Asiatics arrived at such a height of knowledge regarding the mysteries of nature, it was only due to the fact that the Chelas have always blindly followed the dictates of their Masters and have never set themselves higher than, or even as high as, their Gurus. The result was that sooner or later they were rewarded for their devotion, according to their respective capacities and merits by those who, owing to years of self-sacrifice and devotion to *their* Gurus, had in their turn become Adepts. We think that our blessed Masters ought to be the best judges how to impart instruction. Most of us have seen and known them personally, while two of the undersigned live with the venerated Mahatmas, and therefore know how much of their powers is used for the good and well-being of Humanity. And if, for reasons of their own, which we know must be good and wise, our Gurus abstain from communicating 'to the world all the knowledge they possess' it is no reason why 'lay Chelas' who know yet so little about them should call it 'a sin' and assume upon themselves the right of remonstrating with, and teaching them publicly what they imagine to be their duty. Nor does the fact that they are 'educated European gentlemen' alter the case. Moreover, our learned Brother, who complains of receiving so little from our Masters, seems to lose sight of the, to him unimportant, fact that Europeans, no less than natives, ought to feel thankful for even such 'crumbs of knowledge' as they may get, since it is not our Masters who have first offered their instruction, but we ourselves who, craving, repeatedly beg for it. Therefore, however indisputably clever and highly able, from a literary and intellectual standpoint, H.X.'s letter, its writer must not feel surprised to find that overlooking all its cleverness, we natives discern in it, foremost and above all, an imperious spirit of domineering—utterly foreign to our own natures—a spirit that would dictate its own laws even to those who can never come under *anyone's.* No less painfully are we impressed by the utter absence in the letter, we are now protesting against, of any grateful acknowledgement even for the little that has confessedly been done.

In consequence of the above given reasons, we the undersigned, pray our brothers of THE THEOSOPHIST to give room in their Journal to our PROTEST

DEVA MUNI.·.·.
PARAMAHANSA SHUB-TUNG .·.·.·.
T. SUBBA ROW, B.A.,B.L., F.T.S. .·.·.·.
DHARBAGIRI NATH, F.T.S.
GUALA K. DEB, F.T.S.
NOBIN K. BANERJEE, F.T.S.
T.T. GURUDAS, F.T.S.
BHOLA DEVA SARMA, F.T.S.
S.T.K. CHARY, F.T.S.
GARGYA DEVA, F.T.S.
DAMODAR K. MAVALANKAR, F.T.S.

APPENDIX E

THE KIDDLE INCIDENT: THE CRISIS OF 1883-1884

(From *The 'Brothers' of Madame Blavatsky* by Mary K. Neff)

ONCE upon a time, shortcomings in a chela's precipitation of a letter for Master K.H. led to a 'crisis' in the Theosophical Society which shook out doubting and uncertain members, as these crises from time to time are apt (and intended?) to do. It was the third controversy that shook the Society and will go down in theosophical history as 'The Kiddle Incident'.

On 10 December 1880, Mr Sinnett received a letter from the Master which contained certain statements relating to ideas. He incorporated them in *The Occult World* when he published it in 1881, while on holiday in England. [See ML, letters beginning on pages 22 and 413, 3rd ed., respectively for the letter in question and the explanation given later by the Master K.H. —Ed.] It seems that a Mr Henry Kiddle of U.S.A. wrote to Mr Sinnett through his publishers about this passage; but either the letter was not received, Mr Sinnett having returned to India, or it was lost amid the mass of his editorial material at Allahabad. Not receiving a reply, Mr Kiddle took up the matter in the press, by sending a letter to Mr Stainton Moses ('M.A. Oxon'), editor of *Light,* the English Spiritualist organ, which letter was published in its issue of 1 September 1883. In it he pointed out that

> On reading Mr Sinnett's *Occult World* more than a year ago I was very greatly surprised to find in one of the letters presented by Mr Sinnett as having been transmitted to him by Koot Hoomi, in the mysterious manner described, a passage taken almost verbatim from an address on Spiritualism by me at Lake Pleasant in August 1880, and published the same month by the *Banner of Light.* As

Mr Sinnett's book did not appear till a considerable time afterwards (about a year, I think), it is certain that I did not quote, consciously or unconsciously, from its pages. How, then, did it get into Koot Hoomi's mysterious letter?[1]

Mr Sinnett promptly answered in *Light* for September 22, explaining his seeming neglect, and adding:

For the moment all I can say is that the passage is introduced by my revered friend with the expression, 'Plato was right'; which seems to point to some origin for the sentences immediately following that may have lain behind both the letter and the lecture. To obtain further explanation of the mystery from India will take time;[2] but meanwhile I may point out that the path leading to acquaintanceship with the Adepts is always found strewn with provocations to distrust them, for reasons very fully detailed in my books; their policy at present is rather to ward off than to invite European confidence.

Naturally, Colonel Olcott took up the cudgels. His line of argument, as published in *Light* for November 17th, was that unconscious plagiarism was not uncommon; or rather, that two persons at a distance from each other not infrequently evolved the same idea. He cited examples:

If M.A. (Oxon) thinks it so funny that a very small patch from Mr Kiddle's robe should have been stitched into the garment of Koot Hoomi's thought, I can give him a tougher nut to crack. In the last number of *The Nineteenth Century* in the article 'After Death', occurs a passage which is word for word identical with what was written by this same Koot Hoomi two years ago in a private letter to myself. ... Again, when the report of one of Mrs Hardinge-Britten's American lectures appeared in *The Spiritual Scientist,* Madame Blavatsky found in it a passage verbatim from the as yet unpublished *Isis Unveiled,* which Mrs Britten had not seen and the manuscript was actually altered so as to avoid the appearance of plagiarism. I do not undertake to explain the Kiddle mystery at all, nor do I think it of much consequence. It is highly absurd to think that a mind capable of reducing to expression in a foreign tongue so lofty a scheme of evolution as that in *Esoteric Buddhism* would be driven to fish for

[1] Quotations from Spiritualist journals used in this chapter are taken from H.P.B.'s scrapbooks.

[2] Mr Sinnett was by this time permanently in England.

ideas in Mr Kiddle's speeches, or the pages of any Spiritualistic journal. When my friend of London has explained away the mystery of his own mediumship, it will be in order for him to throw stones into his neighbour's garden.

Meanwhile, Mr William Q. Judge in America, in the *Religio-Philosophic Journal,* took the position that

> It is not proven that Mr Kiddle was the first to use the form of words advertised. It is an idea which has been common property for a long time...In the Inaugural Address of the Theosophical Society, 17 November 1875 (in print) the same ideas, inspired by Koot Hoomi, may be found.

What Madame Blavatsky thought of all this she vividly expresses when writing to Mr Sinnett, 17 November 1883:

> K.H. plagiarized from Kiddle! Ye gods and little fishes! ... If they knew what it was to dictate *mentally a precipitation* as D. Khool says—at 300 miles distance; and had seen as all of us—General Morgan, I, the chelas here (of whom we have three)—the original fragments on which the precipitation was photographed, from which the young fool of a chela had copied, unable to understand half of the sentences and so skipping them; then they would not be idiotic enough to accuse an Adept...of such an absurd action. Plagiarism from the *Banner of Light* !!... K.H. blows me up for talking too much—says He needs no defence and that I need not trouble myself. But if He were to kill me I cannot hold my tongue—on general principles and as a sign of loyalty to them. ... Ever since Subba Row brought to us the original scrap of Kashmir paper (given to him by my Boss) on which appeared that whole page from the letter you published (in *The Occult World*)—I understood what it meant. Why, that letter was but one-third of the letter dictated and never published, for you have not received it...

[Here several lines of HPB's writing have apparently been completely erased, and the following note precipitated in KH's writing]:

> TRUE PROOF OF HER DISCRETION! I WILL TELL YOU ALL MYSELF AS SOON AS I HAVE AN HOUR'S LEISURE.

[HPB goes on]: But since they don't want me to speak of this I better not say a word more lest M. should again pitch into me![1]

[1] *Letters of H.P. Blavatsky to A.P. Sinnett*, pp. 66-7.

Here we have a hint of the true explanation, and in the December *Theosophist* Mr T. Subba Row guardedly advanced it:

> If anybody has committed literary theft, it is the complainant himself and not the accused. I find no reference to Plato in the passages quoted from Mr Kiddle's lecture... Also there are certain alterations of Mr Kiddle's language in the passage which show that the Mahatma never intended to borrow Mr Kiddle's ideas and phrases, but that he rather intended to say something against them.... Thus, where the lecturer says that 'the agency called Spiritualism is bringing a new set of ideas into the world', the Mahatma emphatically affirms that 'it is not physical phenomena' that he and his brother Occultists study, but 'these universal ideas' which are, as it were, the noumena underlying all physical manifestation. The contrast between the Mahatma's view of the relationship between these ideas and physical phenomena and Mr Kiddle's views is striking...
>
> It is quite evident from the wording of the passage that there *is* 'something wrong somewhere'. Plato is introduced into it rather abruptly and the grammatical construction of the last sentence is by no means clear. Apparently there is no predicate which refers to 'ideas larger', etc. A part of the sentence is thus evidently lost... Therefore, from a careful perusal of the passage and its contents, any unbiased reader will come to the conclusion that somebody must have greatly blundered, and will not be surprised to hear that it was unconsciously altered through the carelessness and ignorance of the chela by whose instrumentality it was 'precipitated'. Such alterations, omissions and mistakes sometimes occur in the process of precipitation; and I now assent that I know it for certain *from an inspection of the original precipitation proof,* that such was the case with regard to the passage under discussion.
>
> The Mahatma against whom the accusation has been brought will, of course, think it beneath his dignity to offer any explanation in his own defence to Mr Kiddle or his followers and supporters. But I hope Mr Sinnett will be so good as to place before the public as soon as possible such explanation or information as he may be permitted by the Mahatmas concerned.... In conclusion I cannot but regret that some writers in the Spiritualistic organs and other English journals have thought it fit to drag our Master's name into public print without any necessity for doing so,[1] using moreover such remarks and

[1] Meaning particularly H.P.B. This was the real point at issue between them, which led to his refusal to cooperate with her in the publication of *The Secret*

> insinuations as are fully calculated to be highly offensive to those who have the good fortune to be personally known to, and acquainted with, the Mahatmas in question. The reproach contained in the *Protest* of 500 Hindu Theosophists—just published in *Light*—may be fairly applied to many spiritualists besides 'B.W.M.D.'

As a matter of fact, in December, the Master did give Mr Sinnett a full solution of the mystery, but under a promise of secrecy....

> (The student is referred to ML-93 [chronological 117], p. 420/413. Pertinent passages are quoted in Miss Neff's book but need not be repeated here.—Eds.)

Doctrine. He, together with most Hindu Theosophists, held that the existence of the Masters should never have been made a matter of public knowledge, and he never forgave H.P.B. for what he considered her desecration of the Masters' names by allowing them to appear in print.

APPENDIX F

MASTER KOOT HOOMI'S TRAVELS

(From *The 'Brothers' of Madame Blavatsky* by Mary K. Neff)

> *Those who work with Shamballa, the initiates and the messengers of Shamballa, do not sit in seclusion—they travel everywhere. Very often people do not recognize them, and sometimes they do not even recognize each other!* [1] *But they perform their works not for themselves, but for the great Shamballa; and all of them know the great symbol of anonymity. They sometimes seem wealthy, yet they are without possessions. Everything is for them, but they take nothing for themselves.*
>
> *Shamballa*, by Nicholas Roerich

The truth of this statement is amply borne out by a study of the letters of the Mahatmas and of H.P.B. We know that in the 1870's Mahatma Koot Hoomi was a student in Europe, a young man securing a Western education. Dr Hugh Wernekke and Professor Fechner speak of his attendance at the University of Leipzig in 1875, and of his later visit to Zurich. H.P.B. specified other cities honoured by his presence:

> I like Würzburg. It is near Heidelberg and Nurenberg, and all the centres one of the Masters lived in, and it is He who advised my Master to send me there.[2]

Beginning with 1880, his journeyings about Asia can be traced.

[1] Thus Mme Blavatsky relates that late in the 1850's a 'Master ordered me to go to Java for a certain business. There were two whom I suspected of being chelas there. I saw one of them in 1869 at the Mahatma's house and recognized him, but he denied.' *Letters of H.P. Blavatsky to A.P. Sinnett*, p. 151.

[2] *Letters of H.P. Blavatsky to A.P. Sinnett*, p. 105.

1880

On the first letter he had from his Guru, Mr Sinnett has noted that it was received about 15 October 1880. Mme Blavatsky, writing in 1881, says: 'Toling is where K.H. was when he first wrote to you.'

She adds that Captain Banon of the 29th Gwalior regiment, describing his travels in Asia, wrote to her about 'the grand monastery of Toling, where the head lamas have great occult powers', and proposed going there shortly. She comments:

> There are only chelas of the first degree there and I doubt whether they tell or show him anything. However, it is a good thing he goes there.[1]

On October 20th the Master wrote:

> Please remark that the present is not dated from a 'Lodge' but from a Kashmir valley.[2]

And on the 29th of that month:

> The other day I was coming down the defiles of the Konenlun—you call them the Karakorum—and saw an avalanche tumble. I had gone personally to see our chief to submit Mr Hume's important offer, and was crossing over to Lhadak on my way home.[3]

1881

About February 20th, Mahatma Koot Hoomi being in 'an irremediable paperless condition' remarked:

> I, being far away from home, and at a place where a stationer's shop is less needed than breathing air, our correspondence threatens to break very abruptly.[4]

Soon after that Mr Sinnett went to England, and in London on March 26th a letter reached him which said:

> It is from the depths of an unknown valley, amid the steep crags and glaciers of Terich-Mir[5] a vale never trodden by European foot since the day its parent mount was itself breathed out from within our

[1] *Letters of H.P. Blavatsky to A.P. Sinnett*, p. 11.
[2] *The Mahatma Letters*, p. 11 [same page in 3rd ed.].
[3] ibid, p. 12 [same page in 3rd ed.].
[4] ibid, p. 33 [same page in 3rd ed.].
[5] Terich-Mir is the highest peak in the Hindu-Kush mountain range which lies between what is now Pakistan and Afghanistan.

Mother Earth's bosom — that your friend sends you these lines. For it is there KH received your 'affectionate homage' and there he intends passing his 'summer vacations'.

During this visit to England, Mr Sinnett published his first book, *The Occult World.* After his return to India he received a long letter (August 5th), the following excerpts from which will indicate something of the Master's travels:

> Just home...I now come from Sakkay-Jung[1]. To you the name will remain meaningless. Repeat it before the 'Old Lady' and — observe the result. ... I hope these disjointed reflections may be pardoned in one who remained for over nine days in his stirrups without dismounting.[2] From Gharlaring-Tcho Lamasery (where your *Occult World* was discussed and commented upon — Heaven save the mark! you will think) I crossed to the Horpa Pa La territory — 'the unexplored regions of Turki tribes' say your maps, ignorant of the fact that there are no tribes there at all — and thence home. In October I will be in Bhutan.[3]

However, by October the Master writes:

> I have given up my projected voyage to Bhutan, and my Brother M. is to take my place. We are at the end of September. ... My chiefs desire me particularly to be present at our New Year's festivals February next, and in order to be prepared for it I have to avail myself of the three intervening months. I will therefore bid you now Goodbye, my good friend. ... January next I hope to be able to let you have good news from me... I have but a few hours before me to prepare for my long, *very* long journey.[4]

1882

In January, 'The Disinherited' (Djwal Khul) wrote a letter to Mr Sinnett beginning with the words, 'The Master has waked and bids me write.'[5]

And in February there came a letter from the Master himself:

[1] Sakkya-Jung is a Buddhist monastery in Tibet on the road from Darjeeling to Lhasa. It lies south-west of Gayantze.

[2] This is the letter precipitated by a chela, which led to the 'Kiddle Incident'. The Master's great weariness induced him to decline to examine the precipitation.

[3] *The Mahatma Letters,* pp. 280-6/276-82.

[4] *The Mahatma Letters,* p. 441 [p. 433 in 3rd ed.]

[5] ibid, p. 248 [p. 245 in 3rd ed.].

My Brother, I have been on a long journey after supreme knowledge; I took a long time to rest. Then upon coming back, I had to give all my time to duty, and all my thoughts to the Great Problem. It is all over now; the New Year's festivities are at an end, and I am 'Self' once more. But what is Self? Only a passing guest, whose concerns are like a mirage of the great desert.[1]

This year marked the beginning of trouble in Egypt which necessitated a very considerable movement on the part of various members of the Brotherhood. Master K.H. at the end of June informed Mr Sinnett that

The Egyptian operations of your blessed countrymen involved such local consequences to the body of Occultists still remaining there and to what they are guarding, that two of our adepts are already there, having joined some Druze brethren, and three more on their way. I was offered the agreeable privilege of becoming an eye-witness to the human butchery, but—declined with thanks.[2]

On which H.P.B. comments to Mr Sinnett:

Your K.H. *refused* going to Egypt and thereby displeased *his* authorities.[3]

She herself, a 'messenger of Shamballa' and a member of the Brotherhood, had been nearly four years in India, and was longing to pay a visit to the ashram of her Master. She obtained his permission, but the troubled state of affairs put a stop to the proposed visit. Master K.H. writes to Mr Sinnett: 'H.P.B. is in despair; the Chohan refused permission to M. to let her come farther than Black Rock, and M. very coolly made her unpack her trunks. Try to console her if you can. Besides she is really wanted more at Bombay than at Penlor.'[4]

Before Mr Sinnett's consolatory letter could reach her, she had written to him, pouring out the vials of her wrath and disappointment:

My plans are *burst*. The 'Old One' won't let me go, doesn't want me. Says all kinds of 'serenades'—bad times; the English will be behind me (for they believe more in the Russians than the Brothers); their presence will prevent any Brother to come to me *visibly*, and *invisibly* I

[1] *The Mahatma Letters* p. 264 [p. 260 in 3rd ed.].
[2] Ibid, p. 116 [p. 113 in 3rd ed.]
[3] *Letters from H.P. Blavatsky to A.P. Sinnett*, p. 27.
[4] *The Mahatma Letters*, p. 116 [p. 112 in 3rd ed.]

> can just as well see them from where I am; wanted here and elsewhere, but not in Tibet; etc.... I had all ready, the whole itinerary was sent from Calcutta. M. gave me permission, and Deb was ready. Well, you won't prevent me from saying, *now* at least from the bottom of my heart—DAMN MY FATE. I tell you death is preferable. Work, work, work, and no thanks.
>
> Well, if I do feel crazy, it is *theirs* not my fault—not poor M. or K.H.'s but theirs, those heartless dried-up big-bugs, and I must call them that if they had to pulverize me for this. What do I care now for life! Annihilation is 10,000 times better.[1]

By September she was seriously ill, and the longed-for visit to the Himalayas became a necessity. She wrote to Mr Sinnett:

> I am afraid you will soon have to bid me goodbye —whether to Heaven or Hell *connais pas*. This time I have it well and good—Bright's disease... and other pretty extras and *etceteras*. This is *primo* brought by Bombay dampness and heat, and *secundo* by fretting and bothering...[Dr] Dudley says that I can last a year or two, and perhaps but a few days, for I can kick the bucket at any time in consequence of an emotion. Ye lords of creation! Of such emotions I have twenty a day—how can I last then?...Boss wants me to prepare and go somewhere for a month or so. He sent a chela here, Gargya Deva from Nilgiri Hills, and he is to take me off—where I don't know, but of course somewhere in the Himalayas.[2]

Later she writes:

> This morning I got up from my bed for the first time this week. But never mind me...Read this: 'I will remain about 23 miles off Darjeeling till Sept. 26th—and if you come you will find me in the old place...K.H.'[3]

After the visit, writing from Darjeeling, on October 9th, she tells of her joyous experience in the Himalayas with the Masters:

> How did you know I was here?...Well, now that there is no more danger from your *blessed* Government and its officials, I was going to write to you myself and explain the motive for the *secrecy* 'which is so very repulsive generally to your European feelings'. The fact is that had I not left Bombay in the greatest secrecy—even some Theosophists who visit us believing me at home but busy and invisible as usual—had

[1] *Letters from H.P. Blavatsky to A.P. Sinnett*, p. 28.
[2] ibid., p. 37.
[3] ibid., p. 34.

I not gone incognito till I reached Sikkim, *I would have never been allowed to enter it* unmolested, and would not have seen M. and K.H. *in their bodies* both. Lord, I would have been dead by this time!

Oh the blessed two days! It was like the old times when the bear paid me a visit. The same kind of wooden hut, a box divided into three compartments for rooms, and standing in a jungle on four pelican's legs; the same yellow chelas gliding noiselessly; the same eternal 'gul-gul-gul' sound of my Boss's inextinguishable *chelum* pipe;[1] the same *entourage* for furniture—skins. and yak-tail stuffed pillows, and dishes for salt, tea, etc., etc.

Well, when I went to Darjeeling, sent away by them—'out of reach of the chelas who might fall in love with my beauty' said my polite Boss—on the following day already I received a note I enclose from the Deputy Commissioner, warning me not to go to Tibet! He locked the stable door after the horse had been already out. Very luckily! Because the six or seven Babus who stuck to me like parasites went to ask passes for Sikkim: they were refused point blank and the Theosophical Society abused and jeered at. But I had my revenge. I wrote to the Deputy Commissioner and told him that I had permission from the Government—the fact of Government not answering for my safety being of little importance, since I would be safer in Tibet than in London; and after all I *did* go twenty or thirty miles beyond Sikkim territory and remained there two days, and nothing happened bad to me and there I was.

Several ladies and gentlemen anxious to see 'the remarkable woman' pester me to death with their visits, but I have refused persistently to see any of them. Let them be offended. What the d— do I care? *I won't see anyone.* I came here for our Brothers and chelas, and the rest may go and be hanged.

Thanks for your offer. I do mean to pay you a visit, but I cannot leave Darjeeling while my Boss is hovering nearby. He goes away in a week or ten days, and then I will leave Darjeeling; and if you permit me to wait for you at your house, I will do so with real pleasure...I am very weak and must stop. Boss gives you his love—I saw him last night at the Lama's house.[2]

Somewhat later in a letter to M. Biliere of Paris, she says of this visit to the Himalayas:

[1] The water-pipe, or narghil, often called 'the hubble-bubble' because of the sound it gives forth.

[2] *Letters of H.P. Blavatsky to A.P. Sinnett*, p. 38.

> My Mahatma and Guru has already twice patched me up. Last year the doctors condemned me. I had Bright's disease in the last phase.... Well, I went to Sikkim, to the entrance of Tibet, and there my beloved Master repaired kidneys and liver, and in three days' time I was as healthy as ever. They say it was a miracle. He only gave a potion to drink seven times a day from a plant in the Himalayas.

That she did actually see the two Masters in their physical bodies is corroborated by Master KH in a letter to Mr Sinnett shortly before her expedition, thus:

> I am not at home at present, but quite near to Darjeeling, in the Lamasery, the object of poor H.P.B.'s longing. I thought of leaving by the end of September, but...I will have to interview in my own skin the 'Old Lady' if M. brings her here. And—he has to bring her or lose her forever—at least, as far as the physical triad is concerned.[1]

We are able to catch a glimpse of that meeting through the eyes of Master K H himself; for in a letter defending Madame Blavatsky against certain accusations made by a Theosophist in Europe, he writes:

> Most undeniably she is given to exaggeration in general, and when it becomes a question of 'puffing up' those she is devoted to, her enthusiasm knows no limits. Thus she has made of M. an Apollo of Belvedere, the glowing description of whose physical beauty made him more than once start in anger, and break his pipe while swearing like a true—Christian; and thus, under her eloquent phraseology, I myself had the pleasure of hearing myself metamorphosed into an 'angel of purity and light'—shorn of his wings. We cannot help feeling at times angry with, oftener—laughing at her. Yet the feeling that dictates all this ridiculous effusion is too ardent, too sincere and true, not to be respected.
>
> I do not believe I was ever so profoundly touched by anything I witnessed in all my life, as I was with the poor old creature's ecstatic rapture when meeting us recently, both in our natural bodies·[2] one—after three years, the other—nearly two years absence and separation in the flesh. Even our phlegmatic M. was thrown off his

[1] *The Mahatma Letters,* p. 190 [p. 188 in 3rd ed.].

[2] Confirmation of the fact that HPB actually saw the two Adepts in their physical bodies but a few times during the years she was living in India. Nearly all of the accounts by various persons of seeing the Adepts relate to their 'illusory bodies' or Mayavi Rupas rather than to their actual physical bodies.

balance, by such an exhibition—of which he was the chief hero. He had to use his *power*, and plunge her into a profound sleep; otherwise she would have burst some blood-vessel...in her delirious attempts to flatten her nose against his riding mantle besmeared with Sikkim mud! We both laughed, yet could we feel otherwise than touched? You can never know her as we do; therefore none of you will ever be able to judge her impartially or correctly. You see the surface of things, and what you would term 'virtue', holding but to appearances; we judge but after having fathomed the object to its profoundest depth, and generally leave the appearances to take care of themselves.[1]

1883

Towards the close of this year and extending into the next, Master K.H. made an extended tour in Asia. It may be traced by a reference here and there in his letters or those of Madame Blavatsky, and in Colonel Olcott's Diary. H.P.B., writing on September 27th to Mr Sinnett, then returned to England, says,

> Olcott is gone day before yesterday on his northern tour. Maharajah of Kashmir sent for him, and K.H. ordered him to go to a certain pass where he will be led to by a chela he will send for him...I believe Mr Brown will rejoin Olcott somewhere...I am glad that Olcott will see and converse with him. He is in raptures with the expectation. It appears that it is Maha Sahib (the big one) who insisted with the Chohan that Olcott should be allowed to meet *personally* two or three of the Adepts besides his Guru M. So much the better. I will not be called, perhaps, the *only* liar when asserting their actual existence.[2]

Colonel Olcott took the Marathi youth, Damodar K. Mavalankar, with him on this tour to act as secretary, while he himself lectured on Theosophy and organized Branches of the Theosophical Society. Many phenomena occurred, of which the Colonel gives a detailed account in *Old Diary Leaves,* Third Series. On November 4th, he reports Master Koot Hoomi as being at Lake Manasarovar[3] in the Himalayas. While the party was at Lahore

[1] *The Mahatma Letters,* p. 313 [p. 309 in 3rd ed.].

[2] *Letters of H.P. Blavatsky to A.P. Sinnett,* p. 62.

[3] This lake is near Mount Meru (or Kailasa) in north-western Tibet, east of the Himalayas. (Ed.)

camped in tents, and Colonel Olcott was busily lecturing and interviewing all day and far into the nights, Master K.H. paid them a visit, having begun his southward journey. This is the entry in the Colonel's Diary:

> November 20th, K.H. came in body to my tent, woke me suddenly out of sleep, pressed a note into my hand, and laid his hand upon my head. He then passed into Brown's compartment, and integrated another note in his hand.
>
> He spoke to me. Was sent by Maha Chohan, 1:55 a.m.
>
> 10 p.m. After lecture K.H. and Benjamin [Djwal Khul] showed themselves back of the camp to Damodar, Brown and myself. Both dressed in white.

At Jammu, the winter capital of the Maharajah of Kashmir, another incident occurred, which is entered thus in the Colonel's Diary:

> Nov. 25th. Dear Damodar left with his Guru K.H. for the Ashrum. Telegraphed H.P.B. and received word that Master promised D.K. shall return.
>
> November 27th. Damodar returned.

Meantime H.P.B. had written excitedly to Mr Sinnett:

> Well, there's news again. Day before yesterday I received a telegram from Jammu from Olcott. 'Damodar taken away by the Masters.' Disappeared! I thought and feared as much, though it *is* strange, for it is hardly four years he is a chela. I send you both telegrams, from Olcott and Mr Brown's second one. Why should Brown be so favoured—is what I cannot understand. He may be a good man, but what the devil has *he* done so holy and good! That's all I know about him, that it seems to be K.H.'s second visit *personally* to him.[1]

Damodar having returned, the little party of three devoted workers went on with their tour. They visited Wazirabad, Jeypur, Baroda, Bombay, Gooty and Kurnool, and only reached Madras on December 15th. Master K.H. had preceded them southward on his long journey. H.P.B. in the same letter says,

[1] *Letters of H.P. Blavatsky to A.P. Sinnett,* p. 72.

> He is expected here or in the neighbourhood by two of his chelas who have come from Mysore to meet him. He is going somewhere to the Buddhists of the Southern Church. 'Shall *we* see him?' I do not know. But there's a commotion among the chelas. Well, strange things are taking place; earthquakes, blue and green sun, Damodar spirited away, and Mahatma coming.[1]

They *did* see him. Mr Sinnett, in England, received a letter from him saying:

> This week I will be in Madras, en route to Singapore and Ceylon and Burmah. I will answer you through one of the chelas at Headquarters.[2]

Mysore is an independent state bordering on Madras Presidency; its capital is also called Mysore. On December 7th, dated from Mysore, the Master wrote a letter to the London Lodge, Theosophical Society[3], enclosed in another to Mr Sinnett in which he declared:

> The journey before me is long and tedious, and the mission nearly hopeless. Yet *some* good will be done.[4]

On the same day, HPB had written to Mr Sinnett:

> Mahatma K.H. sent a letter from Sanangerri to Damodar and Dharani Dar Kauthumi, with a copy of some passages from his big letter to you.... On February 17th Olcott will probably sail for England on various business, and Mahatma K.H. sends his chela, under guise of Mohini Mohun Chatterjee, to explain to London Theosophists of the Secret Section every or *nearly* every mooted point....You better show Mohini all the Master's letters of a non-private character, saith the Lord my Boss....Do not make the mistake of taking the *Mohini you know* for the Mohini who will come. There is more than one Maya in this world of which neither you nor your friends are cognizant. The ambassador will be invested with an *inner* as well as an *outer* clothing. *Dixit.*[5]

That the Mahatma's visit to Mysore preceded his visit to Madras is indicated by a letter which he wrote to Mr Brown, December 17th.

[1] *Letters of H.P. Blavatsky to A.P. Sinnett,* p. 72.
[2] *The Mahatma Letters,* p. 428 [pp. 421-2 in 3rd ed.].
[3] ibid, p. 402 [p. 396 in 3rd ed.].
[4] ibid., p. 405 [p. 399 in 3rd ed.].
[5] *Letters of H.P. Blavatsky to A.P. Sinnett,* p. 64.

> I have left Madras a week ago, and where I am going you cannot go, since I am on my journey and will cross over at the end of my travels to China and thence home.[1]

As to the Master's visits to China, HPB says in a letter addressed to a member and dated 29th November 1889:

> Master K.H. every two years goes to Japan and China, and my own blessed Master comes sometimes to India.[2]

The last news of Master Koot Hoomi's long journey is furnished by his Brother, Master Morya, who in his absence once more carried on the correspondence with Mr Sinnett:

> He is in the far-off woods of Cambodia now.[3]

[1] *Letters from the Masters of the Wisdom,* First Series, p. 64.
[2] *The Canadian Theosophist,* November 1923.
[3] *The Mahatma Letters,* p. 432 [p. 425 in 3rd ed.].

APPENDIX G

PHYSICAL APPEARANCE OF THE K.H. LETTERS TO SINNETT

THERE is a great deal of interest among students of the Mahatma Letters concerning how they were written and transmitted. It seems advisable to consider the two aspects separately, and this appendix will be limited to the physical appearance of the letters emanating from the Mahatma Koot Hoomi.

Each of the two Mahatmas used definite and distinctly different types of calligraphy throughout the correspondence. The Mahatma Morya's letters are nearly all in what appears to be red ink and in a peculiar type of scrawl that is at times very difficult to decipher. The letters from the Mahatma KH are generally in blue, either in what appears to be ink or pencil, but there are quite a number of exceptions. His writing is smooth and even and quite easily read. In order to give the student a better picture of the appearance of his letters, a tabulation has been made, arranged in chronological sequence to give a clearer picture of when and how the variations occurred.

In some of the letters there are indications of deletions having been made, some with reinsertions, sometimes smears, and in a few instances what appear to be definite blots.

Type of paper used

There is a great variation in the types of paper used and no uniformity in the size of the sheets. Much of the paper in use in India at that time was of a type generally referred to as 'rice paper', some of which was of smooth finish and some having a rippled appearance. Most of the letters are on white paper, some in off-white, and a few on paper of different colours. Some are on a sort of waxy type of vellum. A few are on what looks like ordinary wrapping-paper, unevenly cut as to size, as if the sheets had been cut by hand.

Another interesting variation is that in a few instances letter-head sheets of Sinnett, Hume, and Sam Ward have been used. In other words, one gets the impression that the Adept made use of whatever paper was most readily available or could be secured by his transmitting agents. The occasional use of imprinted letterhead stationary belonging to another person may have been for the purpose of making a point with the recipient.

Filed with the letters in the British Museum are several envelopes in which the letters were transmitted, a few of which are Chinese in appearance, with line drawing picture imprints which are either Chinese or Tibetan in nature.

When Sinnett was asking questions, he usually wrote the question on the left-hand side of his heavy folded notepaper, leaving the right side of the sheet for the reply. In most instances, however, the Adept could not accommodate his reply to this small space and added additional sheets as needed of paper of different size, type, and sometimes colour.

Type of media used

There is considerable difference of opinion among students of the Letters as to the method of their production and transmission. Within the letters themselves, and based upon explanations given by HPB, there are some indications as to these points. These are not especially specific, and one may conclude with some reason that several means were employed; further that we may not yet be privileged to understand fully about these aspects. A superficial glance leads one to think that they were originally handwritten, either by the Adept or by one of his chelas or agents. However, this may not be the case, and in instances of direct precipitation by a chela, it is possible that the message was passed direct from the Mahatma's mind to that of the chela. In some instances it seems that the letter was definitely written by hand by the Adept. It is possible also that sometimes the message was directed mentally to the chela, who received it visually and wrote it down by hand.

We are told by HPB and others that few of the letters were actually written by the Adept. Why the selection of colour and why some letters appear to be in ink and others in pencil is not explained. In one letter the Mahatma indicates that the writing was actually by hand, either by himself or by his attendant chela. He also requests Sinnett to furnish him with a recipe for making blue ink, and further states that he has to close the letter because of a shortage of paper.

In a letter from HPB to Sinnett, written while on board ship at Algiers, she describes clearly how Djual Khul, one of K H 's principal assistants, appeared in his Mayavi Rupa in her cabin and asked for paper on which to write to London a message which he was to receive from his Master. Having received the paper, he materialized a hand sufficiently to write the message, which appeared in the air before him. In other instances, especially those in which a blue pencil seemed to be used, it seems quite certain that the colour was driven into the paper by precipitation rather than having been written.

All this leads one to conclude that the Adepts used the method most feasible at the time and requiring the least expenditure of energy; further that there is much we do not know about their methods.

Sending of telegrams

During the years the correspondence was in progress, the Adepts sent a few telegrams to several different persons. Not all of these have been printed as yet. Presumably, when the commercial telegraph system was used, it was necessary for the message to be written out on the standard telegraph forms.

It is interesting, and somewhat amusing, to note how the Adepts signed the telegraph forms. In the case of the Mahatma K.H., three different types of signatures were used: Koothoomi LalSingh; K.H.L. Singh, and Kaytch. The Mahatma Morya signed his M. Orya and M. Orya, Boss for T.S.

Just as a note in passing, it is stated in the letters that the Adepts do not give direct orders to persons who are not their chelas. However, in two of the telegrams from the Mahatma KH he issued direct instructions to both Sinnett and the members of the British Theosophical Society.

LIST OF LETTERS FROM MAHATMA K.H. IN CHRONOLOGICAL ORDER SHOWING TYPE OF MEDIA

Letter No. *Chro.*	*Book*	*Date*	*General appearance and type of medium. (On white paper unless otherwise stated.)*
		1880	
1	1	Oct. 17	Dull black ink
2	2	" 19	" " "
3	3	" 20	" " "
4	143	" 27	" " "
5	4	" 29	" " "
6	126	Nov. 3	Black ink
7	106	"	Blue ink
8	99	Nov. 20	" "
9	98	Dec. 1	" "
10	5	Dec.	Dull black ink
11	28	"	Black ink To Hume
12	6	"	Blue ink (precipitated by a new chela)
		1881	
13	7	Jan.	
15	8	"	Blue ink. K.H. requests recipe for blue ink

16	107	March	Blue ink K.H. requests recipe for blue ink
17	31	"	" "
18	9	July	" "
19	121	"	" " Ink blot from folding paper
20	49	Aug.	" "
21	27	Sept.	" " Blotched appearance
22	26	"	" "
23	104	Oct.	" "
		1882	
49	48	March	" "
50	88	"	" "
51	120	"	Blue pencil
52	144	"	Blue ink
54	35	"	" "
55	89	"	" "
56	100	March	Blue ink
57	122	April	" "
59	132	June	" "
60	76	"	" " (on rough parchment, hand cut)
61	17	"	Dull red ink
62	18	"	Blue ink (heavy rough paper, hand cut)
63	95	"	" "
68	16	July	Black ink. (question and answer)
69	69	"	Blue pencil (waxy paper)

70	20	”	Blue pencil (first with grained appearance)
71	19	August	” ” (grained)
73	113	”	” ” ”
74	30	”	Blue ink
75	53	”	Light blue pencil (grained)
76	21	”	Blue pencil (grained)
77	50	”	” ” ”
78	51	”	” ” ”
79	116	”	” ” (on an envelope)
80	118	”	” ” (ochre paper with Chinese print)
81	52	”	Blue ink (one sheet in blue pencil)
82	32	”	Blue pencil
84	111	Sept.	Black ink, coral paper, Chinese print
85	24 a + b	”	Famous contradictions. Reply is in sepia ink, some underlining in red.
86	112	”	Blue pencil (grained), bluish paper
87	34	Autumn	” ” (glazed paper)
		1882	
91	110	Oct.	Blue pencil
92	54	”	Blue ink. Erasurers and corrections
93 B	23-B	”	Black ink changing to pale blue. White paper changing to bright pink
94	117	”	Blue pencil on a postcard.
95	72	Nov.	Blue pencil
96	92	”	Bright red ink, canary yellow paper
97	70	Dec.	Blue pencil
98	105	”	Black ink

99	78	”	” ” —pink paper
100	79	”	Blue pencil
		1883	
101	57	Jan.	Black ink changing into sepia to red
102	56	”	Blue ink
103	91	”	Blue pencil, and blue ink
104	80	”	Blue pencil on Sinnett's letterhead paper
105	25	Feb.	Blue ink (some bluish grey paper)
106	103	”	Blue pencil on canary yellow paper
107	77	March	” ” (cream coloured paper)
108	58	”	” ”
109	119	”	” ” (on Sinnett's letterhead paper)
110	67	May	Blue ink
111	59	July	” ”
112	81	”	” ”
113	82	Aug.	First 4 lines in blue ink which changes in 3 lines to green ink, remainder green
114	83	Sept.	Blue ink changing to green ink
117	93	Dec.	Mostly blue ink. Latter part in red ink
		1884	
119	86	Jan.	Blue ink
120	85	”	” ”
121	84	”	Green ink
122	87	”	” ”

123	68	Feb.	Blue pencil
124	94	”	Green ink
126	62	July	Blue ink
128	63	”	Blue pencil
129	60	Sept.	” ” (on rough hand cut paper)
130	55	Oct.	” ” (on L.C. Holloway note paper)
131	66	”	Blue pencil
134	64	Nov.	” ”
		1885	
136	65	March	Blue ink
A	33	”	Blue pencil
B	75	”	” ”
C	123	”	” ”
D	124	”	Blue ink

Based upon the listing of the letters in chronological order as given in this appendix, it is evident that no definite pattern can be assigned to the appearance of the media in which they were imprinted or the type of paper on which the messages were received. Neither was there any consistent method by which they were transmitted. In general, one may summarize the appearance in time sequence as follows:

The first ten letters or so were received while HPB was still at Simla or thereabouts with Sinnett. They are mostly in black ink. Undoubtedly they were precipitated by HPB.

The twelfth letter chronogically (6th in the book) was precipitated by a young chela inexperienced in the process, who made a number of mistakes which resulted in difficulties. It seems that this change in agent was due to HPB's having left Simla.

Throughout the year 1881, the letters were all in blue ink. In January of that year, KH requested Sinnett to furnish him with a recipe for making blue ink (Letter 8 in the book). He remarks in this same letter that precipitation of letters to Sinnett had become 'unlawful'. However, we are not told specifically how the letters were transmitted during that year. In the year 1882 and thereafter, the pattern of transmission becomes mixed. Some are in blue, red, sepia, or black ink, or blue pencil; some have a granular appearance. Also, various coloured papers were used occasionally, some seemingly cut from ordinary paper by hand and a few on paper with printed letterheads.

In other words, it would seem that the Adept used whatever means was most readily available and required the least expenditure of energy. As to the means of transmission, it is doubtful whether we shall ever know the details, but apparently a variety of methods was used. HPB undoubtedly precipitated some of the later letters, but indications are that towards the end of the correspondence, after Sinnett had moved to England, the Adepts relieved her of this work, due to her ill health, and that other agents were utilized.

G.E.L.

APPENDIX H

SOME INCIDENTS IN HPB'S LIFE AS RELATED IN THE LETTERS

IN Mahatma Letter 26 the first letter in the section of *The Mahatma Letters to A.P. Sinnett* under the heading 'Probation and Chelaship', p. 203 in the first and second edition; (p. 201 in the third edition), designated by Sinnett 'K.H.'s Confidential Memo about Old Lady' we find some frank and extremely important comments about H.P. Blavatsky. This 'Confidential Memo' is obviously meant for both A.P. Sinnett and A.O. Hume, the two Englishmen involved in the correspondence with which the volume is concerned. Both were at that time in Simla at the Humes' residence. Something had taken place in the room occupied by Sinnett which is not explained in detail here but is more fully described in a subsequent letter (ML-29, p. 217/215) It is suggested that, in any study of this situation, both letters be read.

Two words used in ML-26 might be explained: *Bod-Las* (low on the first page) is translated 'divine rulers'; and the term 'the real baitchooly' on the second page can be taken to mean something similar to the American idiom 'the real McCoy'.

The Mahatma mentions also HPB's 'occult training in Tibet'. As Geoffrey Barborka points out in *The Masters and Their Letters,* p. 121, somehow, even during her lifetime, word had got around that she had been in Tibet for seven years. We have her own explanation of this.

The 2 August 1884 issue of *Light,* a Spiritualist journal published in England and edited by Stainton Moses, carried an article by a Mr Arthur Lillie entitled 'Koot Hoomi Unveiled' in which he said, among other things, that he had never heard of an initiation lasting for seven years. HPB replied to this article, and her reply appeared in the 9 August 1884 issue.[1] In this reply she said:

> I will tell him [Arthur Lillie] also that I have lived at different periods in Little Tibet as in Great Tibet, and that these combined periods form more than seven years. Yet, I have never stated either verbally or over my signature that I had passed seven consecutive years in a convent. What I have said, and repeat now, is, that I have stopped in Lamaistic convents; that I have visited Tzi-gadze, the Tashi-Lünpo territory and its neighbourhood, and that I have been further in, and in such places in Tibet as have never been visited by any other European, and that he can ever hope to visit.

Undoubtedly she was in Tibet several times. It is likely that one of those times—perhaps not the first—was in 1868. In the reply to Mr Lillie mentioned above, she says that she had never seen the Mahatma KH before 1868.[2] Since he seems to have participated in her training, this *may* indicate the time at which it began. This is only an assumption and may be wrong. She was in Italy for part of that year, and she was definitely in the Battle of Mentana on 2 November 1867,[3] when she fought as a man in the army of Garibaldi, the Italian patriot. In the fighting 'her left arm was broken in two places by a sabre stroke, and she was badly wounded by musket shots in the right shoulder and one leg. When she fell in the heat of the battle, her companions thought she had been killed and left her behind. Later she was found and rescued.[4]

However, when she was in Italy in 1868, she received a letter from her Master 'directing her to wait in the Serbian mountains until she had definite word from him to go to Constantinople and meet him there. She had high hopes that the meeting would be soon and that he would take her to India and Tibet.'[5]

This *may* have happened. According to the source just quoted (p. 58) she left Tibet in 1870.

Geoffrey Barborka, in *H.P.B. Tibet and Tulku,* devoted Chapter 6 (p. 108 et seq) to HPB's Tibetan experiences. He believes that, at least on one occasion, she entered Tibet through China, and he develops this theory (which he says no one else has advanced) in a fascinating manner. He does not solve the mystery; probably that will never be solved, but he does give considerable insight into that phase of her life.

Even Col. Olcott, who knew her so well during the years they worked together for the Theosophical Society, calls her 'a personality puzzle' (ODL 2:vi-vii) and says that just because he did know her so much better than most others did, she was to him a greater mystery.

> To me, her most intimate colleague, she was from the first and continued to the end an insoluble riddle. How much of her waking life was that of a responsible personality, how much that of a body worked by an overshadowing entity, I do not know.

Olcott mentions a number of times in ODL how charming and warm she was on many occasions, so that she endeared herself to everyone who happened to be in her presence at such times. As a further delightful light on her personality, he quotes a Hartford, Connecticut, reporter describing her laughter:

> Madame laughed. ... When we write that Madame laughed, we feel as if we were saying that laughter was present! For of all clear, mirthful, rollicking laughter that we ever heard, hers is the very essence. She seems, indeed, the Genius of the mood she displays at all times, so intense is her vitality.[6]

Countess Constance Wachtmeister, who was so closely associated with HPB for a number of years later on, pays tribute to her in her book *Reminiscences of H.P. Blavatsky and The Secret Doctrine* (p. 42):

> All who have known and loved HPB have felt that unique charm there was about her, how truly kind and lovable she was. At times a bright childish nature seemed to beam around her, a spirit of joyous fun would sparkle upon her whole countenance, and cause the most winning expression that I have ever seen on a human face.

And, again, pp. 61-62:

> None of those who knew her really understood her. Even to me, who had been alone with her for so many months, she was an enigma, with her strange powers, her marvellous knowledge, her extraordinary insight into human nature, and her mysterious life spent in regions unknown to ordinary mortals, so that though her body might be near, her soul was often away in commune with others. Many a time I have observed her thus and known that only the shell of her body was present.

If one may judge by some of HPB's own comments, she herself had some questions about her psychological make-up. She seems to have passed through a number of strange crises in her life. In 1854, before her near-death in the Battle of Mentana already mentioned, she had a strange illness. This is related in *When Daylight Comes,* beginning on p. 51. She was on one of her visits to Russia and had bought a house in a military settlement in Transcaucasia, where she was engaged for a time in a commercial enterprise involving the sale and export of lumber products. She became very ill. The symptoms were curious:

> Physically, she had a mild fever and a complete loss of appetite. She refused everything except a little water and was most of the time in a half-dreamy, disinterested state, though not completely unconscious. But mentally she appeared to have reached a great crisis, so that she became a double personality. When a friend or servant called her name, she opened her eyes and answered, as Helena Blavatsky. But as soon as left alone, she closed her eyes and became, she said, somebody else in 'another far-off country. A totally different individuality' who seemed, indeed, even to live in a different dimension of time.
>
> She later described it in this way: 'In cases where I was interrupted, during a conversation in the latter capacity (in my other self), say, at half a sentence either spoken by me or some of my *visitors,* invisible of course to any other, for I was alone to whom they were realities—no sooner I closed my eyes than the sentence which had been interrupted continued from the word it had stopped at. When awake and *myself,* I remembered well who I was in my second capacity, and what I was doing. When somebody else, I had no idea of who was H.P. Blavatsky.

The army doctor who attended her was completely out of his depth, but he was certain she would die without greater help than he was able to give. So he arranged to have her sent to Tiflis in a native boat travelling down a narrow river which ran by the military settlement. She lay there close to death, and the boatmen were very frightened.

> During the night they saw—they vowed—the patient glide off the boat and cross the water toward the forests, but at the same time her body was lying prostrate on the bed at the bottom of the boat.
>
> The same thing occurred on the second night and they were ready to abandon both the boat and the patient. Only the courage of the man in charge kept them at their posts. Even he wavered, the third night, when he saw *two* phantom figures while HPB herself lay sleeping before his eyes.

However, they did manage to complete the journy and, at

Tiflis, the boat was met by her family and she was taken to the family home. Gradually she improved. 'She had been through a great battle with occult forces that had almost killed her, but she emerged from the crisis complete master of those forces.'

In a letter to a relative she wrote: 'I am cleansed and purified of that dreadful attraction to myself of stray spooks and the ethereal *affinities*. I am free, free, thanks to those whom I now bless at every hour of my life.' Somehow, says her biographer, during that dreadful crisis, she had thrown off the curse of unwanted mediumship and had become a magician. Now psychic phenomena would be the subject of her own will.

HPB herself wrote in a letter to Sinnett (LBS p. 145): 'Between the pre-1865 and the post-1865 Helena Petrovna Blavatsky there is an unbridgeable gulf.' Prior to 1865 she had been quite mediumistic and unable to control the odd things that happened when she was in the vicinity. Now she had thrown off that burden—perhaps a necessity before she could go to Tibet for her real occult training.

Concerning the Mentana crisis, Olcott believed this was a critical time. In ODL 1:263 he mentions how various Mahatmas occupied HPB's body, especially in the writing of her great works, but says there were times when this was not the case. 'There were intervals', he says, 'when her body was not occupied by the writing Mahatmas;[7] at least I assume it to be so, although I have sometimes been tempted to suspect that none of us, her colleagues, ever knew the normal HPB at all, but that we just dealt with an artificially animated body, a sort of perpetual psychic mystery, from which the proper *jiva*[8] was killed out at the battle of Mentana, when she received those five wounds and was picked out of a ditch for dead.'

Still another crisis took place much later, in May and June of 1875, when HPB was living in Philadelphia.[9] We have HPB's own words to describe this strange experience, for she wrote of it to her aunt and her sister in some detail. Later, William Q. Judge, editor of *The Path,* prevailed upon Mrs Charles Johnston, HPB's niece and daughter of the sister to whom she had related the events, to translate HPB's letters from the Russian. He published them in *The Path* from December 1894 to 1895. Again, this happened during an illness, or following an illness, and an instantaneous cure after the doctor had given up hope. Again, also, HPB experienced a sense of duality.

'Several times a day,' she says, 'I feel that beside me there is someone else, quite separable from me, present in my body. I never lose the consciousness of my personality; what I feel is as if I were keeping silent and the other one—the lodger who is in me—were speaking with my tongue.'

She spoke of this 'other' as No. 2, and said that during the night, 'the whole life of my No. 2 passes before my eyes and I do not see myself at all, but quite a different person—different in race and different in feelings....There is no mediumship, and by no means an impure power...this is altogether of a higher order.'

'Do not be afraid that I am off my head,' she says in one letter. 'All I can say is that someone positively inspired me—more than this, someone enters me. It is not I who talk and write: it is something within me, my higher and luminous Self, that thinks and writes for me...The one thing I know is that now, when I am about to reach old age, I have become a sort of storehouse for somebody else's knowledge...'

She goes on to say, 'I am perfectly conscious of what my body is saying and doing—or at least its new possessor, I even understand and remember it all so well that afterwards I can repeat it and even write down *his* words...'

G.D. Purucker, in his book, *H.P. Blavatsky: The Mystery,*[10] discusses the strange duality of HPB and says that her case rests upon 'foundations laid in some of the most mysterious and, to the Occident, utterly unknown secrets of human spiritual psychological economy'. 'The Inner self of her was one of the Great Ones of the ages,' he adds, 'an actual, real, self-consciously energetic Individuality or Power, which worked through her and used her both psychologically and physically as the fittest instrument for the saving of the souls of men that the Occidental world has seen in many ages.'

In view of all the above—as well as in many other references which might be cited, but perhaps these are sufficient—it seems that one is justified in concluding that HPB was both H.P. Blavatsky, the personality, and also someone very much greater—her Egoic Self.[11]

The Mahatma mentions (ML, p. 203/201) that no one can leave the precints of Bod-Las and be sent out into the world without being to some extent a psychological cripple, because of the necessity to leave behind the specific link mentioned in the letter. It has come more or less to be taken for granted that HPB left one of her 'principles' in Tibet. If we are to judge from some comments by the Mahatma Morya, it was more than that. In LBS, p. 305, there is a letter from Hume to HPB in which he expresses his scepticism about this whole matter—very rudely, as a matter of fact. He says: 'Now I know all about the Brothers' supposed explanation that you are a psychological cripple...' The Mahatma M. interposed his own comments while the letter was in transit, and of this statement he says: 'He is mistaken; he does *not*.' There are some further words by Hume which end with 'Therefore to me this explanation is not only not satisfactory—but its having been offered—throws suspicion on the whole thing.' Here the Mahatma M. has inserted: 'Very clever—but suppose it is neither *one of the seven* particularly but all? Every one of them a "cripple" and forbidden the exercise of its full powers? And suppose such is the wise law of a far foreseeing power?' This is almost like saying it is the cream skimmed off the top of all of them.

So, it is said, that the 'vacancy' created by the temporary abstraction of that portion of her consciousness, whatever it was, was occupied from time to time by various Adepts, such as M., KH, and others. Sometimes this 'gap' was bridged by her own Higher Self. At other times, it has been said, it was occupied by a very high Initiate, vastly higher than the Mahatmas who were writing the letters. 'This Initiate is a Slavonian in his latest incarnation, and it is precisely because of his peculiar type of psycho-mentality, due to his racial stock, that the Messenger of the present era had to be chosen, if at all possible, from among the Slavic people. This permitted HPB to be "attuned" to his vibratory rate, as it were.'[12]

From all of the above it will be seen that a great many words have been written in attempting to explain the mystery of HPB. Also, it is apparent that the Mahatmas were forever grateful to her; it is extremely moving that the Mahatma KH should rise to her defense as he does in Mahatma Letter 26 (ML 203/210).

The vitality of HPB's memory is attested by the fact that even today writers attack her; since they cannot tear apart her message, they use 'argumentum ad hominem': if you can't destroy the message, attack the messenger.

Foot Notes

[1] It is now found in the Collected Writings, Vol. VI, pp. 269-280.

[2] See *Personal Memoirs of H.P. Blavatsky* by Mary K. Neff; Wheaton, Theosophical Publishing House, 1967, p. 213.

[3] Mentana: a village north-east of Rome, where Garibaldi was defeated by French and papal forces.

[4] *When Daylight Comes,* biography of H.P. Blavatsky by Howard Murphet; Wheaton, Theosophical Publishing House, 1975, p. 55.

[5] ibid, p. 55.

[6] ODL 1:417.

[7] See Neff, op cit., p. 291.

[8] A living being *per se; Occult Glossary,* G.D. Purucker.

[9] Neff, op cit., p. 241.

[10] San Diego, Point Loma Publications, 1974, p. 6.

[11] *Reminiscences of H.P. Blavatsky,* Wachtmeister, p. 111, gives some interesting incidents following HPB's death.

[12] Boris de Zirkoff, HPB's only known living relative, in the January-February 1948 issue of *Theosophia,* p. 13.

V.H.

APPENDIX I

THE TRIUMPH OF GERMANICUS

THERE is a very interesting little item in the folios of the *Mahatma Letters* material in the British Museum which was not published in the book compiled by A.T. Barker, but which seems to have a bearing on an incarnation of Sinnett's in Rome during the very early years of the Christian era.

It will be recalled by the student of the Letters that early in the course of the correspondence, Sinnett inquired of the Mahatma KH if he could give him (Sinnett) some information regarding his previous incarnations. The Mahatma replied that although he could do so, he did not wish to. He added, however, that some day he might give Sinnett a few hints but no details. This is found in Mahatma Letter 23A (p. 144/141),

On p. 175/171 of Mahatma Letter 23B, the Mahatma drops a hint in this direction in his answer to one of Sinnett's questions, indicating that Sinnett might have been a Flamen or priest (even possibly a high priest) in Rome in the early days of the Christian era.

The above mentioned item in the British Museum is a postcard size photo copy of a painting presumably made in Europe (probably Germany) which bears the title: *Thusnelda im Triumphzuge des Germanicus,* meaning, in English, 'Thusnelda at the Triumph of Germanicus'. What the picture illustrates is the scene of the triumph accorded Germanicus when he returned to Rome in the AD 17 after his successful war against the German tribes. In such triumphs the booty and prisoners which the conqueror had brought back were paraded before the officials and populace of Rome.

One of the prisoners depicted in the painting is Thusnelda, the young wife of the leader of one of the principal tribes conquered by Germanicus in Germany.

From Anton's Classical Dictionary we learn the following:

> Germanicus Caesar, born in 14 BC was a nephew of the Emperor Tiberius and a brother of Claudius. He was sent to Germany in AD 16 to subdue the German tribes, which he did with considerable success. He defeated Arminius, one of the leading German chieftains, but was unable to capture him. He did, however, capture the wife of Arminius, a young woman by the name of Thusnelda, whom he took back to Rome in AD 17 when he returned from his campaign.

The painting depicts Germanicus at this triumph together with Thusnelda and other prisoners. It is a large painting and hangs in a museum in Europe and has a date of 1880 on it.

The question naturally arises as to the significance of this picture postcard in connection with A.P. Sinnett. The envelope in which Sinnett apparently received the postcard is in the British Museum and bears the notation, 'Photograph, received at Allahabad July 10'. On the back of the postcard in KH script in blue pencil is the following note:

> Left behind, it is from Mali's dust basket that I save the fair Thusnelda—with whose beauty you were so struck—and Germanicus, for both of whom he had already prepared a bed of infamy in a neighbouring gutter.
>
> K.H.
>
> How about Simla?

The mali, or gardener, was about to throw the postcard, along with other material, into the gutter.

The date of July 10 would seem to indicate that the incident occurred in 1881 just after Sinnett had arrived home in Allahabad on his return from vacation in England. His family had remained in London.

The footnote, 'How about Simla?', was a suggestion to Sinnett that he go to Simla, the summer capital of India, where Hume resided and where HPB was soon to arrive, also to stay at the Hume residence.

The question arises as to the significance of this picture and the Mahatma's note on the back of it which would move the Mahatma to retrieve it from the servant's wastebasket and mention that Sinnett had been struck by Thusnelda's beauty. Referring back to Mahatma Letter 23B, one may be permitted to surmise that this was one of the 'hints' promised to Sinnett concerning a past incarnation. The dates seem approximately to coincide. At least it is an interesting little item in connection with the letters. There seems to be no information as to why or how Sinnett happened to have the postcard.

G.E.L.

FACSIMILE OF LETTERS
FROM
THE MASTERS AND
H. P. BLAVATSKY

ML-32 p. 242/239

The beginning of ML-32 from KH to APS in which he discusses the famous HX letter which the adepts instructed HPB to publish in *The Theosophist* against her wishes.

Large KH script in blue pencil without noticeable 'graining' appearance.

Text of Letter

LETTER No. 32

I am sorry for all that has happened, but it was to be expected. Mr. Hume has put his foot in a hornet's nest and must not complain. If my *confession* has not altered *your* feelings—I am determined not to influence you and therefore will not look your way to find out how the matter stands with you, my friend—and if you are not entirely disgusted with our system and ways; if in short it is still your desire to carry on a correspondence and learn something must be done to check the irresponsible "Benefactor." I prevented her sending to Hume a worse letter than she wrote to yourself. I *cannot* force her...

XXIII   95

I am sorry for all that has happened, but it was to be expected. Mr Hume has put his foot in a hornet's nest and must not complain. If my confession has not altered your feelings— —I am determined not to influence you & therefore will not look your way to find out how the matter stands with you, my friend—and if you are not entirely disgusted with our System and ways; if in short, it is still your desire to carry on a correspondence and learn, something must be done to check the irrepressible "Benefactor." I prevented her sending to Hume a worse letter than she wrote to yourself. I cannot force

ML-37 p. 248/245

A-37 The beginning of a letter from Djual Kul to APS advising him that the Master KH had completed his 'retreat' and would soon be able to resume his correspondence.

Text of Letter

LETTER No. 37

Received at Allahabad, January 1882

Private

Honoured Sir,

The Master has awaked and bids me write. To his great regret for certain reasons He will not be able until a fixed period has passed to expose Himself to the thought currents inflowing so strongly from beyond the Himavat. I am therefore, commanded to be the hand to indite His message. I am to tell you that He is "quite as friendly to you as heretofore and well satisfied with both your good intentions and even their execution so far as it lay in your power. You have proved your affection and sincerity by your zeal. The impulse you have personally given to the Cause we love will not be checked; therefore the fruits of it (the word "reward" is avoided being used but for the "goody-goody" will not be withheld when your balance of causes and effects—your *Karma* is adjusted. In unselfishly and at personal risk labouring for your neighbour, you have most effectually worked for yourself. One year has wrought a great change in your heart.

private

Honoured Sir — The Master has awaked and
bids me write. To his great regret for certain reasons He will
not be able until a fixed period has passed to expose Himself
to the thought-currents inflowing so strongly from beyond the
Himavat. I am therefore, commanded to be the hand to
indite His message. I am to tell you that He is "quite as
"friendly to you as heretofore and well satisfied with both your
"good intentions and even their execution so far as it lay in
"your power. You have proved your affection and sincerity by
"your zeal. The impulse you have personally given to the cause
"we love, will not be checked; Therefore the fruits of it (the word
"reward" is avoided being used but for the "goody-goody")
"will not be witheld when your balance of causes and effects —
"your Karma — is adjusted. In unselfishly and at personal
"risk labouring for your neighbor, you have most effectually worked
"for yourself. One year has wrought a great change in your heart.

ML-66 p. 366/360

A portion of ML-66, KH to APS. It is interesting because of the rather remarkable statement by Master KH that the Coulomb affair and the SPR investigation were 'rather fanned than weakened from Shigatse'.

Text of Letter

...but for united struggle. Whomsoever has sown the seeds of the present tempest, the whirlwind is strong, the whole Society is reaping it and it is rather fanned than weakened from Shigatse. You laugh at *probations*—the word seems ridiculous as applied to you? You forget that he who approaches our precincts even in thought, is drawn into the vortex of probation. At any rate your temple totters, and unless you put your strong shoulders against its wall you may share the fate of Samson. Pride and "dignified contempt" will not help you in the present difficulties. There is such a thing—when understood allegorically—as treasures guarded by faithful gnomes and fiends. The treasure is our occult knowledge that many of you are after—you foremost of all; and it may not be H.P.B. or Olcott or anyone else individually who has awakened the guardians thereof, but yourself, more than they and the Society collectively. Such books as the *Occult World* and *Esoteric Buddhism* do not pass unnoticed under the eyes of those faithful guardians, and it is absolutely necessary that those who would have that knowledge should be *thoroughly* tried and tested. Infer from this what you will; but remember that my Brother and I are the only among the Brotherhood who have at heart the dissemination (to a certain limit) of our doctrines, and H.P.B. was hitherto our sole machinery, our most docile agent. Granting that she is all you describe her—and I have already told you that the ricketty old body becomes sometimes positively dangerous—still it does not excuse in you the smallest relaxation of effort to save the situation and push on the work (and especially protect our correspondence) all the faster. Deem it, what it is, a positive advantage to the rest of you that she should have been what she is, since it has thrown upon you the greater stimulus to accomplish...

for mental strength. Let me [illegible] the [illegible] of
the present tempests, the atmosphere is stormy, the [illegible]
society is [illegible] it and it is rather [illegible] than [illegible]
from Intelligence. You must at first have the [illegible]
and [illegible] as applied to you? You forget that the rule of
probation [illegible] precedes ever a thought is drawn into
vortex of probation. At any rate your temple totters, &
unless you put your strong shoulder against the wall
you may share the fate of Samson. Pride & "dignified
contempt" will not help you in the present difficulties.
There is such a thing even understood allegorically — as
treasures guarded by faithful gnomes and fiends. The
treasure is our Occult knowledge that many of you
are after — you foremost of all, and it may not be H.P.B.
nor Olcott or any one else individually who have awakened
the guardians thereof, but yourself more than any and the
Society collectively. Such books as the Occult World & Esoteric Buddhism do not pass unnoticed under the eyes
of these faithful guardians, & it is absolutely necessary
that those who would learn that knowledge should be
thoroughly tried & tested. I infer from these what you write,
intimating that my Brother & I are the only [illegible]
the T.S. [illegible] at least the dissemination
[(to a certain extent)] of our doctrines, and H.P.B. [illegible]
to our sole machinery, our most docile agent. Granting that
she is all you describe here — & I have already told you
that the rickety old body becomes sometimes positively
dangerous — still it does not excuse in you the [illegible]
least relaxation of effort to save the situation & push on
the work and especially protect our correspondence. [illegible]
[illegible] of what it is, a positive advantage to the
[illegible] of you that she should have been what she is, [illegible]
[illegible] upon you the greater [illegible]

ML-73 p.375/368

The first of several short letters from M to APS after he had taken over the correspondence from KH, who had started on his 'retreat'. Typical 'M' script and signature—M with a long tail and three dots over the tail in the form of a triangle.

Text of Letter

LETTER No. 73

Mr. Sinnet—you will receive a long letter—posted Sunday at Bombay—from the Brahmin boy. Koot-hoomi went to see him (as he is his *chela*) before going into "Tong-pa-ngi" [1]—the state in which he now is—and left with him certain orders. The boy has a little bungled up the message so be very careful before you show it to Mr. Hume lest he should again misunderstand my Brother's real meaning. I will *not* stand any more nonsense, or bad feeling against him, but retire at once.

We do the best we can. M.

[1] Tibetan. The 'Void'.

Mr. Sinnett — You will receive a long letter posted Sunday at Bombay — from the Brahmin boy. Koot-Hoomi meant to see him (as he is his Chela) before going into "Tong-pa-nyi" — the State in which he now is — & left with him certain orders. The boy has a little bungled up the message. So be very careful before you show it to Mr. Hume, lest he should again misunderstand my Brother's real meaning. I will not stand any more nonsense, ill feeling against him and later abuse. Do the best we can.

M.

ML-96 p. 431/424

Beginning of letter from M to APS in London. Rather typical Morya scrawl and difficult to read. Sinnett was attending a seance by Eglinton in the office of American businessman Sam Ward. Master M was in Tibet. He says that his attention was attracted to the seance by the forging of HPB's handwriting, so he went there and watched (in his Mayavi Rupa), and to prove to Sinnett that he had been there, he abstracted a sheet of Sam Ward's monogrammed paper on which to write his letter. The logotype of Sam Ward appears in the upper left hand corner of the sheet and is quite an unusal one, being a compass face with the initials S.W. in the south-west quadrant of the compass, which the casual observer might mistake for a compass direction. It is interesting to note the unevenness of the weight of the lines and several blobs as though the letter had been written by hand with pen and ink.

Another interesting feature of this letter is the intimate relationship existing between adept and chela, in that the forging on the other side of the world of HPB's handwriting instantly attracted the Master's attention.

LETTER No. 96

Received 1883 or '84?

My humble pranams, Sahib. Your memory is not good. Have you forgotten the agreement made at Prayag and the pass-words that have to precede every genuine communication coming from us through a भूत डाक *Bhoot-dak* or medium? How like the seance of December the 15th—coroneted card, my letter and all! Very similar—as a Peling pundit would say. Yet, first a loving greeting from old woman to *Lonie* misspelled on card Louis, then to C.C. Massey whose name she now never pronounces, and that greeting coming after supper—when C.C.M. had already left. Then my message in a feigned hand when I am at dead loggerheads with my own; again I am made to date my supposed message from Ladakh December 16th, whereas I swear I was at Ch-in-ki (Lhasa), smoking your pipe. Best of all my asking you to "prepare for our coming as soon as we have won over Mr. Eglinton Sahib!!!" "One Saturday and Lord Dunraven having failed why not *try* again...

XCVII 137 N.2

My humble pranams
Saheb.—Your memory
is not good. Have you
forgotten the agreement
made at Prayag & the pass-words
that have to precede every genuine communication coming from us through a
[illegible] "Chela dak or medium? Most
likely the seance of Dec. 15th — Colonel's
card, my letter & all! Very similar
as a Kashmiri pundit would say.
Yes—first a loving greeting from
old woman to Louie misspelt on card
Louis, then to C.C. Massey—whose name
she never pronounces, & that greeting coming after supper—when
C.C.M. had already left. Then my
message in a feigned hand when I
am at dead loggerheads with my boss
again & am made to date any
supposed message from Ladakh
Dec. 16, whereas I was gone at
Chini-ki (Lhasa) smoking your
pipe. Best of all my asking you
to "prepare for our coming as soon as
we have done over Mr. Eglinton" Saheb
!!! on Saturday & Lord Lindsay's
having failed why not try again

ML-121 p. 452/445

KH to APS upon his return to Allahabad from his vacation in England; wife Patience and son Denny were still in London. KH urges APS to go on up to Simla as HPB was going there also for the summer.
Large KH script in dark blue ink.
A noticeable and interesting feature of the letter is the obvious blotting of the capital 'P' in Patience onto the upper line of the letter when the paper was folded.

Text of Letter

LETTER No. 121

Received at Bombay on return to India, July, 1881.

Thanks. The little things prove very useful, and I gratefully acknowledge them. You ought to go to Simla. TRY. I confess to a weakness on my part to see you do so. We must patiently await the results, as I told you, of *the* Book. The *blanks* are provoking and "tantalizing" but we cannot go against the inevitable. And as it is always good to mend an error I already did so by presenting the *Occult World* to the C—'s notice. Patience, patience.

Yours, ever

K.H.

CXXI

Thanks. The little things prove
very useful, and I gratefully acknowledge them. You ought to go to Simla
Sry. I confess to a weakness on my
part to see you do so. We must
patiently await the results, as I
told you of the Book. The
"blanks" are provoking and "tanta-
-lizing" but we cannot go against
the inevitable. And as it is
always good to mend an
error I already did so by
presenting the Occult World to
the C——s notice. Patience,
patience. Yours, &c.

K. H.

ML-137 p. 467/459

The first part of a letter from HPB to APS in London, written while on board ship at Algiers, Africa. It is interesting because of her vivid description of the method by which Djual Kul appeared in her cabin and wrote down a letter that was to be sent to England.

Text of Letter

LETTER No. 137

Clan Drummond: Algiers.

Sunday 8th.

My dear Mr. Sinnett,

You see I am as good as my word. Last night as we were hopelessly tossed about and pitched in our Clan wash-tub Djual K. put in an appearance and asked in his Master's name if I would send you a chit. I said I would. He then asked me to prepare some paper—which I had not. He then said any would do. I then proceeded to ask some from a passenger, not having Mrs. Holloway to furnish me with [it]. Lo! I wish those passengers who quarrel with us every day about the possibility of phenomena could see what was taking place in my cabin on the foot of my berth! How D.K.'s hand, as real as life, was impressing the letter at his Master's dictation which came out in *relief* between the wall and my legs. He told me to read the letter but I am no wiser for it. I understand very well that it was all probation and all for the best; but it is devilish hard for me to understand why it should all be performed over my long suffering back. She is in correspondence with Myers and the Gebhards and many others. You will see what splatters *I* will receive as an effect of the causes produced by that probation business. I wish I had never seen the woman. Such treachery, such a deceit I would never have dreamt of. I was also a chela and guilty of more than one flapdoodle; but I would have thought as soon of murdering physically a man as to murder morally my friends as she has. Had not Master brought about the explanation I would have gone away leaving...

CXXXVI

A214

[illegible]

chat. I said I would. He then asked me to prepare some paper — which I had not. He then said my wa[illegible] then proceeded to set down from a passenger not having her Holl[illegible] any to furnish me with. So I wish those passengers who quarrel with us every day about the possibility of phenomena could see what was taking place in my cabin on the foot of my berth! How D. K.'s hands, as well as [illegible], [illegible] expressing the [illegible] of the sister's dictation which came out in raps between the wall and my legs. He told me to send the letter but I see no reason for it. I understand very well that it was all probation and all for the best, but it is very hard for me to understand why it should all be performed over my long suffering back. She is in correspondence with Meyers & the Gebhards and many others. You will see what splutters I will receive as an effect of the powers produced by that probation business. I wish I had never seen the woman. Such treachery, such a deceit I would never have dreamt of. I was also a chela guilty of more than one flapdoodle; but I would have thought no less of myself, if [illegible] physically a man as the murderer morally my friends as she has. Had it not been brought about the explanation I would have gone away, leaving

SUMMARY CHRONOLOGY OF THE LETTERS

(Some dates are approximate or estimated. In most instances the date given is the date of receipt of the letter. Occasionally an incorrect date of receipt has been noted. In such instances the date has been determined by the context.)

Chr. No.	*ML No.*	*Page 2nd ed.*	*Page 3rd ed.*	*Date*	*1880*
1	1	1	1	Oct. 17	
2	2	6	6	Oct. 19	
3A	3A	10	10	Oct. 20	
3B	3B	10	10	Oct. 20	
3C	3C	11	11	Oct. 20	
4	143	488	481	Oct. 27	
5	4	11	11	Nov. 3	
6	126	454	447	Nov. 3	
	(This is a postscript to ML-4)				
7	106	443	436	Nov.	
8	99	435	428	Nov. 20	
9	98	434	427	Dec. 1	
10	5	17	17	Dec.	
11	28	207	205	Dec.	
12	6	22	22	Dec. 10	
13	7	25	25	Jan 3	1881
14A	142A	486	479	Feb.	
14B	142B	488	481	Feb.	
15	8	26	26	Feb. 20	
16	107	444	436	Mar. 1	
17	31	240	237	Mar. 26	
18	9	38	38	July 5	
19	121	452	445	July 11	
20	49	280	276	Aug. 5	

21	27	204	202	autumn	
22	26	203	201	autumn	
23	104	440	433	Oct.	
24	71	374	367	Oct.	
25	73	375	368	Oct.	
26	102	439	432	Oct.	
27	101	439	431	Oct.	
28	74	375	369	Oct.	
29	29	217	215	Oct.	
30	134	461	454	Nov. 4	
31	40	254	251	Nov.	
32	114	449	442	Nov. 13	
33	38	250	247	Dec. 10	
34	39	253	249	Dec.	
35	41	256	252	Dec.	
36	36	248	244	Jan.	1882
37	37	248	245	Jan.	
38	90	412	406	Jan.	
39	115	449	442	Jan.	
40	108	444	437	Jan.	
41	109	444	437	Jan.	
42	43	258	255	Jan.	
43	42	257	253	Jan.	
44	13	70	70	Jan.	
45	44	263	259	Feb.	
46	12	66	66	Feb.	
47	45	264	260	Feb.	
48	47	271	267	Mar. 3	
49	48	273	269	Mar. 3	
50	88	410	404	Mar. 11	
51	120	452	444	Mar.	
52	144	488	481	Mar. 14	
53	136	464	457	Mar.	
54	35	246	242	Mar. 18	
55	89	410	404	Mar. 24	
56	100	438	431	Mar. 25	
57	122	452	445	Apr. 27	
58	130	457	450	May 7	

59	132	459	452	June 3
60	76	376	369	June 3
61	17	117	113	June
62	18	119	115	June
63	95	429	423	June
64	131	458	451	June 26
65	11	59	59	June 30
66	14	78	77	July 9
67	15	88	87	July 10
68	16	99	97	July
69	69	373	366	July
70A	20A	123	120	July
70B	20B	125	121	July
70C	20C	127	123	July
71	19	122	119	Aug. 12
72	127	455	447	Aug. 13
73	113	448	441	Aug.
74	30	228	225	Aug.
75	53	294	290	Aug.
76	21	134	131	Aug.
77	50	286	282	Aug.
78	51	287	283	Aug. 22
79	116	450	443	Aug.
80	118	450	443	autumn
81	52	288	284	autumn
82	32	242	239	autumn
83	125	453	446	autumn
84	111	446	439	Sept.
85A	24A	178	175	Sept.
85B	24B	180	177	Sept.
86	112	447	440	Sept.
87	34	245	242	autumn
88	10	52	52	autumn
89	46	268	264	autumn
90	22	137	133	Oct.
91	110	445	437	Oct.
92	54	302	298	Oct.
93A	23A	144	141	Oct.

93B	23B	149	145	Oct.	
94	117	450	443	Oct.	
95	72	374	368	Nov.	
96	92	419	413	Nov. 23	
97	70	373	367	Dec. 7	
98	105	441	434	Dec.	
99	78	378	372	Dec.	
100	79	382	376	Dec.	
101	57	327	322	Jan. 6	1883
102	56	325	320	Jan.	
103A	91A	415	409	Jan.	
103B	91B	416	409	Jan.	
104	25	191	188	Feb. 2	
105	80	383	377	Feb.	
106	103	440	432	Feb.	
107	77	377	371	Mar.	
108	58	336	331	Mar.	
109	119	451	444	Mar.	
110	67	371	364	May	
111	59	338	333	July	
112	81	383	377	July	
113	82	387	381	Aug.	
114	83	393	387	Sept.	
115	128	456	449	Nov. 25	
116	129	456	449	Nov. 25	
117	93	420	413	Dec.	
118	96	431	424	Dec.	
119	86	403	396	Jan.	1884
120	85	398	392	Jan.	
121	84	397	391	Jan.	
122	87	406	399	Jan.	
123	68	372	366	Apr. 7	
124	94	429	422	Apr.	
125	61	349	344	Apr.	
126	62	351	345	July 18	
127	133	460	453	July	
128	63	356	350	summer	
129	60	349	343	Sept.	

130	55	322	317	Oct.	
131	66	366	360	Oct.	
132	135	464	457	Oct.	
133	137	467	459	Nov. 8	
134	64	358	352	Nov.	
135	138	468	460	Mar.	1885
136	65	362	356	Mar.or April	
137	97	433	426	autumn	
138	145	488	481	autumn	
139	140	478	470	Jan.	1886
140	141	482	474	Mar.	
141	139	475	468	Mar.	

Letters for which dates cannot be determined

Chr. No.	*ML No.*	*Page 2nd ed.*	*Page 3rd ed.*
A	33	244	241
B	75	375	369
C	123	453	446
D	124	453	446

CROSS REFERENCE—MAHATMA LETTERS

ML No.	*Chr. No.*	*Page 2nd ed.*	*Page 3rd ed.*
1	1	1	1
2	2	6	6
3A	3A	10	10
3B	3B	10	10
3C	3C	11	11
4	5	11	11
5	10	17	17
6	12	22	22
7	13	25	25
8	15	26	26
9	18	38	38
10	88	52	52
11	65	59	59
12	46	66	66
13	44	70	70
14	66	78	77
15	67	88	87
16	68	99	97
17	61	117	113
18	62	119	115
19	71	122	119
20A	70A	123	120
20B	70B	125	121
20C	70C	127	123
21	76	134	131
22	90	137	133
23A	93A	144	141
23B	93B	149	145
24A	85A	178	175

24B	85B	180	177
25	104	191	188
26	22	203	201
27	21	204	202
28	11	207	205
29	29	217	215
30	74	228	225
31	17	240	237
32	82	242	239
33	A	244	241
34	87	245	242
35	54	246	242
36	3C	248	244
37	37	248	245
38	33	250	247
39	34	253	249
40	31	254	251
41	35	256	252
42	43	257	253
43	42	258	255
44	45	263	259
45	47	264	260
46	89	268	264
47	48	271	267
48	49	273	269
49	20	280	276
50	77	286	282
51	78	287	283
52	81	288	284
53	75	294	290
54	92	302	298
55	130	322	317
56	102	325	320
57	101	327	322
58	108	336	331
59	111	338	333
60	129	349	343
61	125	349	344

62	126	351	345
63	128	356	350
64	134	358	352
65	136	362	356
66	131	366	360
67	110	371	364
68	123	372	366
69	69	373	366
70	97	373	367
71	24	374	367
72	95	374	368
73	25	375	368
74	28	375	369
75	B	375	369
76	60	376	369
77	107	377	371
78	99	378	372
79	100	382	376
80	105	191	188
81	112	383	377
82	113	387	381
83	114	393	387
84	121	397	391
85	120	398	392
86	119	403	396
87	122	406	399
88	50	410	404
89	55	410	404
90	38	412	406
91A	103A	415	409
91B	103B	416	409
92	96	419	413
93	117	420	413
94	124	429	422
95	63	429	423
96	118	431	424
97	137	433	426
98	9	434	427

99	8	435	428
100	56	438	431
101	27	439	431
102	26	439	432
103	106	440	432
104	23	440	433
105	98	441	434
106	7	443	436
107	16	444	436
108	40	444	437
109	41	444	437
110	91	445	437
111	84	446	439
112	86	447	440
113	73	448	441
114	32	449	442
115	39	449	442
116	79	450	443
117	94	450	443
118	80	450	443
119	109	451	444
120	51	452	444
121	19	452	445
122	57	452	445
123	C	453	446
124	D	453	446
125	83	453	446
126	6	454	447
127	72	455	447
128	115	456	449
129	116	456	449
130	58	457	450
131	64	458	451
132	59	459	452
133	127	460	453
134	30	461	454
135	132	464	457
136	53	464	457

137	133	467	459
138	135	468	460
139	141	475	468
140	139	478	470
141	140	482	474
142A	14A	486	479
142B	14B	488	481
143	4	488	481
144	52	488	481
145	138	488	481